McDowell's Directory

of

TWENTIETH CENTURY FASHION

McDowell's Directory

of TWENTIETH CENTURY FASHION

Colin McDowell

Frederick Muller

First published in Great Britain in 1984
by Frederick Muller.

Second revised edition published in Great Britain
in 1987 by Frederick Muller, an imprint of
Century Hutchinson Ltd, Brookmount House,
62–65 Chandos Place, London WC2N 4NW

British Library Cataloguing in Publication Data

McDowell, Colin
    McDowell's directory of
    twentieth century fashion.
    1. Fashion – Dictionaries
    I. Title
    746.9'2   TT503

ISBN 0-584-11167-3

Editing, picture research, design and production
by Clark Robinson Limited, London

Printed and bound in Great Britain by
Purnell Book Production Ltd, Paulton, Bristol

CONTENTS

AUTHOR'S NOTE

A book of this kind cannot be written without a great deal of help and co-operation. I have had a considerable degree of support from designers, publicity offices and public relations personnel in all the major fashion capitals. To all of them I owe a great debt of gratitude. I have attempted to make this book definitive but I have also taken a critical stance: if any reader finds that his favourite designer is not included I am sorry. However, names are not omitted to gratify a whim. Either the individual is of insufficient interest to merit inclusion or it proved impossible to obtain facts. In the case of one or two living designers, information was simply unavailable. Some PRs did not do their job; some designers gave bland assurances but nothing else; some ignored repeated requests. The record is held by an English-born designer now in America who failed to respond after five transatlantic telephone calls and two letters!

Of those who did respond with great generosity I would like to mention especially: Grazia Gay, Betty Missoni and Bepe Modenesi in Milan; Kevin Fidler in Munich; Peter Mulvey in Rome and New York; Marina Sturdza in Toronto; Brigit McCarthy, Brian Williams and Jocelyn Mason in Rome; and Sally Brampton, Mary Brogan, Roy Callow, Peter Crown, Kate Franklin, Monique Hay, Peter Hope Lumley, Jaine McCormack, Jackie Moore, Brenda Polan, Fiona Robinson, Julia Wilkins and Lindy Woodhead in London. My thanks also to Penelope Byrd of the Bath Museum of Costume. I would like to make special acknowledgement of the help given by Sarah Harrison and the press office of Browns and Paul Davies of Harvey Nichols. Picture researchers Celia Dearing, Anne Marie Ehrlich and Kate Duffy produced exciting illustrations which were ably incorporated by my designer, Eric Drewery; Nathalie Lamoral Cavendish and Christopher Moore spent hours finding just the right shots for us and my editors Robert Stewart and Hal Robinson pulled everything into shape with the greatest efficiency. The personal support I have received from Gloria Ferris, Tony Talbot (ably assisted by Joyce Goode) and my family cannot be overstressed. Without the support and endless trouble taken by Muriel Ross and her colleagues at the London College of Fashion library this book could not have been written — which is also true of my typist Chris Motley who unravelled everything I wrote and produced a manuscript that made sense; my researcher Judy Rumbold and, most importantly of all, Daniella Gluck of Frederick Muller. Her steadfast belief in this book, her determination to get it right and her unwavering personal support made it all possible.

For Ibi Farkas

For, what was well done for a time,
in half a year became a crime

Bernard de Mandeville
(1670–1733)

CLOTHES AS A WEAPON

Fashion is the imposition of a prevailing mode or shape. It is a largely arbitrary imposition and it precludes all other modes or shapes although, of course, variations on the basic theme are permitted. Being fashionable or 'in fashion' means that you obey the rules and willingly follow the laid-down mode simply because you care about it. The fashionable person sees fashion as a way of telling the world of his or her success, importance, attractions and desirability. Fashion is for the privileged. It can be indulged in only by those with money to spare after other, essential, items have been paid for.

To follow fashion the devotee must be able to discard clothes, before they are worn out or destroyed, simply because someone calls them un-fashionable. People with no money to spare have clothes to cover and protect them. They cannot afford fashion. The poor discard clothes only when there is no more useful life left in them. It follows that throughout civilization fashion has been the concern and interest of a minute pro-portion of the world's population. The great majority of the people living at any one time were poor. They found it difficult enough to avoid death by starvation, to keep themselves clean and to protect their children from disease whilst managing to avoid 'the frown o' the great'. For them fashion was irrelevant. The same is true today: although there are more people than ever before with the money to follow fashion, especially in Europe and America, the vast majority of people in the world still spend much of their time and energy fighting starvation, dirt, disease and tyranny. The average Westerner spends more money in a week and has more variety of movement, scene and experience in a day than the world's peasants do in many months.

The traditional centre for the fashionable coterie was the court. Fashion flourished in court circles because there were found the people with money to spend at whim and the time to indulge that whim: the freedom from physical toil which creates leisure having been 'bought', but rarely fully paid for, from the peasants who toiled for them. The more magnificent and detached from the reality of the life of the masses a court became, the more scope there was for indulgence in fashionable attitudes in appear-ance, manners and demeanour. The more remote fashionable people be-come, the more powerful and awe-inspiring they seem to the unfashion-able majority. In the past this meant that clothes became not only the trappings of power, but part of the exercise of power itself. Magnificent clothes helped to frighten the peasant into submission, so that he worked harder, took less and gave more so that the process could be perpetuated. Stand in any art gallery and look at the portraits of European and British aristocrats, serene in their security, often dressed for promenading their empty acres, and imagine the milk-maid or shepherd boy of the time dressed in the filthy, smelly clothes which they wore all day, every day, and even slept in too. When they gazed in awe at the bejewelled, bewigged, perfumed figures of their lords and masters, they must have seen what seemed to them creatures from another planet. The rich must have appeared to be gods and goddesses, moving through their Elysian fields to their magnificent garden temples (which, although serving no real purpose, were bigger and better structures by far than the peasant's crowded, malodorous cottage): if not gods and goddesses, then at least God's anointed, His chosen ones here on earth. It is hard to revolt against people of whom you are afraid and even harder to raise a fist to a god. . . . Which is one reason why the life of privilege continued unquestioned for such an incredibly long period in the history of the world.

Clothes were a tool of oppression, a weapon wielded against the poor. They were used to drive home the lesson that the grand were not simply different, they were better, *because* they were rich. They wore on their backs the proof that they were superior intellectually, morally and socially. Even in today's much more sophisticated atmosphere the super-rich give rise to awe, envy and a faint feeling of inferiority in many people. The woman who is perfectly turned out and expensively dressed is still considered a superior and better person than the woman who cannot spend a great deal of time or money on her appearance. The lessons inculcated centuries ago were well learned and their legacy is still with us today.

Of all the courts, that of the Sun King was possibly the most sumptuous, artificial and remote from the people. At Versailles, Louis XIV created not only a way of life, but a small world where he was the arbiter in art, fashion, beauty, and manners. The ritual, formality and pomp of the life surrounding him and his aristocratic minority were the result of the totally inward-looking life of the court, which enabled fashionable attitudes to flourish by excluding all thought of the rest of the population. People outside the court circles simply did not exist. They were as irrelevant to the fashionable ones inside the circle as fashion was to them. Although at Versailles we see the pattern at its extreme (so extreme that it had to end) it is the same in all fashionable worlds. There is a 'king' and a 'court'. Someone must decree what is fashionable and there must be people willing to obey the edict. The court must be exclusive or it cannot be fashionable. People are excluded or welcomed according to birth or wealth or, preferably, both. Being 'in fashion' is meant to make one feel superior to those who are not.

The real kings are dying out. In the stock-taking after World War I it was noted that four kings had been deposed, three new republics had been

Opposite: *Aggression and power glamorized. This portrait of Napoleon by David is like a fashion photograph of the established order. The streamlined appearance of horse and rider are so far removed from reality that the ideal they present is unobtainable for the ordinary person. Thus rulers perpetuate their reign.*

10

BONAPARTE

created and two empires had vanished. However, pretenders to the throne of fashion-king and leader were in healthy supply and a pattern was appearing: since the days of Beau Brummell in the Regency and of Charles Worth later in the 19th century, royalty had been more and more inclined to allow upstarts to dictate the fashionable message. In fact, it seemed logical that the couturiers, now themselves elevated to some social standing largely through the determined efforts of Worth, should be the arbiters of fashion in clothing. Yet, although by the turn of the century they were accepted by society, it was not forgotten that they had been mere dressmakers. So, at this stage, any edicts they made on manners, morals and polite behaviour were not taken seriously by 'the quality'. Later, thanks to the efforts of Paul Poiret who, as the first major fashion-king of this century, wielded considerable social as well as sartorial power, the upstart fashion 'royals' were accepted as arbiters of all aspects of fashionable life. By the 1970s Andy Warhol could hold sway over his court with all the absolutism of a latter-day Louis XIV.

'Uneasy lies the head that wears a crown'. To guard themselves against the princes waiting to topple them from power, fashion-kings issue more and more edicts. Fashions are changed ever more rapidly. The royal boot is on the neck of the faithful fashion-follower, defying him not to obey and forcing him to enjoy obeying. Only by the exercise of this power can competition be kept at bay. Fashion-power has been held in many hands: the male designers, like Worth and Poiret, who made women sexually desirable; the female designers, like Vionnet and Chanel, who knew how women felt in clothes; the male designers, like Dior and Balenciaga, who created romantic, fantasy women. These kings and queens have always been eagerly helped by their 'victims', the customers who have wished to impress their personalities on their generation. Just as there are new kings, so new courts have arisen during this century. The aristocrats have largely gone and in their place the plutocrats have arrived. Old attitudes, however, have not died. Following fashion is still part of most rich people's lives. It remains irrelevant to the majority of the world's population, yet, strangely, the fashionable life continues to be a potent attraction for many. They are eager to be welcomed into the twilight ghetto world of the fashionable: the world of discotheques, restaurants and fashion shows, peopled by models, hairdressers, starlets, designers and window-dressers.

For the major part of the 20th century these kings, queens and courtiers have been based in Paris because it has been the traditional centre of serious fashion. The catalogue of the 1925 Paris Exhibition boasted that 'there is no woman who does not dream of being dressed in Paris' and it is probably true even today. She may find herself being dressed in clothes stolen wholesale from the far-from-fashionable Third-World countries, but those clothes will be elevated by a Paris label. It is an interesting fact that, while Western fashion-designers find ethnic looks endlessly exotic and manage to persuade women that dressing like Indians, Chinese or

Russians is suitable for occidental streets, the Third World is excited by our blue jeans. They have become such a status symbol that modern travellers in the East are importuned by people eager to buy them off their bottoms.

Until comparatively recently, the world looked exclusively to the salons of Paris for fashion direction. Not only were the greatest designers there, but they were backed by an enormous concentration of talent. The designers were by no means all French: Worth and Molyneux were British; Mainbocher was American; Schiaparelli was Italian; and Balenciaga was Spanish. Had they worked in their own countries they would probably not have reached the level which they achieved in Paris, because couture required an army of highly skilled, traditionally trained cutters, seamstresses and tailors who could work to the highest standards for the most demanding clientele in the world. French women were experts, initiates in all the rites of fashion, whose tastes and fastidious judgement made the

A Winterhalter painting of the Empress Eugenie and her maids of honour relaxing securely in a sylvan glade wearing dresses by Worth. Paintings like this were a rich quarrying ground for future dress designers such as Hartnell and Dior, who were inspired by the artist's romantic interpretations of Worth's creations.

greatest demands on couturiers. These women cared so much about fashion that they had time, patience and vanity enough to stand for long fittings and to wait weeks for delivery. They were in willing co-operation with their couturier in a joint search for the perfectly lying collar, the perfectly cut armhole. Theirs was a creative partnership which, although it may have sprung from vanity, produced beautiful clothes and developed an art form, albeit a minor one.

When we condemn the vanity of the rich we frequently forget that it can also be the source of great pleasure for the non-rich. The portraits of the grand, to which we have already referred, may have been the product of vanity, megalomania and arrogance, but although the reasons can be questioned, the results, when by the hand of a Goya or a Van Dyck, totally transcend the sitter and his motives. The great portraits enhance our lives. Again, many of the great houses and parks of Western Europe were conceived as much to impress as to be enjoyed — yet they give great pleasure to the modern visitor. So there is something positive for the majority in all of this vanity. The same is true of the self-indulgence of haute couture. It is as a result of the *hubris* of customer and grand couturier, who treated dress-making as art, that modern women are dressed with such variety, style and flair in ready-to-wear clothes which are often amazingly inexpensive.

It should also be remembered that the division between the decorative and fine arts was far less clear-cut in France than in other European countries. Artists have always taken couture seriously in France and have frequently lent the couturier their skills. Renoir advised his dressmaker friends on colour. Dior, Chanel and Schiaparelli were all closely involved with artists, writers and intellectuals and Dior actually ran an art gallery for a time. Customers, artists and couturiers, joined by milliners, shoe-makers and jewellers, kept Paris couture supreme. Paris alone had the clientele, the craftsmen and the time and money to produce couture. It was the only city where couture was taken seriously and where new styles or new designers were discussed and analysed in a way that only 'serious' art and artists were treated in other countries. Only when couture began to crumble in the face of an increasing need for ready-to-wear was the power of Paris weakened. Any city can produce ready-to-wear clothes, levelled down to a standard which suits a price. In fact, more and more clothes are being made in Third-World countries where no traditional Western dressmaking skills are found.

Only in Paris and (briefly) Rome was the creation of 'one-off' garments considered a form of art. Yet there is no question that the best creations of the great couturiers can be considered works of art. That they are minor has already been conceded, but the craftsmanship and skill which they show are surely equal to those found in the design of furniture, jewellery and clocks. In addition, they contain the 'artistic' elements of colour and form found in painting. Why serious commentators refuse to concede this is puzzling. Possibly it has something to do with the ephemeral nature of fashion but, from the creative point of view, there is no reason why a screen by Eileen Gray or a chair by Magistretti should be taken more seriously as a work of art than a dress by Chanel or Fath. Each solves design problems in an artistic, but practical way. Furniture and clothes are both utilitarian objects, but the good craftsman or designer creates something which transcends this humble basis.

Why is it, then, that the furniture designer and even the interior decorator are taken seriously as practitioners of the minor arts while the couturier is not? There are two explanations. The first is visual: a chair or a silver rose bowl has an independent existence which is not changed by being sat upon or having flowers placed in it. Each is an autonomous object. A dress, on the other hand, loses a great deal of its point when hanging in a wardrobe. It becomes a rounded and convincing creation only when there is a body inside it. The other explanation is more sinister and springs from the feeling that fashion is frivolous and not to be taken seriously because it is within the domain of women. Unthinking male attitudes have been with us for so long that it is often hard to disentangle ourselves from them but, at last, the feminist movement is attempting to do so. As feminists see it, men have manipulated women and treated them as objects, frequently using dress as a bait and as a reward. An interest in clothing has become a symbol of suppression. The 'little woman' is bought with an expensive dress and by wearing it she feeds a man's ego. She is telling her friends, by her expensive appearance, how rich and powerful he is to be able to buy and possess such a beautifully caparisoned object. All of this may be true, but it is sad that many intelligent and educated women have deliberately turned their backs on fashion. To refuse to acknowledge the artistic achievements of the couturiers of the past, because one objects to the politics behind them, is as shallow as to condemn St. Peter's, in Rome, as a work of art because the Catholics were fond of burning those who did not agree with their dogma. A work of art should not be used as a symbol: it has an existence totally independent of the reasons for its creation.

With couture virtually gone, the fashion map has been re-drawn. London, Milan and New York have joined Paris in importance, while Los Angeles, Florence, Tokyo and Rome have found a place on the map too.

Although spectacular, London's time in the sun was brief, lasting as it did for less than ten years in the 1960s. During this period everything fashionable, lively and 'new' seemed to emanate from Britain. Pop music in the form of *The Beatles* and *The Rolling Stones*; fashion in the shape of Mary Quant and Biba; photography created by David Bailey with Jean Shrimpton: the whole world wanted them. But now much of the London fashion world looks tawdry; little has survived from its heyday except the faintly disquieting feeling that the young were being taken advantage of,

Chanel 1928

Mainbocher 1922

frequently by people of their own age. A great deal of the fashion produced by those hot off the art-school production line was self-indulgent and narcissistic: a privileged group of self-centred young people designed clothes for a clientele limited by age, geographical location, life-style and, perhaps, intelligence. With the advantage of twenty years' hindsight, the London influence seems banal and self-defeating. In the long term it is probably true that anything of lasting worth from the decade came from Paris.

In fact, however, London's fashion position is unique and rests on two foundations. First, and most famous, is the classic, high-quality clothing which has always symbolized British excellence throughout the world. This type of clothing springs from the tradition of men's tailoring which made Savile Row a byword for all that was excellent, elegant, seemly and understated in male dress. It takes the very best natural materials such as cashmere, lambswool, tweed and leather, and treats them in a traditional way to produce classic looks that hardly vary. In fact, so perfectly are they conceived, that variety becomes totally secondary. Burberry and Aquascutum are the two most famous names in this field, along with classic Scottish knitwear firms like Pringle and Hogg of Hawick. These looks are, strictly speaking, outside the province of 'fashion', since they are largely unchanging.

The second major contribution of London to the fashion world is directly opposite to the traditional English classic look. In fact, it is possible to imagine that it is a reaction to that very look. This is the 'way-out' design with which the young break the rules of taste quite deliberately and produce clothes of great vulgarity and great originality. Here the independence and iconoclasm of the young Britisher is seen to be unique. No other country produces such totally underivative and original young thinkers. The young French, Italian and American designers are conformists lacking courage compared to their British counterparts. The sad thing is that so much of this talent evaporates before it can be channelled into designing commercially viable clothes. The fashion contribution of the young in London is vibrant and strong. Like anti-museum artists, they find their ideas not in the salons, but on the streets.

Street-fashion in London is a unique phenomenon. It exists nowhere else so strongly. The young have, for the last few years, been producing their own anti-fashion looks which are totally removed from the world of the fashion magazines. Their clothes are a form of social and political commentary and have become a uniform for those who wish to stand outside a society which they find inadequate and negative. They are stronger and more powerful than anything produced in London during the 1960s. Sixties-fashion sought and gained approval from society. Today's street-fashion is darker and grimmer: it neither seeks nor meets with the approval of any but the wearer's peers. This English phenomenon is subversive and anarchic. Whether it is purely negative and sterile or the first stirring of a completely new approach to clothes within society remains to be seen, but it seems likely that it is at this level that London's fashion contribution will remain most powerful.

The Italian challenge to the hegemony of Paris has proved of much more lasting commercial quality and has been of sufficient worth to cause buyers and the press to change their migratory pattern. Since the mid-1960s they have always included the Italian scene in their itineraries. Today, everyone goes to Milan. Milan, however, did not achieve its status as the Italian fashion-leader without a struggle. Italy is in many of its attitudes still a Renaissance country. Over a hundred years after unification, it is still a country of cities which view each other with suspicion and contempt. No Italian sees himself as an Italian; he sees himself as a citizen of his city which, in his volubly expressed opinion, is the best city in Italy. Rome, Florence and Milan are separate and different entities and the fashions which they produce are divergent.

The Italian fashion boom began slowly in Florence in 1951 under the guidance of Giovanni Battista Giorgini. For some years Florence was the host to buyers and press who came to see what the Italian designers were doing, to enjoy the sun and to be entertained in palazzo after palazzo with almost mediaeval magnificence. Ground so liberally scattered with counts and princes was particularly attractive to the egalitarian American press. By 1966 *alta moda*, or high-fashion, houses were based in Rome, clustered in the Via Condotti area around such luminaries as Valentino, Schon and Capucci. In the 1970s Milan became the centre for high-quality ready-to-wear, wresting this role from Florence and leaving high fashion to decline slowly in Rome. Today, the three cities eye each other cautiously and guard their positions. Milan is the international centre for the best Italian ready-to-wear; Rome contains what is left of *alta moda* (a surprisingly large number of houses, in fact); and Florence presents cheaper ready-to-wear, men's wear, children's wear and knitwear. Despite the despairing feeling one has that every Italian who has reached man's estate is a dress designer, the fact is that Italy *has* many designers, most of whom reach a remarkably high standard and all of whom manage to survive professionally and economically: the 'Italian miracle' in fact.

That the Italian ready-to-wear designers cause worried frowns in Paris salons is not surprising. The clothes shown in Milan are usually well-designed and perfectly made, original without being fantastic, and show a superbly subtle colour sense. Until recently they were also very competitively priced. As yet, Paris has not been so alarmed by the other fashion growth area, which is America. The American fashion scene is spread across the continent. The West coast has its own designers, some catering for the luxury, almost couture, end of the business and, of course, a huge ready-to-wear industry providing sports, play and beach wear. The East coast is New York: on the one hand it has famous-name designers whose importance rivals that of the Europeans and, on the other, there is the vast Seventh Avenue garment industry. The American fashion industry (as opposed to its clothes industry, which all Western countries have) began in the early 1940s when war cut the United States off from Europe and prevented the French designers from continuing to show in Paris. A very strong indigenous fashion began to emerge under the highly professional and gifted guidance of Norman Norell, Hattie Carnegie and Mainbocher in New York. Had that glorious and glamorous blind alley, the 'New Look', not put Paris so firmly back in the fashion lead, it is possible that New York, benefiting from stability and a buoyant economy, would have taken the world lead and kept it permanently.

As it is, American design began to cross the Atlantic only in the late 1970s, by which time it had become very distinct and healthy. When we talk about American fashion we must take into account the fact that it has two distinct roots, which reflect the differences between urban and rural America. On one side there is the country-based, down-to-earth, healthy America of Audubon, Thoreau and Whitman. It produces designers like Cashin and McCardell, who create simple yet sophisticated natural looks based on outdoor work-clothes and clothes evolved for country living. The other side reflects the slick pace of modern city life (and no cities are more 20th-century than America's) — the General Motors, 'high tech.' gloss. Elegant, urbane clothes for elegant, urbane and rich women living lives almost totally city-based, produced by Mainbocher and Norell in the past, are now the looks created by Halston, Blass and de la Renta. The influence of both these streams has grown and, in London especially, the American way of dressing is attracting more and more devotees. A measure of the transatlantic influence – or at least of European interest in American fashion – can be gained from *Le Grand Divertissement à Versailles*, held in November 1973, in which five leading French couturiers (Bohan, Cardin, Givenchy, Saint Laurent and Ungaro) with the Baronne Marie-Helène de Rothschild invited five leading American designers (Blass, Burrows, de la Renta, Halston and Anne Klein) to present a special collection for the benefit of the Château de Versailles. This major social event was held in the Théâtre Royal at Versailles.

It must be said that America's great contribution is ease: the best American looks are sophisticated and glamorous but also – perhaps above all – relaxed and nonchalant. Many would agree with Charles James that blue denim is America's great gift to the world. Certainly the way American designers (like McCardell in the 1940s) took this heavy-duty work material and created a lasting fashion from it is amazing. They were years before their time, although in the last fifteen years the rest of the world has learned that denim is one of fashion's ideal materials: it is smart and classless; it also seems healthy and in American healthy means sexy too.

As the 1970s continued, the fourth, and possibly the most lasting challenge to Paris was the growth of Japanese fashion, not only in Japan, but also in the French capital itself. Will the future of fashion lie in the East and, if so, what sort of fashion will it be? When the Japanese first appeared in Paris in the persons of Kenzo and Mori, their approach to fashion was within a Western framework — although even when they designed in a consciously Western way they still produced something very Japanese to occidental eyes. The elements of Japanese fashion until the early 1980s have been functional simplicity and adaptability of the kind associated with kimonos, sliding partitions and screens (which are so much a part of Japanese architecture) and that most perfectly elegant poetic form, the *haiku*. Certainly the Japanese revolt against figure-hugging status clothes and the emphasis on the layering and wrapping of the body suggested a new way of dressing for the women of the 1980s. With their respect for the beauty inherent in the materials they use, their design adaptability and their austerely selective visual sense the first wave of Japanese designers, such as Miyake and Kenzo, have had a very positive influence not only in Paris, but throughout the West generally.

The second wave of Japanese designers in Paris has been much more aggressively indifferent to Western mores and more uniquely Japanese in

Miyake 1984

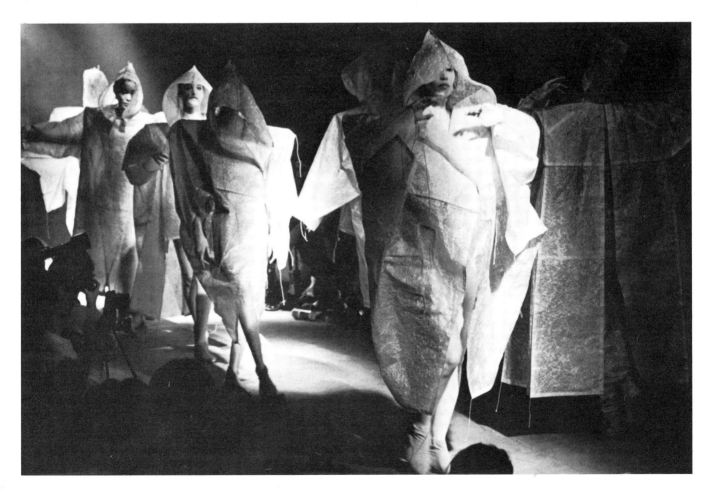

its approach. Designers like Rei Kawakubu of Comme des Garçons and Yohji Yamamoto have perversely chosen Paris, the traditional home of elegant and perfectly made clothes, as the beachhead for their new, anti-designer looks. They have done so because Paris is still the pivot of world fashion and for the Japanese fashion contribution to have credibility it must conquer at the highest point. Certainly the Japanese look of the 1980s could not be further removed from the traditions of Paris, but it has been taken seriously by press and buyers alike. Growing from the layered and wrapped looks of Miyake and Kenzo, it has moved further along the path leading to the importance of texture rather than form. Materials are knotted, twisted, wrapped and draped to create a Christo effect of *trompe l'oeil*. The smooth satins, refined wools and soft silks have been supplemented, and often replaced, by crumpled, slashed and rough torn cotton, canvas, rubber and denim. All of this is surprising, when placed in the context of Paris, but it is closely linked with the approach to dress which has been evolved by the young in London over the last few years. Vivienne Westwood and Rei Kawakubo share a radical approach to materials, shapes, people and society which could point the way for the future.

The final and most fundamental question for fashion in this century is whether it can survive at all in the welter of looks and styles which seem to increase annually and which have often very little to do with what designers and fashion magazines are saying. The Punk phenomenon in London (which was taken up, though to a far lesser degree, in New York and Paris) was largely created on the streets in opposition to what the designers wanted. Is this the future? Is fashion, without the lead of couture, doomed to rush around crazily like a chicken without a head before it dies? Do women want a fashionable, imposed look or are they happy with odd clothes which they put together as they wish? Fashion design in the French way meant elegance, beauty and glamour; it meant women, not girls; it meant clothes as status-makers and for over fifty years the rest of the world accepted these limitations. Elegance and glamour are now almost taboo, because they are not only elitist, they are also increasingly dangerous. The socially confident, financially secure fashion-leaders of the past, who were prepared to use their appearance to proclaim their superiority and their wealth, are increasingly reluctant to do so. Muggers, kidnappers and taxmen impose circumspection. It becomes more and more obvious that the socially underprivileged, who in the past gaped in awe at the gilded ones, no longer intend to do so. Fashion is also endangered by the emergence of the girl as fashion-leader. Elegant, structured clothes are for women who wish to look like women. Now women wish to look like girls and, just as girls would look ridiculous in couture, so women look ridiculous in things like the mini (the classic example of manipulation masquerading as emancipation). Therefore no fashion look can be imposed and fashion design has become a free-for-all.

Status and clothing are no longer linked and what is being done by the designer is of very little general interest. No longer are there reactions like that of the Archbishop of Naples, who blamed the 1925 Amalfi earthquake on the scandalously short new skirts. No longer do newspapers give the collections front page headlines. Clothes are merely clothes. Fashion is what you make it and the fashionable 'court' shrinks almost into insignificance.

Perhaps the fashion industry, which is an essentially 20th century phenomenon, will not even reach its centenary. By the end of the decade every individual will perhaps be making his or her own look taken from any period or country at whim. Will the dictates of Paris, Milan, New York and Tokyo be of no significance to anyone except the manufacturers?

Predictions are dangerous, but some comment must be made on the Punk phenomenon. Has it any real relevance to fashion in the sense of imposed but non-static modes of dressing? Punk is part of the street revolution which began many years ago in London — home of the subversively original and aggressively uncommitted. In the first three years of this decade the strongest development has been the desire to look poor, but behind this is a movement which could have a much more lasting and far-reaching influence. This is the boy/girl look phenomenon. Slowly it is becoming more acceptable for boys to look like girls, just as girls have dressed like boys with increasing frequency in the post-fifties era. It began with Mick Jagger wearing dresses to shock us and force us to question stereotypes. This is still the motive. But the effects are less shocking. Ten years ago people were startled when a boy wore an earring. Forgetting the traditionally virile swashbuckling pirate and *his* earring, people assumed the boy was homosexual. At the time it was probably true. Now earrings are worn by all types of boys and the gay stigma has gone. Today, the new way to shock the old is for boys to wear make-up. Again, though homosexuality is suspected, it cannot be taken for granted. Brightly coloured hair is frequently aggressively heterosexual.

The layered, draped look could be the real unisex fashion for the unisex future. Sexual stereotypes have become loosened and with this has come a loosening of the approach to dress. The girl/boy look has been joined by the boy/girl look and, more and more obviously, the young are using clothes to make statements of their power. In this, they are like their 18th-century counterparts. The punk and the boy/girl frighten and distance society every bit as much as the courtier and his lady intimidated the peasants of the past. They use the same weapon, their clothes. The wheel has come full circle.

Piguet 1937

FASHION AND THE ARTS

When Elsa Schiaparelli burst upon the fashion world with a sweater that had a *trompe l'oeil* bow incorporated in the knitting, she was consciously echoing the surrealistic artist's delight in things not being what they at first appear to be. Coco Chanel simplified the shape of women's clothes to a square cardigan and rectangular skirt. This was a Cubist concept: geometric simplicity to give a line of strength and force. Yves Saint Laurent produced an instant fad when he created dresses which were like Mondrian paintings that moved. Dress designers have always been aware of what is happening in the arts and have always been able to use the discoveries and ideas of the artist to help them solve design problems and create clothes which are new, inventive and reflective of their time. In the first fifty years of this century the artistic world was constantly producing new ideas and movements and the world of fashion responded to and reflected them all in greater or lesser degree.

Central to any discussion of the arts and fashion in this century is Paris. The capital of France became the capital of the world, as far as art was concerned, in the first decade of the century and continued to be so right up to the start of World War II. It was the Mecca to which everyone turned. Russian emigrés, American musicians, Irish writers, Italian painters all flooded into the most exciting city in the world. Paris had always been the crossroads for refugees, fugitives, the unwanted and the persecuted, and in their number were included people of the highest talents upon whose abilities fashion-empires were based — the tailors, cutters and dressmakers without whose skills no designer can succeed. The pre-eminence of Paris in the fashionable world sprang from the nature of French life and society. Whereas in England, for example, the rich and aristocratic have traditionally been in love with their acres, spending as much time as possible in the country, their French counterparts have since the days of François I preferred the life of the city. So Paris became a smart and sophisticated city in ways that London did not. It was a fashionable city where the needs of the fashionable had to be catered for. Fashionable people are very demanding and to meet their demands couturiers had to aim for perfection. Anyone with aspirations to be a dress designer had to conquer Paris, were he from the provinces, like many of the French designers, or from abroad. Its pre-eminence as a fashion city was unassailable for the first sixty years of this century and, even today, although its power is weakened, it still remains of vital importance.

When Diaghilev's Ballets Russes arrived in Paris from St. Petersburg in 1909, it took the fashionable world by storm. The Company consisted of a group of avant-garde musicians, painters and dancers whose combined efforts created a new form of ballet: barbaric, exotic and colourful. It shocked the West and the shock waves reverberated for years. It created such an impact, not because its oriental and exotic themes were a dazzling revelation, but because the treatment of them was. The craze for *Chinoiserie* and *Japonaiserie* in porcelains and lacquers had been long established; Persian rugs, Orientalist painting such as portraits by Delacroix of Algerian women, and the exotic writings of Baudelaire and Rimbaud were all familiar. What electrified Paris was the unfamiliar music, the amazing costumes and decor and the aggressively sensual dancing of Nijinsky. The effect was so overwhelming that it led to a complete re-appraisal in the arts of decoration, fashion and jewellery.

Diaghilev's strength lay in his ability to spot the talents of everyone of any importance in the arts. His music was provided by Stravinsky, Satie, Poulenc, Milhaud and Hindemith, while the artists who worked on his costumes and sets included Picasso, Derain, Matisse, Braque, Ernst, Miró, de Chirico, Pevsner, Gabo and Bakst. From the fashion point of view, Bakst had the most direct impact, especially on attitudes towards colour and pattern, but the importance of the Ballets Russes in re-shaping attitudes to all aspects of the decorative arts cannot be overstressed. Its effect upon fashion was to create a new approach to colour and a new feel for fabric and, even as late as the 1970s, it was still proving a rich quarrying ground for fabric and dress designers. It is probably the single most important influence on fashion this century. Its impact was seen most obviously in Poiret's enthusiastic response, but it is not too far-fetched to say that ballets like *Le Train Bleu* and *Les Matelots* even helped to create a new demand for beach and casual wear that Chanel was soon to exploit.

In the first twenty years of the 20th century the art world was turned on its head so many times by so many different schools that it is almost impossible to keep track of the changes. In the first decade Matisse and a group of friends that included Derain, Vlaminck and Rouault found themselves labelled 'Fauves' (wild beasts), because of their dramatic breaking of previously held rules about colour. No longer could grass be relied upon to be green: blue or red were equally acceptable to the Fauves. In the same decade fashion's Fauve, Paul Poiret, began to menace the cosy hegemony of Worth and the other designers. He was excited by the power of colour in the same intense way as the 'wild beasts' of art. Fauvism was the song of pure colour. It was not a school and it had no theory, manifesto or programme. It burst on the art world at the 1905 Salon d'Automne, where the work of Matisse and his followers was shown. Its liberating effect for all who saw it cannot be overestimated. Two years later, the Cézanne retrospective at the Salon, together with the growing interest in African sculpture and primitive art, stimulated Braque, Picasso,

Molyneux 1938

Patou 1939

Gris and Derain towards their experiments with the simplification of form which led to Cubism.

No less intellectually probing and radical were the artistic anarchists who were re-thinking the whole approach to fine art and unsettling the bourgeois desire for the preservation of the *status quo*. The Italian influence was seen in Paris in 1909, when Marinetti published the manifesto of Futurist poetry in *Le Figaro*. It extolled the beauty of speed and violent movement. The artistic expression of these views was seen in the Futurist paintings of Boccionic and Carrà, whose work influenced the Surrealist, de Chirico. Dada, Constructivism, Expressionism, Neo-plasticism and Elementarism all had their effect. Dada was especially important for fashion in that it led to surrealism in dress design. The term, Dada, was first used in 1916 by Tristan Tzara, the Romanian poet who, along with Arp, founded the movement. Their approach to art owed much to the implacable logic of the anti-aesthetic Duchamp and had at its core a desire to undermine by any means the traditional bases of social and cultural order and stability. From this movement came the themes provided by unconscious dreams and hallucinations, which were the basis of the surrealism of Ernst, Breton, Dali, Man Ray and Magritte. Dali, as a designer who collaborated with Schiaparelli, and Man Ray, as a fashion photographer, had a far-reaching and lasting influence on fashion.

Before World War I, the move away from representational art was based on a rejection of naturalism. Then abstraction for its own sake took over and led to the non-representational approach which has largely dominated the art of this century. It can be said to have begun in 1910 when Kandinsky was inspired by a brilliantly coloured dress fabric (it is tempting to imagine it being by Poiret, under the influence of the Ballets Russes), combined with the unexpectedly liberating effect of seeing one of his pictures lying on its side, to produce a watercolour which was the first totally abstract painting in the history of Western art. It had no recognizable point of reference and no representational purpose. From then on the song was clear for artists, decorators, designers and couturiers and simplification was the tune. Let the melody linger on, but get rid of the twiddly bits. Kandinsky's Munich-based movement, the *Blaue Reiter*, embraced all the arts and was enthusiastically revolutionary. So was *Die Brücke*, the German equivalent of the Fauves. Together, these movements included Macke, Marc, Jawlensky, Nolde, and van Dongen — a handful of giants whose influence was enormous.

These first years of the century were fascinating and the period prior to World War I was surely more inventive and revolutionary than any other period in the history of the arts in the West. Never had artistic thinking moved so quickly and fundamentally to question all previously held assumptions and to make so many of them invalid for the new century. This was the era of the radical re-thinking of volume, mass and colour which produced the first experiments in abstraction by Picasso, Braque,

Brancusi and Delaunay. Their conclusions were unlike any solutions to the acts of painting and sculpture which had ever been proposed before. Non-representational painting, which even today is generally known as 'modern', is unique to this century. The artist's age-old concern to express himself in plastic terms had always been central to civilization. Only in this century has he considered it valid to express himself in abstract, non-representational terms. Accurate representation of appearance was previously considered desirable and control of the traditional media of canvas, paint or marble was a vital part of the process. No longer can this be expected: conceptual and minimal art, if indeed they can be considered to be art, have pushed to the limits the alienation between man and his materials. For the first time in history a man can be taken seriously as an artist even though he lacks manual dexterity and is the master of no medium. Art has become the victim of cerebralism.

If the Ballets Russes was exotic, the Bauhaus was, with typically German precision, thorough. This movement was begun in Munich in 1911 by Walter Gropius, who believed in the virtues of a modern, clean, radical approach to design, based on simplicity and craftsmanship. In many ways Gropius followed the teachings of William Morris and what he offered to the fashion world was the concept of suitability of purpose in design and a rigorous simplicity of line and decoration. The Bauhaus approach was scientific: an object which functioned efficiently was automatically successful and also beautiful. The movement had grown from the *Deutscher Werkbund*. Established in 1907 by Hermann Muthesius it may be considered the first real movement in Europe to attempt to reconcile the arts and industry. The Bauhaus continued this philosophy of destroying the barriers between artist and artisan and affirming a faith in good design at all levels of life. Its effect on all aspects of design throughout the 1920s and 1930s was considerable and is still evident. After the exoticism of the Ballets Russes, it created a purer approach to design which resulted in the streamlined, 'machine-turned' hardness of the 1920s fashion stereotype.

The functional approach to all areas of design, involving fundamental reappraisals of purpose in creativity, was developed at the Bauhaus between the wars. In fashion terms it produced an increased desire for a slim, uncluttered profile (clothes as machines to live in, to adapt Le Corbusier's famous adage about houses). There was also a vogue for machine-turned accessories, whose attraction lay in their factory-made, non-craftsman feel and appearance. The enthusiasm for African art, newly discovered by Picasso and Braque, soon showed itself in fashion with the appearance of the smooth shingled head and the long neck: half African princess, half Modigliani portrait. Chanel's imitation jewellery may be said to have sprung from the same source. Modernism, with its interest in new materials, stimulated jewellery designers to use plastic, metal and glass. New dress materials such as wool stockinet and charmeuse appeared. The fascination with metallic, shiny surfaces in fashion

Right: *West African wooden sculpture*

Far right: *Bronze head, by Brancusi (1912)*

is a reflection of the excitement generated by the sophisticated machines and machine-made artefacts which were influencing Pevsner, Arp and Léger.

Man, however, has a need for the decorative and the discursive. The austerity of line and the rejection of detail which characterized the Bauhaus style could not satisfy for long. The depersonalized, mechanical aspect of design which had developed under its influence began to seem too sterile in the 1930s. The hard logic of the Bauhaus approach to design was too austere for a world which had endured financial crashes and mass unemployment. People viewed the future with less and less confidence. They required the comfort and luxury of applied decoration and a personalized environment. Furniture and interiors became almost baroque; fashion and personal appearances softened; romance became fashionable again. People wanted a degree of fantasy to take their minds off the worrying and confusing realities of finance, politics and international tensions. They found it in the highly personal vision of the Surrealists, whose juxtapositioning of unexpected images was disarming, but whose use of recognizable non-abstract symbols and objects was at the same time reassuring.

Art and fashion probably held hands closest in the 1930s, when Schiaparelli was creating clothes directly influenced by the Surrealist thinking of her friend Salvador Dali and using prints designed by Dufy and Berard.

The purity of line and design strength which appeared in Europe early in the century for the first time with the discovery of Primitive — particularly African — art had an immediate effect on avant-garde artists, especially sculptors. When the public eye had become accustomed to the simplified lines of abstract shapes, fashion exploited and popularized them.

Although by no means the greatest Surrealist, Dali was the most influential in the field of fashion. His humorous conceits, almost metaphysical, often lent a nightmare quality of illogicality to his paintings — watches melted and people's bodies consisted of drawers. His sense of humour, his ability to shock and his irreverence appealed enormously to Schiaparelli, who also had these characteristics. Together they worked closely to amuse and delight the fashionable, designing fabrics, clothes and accessories which gave free rein to their love of *trompe l'oeil*. Their clients slid laughing towards war without, apparently, even noticing.

The Ballets Russes, Surrealism and the Bauhaus all had considerable effects on fashion. They permanently changed people's ways of looking and thinking. Our perception of colour and shape, as we view all aspects of design in our daily lives, comes from the experiments of the artists who, without our realizing it, push forward our visual awareness. The process is simple. It begins with public outrage and uncomprehending shock at the unfamiliar. This is followed by commercial design exploitation of the artist's vision. From this comes visual familiarity with the new imagery and, finally, public acceptance. So developments in colour, pattern and texture reflect the major movements in the fine arts.

World War II brought to a close the period when Paris was indisputably the art centre of the world. After 1939 those key artistic figures who were

McCardell 1946

still alive joined the stream of political and ethnic refugees which flowed from war-torn Europe to an America offering social and artistic freedom. Immediately after World War II the softening of fashion, which had been a growing force throughout the 1930s, continued with Dior's 'New Look', possibly the most inaptly named fashion of all time. It was really an old look derived from appearances of a past which could never be recaptured. Here the artistic influences were the 18th-century paintings of Boucher and Fragonard together with the 19th-century paintings of Winterhalter and Sargent.

It was not until the late 1950s that modern art began to reassert its influence on fashion and the other minor arts with the spin-off from Op Art. Op Art, a movement which was strongest in Great Britain and the United States, delighted in the optical effects caused by paint laid in thin lines or circles to a totally abstract pattern. The results were shimmering 'movements' on the canvas as the viewer's eye tried to adjust to what it saw. The influence of this movement on designers was considerable. Not only did it affect colour and pattern in the design of material but, more broadly, it changed attitudes to what could or could not be done with pattern generally. Stripes, polka dots and waving lines could now all be used together in the same outfit — before Op Art it would have been a solecism to combine them. The geometric feel of much Op Art helped lead designers to a geometric approach to fashion in the 1960s. The designs of Courrèges and Quant were based on a strange (and probably subconscious) mixture of Cubism and Op Art. Their shapes were stiff and static: short rectangular skirts, tubular torsos and trousers with abstract, optical patterning in strong colours contrasting with pure white backgrounds. These hard shapes, like the sculpture of Calder and Caro, were almost an end in themselves and frequently made few concessions to the body inside — a body which had to be very young if the clothes were to reflect the dream of their designer.

A century which had dawned at a high point of ostentation, excess and extravagance had streamlined itself, stripped itself down to essentials in both the major and minor arts, and begun to build up to the glorification of all things youthful which is still continuing today.

Throughout the century, influences other than art have also been working on fashion. Two of the many remarkable changes which differentiate the 20th century from all previous centuries are in transport and in the appearance of women. Since the beginning of time mankind had been tied to the earth and had moved across its surface either on foot or by using horses. This century has seen the internal combustion engine replace the horse as a means of transport and it has witnessed man's rise to the skies and beyond. Intercontinental flight has led to interplanetary flight. The effects of these changes on our attitudes have been profound: alongside growing confidence is an increased uncertainty, as the boundaries of the familiar change and the environment expands, forcing us to do so too. How men and women view their own roles and those of each other has also altered significantly throughout the century. From these changes has come a new concept of how women may be permitted to look, though even now this is still decided largely by male attitudes towards them. For the first time in history women living normal lives have bared not only their knees, but even their thighs, with only a minimum of social disapproval. Previously such behaviour was confined to the Amazon or the whore. Again, only in this century have women who are not on the stage or impersonating men been permitted to wear trousers. These changes in the appearance of women occurred in the 1920s, a period of instability and confusion equalled only by the 1970s, which shared its excesses and uncertainties and the female addiction to wearing trousers.

Parallel with the intense artistic activity of the first quarter of the century was an increasingly liberal view of a woman's role in society and what she could or could not be permitted to do. One of the most liberating influences, which had a considerable effect on fashion, was the growth of interest in sport and leisure activities. Women were allowed more and more opportunities to be actively involved in sports previously considered too manly or, at least, not sufficiently polite or ladylike for them. Sweating, although never to be directly named, was even considered acceptable! Women slowly began to enjoy their own physicality and, although the days of accepting even the possibility of female orgasm were still a very long way off, they began the long love-affair with their bodies which was so eagerly fuelled by commercial interests and is still going strong today. By the mid-1920s women enjoyed a freedom undreamed of just fifteen years before. They no longer had to wait for the safety of middle age to achieve an individual identity. Suddenly, youth was all. However, not only youth but, paradoxically, male youth seemed the ideal.

The long neck and tiny head of the Mannerist school, seen most characteristically in the female figures in the paintings of Parmigianino, became the new ideal through the medium of fashion illustrations. At the same time, the illustrations reflected Cubist discoveries in their tendency to draw the female body in terms of simply treated, cylindrical forms. This also echoed the new interest in African art which had been stimulated by the Colonial Exhibition held in Marseilles in 1922. The bird-like silhouette, skinny as a young boy with tiny shingled head, destroyed the Edwardian mono-bosom for ever. With the birth of the 'new woman', personified by Nancy Mitford's Mrs. Chaddesley Corbett, no woman of elegance could ever be plump again. In *Love In a Cold Climate* even such an apparently hopelessly unfashionable figure as that cut by Lady Montdore could be kneaded, starved and exercised into androgynous simplicity of line under the right stimulus and direction. The whole look was bisexual: no bosom, no hair, trousers, cigarettes and a highly aggressive approach to sport

Fath 1947

were the hallmarks of the new woman. This strange new development must have had something to do with World War I. Was it some sort of compensation for the thousands of young men who were lost? Did girls wish to take on the roles that would have been played by their lovers and brothers? They certainly took up their brothers' sports – swimming, skiing, golf and tennis became increasingly popular and their specialist clothing had distinct effects on women's day-to-day dressing. Modesty became unfashionable and the new pastime of sunbathing, on the newly-discovered beaches of the South of France, began the passion for backless evening dresses which were a feature of the 1920s and 1930s. It was considered glamorous and sexy to bare the back, all the more so if the back were tanned. The days when ladies shunned the sun in order to keep their refined pale looks were gone. Suddenly everyone wanted to look as if they spent their days toiling in the fields under a Mediterranean sun. At the same period it became *chic* to have been born black. In Paris, especially, black musicians playing ragtime, black beauties like Josephine Baker and even the 'black bottom' dance were *le dernier cri* in smartness.

All this healthy sporting activity, and women's desire to occupy their days in more interesting ways than dragging around a heavy and cumbersome outfit, weakened the power of the couturier to treat his customers as objects upon which to hang his marvellous creations. Although it was to be a long time dying, the 1920s saw couture at the beginning of its terminal illness. The disease was social: women began to see that there were advantages to putting clothes in their place, which men had done for many years, rather than being put in their place by clothes. At the beginning this was a largely Anglo-American feeling. Not until after World War II did French women seriously begin to wish for freedom from fashion's dictates.

Throughout the twenties the fashionable mood was informal, if a little frenetic in its pursuit of fun. The talkies were exciting, cocktails 'divine' and international travel *de rigueur*, especially cruising, which produced a new relaxed form of clothing. The 'Expo Deco' in Paris in 1925, the architecture of Le Corbusier and the teaching of Walter Gropius made fashionable folk very aware of the cross-fertilization between art and design. Dufy and Delaunay designed fabrics; Derain designed the sets for *Le Train Bleu*, which, along with Pruna's sets and costumes for *Les Matelots*, had profound effects on dress design; Giacometti designed lamps for Jean-Michel Franck. The artists were at the centre of the fashion world. Poiret was in decline and Chanel, Patou and Lelong were in the ascendant. Things had moved a long way from the Big Bertha bang of Bakst's cacophony of colour. Sarah Bernhardt, Eleanora Duse and Isadora Duncan, once such fashionable examples to smart dressers, seemed as remote as Egyptian mummies. Poor Poiret, who still dearly loved a tassel, could only blame income tax and dieting for what he saw as the destruction of fashion. He could not understand that dancing (people danced at virtually any hour) and skinny, nimble girls who were 'sports' were now 'in'. Fashion shows were smart social occasions, like theatrical first nights, for *tout Paris*, and only the grandest press and buyers were asked to attend. Dressmakers' boutiques became social meeting-places. Patou even had a cocktail bar for husbands and lovers to wait in. Then Wall Street crashed and the dining and dancing stopped. After 1929 fun suddenly became unfashionable.

Curiously, the effect of the world-wide financial crisis on fashion was not as great as one would expect. Although, in the season after The Crash, not one American buyer went to Paris and there was no full return until 1932, the dress houses weathered the storm. They were even able to adapt to the dramatic drop in the number of private customers and the changed buying pattern of the trade. Before the slump a buyer purchased from a Paris house individual dresses in the original material to resell to private customers. After the slump the American government imposed a duty of up to ninety per cent of the original cost on all the dresses being brought from Paris. Toiles, however, were duty free, so that buyers turned to buying more and more of these calico models to make up (often in the original Paris material) in workrooms in America.

The reason the French dressmakers could survive the crisis lay in the nature of the French fashion industry. It was far less industrialized than its English or American counterparts and therefore was less affected by the slump. Most of the French fashion-workers were women, often part-time, who worked for very low wages. Production costs were kept low and the drop in revenue could be absorbed. Nevertheless, the crisis was real enough: Vionnet, a highly admired couturier, was forced to halve her production in the ten years after 1928.

Although fashion production was not changed as much as expected by the Depression, fashion and fashionable attitudes were. A new softness, formality and dignity came in. Girls stopped being tough. They were not called 'baby' any more; 'darling' seemed more appropriate. They no longer looked like adolescent boys and they clearly wished to recapture the joys of femininity. Throughout the decade glamour and luxury were what everyone craved. They obtained them from the Hollywood dream factory. This was the age of the cinema. As life became more sombre and serious, with Hitler in power by 1933 and democracy endangered by the spread of Fascism and Communism in Europe, the movies became the means of escape from reality. Alongside the increasingly grim figures for unemployment came ever more sumptuous and magnificently-costumed films as a means of escape from cruel fact: the popular gods and goddesses were film stars. The importance of Paris as the maker of fashion was obviously affected by this: a Travis Banton costume for a Hollywood film seen by millions would have more fashion impact in numerical terms than a photograph of a Molyneux dress in a magazine seen only by a few thousands.

Length returned: women's hair became longer; so did their skirts. Decoration returned: sterile, blank surfaces gave way to the opulence of

Erogenous zones come and go but no matter what is required the female form can always be adapted to deliver the goods. The bosom has had a particularly chequered time. The Edwardian mono-bosom, emphasized by a tightly laced waist, slowly deflated until, by the mid twenties, it had entirely disappeared . . .

. . . Mae West's hourglass figure re-instated the big-busted look with sufficient conviction to fulfil any male fantasy, as the naming of the inflatable life belt clearly shows . . .

antiques; walls were covered, not with Eileen Gray lacquers, but with what Osbert Lancaster has called 'a surprisingly abundant supply of suspicious Canalettos'. Gold returned: in place of the hard, machine-turned jewellery of the 1920s in silver, aluminium and glass, gold chains and gilt enamel brooches were worn. Hats returned: frivolous ones with veils, feathers, ribbons and flowers, either tiny or broad-brimmed. The 'little black dress' was born and soon became the basis of any *chic* woman's wardrobe. Although Paris talked of *la crise*, and it was smart to pretend poverty, clothes and interiors became more sumptuous as the years went by. Syrie Maughan's all-white rooms were the epitome of luxury, as was the baroque figure of Mae West, whose fame and popularity were world-wide. The story goes that Schiaparelli murmured 'shocking' when she saw the mannequin made to the star's measurements, thus creating the name and bottle-shape for her most famous scent. Mae West's popularity revealed how completely attitudes towards women had changed since the 1920s. Her figure would have been considered grotesque by the flappers. Now there were no more women masquerading as youths. Femininity was back and glamour, fed by Hollywood movies, was in. Make-up was no longer hard and dramatic, but soft and more natural. The twenties mask had gone. All of this showed an increasingly mature self-realization on the part of women. They knew that they could be feminine and not

. . . It was Monroe and Mansfield who brought it back to its overblown baroque magnificence. But in the sixties little girls with naughty mini-skirts and unlikely hair made the bosom take second place.

Opposite: Scenes like this became commonplace in Europe during the war. Such devastation and the despair it caused led to the instant response to Dior's romantic gesture to make the horrors of war less potent. The acceptance of The New Look was a rejection of the memories of bombs, starvation and concentration camps.

risk losing their new freedoms. They no longer had to act tough to face up to men. This emancipation was to be dramatically advanced in the next decade.

The 1940s, dominated as they were by World War II and its aftermath, saw fashion frozen for over half the decade. At the same time, however, attitudes changed dramatically. These changed attitudes were to affect fashion permanently from the 1950s onwards but, before they did, the most amazing development in the history of 20th-century fashion took place. After the austerity of the war, Dior's 'New Look', launched in 1947, burst upon the world like a phoenix from the ashes. But this was a phoenix singing like a lark. It was one of couture's greatest moments but, at the same time, possibly its silliest. Dior's 'New Look' was fighting a rearguard action. It was an anachronism. It required corsets and padding and it made women once more subservient to their clothes. It was successful because of its timing. Bringing back prettiness and femininity, as it did, it was eagerly taken up by nations exhausted and debilitated by war. It was a much-needed salve to their wounds. Launched at any other time, it would not have had half the impact it did. Dior's name became one of only two or three known throughout the world, as familiar as those of Hitler and Churchill.

Dior was the first and last couturier to whom this has happened. His 'look' with its long full skirts and tight waists was not really new. It grew logically from the immediately pre-war fashions, but its impact came from an almost 18th-century exaggeration. It became the only look for the late forties, but by the beginning of the fifties, Dior's supremacy was overshadowed by Balenciaga, whose amazingly powerful, forward-looking approach to haute couture slowly began to soften and unstructure clothes. Balenciaga's innovations led eventually to the relaxed shapes of the last two decades. All in all, the 'New Look' and the couture clothes that developed from it proved to be the most glorious of blind alleys in fashion history.

The 1950s saw many changes, not the least surprising being the re-emergence from retirement in Switzerland of one of the great names of the past: Coco Chanel. She was persuaded to make her comeback because of Dior. She wanted to stop him. At the age of seventy-one she still believed that only women could design for women. Dior's new romanticism, she believed, went against what women really wanted. With her canny peasant instinct, she sensed that women would not put up for long with corsets, padded bras and moulded jackets. Her re-opening in 1954 was sombre. Most of the press felt her clothes to be old-fashioned and provincial and said that she was too old to understand the new woman. But in fact the new woman began to buy, first in America and then in Europe, and the press had to follow the lead. Her second collection was a sensation. Interviewed by *Life* about her victory, she said 'a garment must be logical'. With that she had said everything about the unreality of most couture clothes in the 1950s.

Although she was still working in couture, Chanel's clothes, by their very simplicity, were easily copied. So they were responsible for yet another death-shudder in couture. Again, women were demanding more accessible clothes. They were no longer interested in standing for at least three fittings, waiting for delivery and paying the earth for the finished result. Even those women who made up the dwindling number of regular couture wearers began to supplement their wardrobes with ready-to-wear outfits. During the 1950s, Paris couture still gave the unrivalled fashion lead, but the Italians were beginning to organize themselves and in Florence Signor Giorgini, backed by his government, began to promote extravagant fashion shows in Palazzo Pitti which were later followed by Rome showings. Soon Rome became the centre of the Italian *alta moda*, as it remains today, with Florence show-casing the less glamorous, but financially very important, areas of Italian fashion.

Throughout the 1950s interest in fashion was stimulated by considerable changes in length and silhouette, but nothing could alter the fact that the world was moving towards the 'now' generation. Fast, instant clothes, cheaply produced and quickly dispensable, were on the horizon. High fashion was doomed. The 1950s also saw the death of formality: hats and gloves lost their importance as part of an elegant woman's 'look' and they never regained it. The era of hair was beginning: rollers and hairspray made the wildest fancies possible and by the 1960s hairstyles were more ridiculous and extravagant than they had been since pre-revolutionary France. Artificiality had become the province of fashion, with these exaggerated heads and the new wildly extreme stiletto heels. Reality was somewhere far away from the perfumed salons. Now it was on the streets of Paris, London and New York. Casual, iconoclastic youth, personified by Bardot, was about to bring about its fashion revolution and bring to a climax the movement begun forty years before. For the first time in fashion history the young were about to lead the old. The rich and grand were ready to ape their social and financial inferiors. Parisian supremacy was shaken because the young turned not to France for inspiration, but to London and in the next decade, increasingly, towards America.

Fighting a rearguard action, French couture struck back at the youth movement in the first year of the decade, when the house of Dior sacked Yves Saint Laurent for attempting to introduce the Beat Generation uniform of black leather into high fashion. Paris had now to share its leadership with London and, for a time, London seemed to be in the lead. Its ascendancy did not last long. As soon as the Paris houses had adjusted to

Charles James 1950

the new era, in which couture was no longer so important and *prêt-à-porter* was, the skill, taste and ideas of the French designers quickly re-established France's pre-eminence. Even in Paris, however, it was a period of uncertainty, fear and anarchy in fashion as the quick succession of mini, maxi and midi length showed only too well. Designers looked everywhere for inspiration. Films like *Dr. Zhivago* and *Bonnie and Clyde* were eagerly quarried for ideas; Mondrian was a major influence for an Yves Saint Laurent collection; foreign travel brought an endless series of ethnic looks. In all it was the classic post-revolutionary confusion.

That there had been a revolution could not be denied. Social attitudes had changed permanently and fashion aspirations had altered irrevocably. The major catalysts of these changes were the Pill and the feminist movement. The importance of their impact on fashion cannot be overstated. Together they changed women's view of their role in society, which has a vital effect on how women see themselves in relation to fashion. The Pill put women in a position of control which had previously been denied to all but the most privileged. With this new position women gained a self-assertiveness which meant that designers could no longer impose their will; they could merely suggest a way of looking which the new women would take or leave according to how they wanted to project their image.

The final point to note is the enormous influence exerted, through the young, by pop music. As an inspiration and force in fashion, it has rivalled the painterly movements and the Hollywood films of earlier decades. As we have seen, up until the advent of World War II art and fashion were closely linked. Designers responded to and reflected the advanced thinking of painters and sculptors. By the end of the 1950s the place of art as a major influence on fashion had been usurped by popular music and the 'pop culture' it spawned. The disaffection of youth, which reached its most extreme form with the Punk culture of the late 1970s and early 1980s, began with the new, bold sounds, the erotic dance movements and the super-charged sexiness of the pop singers. Suddenly, the young realized that, although their parents and society generally might disapprove of the suggestive gyrations of Presley and Jagger, they were powerless to do anything about them. From this revelation grew the anarchy and iconoclasm of the Sex Pistols who, twenty years later, personified the feeling of the young that they could and would make their own rules. It was a part of youth's rejection of the grown-up world as culturally irrelevant. With the new music went new attitudes to clothes and sexuality. Teddy Boys, Hell's Angels, Mods and Rockers were all male-orientated. The clothes they wore influenced, and were influenced by, stage performers. The fashion story of the late 1950s and the 1960s was a reflection of the power of Jimi Hendrix, the Beatles and the Rolling Stones. It was the beginning of the fashion reversal: no longer from couture to street but, increasingly, from street to couture house.

After the confusion of the 1960s, with its space-age looks, unisex

Balenciaga 1951

clothes and perverse little-girl clothes, the 1970s began exhausted. London's brief light as a fashion leader guttered and died. Paris ready-to-wear became indisputably more important than haute couture and Milan began its powerful thrust to rival Paris as the European ready-to-wear capital. As the decade grew the American designers, who had slowly been building up a powerful indigenous fashion scene in New York and, to a lesser degree, Los Angeles, achieved world status and a considerable degree of fashion influence in London and Europe. As the decade drew to its close the Japanese became more and more important in Western fashion. Alongside these developments the movement, which had begun in the 1960s, for looks that bore no relation to fashion designers' ideas continued to grow.

More than ever, the young turned their backs on 'designed' clothes. They took their inspiration from two major sources: war and work. Army-surplus combat gear, especially if from America and previously worn by real soldiers, had a potent appeal for the young, alongside the considerable attraction of black leather and Nazi-style uniforms. S & M, bondage, chains, and tattoos all became popular alternative fashion symbols in London which, since its 'swinging' days, had sometimes seemed to many to rival inter-war Germany for depravity and deviance and yet, perversely, had produced ideas which had exerted real influence on fashion. Along-

Left: *Sonia Delaunay's experiments with abstract patterns taken from cubist paintings and used in clothing have had a persistent influence since she began them in the early twenties. As recently as 1980 Janice Wainwright returned to this rich vein for the abstract patterns seen on these silk dresses (below).*

side the uniform-cult young walked the denim freaks who, male and female alike, tried to look like American long-distance truck drivers. England, always guaranteed to go over the top with a suspect look, produced Punks. The streets of most major cities were awash with waif-like, pale adolescents with spiky hair, looking like animated drawings by Schiele, an artist of whom one in a thousand of them might have heard. The inspiration for much of this sprang from the increasingly influential gay sub-culture which, consisting of narcissistic and comparatively wealthy young men who did not have the traditional demands made on male pockets to support a family, buy a house and educate children, exerted considerable commercial power. In addition, the desire of many homosexuals to play an unreal, fantasy role in life clearly had an influence on the dressing-up and hiding-from-reality aspect of much of the young street fashion.

Economically the 1970s rivalled the 1930s as a time of recession. Although there was no dramatic crash like that of Wall Street, the unemployment figures crept up over the years and the 1980s began in sombre mood. Fashion was in crisis. Lack of money bred lack of confidence and in the second half of the 1970s designers seemed to take to heart Diaghilev's opening comment to Cocteau: 'astonish me'. We were astonished by extremes of shoulder treatment that made Schiaparelli look a total tyro; a Milanese designer copied American baseball shirts and got away with it; the same man attempted to turn women into Samurai warriors, to the delighted applause of the fashion press; an American designer produced skirts made from old patchwork quilts; work-out clothes were made in the most costly cashmere and actually found buyers. It seemed that no historic period or remote corner of the world was safe from the scouring hands of the desperate designer. Wave after wave of retrogressive fashion looks were revived and more and more ethnic styles paraded the runways.

As the 1980s unfold, the signs are that the confusion of the previous two decades will continue. Women are now perfectly secure in their right to reject, their ability to choose and their power to control their appearance. Subservience to the fashion dictators has gone and with it, perhaps, the concept of fashion altogether. No longer do fashion stories really exist; the twice-yearly parading of new styles has less and less relevance to all but the most specialized coterie. What, if anything, has been lost?

CREATING THE LINE

Like Hamlet's mother, the dress designer takes a new spouse with indecent haste. Twice a year, the moment he has shown his collection to the press and buyers of the world, his relationship with it is dead and the search for something new begins. Almost immediately after his show the designer and his team will begin sketching shapes and playing with ideas. Soon the fabric designers will bring him their latest weaves, prints and colours in the hope that they will capture the imagination of the maestro to such a degree that he will use them liberally in his new designs. Also the designer, or his assistants, will probably visit the fabric shows such as 'Idea Como' in Como, Italy, in search of the beautiful materials in which to realize his new ideas for the next season's creations.

With last season's sales figures to guide him, plus the details of those outfits which have been chosen to be photographed by the top fashion magazines, the designer thinks of shape, colour, texture and pattern. His is a strange form of creativity: in one respect he has an almost Olympian freedom, but in another he is as proscribed as Tantalus. The ultimately important thing in his world is the volume of sales. The desire to make something beautiful must very often take second place to commercial considerations. The designer's job is a difficult one. He has to satisfy two different groups. The press demands something new and forward-looking which will photograph well and look as different as possible from last year's look. The buyers also demand something new, but they want something as near as possible in spirit to the successful lines of last season. It is the classic 'art versus commerce' battle and it must be solved more or less successfully well before the collection is shown. The colours and textures must be ordered in advance so that deliveries will be on time – or at least not too drastically late! To do this successfully the designer should have laid down his broad ideas for the coming season quite soon after his last collection. Some designers actually begin to work on their new line on the very day that their fashion show takes place.

The difficulty of the designer's situation becomes apparent when it is remembered that he holds his show six months before any of his designs will appear in the shops. In fact, therefore, the designer is trying to project a look one year in advance. How does he know what women will want in a year's time or what the social and financial climate will be by then? Of course, he does not, so he makes an inspired guess. It is based on what he designed last season and what the fashion magazines show him of the work of his colleagues and rivals. 'Now thrive the armourers': that busy little band of court clerics, the hairdressers, make-up artists and models, mincing from one house to another, come into their own as providers of gossip about what rivals are doing to help the designer make his guess. Making the right guess is both harder and easier today because there are no rigid lines. Skirts can be short or long, full or straight, and many designers play safe by including so many alternatives that their show does not have a 'line' as such at all. From this point of view, things are easier for the designer: he can, in theory, do anything. The hard part is trying to assess what will be taken up by the press and the buyers. They will make a 'line' from the plethora of confusing and sometimes confused ideas presented to them, and the designer is 'out' if he has not included what other designers have or has not emphasized it in his presentation.

In fact, of course, the designer does not depend on pure guesswork. He has the intuition of the trained eye and mind, and is a highly aware and intuitive creature. Nevertheless, if he is wise, he takes advice and suggestions from others. The fabric manufacturers who visit him help considerably; it is often forgotten that they have a real influence on the new looks for the coming season. Materials can be used only to do certain things that are within their nature. So if many manufacturers produce, for example, a special mohair which is bought by several top designers, this is the beginning of a 'look'. Mohair can be made to behave in only a limited number of different ways and the designers will be able to exploit its properties only in certain directions. The similarity between the work of two designers is not the result of collusion or piracy: it is the result of their both being attracted to similar fabrics, colours and patterns. In the days when haute couture was important as a source of ideas, the logic of fashion ensured that different designers would produce similar shapes and lengths.

By logic of fashion is meant the development of ideas to exploit their potential fully. It might take two or three seasons of refinement before their capabilities were fully realized. Today, this luxury is not automatically allowed the designer, to the great detriment of the industry generally. The modern designer is one of two types: the evolutionary or the revolutionary. All too often it is the revolutionary who, no matter how spurious his search for novelty, obtains the coverage in fashion magazines and newspapers.

Encouraging the good designer, as opposed to the 'shocker', is made more difficult by the proliferation of fashion coverage throughout the world and the consequent lowering of journalistic standards. Far too many of the modern fashion writers are artistically and intellectually shallow; they know little of the history of fashion design. Without this knowledge it is hard for them to assess what a designer is attempting to achieve. The great journalists of the past not only had fashion understanding and design intelligence, but they saw themselves in partnership with the designer. By their judicious and informed choice of which of his

Norell 1951

creations they should decide to photograph and write about they helped him to develop his line. Today, novelty is frequently so all-important that ideas are pushed out and gobbled up at lightning speed with very little hope of their potential being fully realized.

But to return to the designer, anxiously poring over his mohair samples. The process of choosing and ordering the fabrics for the new collection can take several weeks. The designer normally sees all representatives personally and discusses their wares with them very closely. He must know exactly what the materials are made of, how they are likely to behave when cut and sewn, whether the price is competitive, how easy it will be to re-order if the materials are used for garments which go into production, whether he has exclusive rights to a material and, if not, who else has ordered. The negotiations are tough. These are important weeks, for a great deal depends on making the right choice. Any mistakes the designer makes at this stage are not easily remedied. As each order is confirmed, a swatch of the material is filed, named or numbered, and its price and quality are noted along with the different colour variations in which it will be produced. This essential, although mundane, work enables a close check to be kept on delivery dates and quality of material when deliveries begin in the succeeding weeks.

During this time the designer is building up his ideas. He and his team produce a considerable number of drawings, which form the basis of any new line, and from them comes the final selection of what is to be made up. At the haute couture end of the business, toiles will be produced for some of these designs, especially if the cut is unusually complicated or the designer and his technical staff are concerned about how a particular design will appear when made up. At the *prêt-à-porter* level this happens less frequently. Paper patterns will be cut and, when the fabrics arrive, the garments will be made up directly. The pattern cutters are, in many respects, the most important members of a designer's team. They are the people who really make possible his ideas. Highly trained and experienced perfectionists that they are, they shoulder a considerable responsibility. On their patterns all production is based, and if they do not get everything right there will be problems with the garments that eventually sell to the public. Their work demands skill and precision along with a full understanding both of the maestro's mind and of the potential of the fabric he is using. Whether production is in the designer's own factory or whether he is using outworkers to make up garments in their homes, the shape of the garment reflects what the cutter has decided is the solution to the problem of interpreting the design correctly in the most suitable material. He and the designer must work together very closely to achieve their ends and, in the event of a disagreement, the wise designer bows to the wisdom of his cutter.

As each model is cut and then made up by trusted and usually long-serving seamstresses, it is brought before the designer for a fitting. These

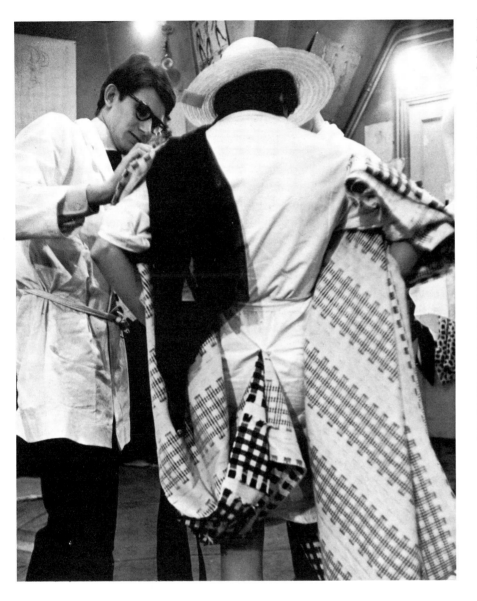

Left: *Yves Saint Laurent, dressed for work as his mentor Dior used to, begins the process of matching fabric and style by draping and pinning materials on the patient house model.*

Below: *A half-finished jacket with Yves Saint Laurent explaining to his seamstress how the back must be adjusted to obtain the exact effect he requires.*

fittings are exciting and important. This is the first time the designer has seen his idea made reality and it is only now that he knows whether it is workable. Along with the designer are the cutter, possibly a seamstress, and his design assistants. The garment will be worn by one of the house models, who will be of standard shape and size, but of a rare degree of patience. Hers is not an easy life. She must stand for many hours while sleeves are ripped out and re-pinned, hemlines altered and pocket-placings changed. Exactly the same things may be done on the same dress the next day, and indeed for many subsequent days, until the designer and his team are satisfied. The fittings are intensely creative: everyone is concentrating, everyone has a particular role (sketching, pinning, noting down alterations) and, at the same time, everyone is looking at the garment in the most critical way possible. Once passed, its next appearance will be on the runway under the discerning gaze of international press and buyers. Cutting and fitting continue in the weeks before the show with increasing momentum. Long hours are worked by everyone, tempers fray, irritations and jealousies surface, the master is frustrated and irritated by the non-delivery of vital materials: the catalogue of problems grows daily.

At the same time other members of the organization are working equally hard, although normally in an atmosphere considerably calmer than that prevailing in the fitting studio. The press office is facing the mammoth task of organizing the seating for the show in order to give the journalists the places that reflect the importance of their publications and their status as individuals. Fashion journalists have powerful egos and can spot a slight at twenty paces – or two places! They are acutely aware of their status and they know that the seat they are given at a show reflects their significance from each designer's point of view. The situation is complicated by the need to balance the importance of national or local writers, whose newspapers may have no sales outside the designer's own country, with that of the internationally famous ones, whose newspapers and journals may not even mention the show.

Major national newspapers are, of course, treated as such and seated accordingly. So are the top international newspapers and fashion magazines. The problems begin for the press office when it comes to consider less clear-cut positions. If the four front rows are filled with the grand ladies of the international and national fashion scene, how do you place the rest? Magazine A, published perhaps in a country such as America with a high sales potential, should perhaps take precedence over newspaper B, with a small but wealthy national readership. However, if newspaper B always mentions the maestro and almost always shows a photograph or drawing of his new line and magazine A is unreliable, who should get the better seat? It is no wonder that the ladies and gentlemen of the press office grow old almost as quickly as they grow hard and cynical! On the day of the show they anxiously scan the rows, looking for the self-satisfied preenings of those whose self-esteem has been gratified, and dreading the frustrated frowns of those who feel they have been slighted. To complicate seating plans further, buyers must also be placed according to their importance, although this is perhaps easier than press placement since their status depends much more clearly on the amount of money they are likely to spend. Those who bought well last season and can be expected to do the same this time are allocated good seats. In addition, seats must be found for suppliers and manufacturers, the designer's friends, especially if they have a 'face' which will attract the *paparazzi*, and, in the case of couture, private clients. Above all, gate-crashers and pirates must be kept out. When all has been decided more or less satisfactorily, strictly non-transferable, named and numbered invitations are sent out and, to ensure a marked and numbered seat, must be acknowledged by the individual journalists. Only with this accreditation will they be allowed entrance to the shows of important designers.

As the date of the show comes near, the question of accessories for the presentation must be discussed by the designer and his manufacturers. How the question is approached depends on whether the designer has accessories made by a licensee to be sold under the designer's name, that is, whether the designer provides the designs or merely lends them his name. Most designers now have a lucrative 'tie-up' with manufacturers who produce accessories under licence, using the designer's name. Stockings, jewellery, make-up and perfume are very commonly marketed in this way and designers are increasingly lending their names to products only indirectly connected with fashion, such as household linen, china and even cars. If the designer is involved with a licensee, then whatever is decided as being suitable for the show must also be suitable for sales afterwards. If the accessories are made only for the show, then life is easier, since quality control and, to a certain extent, cost are not serious considerations. Most designers have a range of hats, shoes and jewellery created especially as accessories for the show, along with belts and handbags. The function of these accessories is to make the show visually exciting and memorable, to set off the clothes in a way that makes them new, interesting and covetable. The accessory manufacturer must talk to the designer and see the clothes (or at least the sketches and swatches), so that he understands the spirit of the collection, knows the colour and textures and is able to go away understanding how to interpret the designs for his particular field of accessories. Usually the designs are provided by one of the master's assistants, but everything is checked and approved by the designer himself before any production begins. The range of specialist manufacturers in the fashion centres of the world is wide and fascinating: old ladies who have spent a lifetime using feathers to create ephemeral additions for dresses; wizened old men who have worked for years with artificial flowers; button-makers, glovers and costume jewellers all play a crucial role as back-up artists to the designer himself.

For the show itself the two most vital elements, after the clothes and accessories, are the music and the model girls. The presentation of clothes has changed considerably since the heyday of Paris couture. Up until the late 1950s, garments were usually shown in silence. The model girl held a card giving the number of the outfit or a compère gave its name and number. The change came with *prêt-à-porter*. Now music is very evident — usually loud, usually disco and usually aimed at exciting the audience while stimulating the models to show the clothes with style and abandon. The type of girl chosen to show the clothes depends very much on the designer's personal taste and the way in which he wishes his clothes to be projected. But it also depends on the prevailing attitudes towards fashion generally. For example, in the late 1970s the clothes and the designers

*Miss Europe 1948 stands whilst the fitter
makes last minute adjustments to her
Maggie Rouff evening dress before it is
shown to the audience.*

seemed to demand a very aggressive sensual movement on the runway
and this was often provided by black models moving to black music. By
the beginning of the 1980s everything had softened: white girls, preferably blond and boyish, showed the new fashions to the accompaniment
of much more gentle sounds.

The choice of girl is important and the designer himself nearly always
makes the final decision. What is required in a good runway model is the
ability to walk and move elegantly or erotically, or both, a look which
reflects the spirit of the clothes, and a figure which by normal standards
might appear slightly bizarre. Height is generally required, long legs are
always necessary, but surprisingly prettiness is rarely a factor. Some of the
most influential and successful runway models have been quite ugly, but
they all have had style and rhythm. A good model can inspire and influence a designer and most of the couturiers have one or two favourites.

The selection of the model girls begins with a close perusal of the composites provided by their agents. These composites are like glossy visiting
cards and contain recent photographs showing the versatility of the girl
and her ability to project a variety of images; they also give her statistics,
which are vital in that shoes must be made for the chosen one and she
must not be so tall or so short that she does not blend with the others.
These composites are looked over by the designer and his assistants. New
faces are noted and prices are negotiated. The price demanded by the
model agencies for good models can be very high indeed, considering the
amount of time spent by them in actually working. The vast majority of
the model girls are known to the designer and he does not need to see
them (although they might well be called in to try on a particular dress
which the designer is not sure about). But he may wish to see one or two
newcomers who seem promising. All of this takes place in the last few
days before the presentation is due. Once booked, the model girl will be
required for a fitting if she is showing an haute couture collection or if
there is something special about the clothes she will wear. She may also,
in certain circumstances, be required to attend a rehearsal.

Frequently, a designer has an arrangement with a cosmetics manufacturer to create, and retail under their joint names, a range of make-up that
complements his new looks and colours for the coming season. Even if
this is not the case, make-up artists must be consulted and colours decided
for the girls' make-up in the show. The same is true for their hair. Particular styles will be decided with a hairdresser to help create the designer's
look. On the day of the show the make-up and hair are done professionally.
The girls will help by preparing head and face in a preliminary way, but
after that they are in the hands of the experts. In fact, nothing is left to
them. They even have professional dressers to get them in and out of their
outfits with the minimum of delay. Nimble-fingered, quick-witted and
deft, these women can strip and re-dress a model in less than three
minutes, including changing tights, jewellery and accessories.

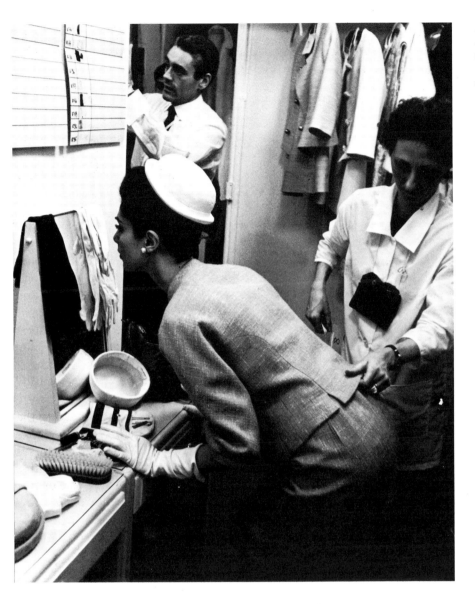

Final adjustments in the cabine before the model girl walks out into the salon to do one of the toughest sales jobs in the world: within a few minutes she must convince a critical audience that this suit is the one!

Modern fashion shows are fast, slick and professional pieces of entertainment and cost a great deal. To enable clothes to be shown with the greatest impact each exit will normally have a minimum of six girls and a maximum of twelve and the clothes they wear will be similar in cut or colour or both. In many cases these figures are dramatically distorted by the designer's insistence on a large number of girls: Calvin Klein once used seventy-two models to show his clothes! The message of each exit must be clear and unequivocal: even the sleepiest and dullest journalist must be able to comprehend. Gone are the days when a dress was shown to viewers completely on its own, the designer having faith in their ability to assess it. Now it is considered necessary to bludgeon the viewer with

Charles James 1955

several girls who behave more or less wildly, supported by insistent music, and who wear variations on a theme. Is this a sign of the designer's lack of confidence in his clothes or in the professional judgement of his audience? Either way, when a designer has to pay for as many as thirty girls, plus hairdressers, make-up artists, dressers and electricians for lights and music, the bill is very large. There are, however, signs that the days of the big theatrical presentation may be over. Already one or two influential designers have started to limit their shows or to scrap them altogether. The cost is simply too high.

The day before the show is one of intense activity. The clothes worn by each girl for every exit she will make must be checked. If creased, they must be pressed; if a button is loose or a hemline has dropped, this is the time to rectify it. Every girl has her own area of the changing room, clearly demarcated, with her name written large. Often, to help dressers to identify their girl in the crush and confusion of the actual show, her photograph is placed alongside her name. It should be remembered that a large proportion of the world's top models speak only English and so, when working in Europe, they cannot communicate with their dressers. To help the dressers in their difficult job, drawings of each outfit are frequently also provided below the girl's name. Each girl's changing area contains a clothes stand on which her outfit for each exit is placed, in correct wearing order. The outfit is clearly labelled with its exit number so that no confusion may arise in the dressers' minds. They have no time for uncertainty. All accessories are placed on or below the outfit so that everything will be to hand the moment it is required. While all this is being done behind the scenes there is also activity at the front of the house. Seat numbers are checked on the master seating-plan and the names of those who rate reserved seats are placed on their chairs; publicity material is also put on all seats; flowers are arranged. All takes place against the noises of music being tested, workmen tacking protective material onto the runway and electricians checking the lighting and amplification systems.

Many designers arrange ancillary delights to excite visiting journalists and perhaps soften their critical faculties. These little treats for already over-excited egos can range from a single bunch of flowers in the journalist's hotel to presents of clothing; from drinks parties to dinners, galas and balls. No trouble is too great. The press must be kept happy and in their contented glow they must remember warmly the name of the designer who paid for all their pleasures. This is the time when all but the grandest and most successful designers feel vulnerable, when they seem to be compelled to join in the costly charade known as entertaining the press.

On the day of the show, the twenty-minute presentation of the work of six months, preparations begin at least an hour before the show is scheduled to commence. Model girls, dressers, make-up men and hairdressers work speedily and professionally while all the details are finally checked by the designer and his team. Staff cope with last-minute problems and alterations to plans, well-wishers arrive to give encouragement and the lists of which girls exit to which music and what they will be wearing are given one last run through. The maestro stands behind the door, ready to check each girl's appearance and to make last-minute adjustments to hats and belts before she goes out. The music begins and the frenzy commences. Fast as they are all working behind the scenes, they are not so involved that they cannot listen for and respond to the encouragement of applause from the audience.

In no time it is over; the applause reaches a crescendo; the model girls drag a supposedly reluctant designer on to the runway to acknowledge the crowd; many guests accompany him backstage to congratulate him personally; the model girls rush off to the next show; the clearing-up begins and the chasm opens in front of the designer: in six months he must repeat the whole process, only it must be even better next time.

Designers are under considerable pressure, but it must be remembered that they do not stand alone. Behind most of the well-known names are two very important props, quite apart from all the workers and publicists who keep the daily motion of the firm going. They are often forgotten, and sometimes wilfully hidden, but even the most megalomaniac designers acknowledge their importance. They are, of course, the financial partner and the design team. A really good financial partner has a measure of creativity in his own right, as well as often being a support, confidant and confessor to the designer. Sometimes he is a close friend and it is certainly on this level of trust and dependence that the really creative partnerships function. Designers must have someone to turn to, if they are to produce their best. Could Yves Saint Laurent function so efficiently without Pierre Bergé? How would Valentino fare without Giammetti at his side? Calvin Klein might not have started without Barry Schwartz and has certainly said that to continue without him is inconceivable.

The young and hopeful who work as designers at the master's side are only rarely acknowledged, are frequently badly treated and are very often underpaid. But, despite all, their role is crucial. Many of them design substantial areas of the collection that eventually appears under the designer's name and, even if they are employed only as sketchers to draw and organize his ideas, their importance lies in the fact that it is through them that he controls his thoughts and imagination. Although almost always overworked, they are greatly privileged. They work so closely with the designer that they learn the realities of their trade in the most intimate of apprenticeships. Not infrequently, they have a technical and practical education far superior to that of the designer: what they take from him is a stylistic approach and a commercial method of working. From him they learn what art schools cannot teach – how to organize a collection and give concrete form to their ideas. It is rather like being in a very tough finishing school which teaches them how to use their practical education. They have usually come from a handful of prestigious art colleges or fashion schools in America and Great Britain and it is amazing how many young English and American designers are to be found in the fashion houses of Paris, Milan and Rome, quite apart from those in their own countries. They bring one specific and important thing to the designer: the cross-cultural influence of the young, the street-fashion approach to design which freshens the designer's ideas and gives him vital creative input.

The designer, his adviser and his design assistants all work hard to produce clothes of which they can be proud and which, most importantly, will sell in large numbers. In addition, the designer has a further responsibility. If he is successful, he becomes public property and must play a public role. By so doing he obtains priceless publicity. The importance of this area of his life varies according to his temperament and the society in which he lives. In Paris and Milan dress designers are sought after and are expected to appear in public reasonably regularly. If not personally glamorous, they must be surrounded by glamour in the form of elegant women dressed by the great man himself. In London, the pressure is considerably less. The few glamorous occasions are usually more 'establishment' than 'show-biz' and no English designer has the status to be considered important in such a situation. No social gathering in London could be dominated by the designers and their friends, because they do not rate the 'superstar' treatment that their counterparts do in other cities.

After Milan, the city where the designer comes into his own as a social star is, of course, New York. Magazines like *W* and *Interview* have given designers a status there that they have nowhere else. To maintain it they must play the social game, be they natives or visitors. They do, however, have their claques to help them in many ways. The claque consists of glamorous and newsworthy women who wear the designer's clothes at grand social occasions where they can reasonably expect to be photographed by the press. In addition, they add their *chic* presence to his fashion shows and, most usefully, allow him to escort them in public. For many designers these women are friends who support and comfort them, while offering artistic stimulation. Their partnership is fruitful and mutually valuable. Calvin Klein and Brooke Shields; Halston and Liza Minnelli; Valentino and Doris Bryner: these friendships transcend the couturier-client relationship. They also help in the battle to keep ahead in publicity and sales. In common with most artistic endeavours, the role of the designer demands that his head be constantly placed on the chopping block. Twice a year the blade is poised. The cliché is correct: he is only as good as his last collection, no matter who his friends may be.

FROM SALON TO STREET

Sharp, experienced and calculating eyes have watched the designer's presentation of his new line: the eyes of press and buyers. In any fashion-show audience there is a certain proportion of uncritical friends and well-wishers: fabric suppliers, accessory makers, boyfriends and girlfriends of the designer's staff. But the *real* audience consists of the professionals. For the friends the theatrical presentation, pounding music and general over-excitement are fun; for the professionals they are largely irrelevant. Buyers and press must see beyond the showmanship of the whole presentation and must isolate from each entrance those individual dresses and looks that may be of interest to them. For them the fashion show is no more mere entertainment than a theatrical performance is for the theatre critic. Like him, they are there to do a job.

The job that they do is vital to the designer. They are the ones who make sure that his new line is discussed, thought about, bought and finally worn in one form or another throughout the world. Without them there is no success. What they are looking for, broadly speaking, is something new and interesting that they can present in a way that interests the fashion-page reader and the potential customer. The ladies of the press (by far the majority of fashion journalists are women) watch every collection with a bi-focal eye. One side is assessing the clothes on their own merits as a fashion statement by an individual designer. The other side is mentally slotting them into a picture which is composed from all the designers' shows. The fashion journalist must look for similarities, or meaningful contrasts, because her job is to give the 'story', from Paris, or Milan, or wherever. This story must have cohesion, it must simplify a complicated overall picture and it must reflect what is new and important in the city for that season. The really professional and experienced journalist can very quickly tell what the story will be. She will soon know what to say about skirt length, shoulder treatment or colour. Part of her professional approach might well be to give prominence to a designer whose work is not especially appealing to her, but whose new clothes are clearly im-portant. Conversely, clothes which she would perhaps love to buy and wear herself might well have to be ignored because they do not fit into the fashion story or are not strong enough to carry a fashion message. The journalist's job is to tell a great deal in a limited space. She does not have the luxury of writing about or photographing everything she sees. From all the mass of looks and variations she will see in one week in the

Cardin 1967

51

world's fashion capitals she must sift out a story which will be communicable to readers who have not seen any of the shows.

The job of the magazine and newspaper journalist is the same, but the method of tackling it is based on different criteria. Newspapers are, by their nature, instant and ephemeral. Normally, during collections week, newspaper journalists file copy daily to be featured in the newspaper the next day or, if the journalist is allotted one day per week for fashion, certainly within the week. This second situation often presents great problems. Agonizing decisions must be made. If her day for fashion is Wednesday, all copy must be with the newspaper by Tuesday night, so if one of the best designers is showing on Wednesday morning she has to gamble. Either she goes for immediacy and publishes as normal or she loses a week so that she can include the maverick designer. In the past the press was coldly received by the great houses, but now all but the most august designers are prepared to co-operate by allowing important newspapers previews and press release photographs to feature – in some cases even before the day of the show. Nowadays, considerable lengths are gone to in order to please the press. In Milan, for example, there are press rooms with multi-lingual secretaries, typewriters, special international telephones and everything necessary to keep harassed journalists happy and functioning.

While the newspaper journalist is rushing around from shows to photographic sessions to interviews with the designers and still endeavouring to file her copy, her colleague covering the shows for a monthly magazine is having a somewhat quieter time. The basic difference between the two lies in the medium. The newspaper journalist tells the story largely in words, with a few photographs or drawings to supplement the points she is making. The magazine journalist is normally thinking visually, and tells her story in pictures with the help of few words.

Nowadays the pictures in newspapers and magazines are normally photographs. Sadly, fashion artists are not often used. For a newspaper the photographer takes 'runway shots' of the girls as they are showing the clothes, and good photographs will have movement, excitement and immediacy, linked with a 'feel' for the clothes and showing as much detail as possible. For the magazine, runway shots will be taken and some will possibly be featured but the majority are used as an *aide-mémoire* for the journalist, because the magazine coverage of the collections is usually six months after the shows. During this time, the magazine journalist will pore over the contact sheets of the runway shots, choose the more important and photogenic looks and arrange to have the garments photographed specially, often by a top photographer. The photographs will be taken in a studio, at leisure, with backgrounds and accessories to suggest the mood of the new fashions as the journalist sees it. The dark side of magazine coverage of fashion is that, in many cases, the journalist must temper her view of what is good in order to fit in with what the advertising

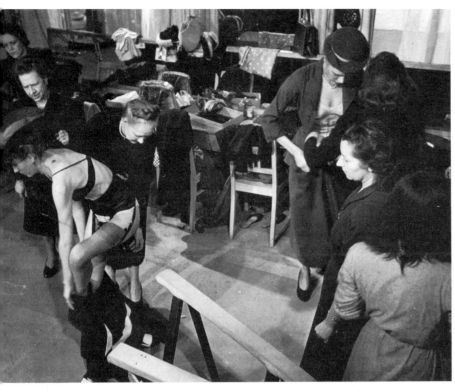

Behind the scenes at a Piguet show, 1948. It all seems very calm and orderly compared with today when the couturier must use many more girls to show more clothes in less time and with much more urgency. Some things do not change, however, and the models are as anorexic-looking as their modern counterparts.

It is important to obtain the right place and to hang on to your seat. Interlopers are firmly admonished above the shouted conversations of buyers and press who greet each other every hour as if they had not seen each other for months.

The ladies from Vogue explain to Mlle Josette of Piguet which dresses from the 1948 collection they have chosen to photograph for their Paris fashion number.

Buyers and press can be relied upon to take a long and critical look at the maestro's creations. Their sharply trained eyes can spot faults which to normal mortals are insignificant.

editor considers important. If a designer spends money on magazine advertising he has done so for two reasons: he wishes his clothes to be brought to the notice of a wide and discerning audience and he also hopes to 'buy' editorial favour. Having spent his money, he expects his collection to be viewed with favour by the fashion staff. Many a designer's clothes have been given more editorial coverage than they deserved simply because of his monthly advertising payments, the costs of which are so high (a colour page in a British fashion magazine may cost £3,000 to £4,000 and in other countries the cost may be much higher) that the designer in turn must weigh all actual and potential benefits before deciding. Frequently, the costs of advertising will be shared with those stores stocking his range or with his fabric manufacturers.

In addition to playing her fashion hunches and keeping her advertisers happy, the magazine journalist must be aware of what has been bought by the stores. There is little point in featuring clothes (unless they are very exceptional) if they are not available for purchase by her readers. So her choice is again restricted by what the buyers have decided will sell in her particular country or city.

While the press corps have been assessing the clothes, the buyers have also been evaluating things from their own point of view. Their approach is practical. 'Will that sell in Munich?' 'Can I push a jacket like that in Bal Harbour?' The clothes presented on the runway are frequently modified before they go into production. The 'look' on the runway is telling a story in the most dramatic way and not even the designer expects his clothes to be worn on the streets in that extreme form. This is sometimes forgotten when the photographs appear in newspapers and magazines and the clothes are condemned as 'ridiculous' or 'unwearable'. It is when the buyer is writing his or her order (men form a significant proportion of buyers) that modifications take place. The job of the buyer is a difficult, but very important, one. She or he must not only have an understanding of fashion and a 'response' to clothes, but must also be able to project six months ahead and try to imagine what women will be prepared to be persuaded to buy at that time. This requires a clear vision and a strong business head. The store entrusts the buyer with considerable sums, every penny of which must be spent, and spent wisely. A buyer is constantly casting bread upon the water and it must come back enhanced a hundred-fold or he will risk losing his job. It is little wonder that buyers command such high salaries to compensate for their knife-edge existence.

The designer's 'look', as finally seen in any one store, is the brainchild of his sales force, working with the buyer. Width of shoulder, skirt length, embroidery and detailing can all be altered to suit the individual client before the garments are put into production. Again, the colours seen on the runway need not be chosen by the buyer. Most outfits come in a choice of three or more colour combinations in the average ready-to-wear range, so that the buyer has a choice which can take account of social and climatic conditions peculiar to any one city. By giving buyers these choices the designer ensures the widest possible diffusion for his new collection. He cannot afford the unbending stance of the dictator. His role now takes him right into the market place. While the clothes are being made on the production line the buyer, back in the home town, is still thinking about them. One of the buyer's biggest headaches is whether the delivery date will be met. Clothes that arrive in the shops two weeks late can produce terrible problems, especially if the store does not have the exclusive right to sell that line in its city and rival stores receive their consignments first. The buyer must also consider how to promote them: which clothes will be featured in advertisements, which will be displayed in the window, which will appear in a show or special promotion. If the answers to these questions are wrong, the buyer's failure will be obvious at the end of the season, when the clothes are still on the racks, not on customers' backs.

Order and calm reign at the climax of a Dior charity presentation. The invited audience applaud the traditional end of the show: the bride flanked by examples of the designer's evening dresses.

Others have been viewing the shows every bit as critically as the buyers and the press. Pirates are still a force in fashion. In the golden days of haute couture the problem of piracy was acute. Huge amounts of money could be made by knowing in advance what a grand couturier's line was going to be. Deep secrecy shrouded everything until the day of the show. People wishing to attend required accreditation and they were made to pay a hefty deposit as a proof of their good faith. In Paris the Chambre Syndicale de la Haute Couture, which grew from the Syndicale de la Couture Parisienne, a union of dress designers founded in 1868, controlled every aspect of the showings to press and buyers. It still does today, although its importance has waned in proportion to couture's weakening as a fashion force.

The issue of couture press cards was begun by the Chambre and they were given only to named, accredited journalists working for newspapers and magazines which had applied for them in advance. This system is in

operation for all fashion presentations in all the major fashion centres even today. No better way of checking who is coming and of controlling the numbers has been found. The checks are rigorous and indeed they must be, as many more people wish to see the opening shows than could possibly be accommodated. Without them, the showrooms and presentation-halls would be overrun by gate-crashers. The Chambre Syndicale also laid down rules for the attendance of buyers. A 'carte d'acheteur' was only issued to buyers on receipt of full details of their firms and a large deposit, known as 'caution' money. This money usually covered the cost of one or two models. If the buyers purchased, it was deducted from the cost of their purchases.

These rules and regulations were instituted to help stop the piracy of ideas. Fashion is, more and more, very big business and designers must ensure that their ideas are not plagiarized and put into the shops in an inferior form before they can be delivered from their own production lines.

This line-up of late fifties Paris looks includes a Dior evening dress at far left and outfits by Lanvin, Laroche and Cardin. The overall feeling is of glamorous, pampered women wearing status clothes to impress as much as delight.

Although the importance of anti-plagiarism policies has diminished with the broadening of the fashion message and the subsequent weakening of 'the line' for any one season, it is still common sense for the designer to check on who is coming into his show and for what reasons. He can still lose a considerable amount of money from cheap copies of his designs flooding the market. The old embargos on sketching and photographing during the show are rarely adhered to any more and certainly a situation like the legendary one in which Dior himself evicted a woman who was using a miniature camera hidden in her hat to photograph his clothes could not happen today.

Nevertheless, piracy of ideas still continues, and is a particularly nasty trade, carried on by people who have the trust of the designer. A person with trained eye and memory can always rush to a bar or hotel room to sketch the clothes that have just been seen, and the more ambitious firms wishing to steal ideas have fielded teams of specialists to note particular design ideas. A really strong team could consist of a sportswear specialist, a coat specialist and an evening-wear specialist, who could come together after the show to pool their ideas and reproduce as much of the collection as they required. Having noticed the cut that makes possible the designer's individual line, such experts could produce technical drawings or patterns without buying a single garment or toile.

The more common form of piracy is committed through photography. Every designer allows runway photographers access to his show, provided that they are with an accredited journalist or are working for an accepted publication. These photographers are in a position to photograph the clothes from close quarters, using as many cameras as they choose. They are uniquely privileged and some abuse their privilege. It is easy to respond to a request to 'lose' a roll of exposed film after the show or make a second set of contact prints – especially when the money offered is high and the risks of being caught relatively low.

As long as fashion is a healthy business and the work of the individual designer is in demand, however, people will wish to steal ideas without payment or credit to the maestro. Reprehensible as such behaviour is, and distasteful as such betrayal of trust is to the designer, it confirms both his position and that of his trade, nevertheless. The *real* worry begins when no one cares about the latest fashion or about the designer.

THE FIRST COUTURIER

No designer's story could be more unlikely or more Dickensian in origin than that of Charles Frederick Worth, acknowledged as the world's first couturier and the undisputed founder of Paris couture. That an Englishman, of mundane background, should achieve these distinctive accolades suggests a truly exceptional man — which indeed he was.

Charles Frederick Worth was born in the Lincolnshire town of Bourne on 13 October, 1825. His father was a solicitor addicted to drink and gambling who, when Charles Frederick was only eleven, was declared a bankrupt. At the age of twelve the boy's desperate mother, who was herself now working as a housekeeper, found a job for him with a printer. Worth loathed it and in 1838 his mother obtained for him an apprenticeship in London with Swan and Edgar, the drapers. He was just coming up to his thirteenth birthday.

Charles Frederick Worth

His training at Swan and Edgar was in helping ladies choose suitable fabrics to be made up by their dressmakers. The hours were long, often twelve hours a day, but the experience was invaluable. He learned to understand fabric and to judge its suitability for a particular design. He also learned the manners and modes of the fashionable world and he began to educate himself by reading and by visiting theatres and galleries. At the end of his seven-year appenticeship he was a country boy no more.

Always ambitious and bold, Worth moved from Swan and Edgar to Lewis and Allenby in Regent Street, who were considered the grandest purveyors of silk to London's quality. But he quickly decided that his real goal was Paris. At the age of twenty he arrived in the French capital with little money and even less French. His first jobs were casual and badly paid, but by 1847 he was in a position to cope linguistically as a salesman and he obtained a job with Gagelin and Opigez, the most fashionable drapers in Paris.

Here he stayed for twelve years, quickly graduating from fabric sales to selling shawls and mantles and then, with the reluctant agreement of his employers, to making dresses for the customers. His approach to dressmaking was radically different from that of the traditional dressmaker. He began with a consideration of the potential of the fabric, used English tailoring techniques and produced a harmonious amalgam of line and material. He demanded perfect fit and finish and his high standards, which formed the basis of couture, won him medals in London and Paris. His future was set fair.

The Empress Eugenie

With his wife, who had also worked at Gagelin, and Otto Bobergh, a fellow salesman, he opened his own house in the rue de la Paix in 1858. This was the perfect time to launch a new business, the period of the Second Empire of Napoleon III. Paris was alive with *nouveau-riche* 'go-getters' with plenty of money to spend. Magnificence, ostentation and grandeur were the order of the day and vast amounts of money were available to achieve it. This was money without knowledge: people insecure in their tastes were perfect bait for experts who wished to dictate their standards to a rich clientele.

Worth did not have long to wait to jump on the bandwagon. To break into court and social circles as a dressmaker needed the help of a socially highly-placed sponsor who would wear his clothes at court. His wife's persistence persuaded Princess Metternich, wife of the Austrian ambassador, to order two Worth dresses. Wearing one to court, she was asked by the Empress Eugenie who had made it. As a result Worth became the Imperial dressmaker and his success was assured.

Amazing as it seems, Worth was soon the arbiter of fashion, able to dictate his views to the highest-born in Europe. Arrogant, and by now probably thoroughly disagreeable, Worth had single-handedly raised the status of the dressmaker from that of artisan to artist. No longer would dressmakers gratefully work for a minute profit simply to keep 'quality' customers. On the contrary. Worth's prices were extravagant but women clamoured for the privilege of buying from him. He gave the couturier power. Although couture has now waned, the designer still exercises that power and it enables him to control multi-million-dollar business empires.

Worth died in 1895. A man of genius, he nevertheless succeeded because he was the man for his time. He was lucky that the court of Napoleon III was the least formal in French history. The demi-mondaine, the self-made and the petit-bourgeois were at ease with Worth for, like him, they were upwardly mobile and, in many cases, had been tradesfolk too. Excess and display were what they required and the man who provided them was the arrogant dressmaker from Lincolnshire.

THE DIRECTORY

A

ADOLFO · ADRI · ADRIAN · AGHAYAN · AKIRA · ALAÏA · ALBINI · ALIX (*See* GRÈS) · AMEY · AMIES · ANDREVIE · ANTHONY
ANTONELLI · ARMANI · ASHLEY · ASSALTY · ATKINSON · AUGUSTABERNARD (*See* PARIS COUTURE) · AUJARD · AVELLINO
AZAGURY · AZZARO

Albini

Amies

Anthony

Armani

Small capitals are used to identify designers with articles of their own — for example, BALENCIAGA in the first article. Image makers, described in a separate collection of articles between pages 275 and 292, are also identified by small capitals but an asterisk is added (thus, FAIRCHILD*) to distinguish image-makers from designers.
Colour illustrations (pp 65–80, 113–128, 161–176, 241–256). Designers whose work is illustrated in colour are identified by symbol □ beside their names.

ADOLFO, Sardina

Born Havana, Cuba, 1933.
Adolfo came from a comfortable middle-class family of lawyers. Destined to join the family firm, he was lucky in that the privileged world of the wealthy pre-war Cubans included many sophisticated fashionables and one of the most elegant was his aunt, Mme Maria Lopez. Wealthy and worldly, having persuaded his family to let him out of law she took him to Paris. Her power opened the stern doors of the Maison BALENCIAGA, who gave Adolfo an understanding of the importance of cut and line which has remained with him throughout his career. In 1948 he moved to New York to work as a milliner. He soon had a devoted following and in 1962 he opened his own fashion house, designing

Originally a milliner, Adolfo was famed for his fantasy creations. He is shown adding the finishing touches to a 1965 confection of violets and feathers.

Adolfo created the cat-woman look in his 1964 collection. A leopard-skin mask and a red fox helmet made an arresting statement for winter sidewalks.

The Adolfo evening look in 1983 showed American dressing at its best: a demure collar and cuffs with a shiny paillette-embroidered top, combined with a full length skirt.

clothes as well as hats. His debut was highly successful and his reputation has grown. He now dresses many of those 'wonderful women from W' (see FAIRCHILD*), including Nancy Reagan. He has won a Coty Special Award twice in his career for his millinery (1955 and 1969) and is a member of the Council of Fashion Designers of America. These accolades are a reflection of the esteem accorded to all his clothes, be they his famous patchwork evening skirts or his ultra-*chic*, Chanel-type suits. He is a consistently good designer, if not a great original.

ADRI

Born St. Joseph, Missouri, USA, 1930s.
Adri's real name is Adrienne Steckling. She studied design in the fine art department of Washington University, St. Louis, and was chosen as guest editor for *Mademoiselle* magazine's college issue, during her sophomore year in 1955. She continued to work at her studies at Parson's School of Design in New York from 1955 to 1956, and was considerably influenced by Claire MCCARDELL, who was one of her lecturers. Eight years with the wholesale firm of B.H.Wragge was followed by a period designing for the Clothes Circuit Division of Anne Fogarty Inc. In October, 1971, she showed her collection at Washington's Smithsonian Institute. In 1972 she broke away from Anne Fogarty Inc. and created her own firm to produce innovative and distinctive clothes in the McCardell manner, using soft and pliable materials to create functional, layered looks. She is a member of the Council of Fashion Designers of America. She won a Coty American Fashion Critics 'Winnie' in 1982.

ADRIAN, Gilbert

Born Connecticut, USA, 1903.
Died Los Angeles, USA, 1959.
Both of Adrian's parents had worked in the fashion trade and they owned a successful millinery shop, so that his entry into fashion was almost pre-ordained. He studied at Parson's in New York and also in Paris. His first work was designing costumes for an Irving Berlin revue, with only mixed success. His opportunity came with

Above: *Maurice Vlaminck's*
Restaurant at Marly *shows the Fauve
indifference to recreating natural
appearances in their paintings. Instead,
colour is used to heighten the viewer's
emotional response. Bold statements
like this had an influence on both fabric
design and fashion alike.*

Right: *Art and design merge in the
field of fabrics. Here a Matisse-style
cut-out, in the shapes of a Robert
Motherwell, echoes the colours of the
sixties art scene.*

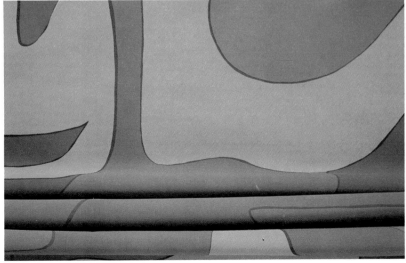

Supreme in her cleanliness and confidence, the Hon. Mrs Graham, painted by Gainsborough, would have been appalled at the crude and dirty peasants from across the Channel. They in turn would be kept in their place by that patrician appearance. Only the desperation of starvation caused them to revolt (right) against the smoothly elegant upper classes.

Left: *The privations of war make the glamour of fashion attractive to the most unlikely audiences. This World War II cartoonist could rely on people recognizing the London milliner referred to, even though only her christian name is given.*

From pure art to functional design: Mondrian's linear experiments with colour and formal design were given practical application in Rietveld's chair and Yves Saint Laurent's dresses based on the artist's paintings.

When he was producing
drawings of people whose
hair suggested that they had
just had a terrible shock,
could Egon Schiele ever have
imagined that hair like this
young lady's would be used
to shock in its turn, 'up
staring, then, like reeds, not
hair'.

Antonio's drawings of these Capucci
evening dresses shows that 'Roman
legion' tufts do not have to be menacing
as they are in punk styles.

Giorgio Armani showed his 1982 collection like a still life ensemble. The subtle but powerful mix of colour and pattern is typical of this Italian designer. It is by producing clothes of this calibre that Armani has deservedly become a world-renowned name in fashion circles.

In his October 1983 collection Giorgio Armani mixed men's shirting and ties with exotic prints, using a masterly hand to create a new way to dress in the evening.

Below: The 1980 leather blouson by Armani. This shape was taken up world-wide.

Baroque swags create a richly moving back on this Balenciaga evening dress. He created clothes which were the architecture of fashion based on a total understanding of the human form.

Opposite page: Balenciaga's structured suit of 1952 (left) is softened in the semi-tailored look of 1954 (centre); his severely elegant tunic (right) is from 1957.

*Fifties' evening glamour from
two masters of the genre,
Balenciaga (left) and Balmain
(right): strictly for the
exceedingly rich and very slim.*

Left: *Balmain's 1957 suit features
a high-waisted jacket; the outfit is
given scale by the outsize hat.*

Right: *A Balmain suit for 1962 in
strong blue has a pie crust looped
wool collar and cuffs.*

Beene uses unexpected pattern and texture for this
glamorous and varied approach involving heavy embroidery
and abstract lining.

A beautifully put together outfit by Geoffrey Beene shows his skill
with subtle colour, shape and texture.

Laura Biagiotti's 1979 oversized coat dress is softly tied at the waist and accessoried with a casually-knotted cashmere scarf. The look is relaxed and easy to wear and is characteristic of the informal, sporty fashion of the time.

Bill Blass added a feather wrap to complete this relaxed evening look for Spring/Summer 1984. Softly draped top and casual tie belt are used to enhance the beauty of the red-dotted material.

*Marc Bohan keeps alive the fifties traditions of opulent
larger-than-life glamour fashion at Dior.*

*As elegant as the little gold chairs which once symbolized
fashion shows, this woollen suit by Bohan for Dior, 1963,
exemplifies the refined chic which used to be the hallmark of
the great Paris houses.*

Adrian, seen here with Joan Crawford in 1933, was responsible for the on- and off-screen wardrobes of many of Hollywood's top actresses.

a commission to design costumes for Rudolph Valentino films. He moved to Hollywood, where his talent and his famed gregariousness guaranteed mounting success. His fashion influence, through the Metro-Goldwyn-Mayer films of the 1930s and 1940s, was wide and profound. He is credited with introducing many looks which even Paris took notice of. Even if he did not originate them all, he certainly made them into 'looks' through the enormous exposure of the films he worked on. The audience for his clothes was unique in size and social composition. In a sense, because of the medium in which he worked, he was the most influential designer of his time. His designs for Crawford and Garbo innovated many looks which were eagerly plagiarized by his fellow designers. His broad-shouldered suits were widely copied.

In 1942 he opened a salon in Beverly

Hills which, after a shaky first show (in his garden, as the salon was not ready), became very successful. Film stars and wealthy socialites flocked to his door. After World War II he reacted badly, and not entirely with dignity, to the ecstatic reception the American press gave to DIOR's 'New Look'. Soft and curvaceous, it was the antithesis of his square-shouldered, narrow-hipped look. He took part in a broadcast debate with Dior, but lost the battle. The New Look overcame all criticism. In 1948 he opened a salon in New York and his success continued. His experience in dressing films made him an all-purpose stylist who could produce sculptural, romantic or sexy clothes. Almost always they worked, although inevitably there were some lapses of taste.

After a heart attack in 1952, until his death in 1959, Adrian lived in a jungle hide-away near Brasilia. At the time of his death he was working on the costumes for the film, *Camelot*. He was married to Janet Gaynor, the actress, and they had one son. Adrian felt that he was never taken seriously by the fashion press. Carmel SNOW* and Mrs. CHASE*, the undisputed fashion arbiters of their time, thought scantily of him. For them his fashion pedigree was impure; his film work precluded him from the temple of fashion worthies. Nevertheless his design skills were recognized by the industry with the award of a Coty American Fashion Critics 'Winnie' in 1945.

AGHAYAN, Ray
Born Teheran, Iran, 1927.

The son of an Iranian couturier for whom he began to work immediately on leaving school, Aghayan went to Los Angeles to continue his education. He studied architecture and drama, before joining NBC. There he designed costumes and, after six years, was made head designer. In 1963 he hired Bob MACKIE to work on designs for the Judy Garland show and this was the beginning of their partnership. In addition to designing together and separately for stage, film and television shows, they produced four ready-to-wear collections per year (with an emphasis on evening wear), although this turned out to be a brief venture.

Draped and sculpted Joan Crawford is packaged as a refined sex-symbol in this crêpe evening dress designed by Adrian for the film Letty Lynton.

In this design by Adrian, Joan Crawford personifies 1930s chic. Elements like these pleated ruffles, exaggerated for the screen, filtered down to the high street in a modified form with remarkable speed.

AKIRA, Maki

Born Oita, Japan, 1949.

After graduating from Oita University, Akira worked for the Olivetti company for six months and then moved to Tokyo to study fashion. After three years working and studying with Reiko Minami in her training school, he moved to America when he was twenty-five. Between 1976 and 1981 he worked with HALSTON as a tailor and learned couture design. Here he was able to develop his interest in bias cutting and diagonal draping, both of which are part of his trademark. In 1982 he showed his own collection and he has a growing clientele of private customers, including Mrs. Ronald Reagan.

See also JAPANESE DESIGN.

ALAÏA, Azzedine

Born Tunisia, date undisclosed.

One of the more interesting names to come into international currency in the late 1970s, Alaïa has been working, almost unknown, in Paris for the past thirty years. He became famous through his black-leather, rivet-studded gauntlets. He carefully shrouds his background in mystery — 'I am as old as the Pharaohs' — but it is known that he studied sculpture at L'École des Beaux Arts in Tunis. Arriving in Paris, he worked with Christian DIOR for five days. Later he worked for two seasons with Thierry MUGLER. From his base in rue de Bellechasse in Paris he has dressed a discerning and wealthy corps of women he liked or admired, such as Paloma Picasso and Garbo. Inseparable from his Yorkshire terrier, Patte à Pouf, and always dressed in a black silk Chinese jacket and trousers, he has become a cult figure. His clothes have developed consistently over the years. They are nearly always black or deeply coloured, usually body-hugging and incorporate net, rivets, industrial zippers and panels of leather and suede. They bear out his belief that 'the base of all fashion is the body'. His tightly draped, little black dresses have hardly changed in years and they epitomize Alaïa's designing. Camp, sexy, fantasy women, like strip-cartoon characters, are his contribution to the 1980s. They are a continuation of the masculine/feminine tartiness of MONTANA and Mugler, and are strongly reminiscent

Albini's 1979 collection presented an uncompromisingly geometric line-up with these two-toned jackets. Variations on a theme strengthen the designer's message in their differences and similarities. The story is clear.

of the long-lost Left Bank of Juliette Greco and Bardot, as one imagines Allen Jones would have viewed it.

ALBINI, Walter

Born Busto Arsizio, Italy, 1941.
Died Milan, Italy, 1983.

After studying illustration in Cremona and fashion in Turin, Albini worked for some years in Paris as a fashion illustrator for Italian magazines, especially *Novità*. In the early 1960s he returned to Italy. He worked as a designer with Mariuccia Mandelli at KRIZIA and also designed ready-to-wear collections for BASILE. He formed his own company in 1965. He designed for both men and women. In his early days he was strongly influenced by CHANEL and he had an abiding interest in thirties and forties fashion and a passionate love of the movies of Dietrich and Hepburn. In 1971 in Milan, he was the first designer to show together five different collections from five different houses. As a stylist, co-ordinator and designer, he had a considerable influence on the international fashion scene. As far back as 1972 *Women's Wear Daily* said that his line was

as strong 'as Yves SAINT LAURENT's and has decided tastes all over Europe'.

ALIX

See GRÈS

AMEY, Ronald

Born Globe, Arizona, USA, 1932.

A scientific education at high school in Superior, Arizona, led to Amey's first job as an assayer for local copper mines. He moved on to Los Angeles, where he followed a fashion course for one semester at Chouinard Institute, and then joined a couture shop to produce exclusive designs. Amey next enlisted in the US Air Force. There he met his future partner, Joseph Burke, and together they designed clothes. On being demobilized, Amey went to New York to study fashion at Parson's School of Design. He was then fired from six jobs before Norman NORELL advised him to work for himself. Burke-Amey was founded in 1959. Ten years later Amey bought Burke out and created Ronald Amey Inc. In 1970 he won the Gold Coast Fashion Award of Chicago.

AMIES, Hardy

Born London, England, 1909.

While most of his contemporaries have long since closed their doors, Amies continues indestructibly into the 1980s. What is his secret? His success is built on a shrewd approach to business, considerable ambition, hard work and talent. Hardy by name and hardy by nature, he is one of Great Britain's most famous designers, sitting securely among the elite who have an international reputation. His early ambition was to become a journalist and, in order to improve his languages, he spent some years on the continent. He taught English in France and then moved to Germany as a representative of Avery's, the weighing-machine company. He returned to England in the early 1930s to work as a travelling salesman. He thus had a valuable commercial training which helped him considerably when he set up in business for himself. That came about through a description of a dress in a letter he wrote. It was shown to the director of the company for which his mother worked. The company had a subsidiary, called LACHASSE, with Digby MORTON as its designer. Morton wished to set up on his

Spring 1949 and the New Look is given the London treatment by Hardy Amies. This fitted coat with full skirt and padded shoulders is in yellow-green diagonal worsted. The 'look' is topped off with an extravagant hat to balance the proportions of the skirt.

own and so, in 1934, Amies was offered his job. Within a year he was manager as well as designer at Lachasse.

In 1939 he joined the army, but his military commitments did not prevent him from designing. In fact, in 1941, he was released to join other designers in creating a collection sponsored by the government, to be sent to South America. This venture led to the formation of the Incorporated Society of London Fashion Designers with MOLYNEUX as chairman, a position held by Amies in 1959. He designed clothes for the government-sponsored Utility Scheme, and not only were they elegant, they were ingenious in the ways they overcame wartime restrictions. On being demobbed in 1945, Amies opened his own house. In 1946 he went on the first of many business trips to America, which resulted in healthy sales there. He began making clothes for Princess Elizabeth and, after her coronation, was awarded a warrant as dressmaker to the Queen.

In 1950 he opened a boutique for ready-to-wear and in 1961 began his long association with Hepworths, the menswear company. It is as a menswear designer that he is now mainly known. As

Hardy Amies' 1947 woollen dress and jacket ensemble exemplifies all that was best in London tailoring. Classic proportions are enlivened by interesting seam detail.

A permanently pleated yellow nylon net evening dress designed by Amies in 1958. The high waist is defined by the velvet bow at the bust and the bodice line is repeated in the backward-sweeping skirt.

Amies took softly textured wool in burnt sugar and cream to create a bias-cut top and gently gathered skirt for Autumn/ Winter 1977–78 – a relaxed and informal way with classic English ingredients.

a designer for women he produced well-cut and refined clothes in the days when such things were required. The women's wear is now designed by a co-director, Ken Fleetwood. His firm was acquired by Debenhams in 1973, but he bought it back in 1981. Today he cuts a quaintly anachronistic figure with his impeccably elegant personal appearance, surrounded as he is in London fashion circles by blue jeans and sweatshirts. He has published two autobiographical volumes: *Just So Far* appeared in 1954 and was followed by *Still Here* in 1984. In 1977 he was awarded the C.V.O.

ANDREVIE, France

Born Montauban, France, 1946.
Died Paris, France, 1984.
After taking a degree, Andrevie began work in 1971 as a stylist for a ready-to-wear firm in Brussels. From here she moved to the South of France and opened her first boutique in St Tropez in 1976. From the beginning her design philosophy was based on the need to combine comfort with style. She always liked a soft silhouette and big shapes. Ease of movement and a relaxed line were the characteristics of her work. Her first collection was in Paris in October, 1976, and by March, 1977 her name was internationally known. Her layered look showed her original sense of colour and fabrication. This she achieved by working closely with textile mills to develop unique, subtly shaded textures. She was an inventive mixer of textiles and her trousers and jackets were probably her strongest statement.

ANTHONY, John

Born New York City, USA, 1938.
Anthony attended the High School of Industrial Arts, where he won scholarships for European travel and for fashion training. After a year at an art academy in Rome, he returned to New York to continue his studies at the Fashion Institute of Technology. He had a twelve-year apprenticeship designing for wholesale fashion firms before founding John Anthony Inc. in 1971 with the manufacturer, Robert Levine. His great interest as a designer is in a high-fashion, sleek look which sells at the top end of the ready-to-wear market.

For Spring 1981 John Anthony shows a look pared down to the minimum.

He is known for his well-cut, understated clothes, which won him the Coty 'Winnie' Award for his second collection in 1972 and a Coty Return Award in 1976. Like HALSTON, he is a minimalist and his unique design intelligence can be seen in the way he edits and confines his ideas to produce lean, logical collections of supple and subtle clothes. In addition to his women's range, he designs menswear, furs, John Anthony Prêt, and John Anthony for Friedrick's Sport.

ANTONELLI, Maria

Born Tuscany, Italy, 1903.
Died Rome, Italy, 1969.
This serious and highly respected Italian couturier began as a dressmaker in Rome in 1924. As a designer she was known especially for her high standards of tailoring for coats and suits – a skill passed on to LAUG, who worked with her before starting on her own. In 1958 she was honoured with the award of 'Cavalier of the Republic', bestowed on her by the Italian government. This civic honour was in recognition of her

Grey and black pin-point check in a wool and silk mixture is used for Antonelli's collarless dress with appliqué belt and patch pocket.

role in establishing Italy on the international fashion map. As one of the pioneers of Italian high fashion when it began in the early 1950s, she participated in the famous Florence shows. She gave the Italian high fashion movement credence by the long and impressive list of her personal clients, which included Italian and foreign actresses and film stars. Antonelli Sport, her ready-to-wear line, was launched in 1961.

ARMANI, Giorgio ☐

Born Piacenza, Italy, 1934.
Armani's father was manager of a transport company. His school studies were geared towards science and he read medicine at Milan University. After military service, he joined La Rinascente, a large Italian department-store chain, working first on window dressing and then in the fashion and style department, where he learned the importance of the correct use of fabric. In 1961 he became assistant to the menswear manufacturer, Nino CERRUTI. In 1970, with his friend

Spring 1982 Giorgio Armani presents brief culottes with a rolled hem and a loosely tied belt — creating a very young, fun look.

Giorgio Armani mixes stripes and checks to create a lively but perfectly controlled casual look.

The Armani proportions par excellence are seen in this androgynous look for summer 1984, consisting of a draped collarless coat and straight pants.

Why can't a woman be more like a man? This seems to be the Armani question in this outfit made up entirely of items borrowed from a masculine wardrobe.

Sergio Galeotti as business manager, he set up on his own as a fashion consultant and worked with UNGARO, Segna and Sicons. Giorgio Armani Co. was founded in 1975 and since then his story has been one of ever more extravagant success. He is now, with VALENTINO, Italy's best known designer, and his clothes are eagerly sought after not only in Italy but also throughout Europe as well as in the United States.

Armani is unusual in having reversed the normal fashion order: he designed for men before he became a women's wear designer. He produces ready-to-wear ranges and jeans under his own name and also designs for Erreuno & Sicons. All show the easy elegance of his understated designs and his dislike of 'important' clothes. His casual, easy-to-wear clothes are beautifully fabricated and perfectly cut, if in the past they have sometimes been marred by his over-prominent eagle logo. His influence is enormous and he has helped to change attitudes to dressing permanently.

Conscious of the high retail prices of Armani clothes, he has opened shops to sell Emporio, his cheaper, mass-produced clothes, at much lower prices than those for his main line. FAIRCHILD* dubbed him King George I and Armani's robust ego has shown signs of believing that he has indeed a royal exemption from the formalities of the complicated courtship dance performed between press and designer. In March, 1982, he emulated BALENCIAGA and refused press showings of his clothes. He presented them to small groups of buyers, declaring that fashion shows were too much shows and not enough fashion. He has since relented. Despite his three homes, Armani lives a 'simple', even ascetic, life, albeit on a rather luxurious level. In 1979 he received a Neiman-Marcus Award.

ASHLEY, Laura

Born Merthyr Tydfil, Wales, 1926.
Died France, 1985.

Laura Ashley would have been the first to admit to the implausibility of her being considered a fashion force. In fact, she always insisted that her product was not fashion. She was right. A look that is worn and copied for several years without any significant change or evolution is not fashion: it is a mode of dress. And yet her success is awe-inspiring, and the paradox is that her influence has in fact been very powerful. The Laura Ashley look is worn world-wide; millions of young women want it and the signature is so strong that everyone forms the same mental picture from the words 'a Laura Ashley sort of dress'. Romantic and innocent, this look harks back to 18th-century milkmaids, purified as Hollywood might see them.

The success of Laura Ashley's clothes says more about the confusion over mid-century female roles than it does about her as a designer. Her early dresses were fancy dress, far removed from contemporary life. The classic ingredients of her improbable recipe were long, soft skirts, floral prints and romantic trimmings. In the eighties, however, she broadened her style to include looks which took more note of current fashion developments. Brilliant marketing and costing have always made the clothes comparatively inexpensive. Her rise was invigorating and heartening because it was so unlikely. From baking dyes in her kitchen in order to produce tea towels and table napkins (a cottage industry which would please the Women's Institute for whom she once worked), she moved with headlong speed and very hard work to be the head of a multi-faceted company, which was started in 1956, moved to rural Montgomeryshire in 1961, and was awarded the Queen's Award for Industry in 1977.

In the eighties, Laura Ashley clothes have become much more a part of mainstream fashion and their appeal has broadened. Her influence on other designers has been real and it is not too fanciful to see a link between her creations and those of certain American designers such as Perry ELLIS and Ralph LAUREN. The success of Laura Ashley is as satisfying as it was unexpected.

ASSALTY, Richard
Born Brooklyn, USA, 1944.
This American designer studied business administration before taking a fashion course at the Fashion Institute of Technology in New York, from which he graduated in 1965. He designed coats and suits for Ginala, a division of Originala, for seven years, before getting his own label for Gino Snow in 1975. He became Richard Assalty Ltd. in 1978. His firm produced sophisticated yet lively town clothes, but went out of business and he now designs for the suit firm, Benton, Ltd. He is a good colourist and his lines are never ponderous or timid. He also designs for Simplicity Patterns.

ATKINSON, Bill
Born Troy, New York, USA, 1916.
Atkinson graduated from Cornell University in 1937, having studied landscape design and architecture there. He had a variety of jobs with big corporations, including Metro-Goldwyn-Mayer and Chrysler, before starting his own private architectural practice in 1945. During World War II he slipped into fashion almost by accident. To overcome government fabric restrictions he made a skirt out of bandanas for his wife. More and more women asked for one, so in 1950 he joined with a contractor to produce this and other designs. The firm was called Glen of Michigan. In 1970 Atkinson's design consultancy was created under the name of Presentation. Bill Atkinson Inc. was created in 1973. He received a Coty American Fashion Critics' 'Winnie' in 1978.

AUGUSTABERNARD
See PARIS COUTURE

AUJARD, Christian
Born Brittany, France, 1945.
Died Paris, France, 1977.
Aujard started his career in fashion as the financial manager of a wholesale firm. In 1968, on a limited but sound budget, he started his own ready-to-wear firm. He died at the age of thirty-two as a result of a fall from a horse and the firm was carried on by his widow, Michelle. Her fresh, up-to-date and rather sporty clothes sell in good stores and boutiques around the world, as do her knitwear and casual ranges for men.

AVELLINO, Dominick
Born New York City, USA, 1944.
Avellino's line is best known as DDDominick, which is the name of the shop he opened in 1969 to sell his jewellery and knitwear. In 1970 he joined Huk-A-Poo, designing sweaters and overseeing their manufacture in Hong Kong. He moved to Benson and Partners in 1973. In 1975 he founded DDDominick Sportswear and his Designer label followed in 1978. Although without academic fashion training, Avellino's zest and lively design approach have made him very successful with the younger age-group.

AZAGURY, Jacques
Born Casablanca, Morocco, 1956.
At the age of sixteen Azagury began to work for a dress company in the East End of London. Nine months later he joined the second year of a three-year fashion design course at the London College of Fashion, from where he moved to the St. Martin's School of Art to finish his education. Immediately on graduating, aged twenty, he began his own business, but production problems caused him to close after only one year, in 1976. By 1978 he was ready to re-open and within a year he was asked to join the LONDON DESIGNER COLLECTIONS. He has remained a member of that organization since then.

AZZARO, Loris
Born Tunisia, 1934.
Azzaro's father was Sicilian and his mother Tunisian. He was brought up and educated in Tunisia. He studied French literature and became a university lecturer in Tunisia and later Toulouse. His years in education, from 1957 to 1962, were followed by five years in Paris. Having finally received a work permit to enable him to work under his own name, he opened a shop in 1966 near the Opéra. He soon became known for slinky evening wear and he created a spectacularly sexy wardrobe of evening clothes for Raquel Welch's disco-dancing show in Las Vegas in 1979. He now has boutiques in Italy, Monte Carlo and the South of France.

B

BAKER · BAKST · BALENCIAGA · BALESTRA · BALMAIN · BANKS · BANTON · BARNETT · BAROCCO · BARRIE · BARTHET
BASILE (*See* ITALIAN READY-TO-WEAR) · BATES · BEAUDRY (*See* PINKY AND DIANNE) · BEENE · BEER (*See* PARIS COUTURE) · BELTRAO
BELLVILLE SASSOON · BENDER · BERANGER · BERETTA · BERHANYER · BIAGIOTTI · BIBA (*See* HULANICKI) · BIKI · BIS · BLAHNIK
BLAINE · BLASS · BODY MAP · BOHAN · BRIGANCE · BROOKS · BURBERRY · BURROWS · BUSVINE

Balenciaga

Balmain

Beene

Blahnik

Blass

Bohan

BAKER, Maureen

Born London, England, 1925.

As chief designer of the English wholesale firm of Susan Small which she joined in 1943, Baker made her name by designing the dress for Princess Anne's wedding to Mark Phillips in 1973. This made fashion history in that there was no precedent for royal dressmakers to be passed over in favour of a ready-to-wear designer. In 1978 she founded her own firm, Maureen Baker Designs, and she continues to provide clothes for the princess and other members of the royal family. She is essentially a practical designer who draws, cuts and sews. Her clothes are therefore always well made with a very high standard of finish.

BAKST, Léon

Born Grodno, Russia, 1866.
Died Paris, France, 1924.

Bakst was brought up and educated in St. Petersburg, where he met the impressario Diaghilev. This meeting, engineered by Alexander Benois, was of vital importance, because from it grew the fruitful co-operation between Diaghilev and Bakst in the Ballets Russes. Bakst arrived in Paris in 1909 with Diaghilev's company and worked with it until 1914, designing costumes for most of its startling and original ballets. The fashion influence of his work on designers like POIRET was immense and has continued up to the present time. His colourful, flowing robes for *Scheherazade* are perhaps his most powerful work, strong and erotic. He designed costumes for fancy-dress balls for the Marchesa Casati and between 1912 and 1915 he produced designs for PAQUIN and WORTH. He and Poiret always quarrelled over who created the oriental line, but the bold, geometric use of colour which had such an influence on fabric design was the invention of Bakst.

BALENCIAGA, Cristobal ☐

Born Guetaria, Spain, 1895.
Died Valencia, Spain, 1972.

Austere and remote, priestly in his devotion to the perfection of cut, Balenciaga stands 'a torch amongst tapers' in relation to his contemporaries. He is unquestion-

'Rialto' by Maureen Baker for Susan Small in polka dot silk shows London's top ready-to-wear version of the New Look worn by Barbara Goalen, doyenne of fifties fashion models.

ably the greatest designer of the century, although frequently his work was too subtle or radical to be understood by the press and his fellow designers. His antecedents were as enigmatic as his persona and much of what we know of him is near the realm of myth. His family was humble and his life in fashion began — so the famous but possibly apocryphal story goes — at a tender age, when he admired the DRÉCOLL dress of the Marquesa de Casa Torres as she walked past him in the street. Intrigued (presumably by his precociousness), she allowed Balenciaga to copy the dress. So well did he do it that she sent him to Paris to meet Drécoll. After this Balenciaga's ambition was fired. When he was eighteen, he opened a shop in San Sebastian and followed this by setting himself up as a couturier, under the name of Eisa, in Madrid and Barcelona. In 1937 he abandoned Franco's repressed Spain and arrived in London. He very quickly moved on to Paris and opened his French house, to mixed response. His approach to

Little American Girl by Léon Bakst. Art and fashion became one at the hand of this genius who created clothes for houses like Paquin and Worth, and costumes for Diaghilev's Ballets Russes.

fashion at this stage was very Spanish: he favoured the dignity and drama of stiff, formal materials of the sort that Goya or Velasquez painted. At the outset of World War II he returned to Madrid.

After the war he re-opened in Paris and began his twenty-year climb to fashion supremacy. His work was completely in the couture tradition and each collection made a crisp and clear fashion statement with clothes which had grown logically from previous collections. His clothes always had a dignified, structural quality, even when made in filmy materials. It is no accident that his favourite material was silk gazar — it has weight and body which gives it great structural possibilities.

Clothes are ephemeral, but Balenciaga left a lasting imprint on the way women look. He changed the shape of garments previously considered standardized. For example, he invented the stand-away collar (reputedly to mask the problem of Carmel SNOW*s' short neck) and the three-quarter-length sleeve. Although a brilliant

This woollen dress with banded hips and pleated skirt has its precision softened by a softly draped pillbox with a medieval feeling in this early example of Balenciaga's sense of scale.

A stunning black lace and taffeta dress which shows Balenciaga at full power: a fan-shaped bodice clings over the hips and bursts in a double frill fan skirt curving up at the front and down at the back, the taffeta ballooning out at the hem, to create a masterpiece.

Balenciaga is seen at his glamorous and Spanish best in this late-day or dinner suit, made of velvet and moiré with wide sleeves and a slightly fitted front. The sophisticated hat is a characteristic Balenciaga touch. The whole outfit is black.

Left: *A gently tailored suit from Balenciaga's Winter 1959–60 collection. The collarless long jacket and asymmetric wrap-over skirt are given definition by the wide collared tunic blouse.*

tailor, he moved away from the close fit of the New Look and created softly unshaped jackets for his suits in the early 1950s. He also evolved the inelegantly named sack-dress. His evening looks were as formal as an infanta, but they also contained a great deal of fantasy. He understood scale and proportion and the importance of the balance of an outfit. Exaggeratedly large or minutely small hats were used to state the silhouette with devastating succinctness. He invented the minute pill-box hat.

The 'Spanishness' of Balenciaga cannot be over-estimated. As the 'true son of a strong country', he followed that long line of artists from Goya and Zurbaran to Miró and Picasso; his colours were those of the bullring, flamenco dancers and the Spanish earth; his cut reproduced the simple perfection of the monk's habit. A religious man, he had a conception of harmony which he wished to create in his clothes. He understood that elegance came from

In 1962, for this romantic evening dress, Balenciaga selected a black lace top with an off-the-shoulder neckline and layers of frills, to complement a skirt in heavy cream silk.

Black silk is used by Balenciaga for this high-necked, sleeveless dress which sweeps to the floor at the back. The dress is cut with a single seam and has a semi-circular cape cut on the same lines (not shown).

elimination of detail and perfection of cut. With his infallible instinct for what was right for its time, his decent use of a material and his faultless taste, he was one of the few designers to elevate dressmaking to the level of art.

Balenciaga made life very difficult for everyone. He moved the time of his press showings and (along with GIVENCHY) presented his clothes weeks after the other designers. He never allowed a dress to leave until *he* was satisfied no matter how pressing the customer's demands (rumour has it that he watched fittings through a peephole in the fitting room so that he could later instruct his tailors how to correct the fit). His customers were in partnership with him to achieve perfection — regardless of time or cost.

Loathing publicity and refusing to compromise, this stiff, taciturn man, who closed his doors in 1968 with the words, 'It's a dog's life', created the most marvellous clothes of this century. His legacy to fashion is the continued influence of his design precepts, carried on by GIVENCHY, UNGARO and COURRÈGES, all of whom were trained by the maestro.

Major perfumes: Le Dix (1948); Quadrille (1955).

BALESTRA, Renato

Born Trieste, Italy, 1930s.

Renato Balestra studied civil engineering in Padua and Trieste and graduated in 1956. Instead of following his trade he took work with the designer, Jole Veneziani. He also worked for FONTANA and SCHUBERTH until 1958, when he founded his own house. His family, who ran a building business in Trieste, did not approve, but he was determined to succeed as a designer. Backed by German and American money, he was in at the beginning of the Roman high-fashion movement. He is a traditionalist and his clothes, with their precision of cut and obedience to the laws of fashion, reflect his engineering and haute-couture training. He sells his clothes worldwide and, in addition to his high-fashion range and Balestra International (his ready-to-wear line), he has twelve lines of accessories, including bags, belts, perfumes, luggage, household linens and sunglasses.

BALMAIN, Pierre ☐

Born Aix-les-Bains, France, 1914.
Died Paris, France, 1982.

No *laide* was ever more *jolie* than the one lucky enough to be wrapped in the elegantly glamorous luxury of a Balmain outfit. He studied at Grenoble University before going to Paris to read architecture. He had already determined to be a dress designer and, after several rebuffs, managed to sell three designs to PIGUET. He then joined MOLYNEUX, initially working for him only in the afternoons, but soon becoming a full-time designer, a post he held for five years. In 1941 he moved to Lucien LELONG, where he worked with DIOR in such harmony that they contemplated opening a house together. This did not happen and Balmain opened alone in 1946, to immediate praise. One of his friends and supporters, unlikely as it sounds, was Gertrude Stein. She, at least, had the wit to realize how bizarre it was for her and her friend, Alice B. Toklas, to be involved in such a glamorous and unintellectual world as that of high fashion, but their loyalty to him was intense.

Fifties chic in a princess-line wool dress by Pierre Balmain with a draped cowl necklace of crêpe and a softly swathed drum hat.

A white lace and tulle short dance dress with a repeat apron effect and layered underskirts by Balmain, in the mid-fifties.

A suit and coat by Balmain in 1957, in fine wool. The coat is cut on relaxed lines and lined with spotted silk which is also used for the scarf which fills the neck of the brief jacket of the suit.

Balmain uses a taupe wool and silk mixture for this model from 1958, with a wrapped skirt which passes through a broad black belt.

Sumptuous hand embroidery highlights this simple but very assured evening gown from Balmain's Winter 1964 collection.

Handsome, ambitious, fond of high life and exotic travel, Balmain and his clothes have always appealed to ladies of a certain age, as the French so tactfully put it, and his success has been considerable. At his apogee as a purveyor of glamorous clothing to the rich in the 1950s and 1960s, he dressed queens, statesmen's wives, stars, and virtually all the members of the international set. In addition, he designed air hostesses' uniforms and created costumes for many plays and films, including his memorable wardrobe for Katharine Hepburn in the stage production of *The Millionairess*. His design credo was that dressmaking is the architecture of movement. Balmain continued for a long time as a major French designer, although he ceased to be newsworthy after the demise of couture in the early 1970s. Since his death, the house has been run by his assistant of more than thirty years, Erik Mortenson.

He won a Neiman-Marcus Award in 1955 and his autobiography, *My Years and Seasons*, was published in 1964.

Major perfumes: Vent Vert (1945); Jolie Madame (1953); Miss Balmain (1967); Ivoire (1979).

BANKS, Jeff

Born Ebbw Vale, Wales, 1943.
Having trained at Camberwell School of Art from 1959 to 1962 in textile and interior design, Banks opened his own shop in 1964 at the time of the 'youth boom'. Called 'Clobber', and carrying the designs of FOALE AND TUFFIN and Janice WAINWRIGHT, his clothes were very successful. But in 1974 a fire at his first 'Warehouse' shop destroyed everything. A year later he linked with the dress wholesaler, Rembrandt, and the London store, Liberty, to produce ranges for them. In 1978 he entered into a new venture by designing a range of bed linen. 'Warehouse' Utility Clothing Company shops became an important chain and Banks' influence on high-street fashion was acknowledged in 1982 when he received the *Woman* British Fashion Award. His skill lies in taking the fashion look of the moment and, by removing the extremes, reconstituting it so that it is not frightening at street-level. His designs are fashionable, wearable and

Jeff Banks for Warehouse uses cotton canvas trimmed with corduroy for two young looks with lots of style and dash at an affordable price.

good value. He was married to the former pop singer, Sandy Shaw.

The influence of 'Warehouse' on London fashion has been considerable. Jeff Banks believes in the importance of sound training in business as well as design areas, and to disseminate his views he takes a small number of fashion graduates each year for training.

The 'Warehouse' mail-order catalogues have changed the shopping-by-catalogue image with their contemporary high-gloss look, created for Banks by top photographers, models and stylists. His By Mail range, in conjunction with Freeman's, has set new standards for shopping by post and has as a consequence spawned several inferior imitations.

BANTON, Travis

Born Waco, Texas, USA, 1894.
Died 1958.
Brought up and educated in New York, where he studied art, Banton's first job came after his naval service in World War I. His design career began with a job as an assistant at the prestigious New York salon of LUCILE. Later moving to Madame

Francis, he continued his basic grounding in the art of couture dressmaking. Banton had by then learned to work to the highest standards for an exacting clientele — a grounding which proved invaluable in his designing for the movie camera. In 1924 he was hired by Walter Wanger to design the costumes for a Paramount fashion film called *A Dressmaker in Paris*. The scope to show his skills was there and he used the opportunity to such good effect that he never looked back: he soon became Paramount Studios' chief designer. When his contract expired in 1938, he moved to 20th Century Fox, and then to Universal, although he worked for them only occasionally while carrying on his own dressmaking business. He designed all of Dietrich's costumes at Paramount, including her famous black dress of feathers and beads in *Shanghai Express*. The clothes he created for her exemplify his design talents. His designs were as finely detailed as any in couture, and they moved and shimmered for the cameras. He created similarly elaborate couture dresses for his private customers.

BARNETT, Sheridan

Born Bradford, England, 1951.
Barnett studied fashion at Hornsey and Chelsea Colleges of Art and worked for several firms before joining Quorum in 1975. After one year there, he and a partner, Sheilagh Brown, formed their own company. It ran from 1976 to 1980, but was forced to close from lack of capital. Barnett then taught fashion at St. Martin's School of Art, and textiles at Chelsea before joining the wholesale firm of Salvador. He is now connected with Reldan. His clothes are classically British. They are often based on a male matrix and are minimalist. Decorative detailing is slight, shape and scale being considered more important.

BAROCCO, Rocco

Born Naples, Italy, 1944.
Study at a *liceo artistico* in Naples was followed by enrolment in 1962 at the Accademia delle Belle Arti in Rome, where Rocco Barocco was due to start a fine arts course. Instead, he obtained work as a sketcher with the Rome-based designer,

DE BARENTZEN, with whom he worked for the next two years learning every aspect of high-fashion design. In 1965 he combined with a group of others to form an atelier producing high-fashion collections under the Barocco label. In 1974 this group was disbanded and in 1977 Barocco began to work independently to produce an exclusively high-fashion collection called, simply, Barocco. One year later he expanded to include a ready-to-wear range using his full name. Like LANCETTI, LAUG and other Rome-based designers, he shows his high-fashion line in Rome and his ready-to-wear in Milan. He added a range of knitwear for men and women in 1982 and, in the same year, began to produce a Barocco line for children.

BARRIE, Scott

Born Philadelphia, USA, 1945.
Barrie's godmother made clothes for Dinah Washington and Sarah Vaughn. Following this influence, Barrie studied fashion in Philadelphia and at the Mayer School in New York. In 1966 he began designing for the Allan Cole boutique, and in 1969 he formed his own company, Barrie Sport, a ready-to-wear firm. His clothes are elegantly sexy, especially his evening looks, for which he frequently uses jersey and chiffon. He also designs furs, lounge-wear and accessories. His extra-fashion activities include designing for films and, in 1973, he created the costumes for the Joffrey Ballet's production of *Deuce Coupe*. At present not designing under his own name, he currently designs for S.E.L., a dress firm.

BARTHET, Jean

See MILLINERS (French)

BASILE

See ITALIAN READY-TO-WEAR

BATES, John

Born Ponteland, England, 1938.
Nothing in John Bates' upbringing or education (he was trained as a journalist) would have suggested a future as a dress designer. He worked for Herbert Sidon, a

An elegant look from John Bates' 1970 collection. The narrow three-quarter length coat goes over a sharply pleated skirt to create a refined outfit.

Right: Sportswear in the Beene manner: beige linen shirt and pants teamed with a black linen three-quarter coat topped off with a deep-crowned linen hat.

Below: Evening glamour with this intricately and elegantly embroidered crêpe dress by Geoffrey Beene from his 1971 Winter collection.

couple designer, from 1956 to 1958, then freelanced until he became chief designer of Jean Varon, which was founded in 1961. In the explosive atmosphere of London in the 1960s, however, along with QUANT, he changed the way women looked in and at clothes. He capitalized boldly on the new freedom from constraints like good taste, sexual modesty and visual consideration for others to produce young, sexy clothes which reflected the mood of the time. Throughout the 1960s his designs for Jean Varon were ceaselessly novel and often revolutionary: he designed 'the smallest dress in the world', re-introduced the bare midriff (until then merely a showbiz cliché in the Carmen Miranda style), and revived *appliqué* by scattering rose petals on stockings. He was perhaps the most influential designer in London in the mid-1960s. His costumes for the popular television series, *The Avengers*, brought the new look in dressing to the notice of millions of people. Since those heady days, Bates has settled down. In 1974 he

launched his up-market range, using his own name, and he continues to produce worthy clothes with popular appeal. He designs dresses and evening wear under the John Bates label, and coats and suits for the London wholesaler, Cojana.

BATH MUSEUM OF COSTUME AWARDS
See FASHION AWARDS, p. 232.

BEAUDRY, Dianne
See PINKY AND DIANNE

BEENE, Geoffrey ☐
Born Haynesville, Louisiana, USA, 1927. Beene began his studies as a medical student at Tulane University, New Orleans but abandoned them and began work in display for I. Magnin, Los Angeles, before moving to New York to study fashion at the Traphagen school. He rounded off his education by studying fashion at the École de la Chambre Syndicale in Paris and working briefly at MOLYNEUX. On his return to New York in 1949 he worked as an anonymous designer until he joined Teal Traina, who put his name on the label. He opened his own business in 1962. From his first collection in 1963, his success was assured. His relaxed easy-to-wear clothes relied for their simplicity on shrewd cut and careful fabrication, and very soon the Beene look was strong and individual. Throughout the 1960s and 1970s the Beene design area expanded to include 'Beene Bag' (his boutique line), menswear, furs, jewellery and bathing suits. In 1975 Beene showed in Milan with such success

Geoffrey Beene uses cotton for this 1965 outfit. The black and white cotton tweed 'smock' jacket has the pockets and front panel defined with black braid and sparked with black buttons.

that he continued to do so in subsequent years. He likes to produce the unexpected and the humorous in his designs and enjoys being mildly shocking with his little touches of fantasy. One feels SCHIAPARELLI would have enjoyed him. His very successful 'Beene Bag' collections have been aptly described by Beene himself as 'romanticized sportswear'.

Beene is a colourist and likes to use unexpected fabrics, sometimes mixing as many as four different ones in a single outfit. In 1964 he received Neiman-Marcus and Coty American Fashion Critics Awards. A Coty Return Award followed in 1966, and in 1974 and 1975 he was given a Hall of Fame and a Hall of Fame Citation respectively. In 1977 he received a Coty Special Award for his contribution to American fashion. He was a nominee in 1981 and in 1982 received his fifth Coty Award citation.

BEER
See PARIS COUTURE

BELTRAO, Anna
Born Brazil, 1946.
Beltrao studied fine arts at Brazil University, then fashion at the London College of Fashion. Her first collection, in 1974, was a great success, especially her flattering and feminine use of jersey for evening wear.

BELLVILLE SASSOON
Founded London, England, 1953.
This popular London fashion house was started by Belinda Bellville, whose grandmother owned a famous dress shop in London. A debutante, she worked in a Bond Street dress shop, on a magazine, and then as an assistant to a fashion photographer before founding her own firm. It was originally called Bellville et Cie (Cie being her dog). She spotted David Sassoon at the Royal College of Art and he came to work for her. They are now partners. Their design success is based on a refined line and they are especially noted for their romantic evening dresses.

BENDER, Lee
Born London, England, 1939.
Born of Austro-Czechoslovakian parents, Bender trained at St. Martin's School of Art from 1955–7 and the London College of Fashion from 1957–8. With her husband, Cecil Bender, she had been designing a wholesale line for their company when in 1968 they decided to open their own shop, called Bus Stop. It was an immediate success and soon Bus Stop branches had spread throughout the country. The look of her clothes was right for the time: they were young, easy, casual. Times changed and the Benders were bought out by French Connection in 1979. In 1982, they began again with Arcade, a boutique in London selling their own designs.

BERANGER, Dan
Born St. Etienne, France, 1945.
Beranger specialized in fashion while studying in St Rochelle in 1968, after three years of studying fine art. He began his working life as a freelance designer with Emesse in France and Pourelle. He has been the stylist for various manufacturers, but now has his own label. He designs ready-to-wear women's clothes, made up in Italy. His approach is eclectic, light-hearted in the KENZO manner.

BERETTA, Anne-Marie
Born Beziers, France, 1937.
Anne-Marie Beretta is a French designer who began her career at the age of eighteen. After taking a fashion course, she joined Esterel as a designer. She left him in 1965 to work for Pierre d'Alby designing for the ready-to-wear market. Her scope is wide and she designs leather, rainwear and ski-clothes in addition to her other ranges. In 1975 she opened her own boutique to present her favourite line, which is city clothes. She believes that fashion must be a process of evolution and considers that a garment's initial attraction lies first in its colour and then in its fabric. Her clear-thinking design attitude produces clothes of ease and accessibility, plus a loyal following. She designs for the Maxmara organization in Italy.

BERHANYER, Elio
Born Córdoba. Spain, 1931.
Berhanyer's background is romantically mysterious. He is reputed to have worked as a shepherd in the country around Córdoba before moving to Seville, at the age of seventeen, to find work as a manual labourer. His next port of call was Madrid, where he arrived when he was twenty-one. He obtained work on a fashion magazine, as a representative calling on the magazine's clients. He worked in a fashion shop, then branched out into creating his own designs and, in 1959, established his own fashion house, with one dressmaker and an apprentice. Although self-taught, he became famous in Spain for his masterly tailoring. Like BALENCIAGA and PERTEGAZ he produced clothes which reflected Spanish costume: the boleros and severely seamed jackets of the matador and the ruffles and lace of the Infanta. In 1974 he headed the first show by Spanish designers to be seen in Japan.

BIAGIOTTI, Laura ☐
Born Rome, Italy, 1943.
Biagiotti has a shrewd business brain, allied with the ability to spot talent and exploit its potential. CRUZ and TARLAZZI have both worked with her. A graduate of Rome University in archaeology, she began her fashion career by helping out at her mother's small clothing company. She then turned to producing clothes for other designers, such as BAROCCO, and in 1972 made her debut in Florence with her own label. Shortly afterwards she bought a cashmere firm in Pisa and with it she found her true strength. She is known in Italy as 'the Queen of Cashmere' and the quality and colour combinations of her Macpherson's range of cashmere for men and women are without rival. In addition to Macpherson's, she produces a women's collection under her own name and a second women's line called 'Portrait'. Her clothes are not in the vanguard of fashion, but they are wearable, restrained and full of interesting details and workmanship. She works and lives, with that improbable grandeur beloved of Italian designers, in a 14th-century castle outside Rome.

BIBA
See HULANICKI

BIKI
Founded Milan, Italy, 1936.
Elvira Leonardi, the founder of the high-fashion business of Biki, is the grand-daughter of Puccini and owner of the powerful *Corriere della Sera*, Milan's most important newspaper. She is quite *La Fanciulla del West*, as grandpa might say! She opened her boutique to immediate success. Her son-in-law, Alain Reynaud, is her designer. An American, he worked for FATH in Paris and had experience in the New York fashion world. The firm is one of the oldest surviving in Italy and continues to trade from its Milan head-quarters.

BIS, Dorothée
Founded France, 1960s.
Dorothée bis is the name of a chain of highly commercial boutiques producing sporty, casual clothes. It was established in the 1960s by Jacqueline Jacobson, the designer, and her husband, Elie, the manufacturer. They produced very successful children's wear as well as easy, relaxed adult clothes in jersey and wool. They were among the first of the French ready-to-wear designers to attempt to sell a co-ordinated total look. As well as the shops in France, there are several Dorothée bis outlets in America. Their successful formula for 'no-fuss' clothes continues.

BLAHNIK, Manolo
Born Santa Cruz, Canary Islands, 1940.
Blahnik's father was Czech, his mother Spanish and his education European. He read literature at the University of Geneva and then studied art in Geneva before moving to Paris in 1968. He spent two years as an art student at L'École du Louvre. In early 1971 he was in New York, where a friend showed his portfolio of theatrical designs to various editors, including VREELAND*. Intrigued by his fantasy (snake straps, cherry fastenings coiling up the legs), they put him in touch with Italian manufacturers. He moved to London in the same year to design shoes, although he claims that it was not until 1978 that he began to take shoe-designing seriously. Disliking the word designer as too pretentious, he says, 'I deal in shoes'.

Manolo Blahnik's drawing of his 'leaf' shoe in emerald green suede and red kid for Ossie Clark's Royal Court fashion show in 1972.

He does so very well: the *New York Times* voted him the most influential shoe designer in the world, and through Zapata, and now his own-name boutiques in London and New York, he has provided shoes for such famous customers as Bianca Jagger for more than ten years. His shoes have been chosen by designers like Ossie CLARK, Zandra RHODES and Jean MUIR to complement their clothes. From 1980 to 1982 he designed shoes for Perry ELLIS and he is now designing them for Calvin KLEIN. In addition, he does four collections each year of his own shoes (two per season). Each collection contains between fifteen and twenty models. He has also designed men's shoes for SAINT LAURENT. He is probably the only truly creative shoe designer in the world today, a worthy successor to the shoemaker he most admires, Roger VIVIER.

BLAINE, Alice
Born New York, USA, 1943.
Born Alice Faye Weber, Blaine was educated at the Pratt Institute and the Fashion Institute of Technology, from which she graduated in 1962. After varied design experience, she started Benson and Partners, a sportswear company. In 1974 she founded her own company, Alice Blaine Corp., followed by a country range in 1976 called Alice Blaine for the Smiths, which embraces her characteristics – classic, simple elegance relying on luxurious, subtle, tailored separates. Currently not designing under her own name, however, she designs a line of active sportswear for Everlast.

BLASS, Bill ☐
Born Fort Wayne, Indiana, USA, 1922.
After studying fashion drawing at Parson's School of Art and Design in New York and spending a period as sketcher for the sportswear firm, David Crystal, Blass was drafted into the army during World War II. He returned to New York to work as designer for Anna Miller and Co. in 1946. In 1959 the company merged with Maurice Rentner and in 1961 Blass became vice-president. He formed Bill Blass Ltd. in 1970, with himself as president. During his career he has been richly re-

The pared-down elegance of this simple dress and jacket by Blass gives the material the maximum impact.

warded. He has won the Coty American Fashion Critics' Award several times: 1961, 'Winnie'; 1963, Return Award; 1968, Men's Fashion Design; 1970, Hall of Fame; 1971, Hall of Fame Citation for overall excellence; 1975, Special Award for fur design; and 1982, Second Coty Award. In 1969 he won the Neiman-Marcus Award. He is a member of the Council of Fashion Designers of America and was a former vice-president of the group.

His forte is producing luxury ready-to-wear clothes, but he has a less expensive range called 'Blassport' and he also does a men's range. He is very successful at producing superslick clothes for rich ladies who live active social lives and wish to be seen in beautifully-cut elegance. If an American woman is rich enough, she buys Blass. He is one of the two or three 'court dressmakers' to the 'ladies who lunch'.

Blass has an empire which encompasses thirty-five licences 'from clothes to hosiery'. He has even designed automobile interiors

for Lincoln Continental. Elegant, worldly and urbane, he produces clothes which reflect the same characteristics, be they his impeccably proportioned suits, his cardigan jackets cut with the ease of a sweater, or his frou-frou cocktail dresses and slinky evening looks.

BODY MAP

Stevie Stewart *Born* London, 1958.
David Holah *Born* London, 1958.
Founded 1982.
Stevie Stewart took her diploma in design at Barnet College and David Holah completed his foundation course at the North Oxfordshire College of Art. They both studied fashion at the Middlesex Polytechnic from 1979 to 1982. On graduating they decided to form their own company, Body Map, which was partially financed by their sales of ex-American army surplus pyjamas, dyed in strong fashion colours and sold at the Camden Town street market in London. The name, Body Map,

Positive and negative images are shown in these identical black and white dresses for Spring 1983 by Bill Blass. The tops are linen and the skirts are point d'ésprit, encircled by silk organza ruffles.

For Summer 1984 Bill Blass takes stripes and drapes and ties them asymmetrically in this full-length, off-the-shoulder evening dress.

This outfit by Bodymap shows why they won the Martini Young Fashion award for 1983 and are set fair for the future.

was inspired by the Italian artist, Enrico Job, who, in 1974, took more than a thousand photographs of every part of his body, cut them up and laid them flat, thus creating a two-dimensional version of a three-dimensional object: a body map, in fact. This work symbolized Body Map's approach to pattern cutting, the object being to re-invent shapes and to sculpt materials.

Body Map clothes are essentially for the young. The look is unstructured and layered with textures and prints which change with the layers. In this way one figure can show the complete range of separates and outerwear. The colours are controlled and revolve around white, cream and black. Body Map won the Martini-sponsored Individual Clothes Show of London Award for the Most Exciting and Innovative Young Designers of 1983.

BOHAN, Marc

Born Paris, France, 1926.

Following two of the greatest design talents of this century, as he did when he became designer at DIOR after SAINT LAURENT, Bohan has been overshadowed by his illustrious predecessors. Nevertheless he came to the job after several years of wide experience. As a child Bohan was encouraged to design by his mother, who was a milliner. His first post was with PIGUET, whom he joined in 1945, thus strangely echoing the career of the man whose house he was eventually to control. Dior himself had started with Piguet. In 1949 Bohan began as assistant to MOLYNEUX, moving from there in 1954 to design PATOU's haute-couture range. So all his pre-Dior experience was with highly established houses which had slightly passed their best by the time he joined them.

On leaving Patou he attempted to work under his own name, but the venture failed owing to under-capitalization. He went to New York early in 1958 to work as a coat designer for an American manufacturer. Having met Dior once or twice, he was asked by the maestro to help with his New York collection, but Dior died before it was designed. However, Bohan did design for Christian Dior,

Shades of the Highlands as no Scot ever saw them: Bohan's 1979 way with plaids, woollen skirts and thick stockings is more Paris than Perth but the overall effect is pleasing.

For Summer 1980 Bohan presented a look of great refinement. The collarless three-quarter coat is severely tailored, the skirt is sharply pleated and the small-collared blouse is completed by a bow to produce an elegantly wearable outfit simple enough to have pleased Chanel.

London, from 1958 to 1960. This was a job of designer as adaptor, following the laid-down Paris line, but altering it to suit a specific market outlet. In 1960 he returned to the main house in Paris, after the Saint Laurent debacle, and became head designer, a post he continues to hold.

Bohan's achievements at Dior have been considerable. When he took over, the business was badly shaken and commercial ruin seemed imminent. He steadied

the boat and to everyone's relief produced a very 'Dior' collection: elegant, romantic and refined. He has continued to produce such clothes to the evident gratification of a satisfied clientele. His *chic*, wearable garments, well-bred and understated, whisper 'Dior'. The vulgar shout is out with Bohan.

Bohan seems to understand and appreciate women in their own right, rather than as objects to be changed at the whim

Ruffles add glamour to this taffeta tent dress by Bohan for his couture collection, Winter 1980.

of the designer. In this he is very like BALMAIN, another producer of glamorous, expensive clothes for pampered ladies. As designers they both find a niche in the Temple of Worthies, although denied entry into the Pantheon of the Greats.

BRIGANCE, Tom

Born Waco, Texas, USA, 1913.
Born into an Anglo-French family, Brigance studied art at Parson's School of Design from 1931 to 1934, then moved to Paris to continue his studies at the Sorbonne. Back in New York he was Lord and Taylor's designer from 1939 until 1941, when he joined the army. On demobilization in 1944, he returned to Lord and Taylor; in 1949 he moved to Seventh Avenue with his own firm. Although an all-round designer, it is for his beachwear and swimsuits that he is best remembered. In 1953 he won a Coty Award for 'revolutionizing the look of American women at the beach'. His approach to fabrics was provocative and his mixing

patterns in an outfit, though now a cliché, was remarkable in the early 1950s. He has lectured extensively in America and received many design awards, including the Italian Internazzionale delle Arti in 1956 for foreign sportswear.

BROOKS. Donald

Born New Haven, Connecticut, USA, 1928.
Brooks has had a career of considerable success as a freelance designer, especially in his costume designs for theatre and films. He has received a number of awards: in 1958, a Coty Special Award; in 1962 a 'Winnie'; in 1967, a Return Award; and in 1963, the New York Drama Critics' Award for the costumes for *No Strings*. He studied fine arts at Syracuse University and fashion at Parson's. His own-name company was founded in 1965 with the fashion entrepreneur, Ben Shaw. When their partnership ended in 1973, Brooks went on to found his own couture business. His involvements cover virtually all areas of design, including household linens and accessories. He also encourages design education as lecturer-critic at Parson's. His look is based on uncluttered lines and very good materials. His 1930s costumes for *Star*, the film about Gertrude Lawrence, had a considerable fashion impact. When he received the Parson's Medal for Design in 1974, Brooks entered the Valhalla of American design along with ADRIAN, NORELL and MCCARDELL. This distinguished designer was out of business for several years, but opened again under his own name in 1983.

BURBERRY

Founded Basingstoke, England. 1865.
This world-famous firm, noted for the high quality of its rainwear, was founded by Thomas Burberry to make waterproof gabardine for outdoor pursuits. He moved to London in 1889 as a maker of rainwear for officers and gentlemen, and at the time of the Boer War (1899–1902) his raincoats were approved by the War Office to be worn with uniform. They were, in fact, the forerunners of the modern army officer's trenchcoat. In 1910 a women's range was introduced. The Burberry is

considered the quintessential English upper-class garment. It has become a fashion 'must' for all nationalities and sexes. It is seen wherever the wealthy gather and the rain falls.

BURROWS, Stephen

Born Newark, New Jersey, USA, 1943.
Having been taught to sew at the age of eight by his grandmother, Burrows studied in Philadelphia then at the Fashion Institute of Technology, New York from 1964 to 1965. After several design jobs he joined H. Bendel in 1969 as house designer. He stayed there until 1973, then moved to Seventh Avenue. Hating the bread-and-butter approach to fashion, he returned to Bendel's in 1977. He made his name with sexy, well-cut dresses in chiffon and jersey, and he is at his best with materials which have movement and cling. His un-hemmed skirts with stitched edges, creating his fluttering 'lettuce' look, became a fashion classic. The fact that he has always been a fashion leader, not follower, is reflected in his Coty awards, a Special Award for lingerie in 1974 and a 'Winnie' in 1973 and 1977. He was one of the five American designers who showed their collections at Versailles, in 1973.

BUSVINE

Founded London 1860.
Busvine, a London-based couture house, was active from the 1860s until the outbreak of World War II. The original Busvine, trained by CREED, became famous as a maker of riding habits. His tailored looks, originally created for Queen Alexandra — he created the first sidesaddle riding habit for her — were 'all the rage', and his staid and stolid clothes appealed to Queen Mary, for whom he designed for much of her life. His grandson, Richard Busvine, studied in Canada and at Oxford before joining the firm. Then he added a branch in New York to the Paris and Berlin shops. In the 1930s he became chief London designer. In 1939, Busvine and Violet REDFERN amalgamated and set up business at Busvine's premises in Brook Street. Their clothes were made-to-measure only, and their clients were measured and fitted in their own homes.

C

CACHAREL · CADETTE (*See* ITALIAN READY-TO-WEAR) · CALLOT SOEURS · CAPPALLI · CAPRARO · CAPUCCI · CARACCIOLO (*See* CAROSA) · CARDIN · CARNEGIE · CAROSA · CARVEN · CASHIN · CASSINI · CASTELBAJAC · CASTILLO · CAUMONT CAVANAGH · CERRUTI · CHANEL · CHARLES · CHAUMONT · CHERUIT · CHONG · CLAIBORNE · CLARK · CLIVE · CLODAGH COMME DES GARÇONS · CONNOLLY · CONRAN · CORREGGIARI · COSSERAT · COURRÈGES · COVERI · CRAHAY · CREED · CRUZ

Capucci

Carnegie

Cashin

Chanel

Comme des Garçons
Rei Kawakubo

Connolly

Courrèges

CACHAREL, Jean

Born Nimes, France, 1932.

The name Cacharel is taken from that of a wild duck, native to the Camargue, but it has come to symbolize a very French sportswear look – clothes 'so young that even the model girls look old in them'. Jean Cacharel studied men's tailoring but, finding menswear too limiting, moved into women's wear and worked as a designer-cutter for a ready-to-wear shop in Paris. In the mid-1950s he started his own business and began modestly enough by making shirts. He employed Emmanuelle KHANH as a stylist and with her evolved the approach which is now his own – pretty colours, feminine details and crisp, matching separates. In 1961 his flower-printed, tight-fitting shirts became status-symbol wear, and in 1965 he signed an agreement with the London firm of Liberty to use their prints to his own modern colourings. In 1966 Corinne Grandval (now Sarut) became his designer for clothes and prints. In 1978 he produced his very successful jeans range. His young, trendy looks for men and women, in the higher-price range, are brisk sellers world-wide. His licenses also include children's clothes and bed linen. He is married with two children. His mini-couture line for children is widely copied and adapted at high-street and chain-store level. *Women's Wear Daily* summed him up succinctly, when it referred to him as a 'kind of middle-brow Yves Saint Laurent'.

CADETTE

See ITALIAN READY-TO-WEAR

CALLOT SOEURS

Founded Paris, France, 1895.
Closed 1937.

The three Callot sisters, daughters of a Parisian antique dealer who specialized in old fabrics and lace, began logically enough with such a background by selling lingerie and ribbons. They opened a couture house which was an immediate and continuing success. Their clothes were luxurious, quality was always maintained, and they moved with the times. The eldest sister, Mme Gerber, was the main designer. VIONNET, who worked as her toile-maker, considered her to be a greater designer than even POIRET. Beautiful materials, and up-to-the-moment yet subtle responses to fashion trends made this house a success for more than thirty years. Reputedly the first house to show lamé evening dresses and lace blouses with tailored suits, Callot produced clothes which were always in impeccable taste.

CAPPALLI, Pattie

Born Providence, Rhode Island, USA, 1939.

Cappalli's working life began in Boston, designing sportswear, after graduation in 1960 from the Rhode Island School of Design. In 1968 she joined Addenda, a sportswear firm, to provide contemporary clothes for the twenty-two to thirty-five year old woman. She joined Jerry Silverman's organization in 1975. Her work has won several awards, including *Mademoiselle's* Woman of Achievement award in 1968. She is a member of the Council of Fashion Designers of America and from 1972 to 1974 she was on the Board of Directors of the Fashion Group.

CAPRARO, Albert

Born New York City, USA, 1943.

After studying at Parson's School of Design, Capraro worked for the milliner, Lilly DACHÉ, for two years and then became a designer with Oscar DE LA RENTA in 1966. He left him in 1974 to form a company with Ben Shaw and Jerry Guttenberg. Something akin to canonization occurred in 1975 when Mrs. Ford, the American first lady, chose his clothes for her spring wardrobe.

CAPUCCI, Roberto ☐

Born Rome, Italy, 1929.

Scion of a wealthy Roman family, Capucci studied at the Accademia delle Belle Arti in Rome and, persuaded by a friend, he then opened a tiny fashion house in that city in 1950, when he was twenty-one. He showed in Florence with great success in the same year. Since then he has been a persistent Italian star. Supported and encouraged by Eugenia Shepherd, he opened in Paris in 1962. Seven years later he closed and returned to stay in Rome.

From the first, Capucci's approach to design was strikingly individual and original. He has always experimented and attempted to extend the perimeters of fashion by a daring use of cut and fabric. For him the dress seems more important than the wearer. This is sacrilege in these modern times and so, although his clothes are becoming more exciting at each collection, press coverage of them appears to dwindle season by season. His cut is architectonic, in the tradition of JAMES and BALENCIAGA. Perfection of line is all-important. He employs no design assistants. A Capucci presentation is mounted on the assumption that the viewers wish only to look at the clothes. The cathedral-like atmosphere as each garment silently appears, often worn by friends of the family, is far removed from the presentational vulgarity of many of his fellow Rome designers.

CARACCIOLO, Princess Giovanna

See CAROSA

CARDIN, Pierre ☐

Born Venice, Italy, 1922.

One of fashion's wayward geniuses, Cardin has the singular distinction in the fashion world of being an intellectual and a polymath. Of French parents, he was brought up and educated in France. He studied architecture in Paris after World War II, but was soon attracted to fashion. His design career began with PAQUIN, where he gained wide experience, even helping to design the costumes for Cocteau's film *La Belle et la Bête*. He moved briefly to SCHIAPARELLI, then spent the last part of his apprenticeship working for DIOR in the heady days of the 'New Look'. It is said that he tried three times to obtain work with BALENCIAGA, but with biblical severity was thrice denied. He headed Dior's coat and suit workroom in 1947, but left to form his own house in 1950 and in 1953 he presented his first haute-couture collection.

Since that time Cardin's name has been synonymous with the *avant-garde*. His approach to design over the last thirty years, both for men and women, has been

A perfectly relaxed woollen coat by Cardin which has all the ease of a nightshirt. This beautifully simple design dates from 1959.

Above: *The maestro, Pierre Cardin, poses with examples from his Winter 1980–81 collection. It is hard to decide what is most amusing: the ideas or their masterly realization.*

Below: *Cardin uses 'Cardine', a mouldable, uncrushable, fire resistant and washable new material, to create these styles of the future first shown in 1968. The coat, incongruously, is Persian lamb.*

A beautifully tailored wool coat by Cardin with the sleeves caught at armhole level by two buttons which, with the belt, are the only interruption.

Left: *Exaggerated scale is taken to its limits for the hood neckline of this high-waisted evening dress from the Cardin couture collection for Winter 1978.*

resolutely and consistently experimental. Hence the references to him as the 'Space Age' designer. Unlike many couturiers, Cardin did not merely lend his name to a menswear range; he personally took a new look at the mid-20th-century male role and produced a line to fit it. He found that many design solutions were interchangeable for the sexes and, as a result, he is often credited with the creation of the glibly named 'unisex' fashion. In many ways Cardin is like an experimental scientist, ceaselessly searching for new solutions to old problems. He has pushed forward the boundaries of fashion with his endlessly inventive innovations of cut, material and scale. It must be said that he sometimes seems to forget the body underneath, but even if the results of his experiments are not always practical, they never fail to stimulate.

Over the years Cardin has developed into a one-man business machine and his interests go far beyond clothes. His name has appeared on everything to do with fashion, from cars and furniture to luggage and wigs. Many of his designs are made under licence in America, but his interests are world-wide and include the Soviet Union and China. Characteristically, he was the first couturier to visit China when the 'thaw' began. The ultimate gesture was probably his purchase of Les Ambassadeurs to convert it into his own theatre complex. It opened in 1971, suitably renamed 'L'Espace Pierre Cardin'. He now owns Maxim's. Despite having so many interests, covering every aspect of design, Cardin is no dilettante, but a hardworking, hard-headed businessman who demands success in all he touches. Because he is aggressively forward-looking he obtains it. His collaborator and fellow-designer is André OLIVER, who joined him in 1971.

Major perfumes: Cardin (1976); Choc (1981).

CARNEGIE, Hattie

Born Vienna, Austria, 1889.
Died New York, USA, 1956.
Carnegie emigrated to America with her parents when she was eleven. In 1909 she opened a hat shop and by 1918, having changed her Austrian surname to Car-

negie, she was producing a full-scale collection. She could not cut or sketch but she had amazing fashion intelligence. With all the flair of the immigrant, this tiny woman was quickly the head of a multi-million-dollar business that included her own factories, wholesale operation and retail stores.

Although Carnegie was not an innovator (she followed Paris and made regular trips there to buy original models from which she made her own adaptations), she was a taste-maker, and her influence in America was considerable. She understood *chic* and she was a perfectionist: her clothes were simply the best of their kind available in America in the 1920s and 1930s. Her shrewd ability to spot a good line in Paris was paralleled by her ability to spot home-grown talent: MCCARDELL, JEAN LOUIS and NORELL all worked with her. Norell said, 'I learned everything I knew from her'.

Hattie Carnegie was a fashion power for almost half a century and she is even credited in some circles with having discovered and encouraged the talents of VIONNET. Her great skill, however, in taking the mood of Paris and giving it her own special American feel was celebrated by her receipt of a Neiman-Marcus Award in 1939 and a Coty American Fashion Critics Award in 1948.

CAROSA

Founded Rome, Italy, 1947.
Closed 1974.
Princess Giovanna Caracciolo, a member of one of the oldest noble families in Italy, opened the house of Carosa in 1947. It quickly became known for its high quality of design and workmanship. This attracted buyers and press to her Pitti Palace shows in Florence and, later, to her salon in Rome. An important house in its time it was in the vanguard of the movement that spread the name of Italian fashion abroad. Carosa was responsible for training much young Italian talent, including LANCETTI. The house was forced to close in 1974, however, because it was not able to support the huge costs of *alta moda* fashion nor to withstand the rising tide of Italian ready-to-wear. Princess Caracciolo died in 1983.

This evening dress from Carven's Summer 1950 collection is tied with a large bow on the romantic full skirt.

'Don Juan' created in black velvet by Carven for her Winter 1956–57 haute couture collection.

CARVEN

Founded Paris, France, 1937.

The story goes that one of the major reasons why Madame Carven Mallet opened her couture house in Paris in 1944 was her frustration, as a small woman, with the fact that beautiful clothes were always created for tall women. Her success rested on the wearability of her clothes. Although not in the first rank of designers, she pleased private customers and ready-to-wear buyers equally, and at a time when many of her contemporaries have been forced to close their doors she is still trading. A great traveller, she uses her voyages as inspiration, and has produced over the years a samba look, Egyptian pleats, the Greek 'amphora' shape and many more. She has a successful line for teenagers and children. Her 'Monsieur Carven' range for men is well known.

Major perfumes: Ma Griffe (1944); Rose d'un Soir (1947).

CASHIN, Bonnie

Born Oakland, California, USA, 1915.

Bonnie Cashin could only have been produced by America. Her clothes reflect a culture which springs from ground-level. Her design philosophy has the same organic basis as that of Frank Lloyd Wright and, like his buildings, her clothes are natural and timeless. Although they are informal and 'country', they are as elegant and sophisticated as a Navajo Indian's weaving or a Georgia O'Keeffe painting.

Her mother was a dressmaker and after studying painting in New York and Paris Cashin returned to California as a costume designer for 20th Century Fox. One of her first assignments was the wardrobe for Gene Tierney in *Laura*, in 1944, and forty years later the clothes she designed still look up-to-date. In 1949 she moved back to New York to concentrate on fashion design, opening her studio in 1953. Her collaboration with the manufacturer Philip Sills, for whom she designed collections, was a truly creative partnership which produced superb clothes.

The 'Cashin look', which is collected by museums and has won several awards for its designer, has always been far-sighted. Cashin pioneered layered dressing and

Bonnie Cashin's timeless way with leather is epitomized by this simple but impeccably cut top. Although it looks totally current it is twenty years old.

Suede and jersey to shrug on and forget about. These easeful clothes are the sort that Cashin collectors wear day after day, year in, year out.

Way ahead of her time, Bonnie Cashin created this look in 1967. The simple triangular shape is glamorized with fur but the really forward-looking details are the fastenings for gloves, hood and coat.

A prophetic 1967 coat from Cashin with two-tone wool and leather trim. This look launched a thousand imitations.

103

In 1971 Bonnie Cashin took jersey and created this directional hooded dress: a vast number of designers have made use of it ever since.

functional clothes like sleeveless leather jerkins, ponchos, hooded dresses in jersey, canvas coats trimmed with leather, studs and buckles, and soft suede. An amazing number of current ready-to-wear looks in the sporty, outdoor ranges sprang directly from Bonnie Cashin's thinking of thirty years ago, and so carefully did she work it out that none of her imitators has surpassed her. Her clothes of over 30 years ago are still perfectly beautiful.

In 1950 she received a Neiman-Marcus award and a Coty 'Winnie', in 1961 a Coty Special Award for leather and fabric design, and in 1968 a Return Award. In 1972 she was elected to the Coty Hall of Fame. Other honours included a retrospective exhibition in 1966 in London and New York.

CASSINI, Oleg

Born Paris, France, 1913.
Of Italo-Russian parents, Cassini was brought up and educated in Florence, where his mother ran an exclusive dress shop. An hereditary count, Cassini would be exotic even without having gained the accolade of being appointed official dressmaker to the White House in Mrs. J. F. Kennedy's days. He began his design career in Paris, sketching for PATOU, and by the age of twenty he had his own private couture customers for a small salon in Rome. He moved to America in 1938, took American citizenship and worked in Hollywood as a costume designer on the films starring his wife, Gene Tierney. He opened Oleg Cassini Inc., a wholesale dress firm, in 1950 and retired from the couture field in 1963. He then set up a ready-to-wear business in Milan. He designs both men's and women's ranges.

CASTELBAJAC, Jean Charles de

Born Casablanca, Morocco, 1950.
When he was five, Castelbajac moved with his parents to France, where his mother started her own small clothes factory. Leaving law school at the age of eighteen, he started to work for her, and produced a successful collection called 'Ko and Co'. At the same time he designed ranges for Pierre d'Alby. In 1974 he joined a group of young designers working under the name of 'Créateurs', then a year later opened his first retail shop. Castelbajac designs for several firms and has worked in Italy, notably for the San Lorenzo mark, with whom he signed a contract in 1978. His clothes exhibit a skilful mixture of fantasy and functionalism, but his attitude is anti-high fashion: he likes natural looks and uses plaids, canvas and quilted cotton to produce rugged, sporty clothes for men and women. He has also produced costumes for theatrical events, most notably the Rolling Stones' Hyde Park concert in the late 1970s. An apt description characterizes him as a space-age Bonnie CASHIN.

CASTILLO, Antonio Canovas del

Born Madrid, Spain, 1908.
Of noble Spanish lineage, Castillo was educated in Madrid. In 1936 he left Spain

for Paris, when he worked for PIGUET and PAQUIN, then moved on in 1942 to become head of the couture department of Elizabeth Arden in New York. He filled this post with great success for five years, until Jeanne LANVIN's daughter, Princesse de Polignac, invited him to design for her mother's firm. In 1950 he began what was to be a thirteen-year collaboration with her. In 1964 he opened his own house, but it closed after five years.

CAUMONT, Jean Baptiste

Born Béarn, France, 1932.
Caumont comes from a military background, but instead of following family tradition he studied fine art in Paris before going to work for BALMAIN. From there he moved on to work freelance as an illustrator for *Vogue* and *Marie Claire*, and as a designer for such prestigious names as the DIOR boutique. At the end of the 1950s he began to work as a consultant for the Italian department store, La Rinascente. This led to more work in Italy and in 1963 he moved to Milan. In 1965 Confezioni Amica, Treviso, for whom he was a stylist, offered him his own-label, ready-to-wear range. From the beginning his designs had elegance and *chic* and from his first show in Milan in 1966 (followed immediately by one in New York) he was a success. He launched his knitwear in 1968 and his menswear range, 'Caumont Monsieur', was inaugurated in 1970.

CAVANAGH, John

Born Ireland, 1914.
From 1932 to the outbreak of World War II Cavanagh worked as assistant and secretary to MOLYNEUX in Paris. During the war he served with the British army, then, in 1946 spent a year in America studying fashion promotion before returning to Paris in 1947 to work as assistant to BALMAIN, whom he had known when both of them worked at Molyneux. In 1952 he opened his own house, which he always called 'the shop', in London and became a member of the Incorporated Society of London Dressmakers, acting as vice-chairman from 1956 to 1959. His clothes were always in the understated and elegant style of Molyneux, many of whose

Perfect elegance from John Cavanagh's autumn 1958 collection. This black cocktail dress is in a wool and silk fabric caught at the bust with a deep red rose. The ostrich feather hat is by Simone Mirman.

customers patronized him. He designed the wedding dresses for the Duchess of Kent and Princess Alexandra but his design name is most closely linked with Princess Marina. He closed in 1974.

CERRUTI, Nino
Born Biella, Italy, 1930.
A cultured, enlightened businessman, Cerruti heads a firm which has been respected since its foundation in 1881 in Biella, the centre of the Italian woollen industry. For over a century the house of Cerruti has produced wool fabrics of the highest quality for all the major European design houses. In 1950, at the age of twenty, Nino Cerruti became head of the

family firm. Determined to expunge its dowdy provincial image, he produced many ideas to publicize his clothes, including the commissioning of four famous playwrights to produce a one-act play each. The plays, which ran in Milan, Rome, Turin and Naples, required many changes of costume and the costumes were designed by Cerruti. Cerruti launched his 'Hitman' men's range in 1957; in 1963 he began a knitwear line, produced in Scotland; and in 1967 he opened his 'Cerruti 1881' boutique in Paris, which led to franchises in Japan and the United States. ARMANI worked for him for a number of years. Cerruti launched his women's range, on an industrial, ready-to-wear basis, in 1977, and in 1979 joined forces with Unilever to produce his men's cologne and cosmetics line, which has proved very successful. The name Cerruti still stands for quality and his men's and women's ranges are classic but sporty, always wearable but never staid. The firm is based in Paris.

Chambre Syndicale de la Couture Parisienne
See FASHION ORGANIZATIONS p. 296

CHANEL, Gabrielle 'Coco' ☐
Born Saumur, France, 1883.
Died Paris, France, 1971.
One of the best-known fashion names of the century, Chanel is unique. She came out of retirement at the age of seventy-one and made as great an impact on fashion as she had when she was a young woman. She was born humbly and her early life is obscure – an obscurity Chanel did everything possible to deepen – but it is known that she spent some of her childhood in an orphanage. Ambitious and determined, she soon realized that men could be exploited. From the beginning she was attracted to wealthy and powerful lovers who were able to provide the money and protection essential to gratify her social and creative needs. Her first lover set her up in a hat shop (the traditional role for the discarded mistress) but it was the Englishman, Boy Capel, who took her to Paris, gave her a taste for the high life and backed her when she wished to open a hat shop in Deauville. In 1914 she opened a

dress shop in Paris, but her ambitions were thwarted by the outbreak of war; she re-opened after the war, in 1919. It was her darkest hour emotionally, for Capel had been killed in a car crash. But it was her first triumph as a designer.

From this time her fame, wealth and importance grew. By 1930 her annual turnover was 120 million francs and she was said to have over three million pounds on deposit in London banks. Her success was based on the simple observation, made very early in her career, that what she liked for herself would appeal to other women. She was a trend-setter and a style-maker and all her designs were based on her personal liking for simple, comfortable and sensible clothes. Unnecessary elaboration and fussiness were anathema to her; practicality and wearability were essential: her clothes had the beauty of fitness of purpose. Through the thousands of

This Chanel dress was photographed in June 1933. The strength of the bodice treatment is vitiated by the uncharacteristically fussy sleeves but Madame Quesnel looks very happy, nevertheless.

copies which sold world-wide, they had a permanent effect, not only on the way women looked, but also on the way they behaved, and it is from Chanel's insistence on easy wearability that the modern woman's clothes have sprung. Uniquely among couturiers, she never objected to her ideas being plagiarized and she was always happy to see copies of her designs on the streets.

What Chanel gave to the world was an uncluttered, relaxed way of dressing. It took much of its inspiration from menswear, amazingly for couture clothes, often working-men's wear — the sort of clothes that she wanted to wear, clothes that suited her active, sporty approach to life. Chanel could never be constrained in clothes that dominated her. She demanded clothes which could be donned and forgotten. This does not imply a slip-shod approach to the quality of material and workmanship, however. On the contrary, a perfectly simple garment requires the highest level of finish, since it exposes faults which can be masked in a more elaborate confection. Chanel understood this and the cunning construction of her clothes reflected her inflexible perfectionism. She hated decoration for decoration's sake, just as she hated change for the sake of change, and throughout the 1920s and 1930s her look became classic. It was relaxed and sporty and its basic ingredients were easy cardigans, wool jersey dresses, pea-jackets, bell-bottomed trousers, demure white collars and bows, hair ribbons and chunky fake jewellery. Chanel's colours were usually sombre: black, grey, white and beige for day and white, black and pastels for evening. Red was also a favourite. She released women from formal dressing, elaborate hair-styles (her own short crop started a fashion) and over-elaborate make-up (she is reputed to be the woman who made a tan acceptable). She was naturally original and supremely confident. She imposed her style and could not fail.

Chanel's private life was as spectacular as her design career. The Duke of Westminster and the Grand Duke Dmitri were her lovers; she was part of the Diaghilev set; she knew every creative artist in Paris from Picasso to Stravinsky; her close friends included Misia Sert and Cocteau;

Above: *This short evening dress by Chanel in 1957 is of golden brown chiffon worked in alternated bands of shirring, which end in a full flounce, over stiffened petticoats.*

Right: *For Autumn 1960 Chanel created her elegant suit in creamy wool tweed braided in black. The boater style hat is in the same materials.*

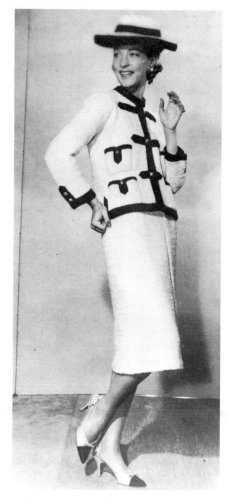

her openings were social occasions; she designed the costumes for the ballet, *Le Train Bleu*, which had a considerable fashion impact; she worked with Sam Goldwyn in Hollywood, designing costumes for Gloria Swanson in *Tonight or Never* and, with Renoir, for *La Règle du Jeu*, in Paris. Her wealth and fame grew all the time. In addition to her clothes, she produced the world's most famous scent, when she launched 'Chanel No. 5' in 1921. In 1939 she closed her doors in the face of war and made her first serious error: she took a German lover and mixed with the Nazi officers who had captured Paris. After the war she was arrested as a collaborator but, owing to intervention on the highest level, she did not have to pay the penalty — having her head shaved and being paraded naked through the streets of Paris — as

some other women did, and was allowed to escape into exile in Switzerland.

This should have been the end of her story, but in 1954 Chanel returned to Paris and re-opened in the rue Cambon. She was persuaded to come out of retirement because it was felt that sales of her perfumes would be boosted if she were once more an active fashion figure. She knew, moreover, that the neo-romantic feelings engendered by the 'New Look' were on the wane and that she could lead women back to *real* clothes. Her first collection was received coolly by the French press, no doubt in some degree because of her wartime behaviour. But the Americans bought and what could have been a disastrous comeback became, within a couple of seasons, a triumph. Over the next few years she evolved the instantly recognizable, timeless look which has become the modern classic: the Chanel suit, in either jersey or soft tweed, was usually collarless and braid-trimmed; the blouse had a softly-tied bow; the shoes were beige with black toe-caps; the hat was a Breton, or the hair was caught with a black bow and white gardenia; and the jewellery consisted of many strands of pearls and gold chains. It was an effortlessly elegant and relaxed look. Once having been perfected, it hardly changed.

So Chanel continued until her death in 1971. She died in the Ritz, alone, as she had lived for years. Her house continued under various designers, including GUI-BOURGE. In 1983 Karl LAGERFELD joined the team as haute couture design consultant and he presented a look based, not on the later Chanel, but on her 1920s look.

Opinions differ as to Chanel's stature as a couturier. Some critics place her on the level of BALENCIAGA, JAMES and VIONNET. Others consider that her strength lay mainly in her ability to market her personality in a way that made women want to copy her. Nevertheless there can be no doubt about her success and influence, nor about her monumental obstinacy and her implacable hatred of those who crossed her. This woman, who coolly sat at the top of her stairs watching her collection being admired by press and buyers below, had, in the words of Mrs. CHASE*, 'the spirit of a Till Eulenspiegel. In coping with her one could never be sure whether her mischief-making was deliberate or unconscious.'

Chanel's uniqueness as a designer lies in the clothes she created in her 'second coming'. She was so in tune with her times that, almost without alteration, her designs have remained *chic* for thirty years. A Chanel suit from the 1950s could be worn anywhere today without appearing to be old-fashioned. No other designer has produced clothes of such long-lived acceptability and influence. They exemplify her own philosophy: 'Let us beware of originality: in couture it leads to costume'.

In 1957 Chanel received a Neiman-Marcus Award; then in 1969 came *Coco*, a Broadway musical (with costumes by BEATON*) based on her life.

Major perfumes: Chanel No. 5 (1921); Cuir de Russie (1924); Cristalle (1974).

CHARLES, Caroline
Born Cairo, Egypt, 1942.
Caroline Charles studied at Swindon Art School from 1958 to 1960, and followed this with a one-year apprenticeship in the London couture house of Michael SHERARD. Here she learnt how to cut and create the two staples of London fashion at that time: the perfectly tailored tweed suit and the romantic ball gown. This was followed by another practical training year in Mary QUANT retail. The final stage of her apprenticeship was a year working with photographer Tony Rawlinson. She founded her own firm in 1963. Having survived London's swinging sixties she became known in the seventies for her evening looks and her strong sense of fabric. Since then she has broadened her approach and neither day nor evening looks dominate. Primarily a dressmaker, she takes beautiful fabrics and creates very English clothes.

CHAUMONT, Marcelle
House founded France, 1939.
Closed 1953.
One of a family of five, Marcelle Chaumont showed a great aptitude for design as a child and in 1912 her mother apprenticed her to VIONNET. Beginning as a seamstress, she soon revealed her talent and quickly became Madame Vionnet's assistant. The two women worked together closely and with mutual admiration until Vionnet's retirement in 1939. Marcelle Chaumont set up on her own in the same year and produced very successful clothes in the Vionnet manner until ill-health forced her to close in 1953. She is credited with pioneering the idea of ready-to-wear boutiques in the early 1950s when she launched her Juliette Verneuil label. Pierre CARDIN worked as a cutter for her early in his career.

CHERUIT, Madeleine
House founded Paris, *c.* 1905.
Closed 1935.
Cheruit, now a rather shadowy figure, was briefly an important and successful Paris designer based in the Place Vendôme. She obtained her training in the 1880s with the couture house of Raudnitz, and opened her own house at the turn of the century.

It was one of the few to remain open during World War I. Her great period of success was during the 1920s but by the end of the decade the fate which had overtaken so many of her contemporaries caught up with her. Fashion moved on and she was left behind.

Although by no means one of the 'Grands Couturiers', she was a successful purveyor of refined day-wear to the sub-aristocratic sector of Parisian society. She is credited with being the first to buy freelance designs from the young POIRET, before he was employed by DOUCET. She retired in 1923, but her house continued until 1935, when the premises were taken over by SCHIAPARELLI.

CHONG, Monica
Born Hong Kong, 1957.
After an education in Hong Kong and Australia, Monica Chong moved to England to study fashion which she did at Chelsea College of Art from 1974 to 1977. She then spent several months working for Browns as a sketcher, window dresser and PR assistant. In 1978 she produced her first collection which consisted of twelve young and inexpensive pieces. From this beginning she has developed into a fully fledged designer. Chong became a member of the LONDON DESIGNER COLLECTIONS in 1980 and in 1982 she joined the Tricoville group to produce a collection for Studio 88. Her designs for day and evening are sophisticated variations on the theme of cut and fit.

CLAIBORNE, Liz
Born Brussels, Belgium, 1929.
Brought up in New Orleans and educated in America and Europe, Claiborne began her fashion career in 1949, when she won the *Harper's Bazaar*-Jacques HEIM National Design Contest. The prize was a trip to Europe to study design. On returning to America, she worked as an assistant designer in a wholesale firm, before becoming assistant to OMAR KIAM. Afterwards she was chief designer for Youth Guild, a post she held for fifteen years, before forming Liz Claiborne Inc. in 1976. Her designs are simple, sporty and based on sound technical skill.

CLARK, Ossie

Born Liverpool, England, 1942.

Raymond Clark, known professionally as Ossie, studied at Manchester School of Art from 1957 to 1961. He went to the Royal College of Art on a scholarship and graduated in 1964. His design career began with Alice Pollock's Quorum in the 1960s heyday of London fashion and his clothes were renowned for their iconoclastic, youthful zest. The superb prints which were a feature of his evening wear were designed by his wife, Celia Birtwell. He was one of the first foreigners to design for the French company, Mendes. His clothes had everything for those heady days when the *jeunesse dorée* of the Royal College seemed able to break all rules and canons of taste, secure in the knowledge that they would receive ever-increasing praise from the press. *Bons mots* attributed to Clark such as 'designing for the future is impossible because the future never comes' and 'fashion is to stop being bored' give us a good idea of the intellectual level of the English designers of the 'swinging sixties'.

CLIVE (Clive Evans)

Born London, England, 1933.

Clive's national service in the navy was followed by study at Canterbury Art School. From there he moved into London couture, working as assistant to MICHAEL, then to John CAVANAGH and LACHASSE, before opening under his own name in 1962. His debut was so successful that after his second collection he was invited to join the Incorporated Society of London Fashion Designers. His haute-couture range was augmented in 1961 by a ready-to-wear collection, called 'Clive Set'. In addition, he designed clothes for films and the theatre and was responsible for the design of the BOAC stewardesses uniform. His firm closed in 1971, but Clive continues to work as a design consultant, specializing in interior decorating.

CLODAGH

Born Galway, Ireland, 1937.

A teenage riding accident forced Clodagh O'Kennedy to spend a year in hospital with a broken back. Seeing an advertisement in a newspaper urging that anyone could be a designer, she decided to do a crash-course at the Grafton Academy, Dublin. Clodagh put on her first show at the age of seventeen. Energetic and ambitious, she opened a boutique, wrote a fashion column for the *Irish Times*, became a fashion co-ordinator for a major Dublin store and designed just about everything. She was discovered by the New York store, Lord and Taylor, in 1963. She subsequently closed her Dublin boutique and now concentrates on 'one-off' designs for private customers in America and Ireland.

COMME DES GARÇONS ☐
(Rei Kawakubo)

Born Tokyo, Japan, 1942.

If the fashion designers of the West hear the faint murmur of 'ancestral voices prophesying war' from the East, one of the Samurai swords is surely wielded by Rei Kawakubo, presiding spirit behind Comme des Garçons. Her anti-status clothes strike at the very base of French couture. Having studied literature at Tokyo's Keio university, graduating in 1964, she joined the textile firm of Asahi Kasei to work in the advertising department. She left in 1966 to work independently as a freelance stylist, then three years later, in 1969, she founded Comme des Garçons. In 1973 it became a limited company formed to produce clothes for specific Japanese women's boutiques. Since then 'Homme', her menswear range, and a knitwear line, 'Tricot', have been added. Rei Kawakubo is president and designer of all. She shows in Paris and Tokyo.

Rei Kawakubo is one of the spearheads of the new iconoclasm. Like Vivienne WESTWOOD in London, she sets out to break down the accepted Western view of fashion and sexuality. Her work is essentially Japanese, but hers is not the formal, restrained Japan of the dry landscape garden, the tea ceremony and the Noh drama. It is the Japan of stylized, ritual violence. Her clothes evoke the world of the Samurai, Sumo wrestling and the Kabuki theatre. The violence, although formalized, is still potent and untamed. Her creased, torn and slashed designs, draped and wrapped around the body, use cottons, canvas and linen, but not to create

An asymmetric top and many-faceted skirt, with gauntlets and medieval shoes, give this Comme des Garçons outfit a troubadour look.

traditional fashion looks. They make the wearers look like the victim of some ritual attack – vulnerable, abandoned and shorn of all sophisticated veneer. Rei Kawakubo could well prove to be a Don Quixote tilting at windmills, but it is more likely that she will emerge as a masterbuilder of the future. The subtlety of her mind is exemplified by her cryptic comments on fashion, of which the best-known is 'I work with three shades of black'.

See also JAPANESE DESIGN.

CONNOLLY, Sybil

Born Swansea, Wales, 1921.

If Eire seems an unlikely place for a world-renowned fashion designer to surface, it seems even stranger when it is discovered that she was born in South Wales. Despite the improbability of it all, Sybil Connolly has kept Dublin firmly on the fashion map for the past thirty years. After working for two years at Bradley's in London, she returned to Ireland on the outbreak of World War II to become buyer for Richard

Sybil Connolly teams a fringed Irish tweed three-quarter coat with a slim handwoven Irish tweed skirt for this unusually textured outfit.

Gossamer Irish linen, finely pleated, is used by Sybil Connolly for her classic evening blouse and skirt.

Alan, a Dublin store. At the age of twenty-two she was a director of the firm and she began to design for them in 1950. She showed a small collection to the Philadelphia Fashion Group, who invited her to America. Success was instant. In 1957 she opened her own couture house.

Sybil Connolly's strength as a designer lies in her ability to combine the homespun with a high-fashion look in an attractive and wearable way. She has exploited the textures, colours and shapes of Ireland and has helped revive many traditional skills. Lace, linen and crochet have all been used by her, along with Donegal tweeds and homespuns. Her clothes are elegant, lady-like and classic.

CONRAN, Jasper

Born London, England, 1959.
Conran's father founded the Habitat chain and his mother is a popular writer. He was educated at Bryanston School in England and was then accepted at the age of only sixteen at Parson's School in New York. He studied there for eighteen months in 1975–1977, then worked briefly for FIORUCCI in New York before returning to London in 1977 to work for Wallis. His first independent show was held in October, 1978. His lively but wearable clothes have greatly helped London to be taken seriously as a fashion centre.

CORREGGIARI, Giorgio

Born Pieve di Cento, Italy, 1943.
Correggiari's father owned a textile mill near Bologna and Correggiari studied political science at the university there. When he was twenty a disastrous fire at the mill meant that his family faced ruin. Having travelled through Germany to England and thence to France, he found work in a mill in Lyon, where he remained for almost a year, learning about textiles and fabric printing. In 1967 he returned to Italy and opened an avant-garde shop to sell his own-design clothes, which were made up by Bolognese seamstresses. After travelling in India, he returned to Italy in 1974 to design the very successful U.F.O. jeans range. In 1975 he designed HECHTER's men's, women's and children's lines, then went on to form his own company.

In addition to his Correggiari line he designs knitwear ('Cleo & Pat'), menswear ('Reporter') and leatherwear for IGI. He also has his own accessories range of handbags, ties and scarves and creates a line in patterned velvet for Cantoni. He has worked as a consultant to the International Wool Secretariat in Paris.

COSSERAT, Kay

Born Hartlepool, England, 1947.
Having obtained first-class honours in fashion and textiles from Goldsmith's College in 1970, Kay Cosserat spent two years at the Royal College of Art. On completion of her course in 1972, she went to India to study dyeing techniques, then spent the next year as a research fellow with the textile department of the Royal College of Art. She was a founder member of the London Designer Collections in 1974 and has since shown two collections a year with this group. In 1982 she became a freelance designer for JAEGER. Her career has included a large commitment to education as a visiting lecturer in art colleges. She sells in England, America, Europe and Japan.

Coty American Fashion Critics Awards
See FASHION AWARDS, p. 298

COURRÈGES, André ☐

Born Pau, France, 1923.
Having studied civil engineering, Courrèges went on to study textile and fashion design at Pau and Paris. Wishing to find a place in fashion, he was attracted to BALENCIAGA, that *éminence grise* from the Spanish Basque, and was engaged by him as a cutter. His years with Balenciaga, from 1950 to 1961, taught him to be a serious, committed perfectionist, and he emerged not just a designer, but also a brilliant tailor. In 1961 he set up under his own name with his wife, also ex-Balenciaga, and slowly began casting off the mould and honing his own ideas. These ideas made him *the* popular designer of the mid-1960s.

The revelation and revolution were launched in the spring of 1964, with crisp,

109

architectural, square shapes (all tailored, no drapes), short skirts and trousers. Meant to be a sexless uniform for space-age living, these clothes were in fact very sexy indeed. Courrèges' 'new look' swept the world almost as dramatically as had DIOR's, except that Dior's had looked back to a bygone era, whereas Courrèges' clothes owed virtually nothing to traditional looks. As *Women's Wear Daily* said, he was 'the Le Corbusier of the Paris Couture'. After his mini-skirt collection of 1965, he was plagiarized world-wide, and as a result he sold his business to L'Oréal and closed his doors to all but individual private customers. A year later he re-opened with three ranges to beat the copyists: 'Prototype', 'Couture Future' and 'Hyperbole'. Despite the name, the last was meant to be a cheap ready-to-wear range.

To everything there is a season, and Courrèges' reign as a leader was brief. By the end of the 1960s the space-age shocker had been grounded. The sexiness of his clothes was taken for granted in a period when publicity-crazy couturiers could design bare-breasted looks and still be taken seriously. Nevertheless, his influence was potent and still continues through his men's and women's ranges, which are sold in his boutiques throughout the world. In 1983 the Japanese group, Itokin, bought sixty-five per cent of Courrèges couture from his backers, L'Oréal.

COVERI, Enrico

Born Florence, Italy, 1952.
One of Italy's fashion 'wonderboys', Coveri is eternally youthful and endlessly original. He studied theatre design at the Accademia delle Belle Arti in Florence and made his debut in 1973 as a designer for a knitwear company. From there he went to Lux Sport as designer. By 1976 he was creating three collections: 'Touche', 'Gentry' and 'Tycos'. He moved to the Espace Cardin in Paris in 1978 and his clothes were strongly featured in the French press – the *Herald Tribune* called him the Italian KENZO – and with this success behind him he returned to Italy to set up his own company. His impact was instant and phenomenal because, although he objects to the idea that he designs only for adolescent girls, he

The look the whole world wanted in the sixties. This Courrèges outfit from 1965 has all the characteristics which made him the most influential designer of the time.

perfectly understands the needs of young customers. His clothes are humorous, light-hearted and bright, and his jeans, shirts and cotton-knits sell well because they are well designed and inexpensive. His strong colour sense, young shapes, witty proportions and well-judged level of fantasy all combine to produce delightful clothes. He shows in Paris, where the 'cartoon character' or 'pop' nature of his decoration is highly appreciated, as it is everywhere where clothes are considered fun.

CRAHAY, Jules François

Born Liège, Belgium, 1917.
Crahay's mother was a dressmaker in Liège and she encouraged the design potential of her son. After studying in Paris from 1934 to 1935 and working for his mother in Liège, he joined Nina RICCI in 1952, working as her designer for eleven years before moving to LANVIN in 1963. His design high point was with Ricci in his 1959 collections, but his understanding of cloth and cut ensured that all that he designed was elegant,

civilized and wearable. Recognition of these qualities came with the Neiman-Marcus Award in 1962.

Crahay is one of many figures who must be called minor, but it is important to remember that for a name to surface at all in such a competitive field as fashion argues a level of talent well above the average.

CREED, Charles

Born Paris, France, 1909.
Died London, England, 1966.
The tailoring house of Creed goes back to the beginning of the 18th century in London and a branch of the firm was founded in Paris in 1854. Charles Creed received a widespread and practical education which took him to places as diverse as Carlisle, Vienna and New York. He returned to the family firm in Paris in the 1930s, but it closed during World War II. After the war, with a contract to design clothes for an American manufacturer, he opened a house under his own name in London. Not surprisingly, his forte was for tailored suits, which were always refined and understated, elegant and meticulous and sold extremely well in America. With his death in 1966 his house closed, thus ending the name of Creed in fashion circles. His book, *Made to Measure*, was published in 1961. Mata Hari elected to go to her execution in a Creed suit.

CRUZ, Miguel

Born Cuba, 1944.
Cruz trained in Paris at the Chambre Syndicale de la Mode and then worked for CASTILLO and BALENCIAGA. In 1963 he moved to Italy, where he worked as a freelance for several designers before opening his own ready-to-wear house in Rome. In addition to his own line, he designs as many as ten collections a year, especially knitwear, for other firms. He is the designer, for example, for Florentine Flowers, a respected and very creative Italian knitwear house. He also designs leather, suede and men's collections. His work for Pitti Filati is usually very influential, and by his many freelance commitments he makes a real impact on Italian ready-to-wear fashion.

D

DACHÉ · DAGWORTHY · DEALEY (*See* ZWEI) · DE BARENTZEN · DE LA RENTA · DELAUNAY · DELL'OLIO · DE LUCA · DE RAUCH (*See* PARIS COUTURE) · DESSÈS · DI CAMARINO · DIOR · DOEUILLET · DOUCET · DRÉCOLL

Daché

Dagworthy

De la Renta

Above: *Doucet*

Left: *Dior*

DACHÉ, Lilly

Born Beigles, France, *c.*1907.

Although born and brought up in France, Lilly Daché is remembered as America's best milliner. She left school at fourteen and became an apprentice in her aunt's hat business, then a year later continued her apprenticeship with the famous Paris milliner, Caroline REBOUX. In 1924 she arrived in New York and set up a millinery business with a friend. Her designing proliferated to take in gloves, lingerie, loungewear and jewellery, cosmetics and perfume. Her husband's retirement as vice-president of Coty in 1969 prompted her to close her doors. She made several 'break-throughs', including half-hats and hats moulded to the individual head. Her work has influenced milliners throughout the States, not least HALSTON. Her autobiography, *Talking through my Hats*, was published in 1946.

DAGWORTHY, Wendy

Born England, 1950.

Dagworthy studied at Medway College of Art from 1966 to 1968 and then took a fashion course at Hornsey College of Art from 1968 to 1971. She graduated with first-class honours, became designer for the wholesale firm of Radley for a year, and then founded her own company in 1972. This venture was successful and remains so because her clothes are totally wearable and finely detailed. Prestigious stores world-wide make up her customers and she exports half of her total output to Italy. She joined LONDON DESIGNER COLLECTIONS in 1975, and takes an active part in fashion education.

DEALEY, Fiona

See ZWEI

DE BARENTZEN, Patrick

Born Copenhagen, Denmark, 1920s.

Brought up in Paris, de Barentzen studied design there before beginning work for DESSÈS. He then spent four years with FATH, until the firm closed on the death of the maestro. Having learned a lot about controlled exuberance from Fath, he took his learning to Italy in 1956, worked briefly

Left: *For Winter 1982–83 Wendy Dagworthy uses strongly textured, loose-woven wool for a gathered skirt with a boldly tied waist.*

De Barentzen uses a wool and silk fabric for a dress and stole. The dress has an inserted belt to mark the slightly raised waistline, the stole is fastened like a cape.

in Milan, then moved to Rome. There he designed for many of the big names of Rome high fashion, including FONTANA, SIMONETTA and CAROSA, before setting up on his own with his partner, Gilles. In the 1960s his *alta moda* house was renowned for its daring and lively innovations, created in much the way one imagines Fath would have, had he lived to develop his fashion philosophy. De Barentzen closed his firm in 1971 and went into retirement.

DE LA RENTA, Oscar

Born Santo Domingo, Chile, 1932.

Born of Spanish parents, de la Renta was educated in Santo Domingo and Madrid, where he studied art with the intention of

becoming a painter. His move into fashion was the result of good luck. He had been designing clothes for friends for some time when one of his sketches was seen by the wife of the American Ambassador to Spain. Liking what he did, she commissioned him to design her daughter's debut dress. Her daughter was photographed, wearing the dress, for the cover of *Life*, so de la Renta the painter gave way to de la Renta the designer. He worked briefly at 'Eisa', BALENCIAGA's Madrid couture house, before joining CASTILLO in Paris at LANVIN in 1961. Two years later he moved to New York as designer for Elizabeth Arden, a post which Castillo had held in the 1940s. In 1965 the foundation of his own organization was laid when he signed a contract with Jane Derby. He married the

Pierre Cardin's skill in tailoring is shown in a finely pleated back, like a refined iguana (left); and an asymmetrically belted coat (right) — both created in 1980.

*Supreme mastery of cut raises
the couturier's craft to the level
of art in the hands of Capucci —
a genius second only to
Balenciaga and James.*

The mobile Chinese pagoda look by Cardin, 1983. This dress shows the exaggerated and complicated cutting for which he is famous.

For Autumn/Winter 1983 the house of Cardin teams a brilliantly shining top with multi-layered skirts for a swishy evening look.

The Lagerfeld way with Chanel in 1984. On the right he retains the traditional look of Chanel's 'second coming' and perfectly recaptures the mood of her famous suit; the elongated proportions of his navy and red outfit update Chanel's twenties' knits with consummate skill and tact.

The uncompromising, undiluted Japanese fashion look from Comme des Garçons, 1984.

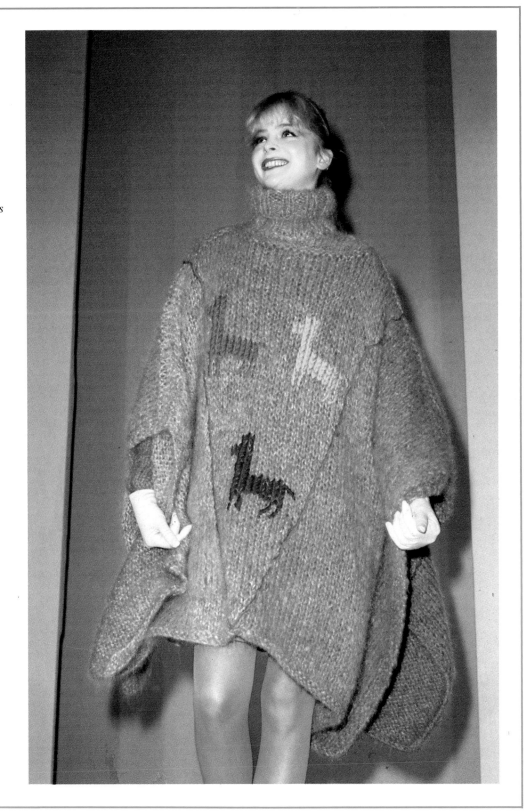

Enrico Coveri's young and amusing knitwear is always in demand. This example from 1980 shows why.

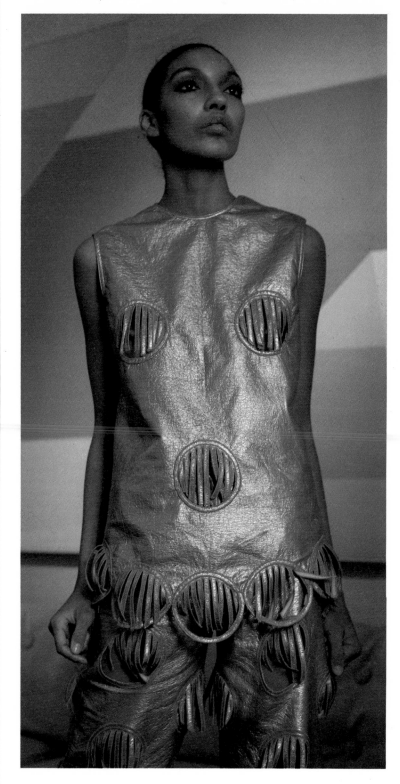

Whether with space-age shine or leather and fur, the scale and proportion of Courrèges' looks were a potent fashion influence in the sixties.

The female gaucho as seen by Cuban designer Miguel Cruz, who works in Italy. His controlled colour palette here shows the sophisticated influence of his adopted country.

*A three-piece dress by
Doeuillet embroidered with
steel thread accompanies
one with a red velvet coat
for a walk through the
pages of Art-Goût-Beauté
for February 1923 where
hopeful spring seems
eternal.*

Art - Goût - Beauté

Youthful verve and vitality are characteristic of Perry Ellis clothes. This colourful outfit from his March 1982 collection has all the attributes that have made his clothes best sellers.

The large-size, long line of 1984 is treated with great skill by Perry Ellis in these understated clothes where neutral colour is sparked with strong accents.

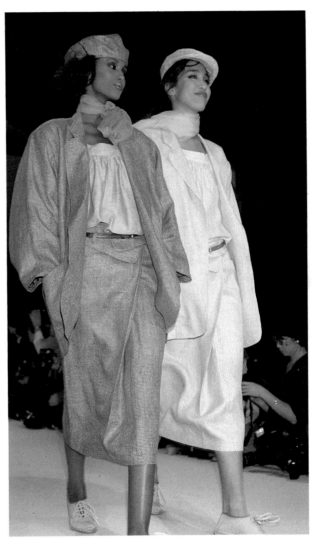

Left: *The throw-away relaxation of the Fendi approach to fur is shown in this characteristically easy belted jacket.*

Below: *Super-slick evening dressing in the Halston way for Summer 1984.*

*In every sense, the classic
Fortuny creation. This finely
pleated silk evening dress
was designed about 1912,
but is still wearable today.*

Jean Paul Gaultier's colourful outfit from his 1984 collection is a mixed metaphor: the trappings of the aggressor are contradicted by the sticking plasters of the victim.

Givenchy's glamorous evening packaging has always been a strong point in his collections. This look is from his 1984 show.

This beautifully draped and controlled evening dress is the apotheosis of Charles James' structural skills.

Charles James designed this 'Four-leaf clover' dress for Mrs William Randolph Hearst in 1953 and subsequently made several copies. He considered it his greatest creation and wrote 'I had intended it to be the last and final statement and it was composed of several parts previously developed as separate designs'.

*A colourful and witty hat by Stephen Jones. The sheer
sophistication and panache shine forth like a good deed in a
naughty world. This is what style is all about.*

Left: *Oscar de la Renta recaptures the honeyed courts of Samarkand in this 1982 outfit. The Persian print is lavishly embroidered at neck, cuff and waist and the stole is bordered with fox.*

Below: *In 1983, Oscar de la Renta used tiered black silk organza for a dress with an embroidered faille bolero for an Americanized Spanish look.*

editor-in-chief of French *Vogue* in 1967, the year a Coty Award was given to him for his luxurious Russian and gypsy looks. His empire has proliferated to take in menswear, jewellery, household linens and perfumes, but his name rests on his richly opulent women's clothes. They are sought after for their glamour and elegance, whether in his couture or up-market boutique range.

The Dominican Republic has honoured de la Renta with the Order of Juan Pablo Duarte, grado Caballero, and the Order of Cristobal Colón, grado di Gran Commandante. He was one of the participants in the historic Versailles show of American designers in 1973. He received a Coty Return Award in 1968 and was elected to the Coty Hall of Fame in 1973. His

Neiman-Marcus Award came to him in 1968.

DELAUNAY, Sonia

Born Ukraine, Russia, 1885.
Died Paris, France, 1979.
Armed with a private income, Delaunay left Russia for Paris in 1905 in order to study art. By 1907 she had come under the influence of the Fauves and had accepted their colour theories. She married in 1909 but divorced her first husband the next year in order to marry Robert Delaunay. In 1917–18 they worked with Diaghilev, designing sets and costumes for the Ballets Russes. As early as 1911 her interest in re-thinking clothes had been apparent and, influenced by Russian

peasant costumes and patchwork, she initiated a total revolution when she created her first 'simultaneous' dress out of multi-coloured samples of material given her by Robert Delaunay's tailor.

From this start she proceeded to mix strong bright colours and fabrics such as taffeta, flannel and organdie. All her fabrics were based on collage: her method 'combined fantasy and elegance' (in Appollinaire's phrase) and was instrumental in changing fabric design. Her influence was considerable: in 1923 she was commissioned by a Lyon silk merchant to design materials using her collage technique and in 1924 she launched her own creations in 'simultaneous' materials and woollen tapestry. Her *Boutique simultanée* at the 1925 International Exhibition of Decorative Arts in Paris showed a variety of 'simultaneous' materials: coats in graduated colours; furs with embroidered panels; and dull, discreet metal with wool and silk. The graduated, harlequin and geometric prints and the embroidery and collage coats reflected artistic thinking of the 1920s and were widely copied – especially the strongly geometric embroidered coat made for Gloria Swanson in 1923. Although she was primarily a painter, she also looked at clothes with a radical eye.

DELL' OLIO, Louis

Born New York City, 1948.
Louis dell' Olio studied on a NORELL scholarship at Parson's and graduated in 1969. He worked as a freelance designer with the wholesale firms Teal Traina and Originala before becoming co-designer with Donna KARAN at Anne KLEIN after Anne Klein's death in 1974. Together he and Karan gave the classic Klein sports look a zesty, modern feel. In 1977 they were awarded a Coty 'Winnie' for their combined work at Anne Klein; a Hall of Fame Award followed in 1982. Since Donna Karan set up on her own, dell' Olio alone designs the Anne Klein range.

DE LUCA, Jean-Claude

Born Paris, France, 1947.
De Luca is of Italo-French parentage. His father was in the ceramics trade. After

studying law in Switzerland and Milan, he met GIVENCHY, who employed him for a year in 1971 and taught him the basics of the designer's craft. He moved to Dorothée BIS in 1972; this was followed by a period of freelance designing; and his first collection under his own name was made by G.F.T. in Italy in 1976. His clothes are glamorous and adult and he designs for the woman over twenty-five — this does not preclude a certain degree of humour and fantasy, however. Traditional, but with a comic twist and witty accessories, his clothes appeal to women with a strong style who are attracted to worldly originality.

DE RAUCH, Madeleine
See PARIS COUTURE

DESSÈS, Jean
Born Alexandria, Egypt, 1904.
Died Athens, Greece, 1970.
Born of Greek parents, Dessès was educated in Alexandria and then went to Paris to study law. Although destined to enter the diplomatic corps, he took up fashion instead in 1925. He designed for Mme Jane until 1937, when he opened his own house in Paris, where his success was considerable. He attracted many rich and discerning clients, who admired the softly feminine fluidity of his clothes, based on his direct draping of fabrics on the dummy. After a visit to America in 1949, he signed an agreement with two American firms for them to manufacture his clothes, and in 1950 his cheaper line, 'Jean Dessès Diffusion', was initiated. This is seen by many as the real beginning of French couture's involvement in mass-production. He closed in Paris in 1960 and moved to Greece, where he continued as a freelance designer until his death.

DI CAMARINO, Roberta
Born Venice, Italy, 1920.
From the unlikely base of Venice, Roberta di Camarino has built a large fashion empire with boutiques and retail outlets on a world scale. Christened Giuliana, she adopted Roberta as her Christian name in 1945, when she and her banker husband

returned from war-time exile in Switzerland. Beginning on a small scale with exclusive handbags, she broadened her scope to include scarves, umbrellas, travel goods and perfumes, finally building up to clothes: in fact, the complete high-quality boutique range. She was early in the field of designer identification marks and right from the beginning signed all her products with an 'R'. In no way in the vanguard of fashion, her clothes are nevertheless creative, elegant and luxurious. Her success was marked in 1956, when she was given the Neiman-Marcus Award.

A very elegant boat-necked dress by Jean Dessès has a tie sash coming from each side seam, tied in the front and falling to the hem. In pure silk, it was designed in 1958.

DIOR, Christian □
Born Granville, France, 1905.
Died Montecatini, Italy, 1957.
Son of a stolid Norman industrialist who manufactured chemical fertilizers, Dior wished to study fine art, but parental pressure forced him to become a student of political science at the École des Sciences Politiques, which he left in 1928. His family wanted to see him in a diplomatic career, whereas he hoped to be an architect. In the event, neither wish was gratified. Christian Dior, became, instead, the most famous couturier of the century. When he finished his studies, he began to run an

The 'New Look' of 1947. Although not using the full skirt associated with this look, Dior's outfit has all the other romantic attributes: picture hat, low neckline, softly gathered skirt and, above all, length.

art gallery with a friend in Paris. This venture was interrupted by the Depression, which ruined his father. Shortly after, his mother died and his brother became terminally ill. Dior tried to escape all of this misery by going to Russia in 1931, but the trip was disastrous. As a young man Dior was an anarchist and he had built up an idealized picture of Russian life: it was shattered by the reality.

Returning to Paris, he lived like a gypsy, sleeping on friends' floors and hardly eating. He became ill and had to go to the South of France to recover. There he learned to weave and his thoughts first

Above: *This romantic evening dress in the grand manner is from Dior's collection of 1949. It shows how assured he is after only two years in his own house.*

Right: *Simplicity, perfectly proportioned, is the mark of good design. This Dior outfit is an excellent example of how less means more when the designer's hand is sure.*

turned to the possibilities of design. In 1935 he returned to Paris, aged thirty and desperately short of money. He began to peddle design sketches around the couture houses and magazines, and managed to get some fashion illustration work with *Le Figaro*, selling his sketches for twenty francs each.

His luck changed in 1937 when, having made a modest success with millinery designs and having worked to improve his dress design, he sold some drawings to Robert PIGUET. In 1938 Piguet hired him as a design assistant, but in 1939 Dior was called up for military service. After the collapse of Paris in 1940, he moved to the country with his family. Piguet re-opened in 1941 and asked Dior to return, but Dior dithered for so long that when he finally arrived in Paris the position had been filled. However, Lucien LELONG offered him a job and he worked there, with BALMAIN, until 1946. It was at this time that he met Marcel Boussac, the fabric millionaire, who was looking for a designer to revive an ailing fashion house. Dior said that he was 'not meant by nature to raise corpses from the dead' and outlined plans for his own house. Boussac decided to finance him and so Dior finally became a couturier, backed by the money and business acumen of the huge Boussac organization.

In February, 1947, at the age of forty-two, Dior presented his first collection, the 'Corolle' line. Named the 'New Look' by an American journalist, it was instantly and spectacularly successful. Dior's name became a household word almost overnight. His place in the history books was secured and, as a result of an agreement by which he received a percentage of all sales, his days of poverty were permanently over.

What he had done to make himself the most famous dress designer in the world was to return to the soft, gentle curves of the Edwardian period. He brought back femininity and glamour after a war-time period of unprecedented privations. The padded hips, nipped-in waists and tight bodices were anachronistic: they could satisfy only briefly. The amount of material used in the skirts, as much as fifty yards a dress in some cases, brought condemnation from Sir Stafford Cripps, President of the British Board of Trade, but the French government supported Dior, happy to see

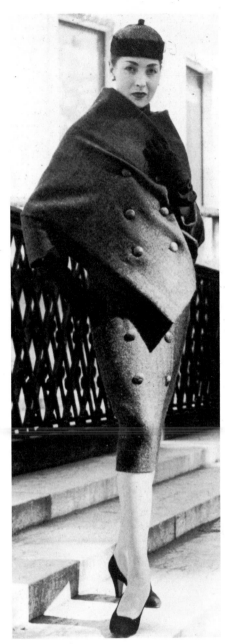

Christian Dior's 'Y' line for Winter 1955 featured a large buttoned stole and a tiny mandarin hat.

Paris re-established as the fashion leader. So great was the impact of the 'New Look' that all couturiers had to follow its shape and proportions in their subsequent collections.

Dior had created a universal look, and

the spectacular advent of the 'New Look' has overshadowed the remaining ten years of his life as a designer. This is regrettable, since later collections produced much more sophisticated and eloquent looks. It was during the 1950s, with his 'H', 'A' and 'Y' lines that he really began to show his level as a great designer, and from the spring of 1954 he grew stronger with every collection. The culmination came in his last collections, shown in 1957. Those last designs showed that Dior had absorbed the design philosophy of both CHANEL and BALENCIAGA, having assimilated the former's practicality and the latter's softly architectured approach to produce clothes which pointed the way to the 1960s. Three months after showing his 'Spindle' line (Dior always named his collections), he was dead. The new designer was the successor he had himself chosen, Yves SAINT LAURENT. Since Saint Laurent's dismissal in 1960, the house of Dior has continued under the leadership of Marc BOHAN.

Dior was a gentle, reticent and superstitious man who, at the time of his death, was the leader of a vast multi-million-dollar international merchandizing organization producing haute couture, ready-to-wear, jewellery, scarves, perfume, furs, stockings, gloves and even men's ties — all to the highest standards. His worth was recognized in 1947 with a Neiman-Marcus Award and in 1956 with a Parson's Medal. His autobiography, *Dior by Dior*, was published in 1957.

Major perfumes: Miss Dior (1947); Diorama (1949); Diorissimo (1956); Diorling (1963).

DOEUILLET □

Founded Paris, France, 1900.
Closed 1928.

After training with CALLOT SOEURS, Doeuillet founded his own fashion house. Always derivative, he survived largely from the publicity accorded the house by the *Gazette du Bon Ton*. This magazine, created in 1912 by Lucien Vogel, was supported by the couture houses of WORTH, CHERUIT, DOUCET, LANVIN, POIRET, REDFERN and Doeuillet. It employed illustrators of the calibre of IRIBE* and LEPAPE* and their drawings of the creations of the contribu-

Below: This Doucet coat, photographed in 1920, is slit down the sides of the skirt to incorporate a second richly patterned material which is used to trim collar and cuffs.

ting couture houses were very important in bringing the designers' new ideas to the public eye. On the death of Doucet in 1929, Doeuillet merged with the house of Doucet to create the Doeuillet-Doucet label. The Doeuillet gowns were over-elaborate and detail was always more important than line. It was a minor, but steadily successful, house.

DOUCET, Jacques

Born Paris, France, 1853.
Died Paris, France, 1932.

Doucet was born above the luxury lingerie shop his grandmother had founded, and when he inherited the same shop he de-

veloped it into a haute couture establishment. He was extremely successful in dressing the more elegant and beautiful members of Parisian society in clothes which were as sophisticated as the persona he projected with his Van Dyck beard and invariable carnation buttonhole. Doucet is remembered today for his encouragement of the young POIRET and also his amazing skill as a fine art collector. He recognized Poiret's talents, offered him a job and taught him his profession: how to cut and drape as well as sketch ideas. He was like a godfather to Poiret and Poiret never forgot his kindness, wanting all his life to be as refined and sophisticated as his mentor. Unfortunately their rela-

tionship ended badly due to Poiret's greed for success. Doucet had allowed him to dress actresses of the standing of Rejane and Sarah Bernhardt and had encouraged him to dress well and become a social success, but things turned sour when, having met an American actress with whom he had an affair, Poiret was unwise enough to make clothes for her although he was employed exclusively by Doucet. His master found out and sacked him instantly.

Doucet the collector was famed for his perception and connoisseurship. Having amassed an impressive collection of 18th-century art he sold it all in 1912 because he was excited by the new painting. In this he was far in advance of most collectors who found Picasso, Modigliani and Miró far too revolutionary. IRIBE* was asked to redecorate Doucet's home to take his new collection and he worked closely on it with Pierre Legraine. Works in his collection included Douanier Rousseau's *The Snake Charmer*, Picasso's *Les Demoiselles D'Avignon* and screens by Eileen Gray all bearing testimony to Doucet's amazing ability to spot good art. His furniture and pictures were bequeathed to the Musée des Arts Décoratifs and his unrivalled collection of 18th-century books of costume went to the University of Paris on his death.

DRÉCOLL

Founded Paris, France, 1905.
Closed 1929.
This couture house was founded in Vienna by the Belgian baron, Christopher Drécoll. His name was bought by his designer, who opened a house in Paris. Although never in the front rank, the fate of the house of Drécoll echoes that of more important houses of the time. Before World War I there was vast wealth and seemingly endless security in Europe; women played a narrow role in society and appeared quite happy to do so. The couturier's job was to recognize these facts and create a certain type of clothing for a certain style of life. With the upheaval of the war, the new ideas about how to spend what wealth remained, and the new attitudes to and expectations of women, couturiers had to change their ideas and adapt to the new situation or be left like stranded whales on a deserted beach. Very few survived. CHANEL and DOUCET managed to move with the times, leading LANVIN, VIONNET and the other essentially post-war talents. Drécoll struggled along, but the taste for his sort of clothes was dead. Over-detailed and elaborate, they were not right for the new woman.

Mademoiselle Nadine Picard looked a little busy in her Drécoll outfit from 1933 which managed to incorporate something for every taste.

A handkerchief skirt, a tucked top and jacket by Drécoll photographed in Deauville's fashionable sunshine, June 1929.

E·F

EDINA AND LENA · ELLIS · EMANUEL · ERTÉ · ESTEVEZ · EVINS · FABIANI · FABRICE · FATH · FENDI · FERAUD · FERRAGAMO
FERRÉ · FERRETTI · FIORUCCI · FOALE AND TUFFIN · FOGARTY · FONTANA · FORQUET · FORTUNY · FOX · FRATINI · FRIZON

Ellis

Fath

Ferré

Erté

Fendi (Carla, Franca, Paola, Anna, Alda)

135

EDINA AND LENA

Edina Ronay *Born* Budapest, Hungary, 1943. And Lena Stengard

Edina Ronay's fashion studies at St. Martin's School of Art, in London, were interrupted by modelling and acting commitments, but she returned to fashion by opening a stall with Lena Stengard in the Antiquarius Antique Market in London. Here they sold old lace, cardigans and Fair Isle jumpers from the 1930s. Realizing that there was a market for nostalgic knitwear, they began to produce designs based on 1930s patterns and by 1979, when they started to show with the LONDON DESIGNER COLLECTIONS, they had forty knitters working for them. The success of their individual look was considerable and their knitwear was in demand in Europe, America and Japan. Edina and Lena shows in London, Milan and Paris and now has almost 2,000 knitters. Two collections are produced each year, covering men's, women's and children's wear. For summer the look is based on cotton and silk yarns and for winter on wool cashmere and alpaca. Although the name is unchanged, Lena Stengard is no longer part of the business.

ELLIS, Perry □

Born Virginia, USA, 1940.
Died New York, USA, 1986.

After taking an MA in retailing at New York University, Ellis worked at the Virginia department store of Miller and Rhoads as a sportswear buyer. He realized that he could design better clothes than those he saw in his job and he began to become more and more involved with design. He moved to John Meyer and worked there for six years, largely involved with selecting colours, prints and fashion. On Meyer's death the company closed and in 1974 Ellis joined the Vera companies. Two and a half years later he was designing his own sportswear for them under the heading 'Portfolio'. This line was such a success that in 1978 Manhattan Industries gave him his own label. Since then his success was always convincing. Bloomingdales, always a barometer of fashion, was the first store to open a Perry Ellis shop. Now clothes bearing his name sell throughout the United States and in London.

Mannish shapes and strong patterns are combined in Perry Ellis' layered look for his Winter 1982 collection.

Interesting proportions make the point in this utterly simple outfit from Perry Ellis' collection for Summer 1984.

Ellis' approach was slightly anti-fashion. 'I don't make fashion', he once said, 'I make clothes'. His designs were young, but they were also bought consistently by older women. He liked to think of them as 'friendly clothes' that improved as they aged. Although very American, his designs had a European sense of scale and colour. He was not afraid to exaggerate, but his clothes never slipped into fantasy. They were always wearable and, for many women, irresistible. A considerable part of their charm lay in the choice of materials. Ellis used natural, even folksy, textures of cottons, linens and wool, with hand-knitted sweaters, to produce a sportswear con-

cept in the Anne KLEIN tradition. His ideas were fully developed and he had the ability to create unusual proportions which not only excited, but also worked.

Essentially informal himself, Ellis designed informally. His approach was practical and idiosyncratic. He liked to swim against the tide and produce clothes which offered an alternative to what most other designers were doing, in keeping with his view that clothes should not be taken too seriously, that they should be worn with humour and that they should exhibit, not inhibit, the wearer's personality.

Recognition of the worth of his views is to be found in his Neiman-Marcus Award

Perfectly cut pants are teamed with a waistcoat and cardigan for this Summer 1984 outfit by Perry Ellis.

and his Coty American Fashion Critics' 'Winnie' – both received in 1979 – in his increased sales, and his continued Coty Awards.

EMANUEL

Elizabeth *Born* London, England, 1953. David *Born* Bridgend, Wales, 1952.
The Emanuels are rather surprising elements in the London fashion scene. They have channelled their talents into the 'dying' field of couture at a time when one would have thought it economically unwise to do so; and yet they have survived. They now concentrate on 'Specials' which are designed and made for one individual as well as ready-to-wear.

Their backgrounds are diverse: she has an American father and English mother, while his family are Welsh. They both attended Harrow School of Art. They married in 1975 and were the only married couple to be accepted at the Royal College of Art, where they both did a postgraduate year in the fashion department. Their end-of-year show in 1977 caused so much interest that they decided to open under their own name in September of that year. Originally they produced two wholesale collections a year, but the increasing demand for individual couture designs persuaded them to close down the wholesale side of their business in 1979 and concentrate on 'one-off' specials. In 1981 they became world-famous with their design for the wedding dress of the Princess of Wales. They have licences for bed linen, sunglasses and perfume, and their book, *Style for All Seasons*, was published in 1983. Their fantasy ball and wedding gowns, which use an abundance of lace, taffeta, organza and tulle, make their wearers imagine they are Scarlett O'Hara painted by John Singer Sargent.

ERTÉ (Romain de Tirtoff)

Born St. Petersburg, Russia, 1892.
Erté's father was an admiral in the Russian navy and inspector of St. Petersburg Naval School. The family background was rich and powerful. In 1912 Erté, whose design name is the phonetic pronunciation of his initials RT, arrived in Paris to study at the Académie Julian, after which he obtained a job sketching for POIRET. How much of his work for Poiret was illustrative, like that of IRIBE*, and how much actual design, is now hard to determine, but there can be no doubt that couturier and illustrator had a considerable influence on each other. Erté also designed costumes for the theatre and the opera and in 1915, began to draw the covers for *Harper's Bazaar*, which he continued to do for the next twenty-one years. During this time he developed a unique personal style. Although it lacked Beardsley's intellectual control, his draughtsmanship rarely degenerated into the merely decorative, wandering line which was a feature of fashion illustration in the 1920s and 1930s.

Erté's theatrical fantasies were given free rein in the 1920s in his designs for the Folies Bergère. He also tried Hollywood, briefly, working mainly for King Vidor. In 1971 he worked with another legendary name: he and SAINT LAURENT designed costumes and sets for a revue starring Roland Petit and René Jeanmaire. As an illustrator and decorative artist Erté has had considerable influence on designers, even though his experience as a practical dress-designer was small.

He was 'rediscovered' on his eightieth birthday, when he selected designs for a retrospective show of his drawings in London and New York. His eye for decorative details and his love of fantasy, so far removed from modern life, made him almost a cult figure: books and articles about him appeared and an Erté poster in the home became the great decorative cliché for a whole section of society. His autobiography, *Erté – Things I Remember* was published in 1975. He lives in Paris and still works.

ESTEVEZ, Luis

Born Havana, Cuba, 1930.
Born into a privileged background, his father being a wealthy sugar magnate, Estevez was educated for a time in America before returning to study architecture in Havana. He took a summer job as a window-dresser for Lord and Taylor in New York City, and the display manager suggested that he should design clothes. This is what he did after a period of study at the Traphagen School of Fashion. He then spent two years in Paris working for PATOU.

In 1955 he set up his own ready-to-wear business in New York, where his name became noted for the wide range of neck treatments he used in his collections. In 1968 he moved to California where, in 1972, he designed collections for Eva Gabor to sell under her name, a venture so successful that in 1974 he signed a contract with her parent firm to design a line called 'Luis Estevez International'. Since 1977 he has had his own firm. His customers are prestigious – he has made dresses for both Merle Oberon and Betty

Ford. His designs are restrained, elegant and very Southern Californian. He won a Coty American Fashion Critics' 'Winnie' in 1956.

EVINS, David
Born London, England.
Having moved to New York at the age of ten, Evins studied fashion design at the Pratt Institute and the Art Students League of New York. This was followed by work as a fashion illustrator and a sketcher for a footwear trade publication. By the late 1930s he was working as a show designer, and after World War II he designed anonymously for the I. Miller company. His own label followed, along with contracts to design for HERMÈS and Delman. Evins received the Coty Special Award in 1949 and the Neiman-Marcus Award in 1953. He was a founder member of the Council of Fashion Designers of America.

FABIANI, Alberto
Born Tivoli, Italy.
At the age of eighteen, Fabiani went to Paris to meet a friend of his family, an Italian tailor, who introduced him to the fashion world. Three years later he returned to the family firm in Italy which his father had established in 1909. In 1952 his lively and eclectic personality found perfect expression in his creation of a distinctly Italian look, free of the echoes of France. He married SIMONETTA and together they opened in Paris in 1961; but Fabiani has called this the darkest period of his life: after a triumphant opening, their venture failed. He went back to Rome alone and there success returned, with clients from Italy, Europe and America. He is now retired.

FABRICE, Simon
Born Port au Prince, Haiti.
Fabrice's mother owned a prominent boutique in Haiti before the family moved to the United States when Fabrice was fourteen years old. On leaving high school he studied textile design and fashion illustration at the Fashion Institute of Technology, then spent the first five years of his working life as a fabric designer. In

A black alpaca and silk fabric is elegantly draped for this cocktail dress by Fabiani.

1975 he began to produce his own hand-painted and hand-beaded dresses under the name of his own firm, and is noted for his luxurious, expensive evening creations that are frequently beaded and always sexy. They won him a Coty American Fashion Critics' Award in 1981.

Fashion Group of America, The
See FASHION ORGANIZATIONS, p. 296

Fashion House Group of London
See FASHION ORGANIZATIONS, p. 296

FATH, Jacques
Born Lafitte, France, 1912.
Died Paris, France, 1954.
Fath's father was a painter and his great-grandmother had been a dressmaker. He

trained in business school and attended a drama school (followed by a brief time in films) before opening as a designer, very modestly, in 1937. His first collection consisted of fewer than twenty pieces, but it contained the seeds of his future. His genius was quickly recognized and he was named one of the most important designers of 1939. On the outbreak of World War II he enlisted in the army; he was taken prisoner in 1940. On his release he reopened his house in rue François 1er. With his wife, Geneviève, he produced clothes for those who could afford them during the occupation until 1944, when he moved to avenue Pierre 1er and began his real period as a couturier. His success was considerable, not only because of his designs, but also because his personality was extravagant, ebullient and theatrical. He was essentially a social couturier — lavish parties, masked balls and outrageous behaviour were all excellent publicity, as Fath, the showman, realized. This is not to suggest that his social activities bought him approval as a designer: his clothes were praised purely on their own merits. He created young and sexy clothes which remained firmly in the haute-couture mould of elegance and sophistication and never slipped into vulgarity. The emphasis in his designs was always on the figure. He worked with a team and frequently draped materials on himself while his assistants sketched the results. His success grew each season, not only as a result of his design abilities and social showmanship, but also because of his shrewd business sense.

Fath's large sales to private customers — among whom was Rita Hayworth, who chose Fath to design her trousseau for her wedding to Ali Khan — were augmented by the custom of wholesalers. In 1948 he signed a lucrative contract with the American manufacturer, Joseph Halpert, for whom he produced two collections a year to be mass-produced in America; Fath Université was one of the first attempts at distributing clothes created to standardized sizes; and nearly half of the Fath revenue came from boutique sales, hats and perfumes. He received a Neiman-Marcus Award in 1949. When he died of leukaemia at forty-two, his wife continued the business, but she closed in 1957.

Above: *This grey silk afternoon dress from Fath's 1948 collection shows the instant effect that Dior's 'New Look' proportions had on the other designers who took them up immediately.*

Right: *Jacques Fath's short evening dress from 1950 is draped from the back with an asymmetric stole caught at the waist and falling to the hem of the skirt.*

Left: *Jacques Fath's tightly waisted dress from 1950 has a buttoned panel but the surprise is in the dramatic sleeve treatment and the theatrical hat.*

Below: *The epitome of French sophistication, this Fath evening dress of 1954 is in black velvet as is the stole, lined with white satin.*

Fath's premature death robbed the fashion world of a remarkable designer who was just coming to the peak of his creative powers. It is interesting to speculate how a man of his genius, originality and forward-looking attitude to fashion would have developed had he lived to work through the 1960s and 1970s. Certainly, it can be taken for granted that his impact on those uncertain decades would have been benevolent and considerable.

Major perfumes: Iris Gris (1949); Fath de Fath (1951).

FENDI (Adele Fendi)

Born Italy, 1897.
Died Rome, Italy, 1978.

Adele Fendi founded her firm in 1918: it is now run by her five daughters with their husbands and children. It is essentially an Italian family firm, with one exception: the chief designer is Karl LAGERFELD. The daughters work together closely and each takes responsibility for an area: Alda (*born* 1940) is in charge of sales; Carla (*born* 1937) is the business co-ordinator; Franca (*born* 1935) looks after customer relations; Anna (*born* 1933) oversees the

The romantic fur by Fendi: this full, softly curving coat in natural fitch is a magnificent example of the art of working with fur.

leatherwear; and Paola (*born* 1931) is involved with the furs. The company is based in Rome, although the Fendi collections are shown with the rest of the Italian ready-to-wear in Milan. The attention to detail and integrity shown by Adele Fendi is reflected to this day throughout the Fendi empire, but it was after the death of her husband in 1954, when she had to call in the girls to support her, that the modern Fendi image was forged. Previously the firm had been respected for its high quality of workmanship and honesty, but her daughters began to inject glamour and fashion into its products. Slowly they moved beyond their mother's confines, she having catered solely for wealthy private customers. Although the importance of private customers was still acknowledged, the daughters realized that to survive and move forward they had to accept the challenge of showing their work to press and fashion buyers. This they did in 1966.

In 1962 they had begun to employ Lagerfeld and it was he who designed the famous 'double F' initials. However, the real success of his collaboration with Fendi has been in the field of fur. Fendi has broken totally new ground in the technique of working fur and must be credited with several pioneering processes. Perhaps the boldest and most interesting is the perforation of the pelt with thousands of little holes to make the fur coat much lighter and easier to wear. They have also woven furs in strips, pleated it like an accordion and created shawls of mink petals. Always they have been inspired by the genius of Lagerfeld, whose baroque and magnificent designs show a total understanding of the medium and an exceptional imaginative power. A Fendi fur is unique, unmistakable and, as befits a status symbol, very expensive. The other great success area is handbags, and although ingenuity sometimes slips over into vulgarity this does not affect sales: they sell extremely well and are much copied. Inventive and imaginative, the Fendi sisters will surely continue to break new ground for many years to come.

FERAUD, Louis

Born Arles, France, 1921.
Feraud opened a dress shop in Cannes in 1955. His couture customers were frequently film stars who came for the film festival, and included Grace Kelly, Brigitte Bardot and Ingrid Bergman. Through contacts like these he began to design costumes for films and he has been responsible for dressing more than eighty movies. He moved to Paris and set up his own ready-to-wear organization, which was a great success. Perhaps because he was affected by the strong light and colour of the Midi, where he was born, he has always been attracted to the art and culture of South America and this is reflected in his designs. Japan was the first foreign country to take his range, but his sales were soon world-wide and he consistently sold more clothes in Great Britain, Germany and the United States than most of his fellow designers. PER SPOOK worked as his assistant before setting up his own business.

Major perfume: Justine (1966).

FERRAGAMO, Salvatore

Born Naples, Italy, 1898.
Died Fiumetto, Italy, 1960.
Ferragamo began to work as a shoemaker at the age of thirteen. In 1923, when he was sixteen, he emigrated to the United States, where he studied factory methods of producing shoes before opening an exclusive shoe shop in Hollywood. He soon became the purveyor of footwear to the stars: Gloria Swanson and Dolores del Rio were on his list of glamorous customers. His hand-made, one-off designs produced for the individual woman were brilliantly original pieces of delicately balanced engineering in leather and suede. They had a truly Italian touch of *fantasia* and flair. Ferragamo not only used traditional materials, but also was endlessly inventive in both fabric and colour. As well as producing haute-couture creations, he also designed ready-to-wear lines in America. By 1936 he was back in Italy with a base in Florence.

The name for quality, style and fit which he had made in America continued until his death, and although as he grew older his designs became more conservative, they never failed to be elegant and sophisticated. Ferragamo is credited with inventing the platform sole and the wedge heel but, despite these lapses, he was one of the world's great shoemakers. His autobiography, published in 1957, was aptly named *Shoemaker of Dreams*. He received a Neiman-Marcus Award in 1947.

His children have carried on the business since his death and the name Ferragamo is now synonymous with luxury boutique items such as scarves, handbags and high-quality ready-to-wear as well as shoes. His European clients have included Queen Elizabeth II and Princess Margaret.

FERRÉ, Gian Franco

Born Legnano, Italy, 1945.
Ferré's approach to clothes is architectural — and, in fact, he did study architecture, in Milan, qualifying in 1967. His first

Understated but strongly individualistic, these coats from Ferré's collection for Summer 1982 concentrate on neck and sleeve treatments which enliven a classic silhouette.

An extremely strong statement from Ferré for Summer 1984, with his exaggeratedly wide 'signature' belt on a large-scale loose outfit.

In this Summer 1982 outfit Gianfranco Ferré shows his mastery of shape in the way he blocks colours and fabrics; also in the folding and layering on the jacket.

job was in the design studio of a furniture company in Milan, then after a period spent in travel, Ferré began to design gold-chain jewellery and by 1970 had made his mark as an accessories designer. His designs for shoes, scarves and handbags were sufficiently good to be bought by ALBINI and LAGERFELD, and a commission from FIORUCCI resulted in his striped T-shirts, which sold so well that they made him famous in Italy. Ferré was now established as a freelance designer and in 1972 he began designing raincoats and sportswear. By 1974 he was showing under his own label and from that time his rise was steady and constant, so that by 1982 he was acknowledged as one of Europe's top ready-to-wear designers: along with ARMANI and VERSACE he is considered every bit as good as all but the greatest French designers. His clothes are powerful statements of shape and have the crisp quality of origami. They have the power and beauty of sculpture. Intricate tucking, pleating and top stitching, combined with involved structures and con-

trolled colours, are the essentials of the Ferré look. If such a thing is possible, Ferré has developed into a fashion intellectual, producing clothes of such a logical perfection that they are like the solution to a complicated engineering equation.

FERRETTI, Alberta

Born Romagna, Italy, 1950.
Alberta Ferretti's involvement with fashion began at the age of sixteen, when she

started work as a fashion buyer. Over the years she found herself increasingly frustrated in her search for interesting and original clothes. To remedy this she formed her own company in 1975 and started to produce clothes to her own designs. She gradually found a place in the market and, by 1981, was sufficiently established to begin to show in Milan.

Alberta Ferretti's clothes are very *per bene* and show a successful understanding of how middle-class Italian women like to dress.

FIORUCCI, Elio

Born Milan, Italy, 1935.

Fiorucci is a one-man fashion revolution. He began in 1962 with the opening of the first Fiorucci store in Milan, which sold only sandals, shoes and boots and was run by Fiorucci himself. In 1967 he expanded and moved to a bigger store, where he began to sell clothes, including imported avant-garde looks from London designers such as Ossie CLARK and Zandra RHODES. By 1969 he was able to go into production with his own-label clothes, but his breakthrough came in the early 1970s with the jeans revolution. Fiorucci jeans, cut by an EX-VALENTINO pattern maker, became a cult searched after by the fashion-conscious not only in Europe, but also in America. They were among the first streamlined, tightly cut, sexy jeans and they made his fortune. They were the start of the Fiorucci phenomenon, which is based on his amazing ability to be attuned to what the young want and to produce it when they want it – always with flair and showmanship. His shops are 'high tech' and sophisticated; their windows are as witty and provocative as his clothes. His expansion in the 1970s was made possible because the Italian chain store firm, Standa, became a part owner in 1974. Fiorucci opened in New York in 1976. Standa sold its share in Fiorucci to Benetton in 1981.

FOALE AND TUFFIN

Marion Foale   *Born* England, 1939.
Sally Tuffin   *Born* England, 1938.

Students of fashion at Walthamstow School of Art, Foale and Tuffin both studied at the Royal College of Art, which they left in 1961. They set up as partners in a private dressmaking business and their chance came in 1962 when their clothes were bought by the London store, Woollands. Their looks were aimed at the young ready-to-wear market and Foale and Tuffin were at the heart of the London fashion revolution. Based on Carnaby Street, they and their designs reflected the fashion influences of the 1960s. Beginning with Pop Art, especially that of Hockney, then Op, they moved through an Art Deco phase towards the romanticism of old lace. In 1972 they dissolved their partnership.

FOGARTY, Anne

Born Pittsburgh, Pennsylvania, USA, 1919.
Died New York City, USA, 1981.

After studying drama in Pittsburgh, Anne Fogarty moved to New York, where she worked as a model and then as a freelance designer for wholesale firms. In 1948 she began work as a designer for Youth Guild and remained there for nine years, followed by five years with Saks Fifth Avenue. Anne Fogarty Inc. was founded in 1962, and traded for twelve years. In 1951 she won the Coty Award for her 'paper doll' silhouette and she received a Neiman-Marcus Award the following year. Her clothes were soft and sensuous, flattering and feminine, and her eye for colour was subtle.

FONTANA

Founded Parma, Italy, 1907.

Forty years ago the Fontana sisters, Zoe, Micol and Giovanna, took over the small dressmaking establishment of their mother in Parma. Zoe and Micol shared the designing; Giovanna was in charge of sales. They moved to Rome in 1936 and, after the war, began to make a name for themselves as high-quality, haute-couture designers. In 1951 they began to sell in the United States. Their glamorous and intricate evening gowns made their name famous, not only in Europe, but in North and South America also. They created Ava Gardner's costumes for *The Barefoot Contessa*, designed President Truman's daughter's wedding gown, and also dressed Mrs. J. F. Kennedy. Their contribution to Italian fashion was extremely important and there are still Fontana boutiques in Rome, Bologna and Geneva, where high-quality scarves, handbags, linen and ties are sold.

FORQUET, Federico

Born Naples, Italy, 1931.

Forquet's family were of French descent, but lived in Naples. As a young man he studied philosophy, literature and music, but his life changed after he met BALENCIAGA when the famous designer was on holiday in Ischia. This led to Forquet's working with the maestro in Paris for two years without pay. Returning to Italy, he worked with FABIANI and GALITZINE, before opening his own house in 1961. After ten years he closed his doors. He now designs fabrics and occasionally creates interior decorating schemes for friends.

In a grand hotel in Rome, before an invited audience, Fontana shows his 1957 look: a strong asymmetric statement in black and white.

FORTUNY, Mariano ☐

Born Granada, Spain, 1871.
Died Venice, Italy, 1949.

Fortuny's full name is Mariano Fortuny y Madrazo. A creator of fashion as art, like DELAUNAY, Fortuny was a painter and inventor who became interested in the possibilities offered by clothes. He was born into a wealthy, privileged and artistic world and his extraordinary intellectual and artistic gifts were apparent very early. A mixture of artisan and alchemist, he endlessly examined, questioned and developed his theories on painting, photography, stage-lighting, architecture and theatre design. He was influenced by the Aesthetic movement, with its emphasis on linear qualities and functional beauty, and also by Wagner's contention that art must be a cathartic experience which should purify and ennoble the spirit. Fortuny's friends and admirers included the poet, D'Annunzio, the novelist, Proust, and the dancer, Isadora Duncan. His complex concepts of clothing were intellectual and far removed from the world of haute couture. The background for his designs was the Greek influence found in the English painters, Alma-Tadema and Lord Leighton, the 'Liberty' style, and above all, Art Nouveau. From these he developed the idea of the natural dress, uncorseted, hygienic and allowing the body freedom of movement.

Fortuny actually considered his dress concepts to be inventions, and had his 'Delphos' dress and his method of pleating patented in Paris in 1909. They were based on the archaic korai sculpture of the 6th century BC. His most famous was named after the Delphic charioteer: the 'Delphos' dress was like the Ionic chiton and its overblouse resembled the Ionic himation. It was very simple: from a boat- or V-neck fell a column of finely pleated silk with batwing, short or long sleeves which were usually caught at the wrist. It always had a cord at the shoulders to adjust the fit – an amazingly modern concept and a surprisingly modern dress. It never lost its pleats and was easily rolled into a tightly twisted ball for storing. Fortuny's 'Knossos' scarf was a large veil of silk, usually printed with Cycladic geometric motifs. It was an item of clothing which could be used in a variety of ways

A Fortuny 'Delphos' dress and tunic show the designer's skill in creating a completely timeless fashion still prized and worn worldwide.

143

Fortuny's 'Delphos' dress, minutely pleated, is worn with a kimono style jacket printed in metallic pigment.

and it always allowed the wearer freedom of movement. Following his work in silk came his work in printed velvet. He created a neo-Medieval style which consisted of two printed velvet panels joined with pleated silk. The design content was minimal and applied decorative additions did not exist. Having created a simple prototype, he did not change it.

The quality of Fortuny's work lay in its total individuality. Everything came from his own head and hand. The dyes he used were his special invention, semi-transparent so that movement and light would affect the colour. At Palazzo Orfei, which was his base, all prints and dresses were made by hand and dyed on the premises. His textiles were inspired by the Renaissance, especially by the Venetian painter Carpaccio. He used silk velvet which was hand-dyed and then hand-printed or stencilled; he also invented and patented his own special way of stencilling. Fortuny was in charge of all processes: he created the vegetable-based colours, the dyes, the blocks and the pattern designs. The results were unique.

In the 1960s Fortuny's dresses began to be collected by museums and therefore became the status symbols that they are today. Like his name, they had sunk into obscurity after his death. His elegant and timeless solution to the problem of clothing, but not constraining, the female form has become classic. 'A Fortuny dress' conjures up a precise mental picture just as 'a Chanel suit' does. For this reason his name will endure.

FOX, Frederick

Born Urana, Australia, 1931.

The eighth of a family of nine children, Frederick Fox was brought up in the country. He became interested in hats at an early age, and by the time he was thirteen he was trimming hats and selling them in the neighbourhood. In 1947 he moved to Sydney to work as a milliner with J. L. Normoyle and, later, Phyl Clarkson. Arriving in London in 1958, he worked for Otto LUCAS before opening his own business in 1964, making hats for private customers and for designers such as Hardy AMIES. It was through Amies that Fox designed his first hats for the Queen, who wore them on her 1970 tour of Brazil. Since then he has created many hats for the royal family and is 'By Appointment' the Queen's milliner.

FRATINI, Gina

Born Kobe, Japan, 1934.

When Fratini was a baby she was brought to England, where she and her family remained until she was seven. During the next five years of her life her family moved to Canada, India and Burma, but she was educated in England. After three years at the Royal College of Art, she spent two years travelling the world with Katherine Dunham's dance company. Back in England, she designed for stage and film productions before starting on her own as a designer in 1964. Her forte is designing romantic, fairytale evening gowns and she does it very well. Customers include the Princess of Wales, Princess Margaret and Princess Anne. Her frothy ballgowns of the late 1970s were perfectly in tune with the spirit of new romanticism which was emerging at that time.

FRIZON, Maud

Born Paris, France, 1941.

Born of an English mother and a French father, Maud Frizon moved into the world of fashion soon after taking her *baccalauréat*, without formal fashion training. She worked as a model in Paris in the early 1960s and did a lot of work for COURRÈGES. A model was expected to provide her own shoes and it was because she could not find any interesting or amusing designs that, after three years of frustration, Maud Frizon began to think seriously about leaving modelling and designing shoes instead. In 1970 she created her first collection, which she showed in a small shop in rue Saint Germain. Its success was instant: her customers, who included Bardot and Queen Soraya, queued to get into her crowded shop. Her success was based on the fact that all the shoes were hand-cut and finished and they were all designed by her. Samples were made in her size so that she could try on the shoes herself.

Although she now has two factories in Padua, Frizon has not changed her original formula. She does all her own designing, tries on all samples and works closely with her pattern cutter. She produces two collections, with around a hundred styles, a year, using materials as diverse as lizard and canvas, satin and snake. Her shoes are characteristically witty, elegant and sexily sophisticated.

She designs ranges for the shows of the French designers, ALAÏA, RYKIEL, MUGLER and MONTANA and for the Italians, MISSONI. She also designs a men's range and a luxury line of soft luggage and travel bags. Her shops are in all the luxurious watering holes of the world from Paris to Bal Harbour. Divorced (and re-married to an Italian), she lives in a château in the Loire and is one of the few women to own a private helicopter and to fly it herself.

G

GALANOS · GALITZINE · GAULTIER · GENNY (*See* ITALIAN READY-TO-WEAR) · GERNREICH · GHIRARDI (*See* ITALIAN READY-TO-WEAR)
GIBB · GILBERT · GIUDICELLI · GIVENCHY · GOMA · GREER · GRÈS · GRIFFE · GROULT (*See* PARIS COUTURE) · GUIBOURGE

Galanos

Grès

Above: *Gibb*
Left: *Gaultier*   Right: *Givenchy*

145

GALANOS, James

Born Philadelphia, USA, 1925.

Of Greek parentage, Galanos studied fashion at the Traphagen School in New York and began selling his sketches to Hattie CARNEGIE. He also worked in California with JEAN LOUIS, but left to go to Paris in 1947, where he stayed for one year, working with PIGUET, before returning to work on Seventh Avenue. Having remained friends with Jean Louis he opened his own business in California in 1951 with the latter's help, a $200 loan. His first show in New York in 1953 caused a sensation and since then his career has never looked back. He is that special being, a designer's designer and, like JAMES and BALENCIAGA, he is admired for his perfectionism and his single-minded development of a theme. Even when out of step with current trends, his approach to design is that of the couturier more than the businessman. His luxurious clothes are very expensive, because he uses superb materials and his flawless cutting and tailoring, the result of a lifetime's search for perfection, cannot be achieved cheaply.

Based in California, he has long been a favourite of Mrs. Reagan and her exceedingly rich friends. After a 1974 exhibition at Los Angeles he was honoured, in 1976, with a retrospective show at the Fashion Institute of Technology in New York, and he has received the 1954 Neiman-Marcus Award, the 1954 Coty Award, a 1954 'Winnie', and the 1956 Coty Return Award. He was elected to the Coty Hall of Fame in 1959.

GALITZINE, Princess Irene

Born Tiflis, Russia, 1900s.

Princess Galitzine comes from a family of Russian nobility, who fled to Italy at the time of the Revolution when she was only one year old, making their new home in Rome. Galitzine studied in English and Italian schools, became fluent in five languages and followed an art course in Rome before turning to fashion design. After working for the FONTANA sisters for three years she opened her own house in Rome and presented her first collection in 1959. Her name was made in 1960, when she presented her 'Palazzo Pyjamas' as a relaxed but sophisticated evening look: they were instant news. Wide-legged, in fluid silks, often fringed and beaded, they became one of *the* looks of the 1960s. In 1962 she was voted 'Designer of the Year' by the Italian press and she won *The Sunday Times* International Fashion Award in 1965. Having closed her house in the late 1960s, she re-opened, to a fair degree of success, in the 1970s, showing simple silhouettes in sumptuous silks and glamorous prints. Her scent has also proved highly successful in a very competitive field.

GALULTIER, Jean Paul ☐

Born France, 1952.

At the age of seventeen Gaultier sent some design sketches by post to CARDIN, who liked them sufficiently to offer him a job. They worked together for two years. Gaultier then spent a year with Esterel, before joining TARLAZZI and GOMA as designers at PATOU. In 1976 he started to work as a freelance, designing ready-to-

Galanos is seen at his high-fashion best in this evening dress and stole, both bordered in lace.

Galitzine's name became famous because of her palazzo pyjamas which were in silk and cut wide. This example from 1964 shows her adapting to the current trouser width.

March 1983 saw Gaultier mixing moods and media to create a confusing look definitely to be worn only by the very young and very assured.

wear ranges, swimwear, furs and leather, in addition to his own label for Mayagor. He is now one of the most influential designers in Paris. Gaultier draws a considerable amount of his inspiration from the London street-scene, taking from it outrageously punk looks which he then glamorizes in the Paris manner. His skill lies in taking the avant-garde and making it acceptable by giving it a kitsch sexiness. He has greatly influenced men's fashion and takes androgyny as far as skirts for men.

GENNY
See ITALIAN READY-TO-WEAR

GERNREICH, Rudi
Born Vienna, Austria, 1922.
Died USA, 1985.
Arriving in America in 1938, Gernreich took American citizenship in 1943. He studied dance in California at the Los Angeles City College and the Los Angeles Art Centre School. Although initially a dancer, he took time, while working as a part-time fabric salesman, to design some clothes to illustrate the potential of the fabrics, and these designs engendered sufficient interest for him to sign contracts with manufacturers. His approach to fashion was radical and, in the 1960s, it became revolutionary. Using as a template the working clothes of dancers, he developed a revolutionary way of dressing which had strong similarities with the work of COURRÈGES and QUANT. A visionary, whose ideas and predictions were far-sighted and original, he is unfortunately best known for his most trite idea: the topless bathing suit. He has received the Coty American Fashion Critics Award three times: a 'Winnie' in 1963; a Return Award in 1966; and the Hall of Fame Award in 1967.

GHIRARDI, Giovanni
See ITALIAN READY-TO-WEAR

GIBB, Bill
Born Fraserburgh, Scotland, 1943.
Educated at the Fraserburgh Academy, Gibb enrolled at St. Martin's School of Art

Bill Gibb's masterly way with material is shown in this skilfully draped back treatment for his silk crêpe evening dress of 1977.

Above: *Bill Gibb's first commercial knits and tweeds collection in 1974 showed the controlled exuberance of mixed pattern which became a popular aspect of British design during the seventies.*

Below: *Soft wool top and pants with a large kimono coat, held at the waist, create Gibb's ethnic look in 1977.*

in 1962 and then went on a scholarship to the Royal College of Art in 1966. He soon became the golden boy, fashion's Hockney, adored by all for his talent and charm. He did not finish his course. Having won the Yardley Fashion prize and having sold his complete collection to Bendel, he was launched. He worked as a designer for Baccarat for the next three years and in 1970 British *Vogue* chose him as 'Designer of the Year'. In the same year he did a collection for the Austrian Embroidery industry to show in Japan. In 1971 his work was chosen for the Paris exhibition, 'British Design', and in the same year he joined with Kate Franklin to create his own label, Bill Gibb Ltd. In 1975 they opened a retail shop and in 1976 his menswear collection was sponsored by the prestigious wool firm of Reid and Taylor. The glitter-

Givenchy's light-hearted way with separates, photographed in 1955, shows the designer in a casual young mood.

ing cavalcade of success culminated in a Bill Gibb retrospective at London's Royal Albert Hall in 1977.

What made Gibb's name so big in London fashion and gave him an international, 'jet-set' clientele was, above all, his approach to evening wear. He was a fantasist. His incredible evening looks, whose intricate embroidery and *appliqué* often incorporated his 'signature', a bee, were extravagant theatrical pieces in the ERTÉ manner. Equally important were the highly original decorative prints produced in collaboration with Kaffe Fasset. Unfortunately his firm expanded too quickly and had to cease trading. New backers were found, but the firm went out of business again. In 1979 he started to have his clothes made up in India and in 1981 he signed with Papillon to create a couture collection. A deal with the *Daily Telegraph* resulted in Bill Gibb patterns being available for the newspaper's readers throughout 1981 and 1982. Also in 1982 Harrods began carrying an exclusive Bill Gibb designer jeans range, complete with bee motif.

GILBERT, Irene

Born Dublin, Ireland, 1920s.
After an apprenticeship in a Dublin haberdasher's shop, Irene Gilbert moved to London to study fashion design. Remaining in London during World War II, she did not return to Dublin until the late 1940s, opening her salon there in 1950. Encouraged by the Irish Export Promotion Board, she showed her couture collection

in New York in 1954. It used traditional Irish materials and methods and its appeal to the Americans was considerable. In 1962 her ready-to-wear collection in New York won similar praise. Her look is a sophisticated, country one, based on tweed suits, woollen coats and capes. She works in linen, lace and mohair.

GIUDICELLI, Tan

Born Saigon, Vietnam, 1940.
Eurasian, with a Vietnamese mother and a Corsican father, Giudicelli arrived in Paris in 1957 to work for the firm of Christian DIOR. After two years he moved as assistant to CRAHAY at RICCI, then in 1961 became design assistant at HEIM, before going freelance in 1962. He worked for several firms in the South of France, notably Mic Mac in St. Tropez in 1968 and also Chloe, before launching a collection of *prêt-à-porter* and evening wear under his own name in 1976.

GIVENCHY, Hubert Taffin de ☐

Born Beauvais, France, 1927.
The last of the aristocrats of couture, and the friend of BALENCIAGA, who influenced and, perhaps, overshadowed him, Givenchy is respected in Paris as a totally dedicated designer. It is said that he begins work on his new collection the day the previous one is shown. Tall, good-looking and impeccably mannered, he is a perfectionist, one whose relationship with Balenciaga was founded on such trust that he was allowed to see the latter's

collections before they were viewed in public – a privilege unique in fashion history.

Givenchy began his fashion career in 1945 with LELONG, moved to PIGUET in the following year, and from 1947 worked for two years with FATH. He also studied at the École des Beaux Arts and the Faculté de Droit in Paris. From 1949 to 1951 he designed for SCHIAPARELLI. He opened his own house, with Balenciaga's encouragement, in 1952. From the beginning it was apparent that he was a designer of lasting quality who, without gimmicks or vulgarity, would create clothes in the great traditions of couture. His clothes were elegant, refined and perfectly made. His designs for daywear were understated; his evening wear was richly glamorous. The same is true of his fashions more than thirty years later: the perfection of cut is the basis of his success. When Balenciaga retired many of his workers joined Givenchy's atelier, and with this work-force Givenchy has managed to retain a very profitable couture business in addition to his Nouvelle Boutique ready-to-wear, which is distributed world-wide.

Like virtually all designers today, Givenchy heads an empire which includes scents, furs, sportswear and home furnishings. He also has a wide network of licences. Although he is not, perhaps, one of the great innovators of Paris, his clothes have had influence, nevertheless. The gentle, small-collared suits and slim woollen dresses worn by Audrey Hepburn (for whose film, *Funny Face*, Givenchy designed the costumes) became a uniform for those

Above: *This Givenchy coat and skirt outfit from 1954 show how close in thinking he was to his friend Balenciaga — the scale of the hat is exactly what Balenciaga would have wished.*

Below: *The grand ballgown created by Givenchy in 1963. The V neck and bodice are echoed on a large scale by the V of the gathered skirt and panel.*

in search of the lady-like look. It was worn by Jacqueline Kennedy and it still influences the looks of a variety of women from Los Angeles socialites to the British Queen. Although he started on a shoestring in 1952, Givenchy was never in danger of failing. Right from the beginning his clothes had the stamp of quality, a fact acknowledged by the Fashion Institute of Technology in 1982, when they honoured him with a retrospective, entitled 'Givenchy: 30 years'.

Major perfumes: L'Interdit (1958). Satis (1984).

GOMA, Michel

Born Montpellier, France, 1932.
Goma's background was Spanish. After a period studying dressmaking and fine art in Montpellier he moved, at the age of nineteen, to Paris, where he was meant to study painting, but instead began to sell his fashion designs. He took sketches to various houses, but received little encouragement until, armed with an introduction from *L'Officiel*, he managed to speak to DIOR. He was encouraged, but not employed, by the maestro. Finally LAFAURIE offered him work and he was designer there from 1950 until 1958, when he bought out the firm and renamed it Michel Goma. He closed in 1963 and moved to PATOU, where he worked for the next ten years, then in 1973 he reverted to freelance work. In no way in the forefront of design, Goma has, nevertheless, produced some outstanding collections.

GREER, Howard

Born Nebraska, USA, 1886.
Died California, USA, 1964.
Greer began his career by working as a sketcher in the New York establishment of LUCILE. In World War I he served in France and, after the armistice, stayed on to work for POIRET and, later, MOLYNEUX. In 1923 he returned to America and began designing costumes for Paramount films, then opened his own couture establishment in 1927. Star-studded and extravagant, it

The classic Grès look, first conceived in the thirties, is still used with total assurance in this example from 1968.

was such a success that he left Paramount in 1930 to set up his own wholesale business. He dressed most of the top Hollywood stars of the time and revealed many of their secrets in his autobiography, *Designing Male*, published in America in 1951. He retired in 1962.

GRÈS, Madame Alix

Born Paris, France, 1910.
The 'Madame' with which Grès' hallowed name is always introduced says everything. She commands respect from the

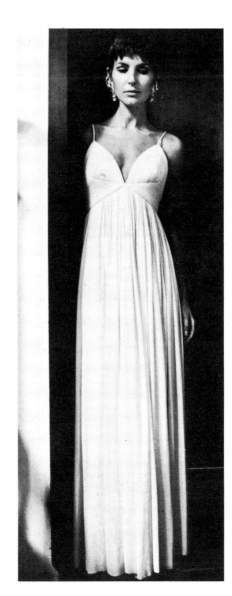

The Grès way with draped silk jersey has been emulated frequently but never surpassed. Her mastery of her medium is clearly seen in this dress which has the purity of Attic sculpture.

youngest to the oldest in the fashion business, not only as a great survivor, but as a survivor who has never compromised her integrity as a designer. She is the last in the line of women dressmakers that began with Bertin and included Jeanne LANVIN and VIONNET: the ones who understood how to make perfect clothes from within themselves, so that their products were unmistakably personal. Alix Grès wished to be a sculptor, but her family's disapproval and lack of money stood in the way of her ambition. Instead, she began to make toiles to sell to fashion houses. Her success encouraged her to open her own house under the name of Alix Barton. As Alix, her sculptural approach to drapery created classically

simple dresses, with the still perfection of a Greek vase. Timelessly pleated and draped, they were always contemporary and had none of the atavism of Fortuny's Greek-inspired dresses. Re-opening her own house in 1942 during the German occupation, she called herself Grès, using her husband's name. She has continued to work in a classically sculptural way ever since, doing all her own designing and cutting.

Grès presents her clothes to press and buyers as sculpture: the models do not cavort around like half-crazed savages, as they do at most fashion shows, and accessories are kept to a minimum. Only the dress matters. Grès has always been attracted to jersey and uses wool for day and silk for evening wear. Her working method is that of the sculptor — she models each dress directly on to the mannequin without any pattern and with the minimum of cutting. In 1970 she became President of the Chambre Syndicale, an honour which recognized her long and highly professional role in French couture.

Major perfume: Cabochard (1960).

GRIFFE, Jacques

Born Carcassonne, France, 1917.
Although his name is in danger of being forgotten today, Griffe deserves recognition for his craftsmanship as a cutter. His workmanship was in the great tradition established by VIONNET, for whom he worked for three formative years. He was born in humble circumstances in a village in the South of France where his mother was a dressmaker. She was ambitious for her son and, when she had taught him all she could, obtained a place for him with a men's tailor. Here he began to learn the science of his trade, sewing and cutting. He continued to train in Toulouse, where he went at the age of sixteen to work with a couturier. After a period of military service, he went to Paris and Madame Vionnet in 1936. Although he did not work directly with her (he saw her only twice) he learned the approach of her house and became a perfect cutter. After World War II, which he spent largely as a prisoner, he worked for some time as an assistant to MOLYNEUX. Then he received backing from Robert Ferrier of Scandal Corsets and was

able to open his own small house, producing modest collections of fewer than thirty pieces. By 1947 press and buyers were showing sufficient interest for him to move into bigger premises — those of MOLYNEUX. Vionnet attended his second collection and thereafter acted as his guardian angel. Griffe never sketched. He draped on a small wooden dummy given him by Vionnet, with the result that his clothes always had a fluid, plastic quality to them. His boutique and ready-to-wear range, called 'Jacques Griffe Evolution', were both very successful.

GROULT, Nicole
See PARIS COUTURE

GUIBOURGE, Philippe
Born Paris, France, 1931.
Study at the École des Beaux Arts Décoratifs in Paris was followed by service in the French army where he met Jacques FATH and showed him some drawings. On demobilization he joined Fath and was trained by him for three years, working at couture and ready-to-wear level. This was followed by a period from 1957 to 1960 as CASTILLO's assistant at LANVIN. 1960 saw the beginning of his long association with the house of DIOR where he stayed for twelve years as Marc BOHAN's assistant. His responsibilities in the Dior empire included ready-to-wear lines for England and boutique accessories, and from 1967 to 1975 he designed all the Miss Dior ready-to-wear line. In 1975 he became director of CHANEL ready-to-wear. His design career is interesting in that, although a man of considerable ability, he has always worked within someone else's framework and nowhere more so than at Chanel where a formula has been evolved which allows very little space for variation or innovation. His design skills and creative tact are exemplified by his success at Chanel: he has consistently produced collections right for their moment and yet indisputably Chanel — no mean achievement. A lesser man might have produced sterile museum pieces or submerged the Chanel image in his own personality. The role of designer at Chanel was taken over by LAGERFELD in 1983.

H

HAIRE · HALLÉE (*See* PARIS COUTURE) · HALSTON · HAMNETT · HANAI (*See* JAPANESE DESIGN) · HANDLEY-SEYMOUR · HARDWICK
HARP · HARTNELL · HAWES · HAYWARD · HEAD · HECHTER · HEIM · HELYETT (*See* ITALIAN READY-TO-WEAR) · HERBERT
HERMAN · HERMÈS · HOLAH (*See* BODY MAP) · HORN · HOWELL · HULANICKI

Halston

Head

Above: *Heim*
Left: *Hartnell*

151

HAIRE, Bill

Born New York City, USA.
Haire graduated from the Fashion Institute of Technology in 1955, travelled to Europe, and on returning to America worked for an evening-wear firm. After fourteen years he left to work for Henry Friedricks as co-designer, with his wife, of a complete range. He now designs alone for Friedricks and has his own label.

HALLÉE, Jean

See PARIS COUTURE

HALSTON, Roy Halston Frowick ☐

Born Des Moines, Iowa, USA, 1932.
Halston attended Indiana University and Chicago Art Institute and began making hats while still a student. He moved to New York in 1957 to work with Lilly DACHÉ and, briefly, as an assistant to Charles JAMES, then in 1958 joined Bergdorf Goodman as their milliner. His hats proved popular and in 1966 Bergdorf allowed him to start designing a ready-to-wear range for them. In 1968 he opened his own couture house for private clients, adding a ready-to-wear range, called 'Halston International', in 1970. Success continued with the opening of Halston Originals in 1972. Halston became part of the Norton Simon organization in 1973 and in 1975 he added menswear and perfume (bottle designed by PERETTI) to his empire. All this activity did not go unrewarded. He won a Coty Special Award in 1962 and 1969, a 'Winnie' in 1971, and a Return Award the year after. He was elected to the Hall of Fame in 1974.

Halston is one of America's top-rated designers, with a very New York sense of sophistication and elegance. There is a laid-back languor about his simple, understated clothes, done in perfect materials and colours, which appeals to the elite of the fashionables. He dresses nearly every noteworthy woman from VREELAND downwards and knows most of his customers socially. His openings and his parties are eagerly-awaited points in the New York social calendar. Through his made-to-order couture and his many licences he has a wide influence, especially on younger American designers. Like NORELL and

Left: *A sculpturally simple evening look from Halston for Summer 1984.*

New York style is seen to advantage in this Halston ensemble for Summer 1984.

BLASS he is in every sense from the middle of America. He was in the right place at the right time and realized in the 1960s that American women were tired of the Russian-peasant and gypsy looks of European designers: he gave them a clean, stripped-down American substitute. In reaction to European eclecticism, the Halston look seemed to be based on minimal and conceptual art principles: cashmere sweaters, shirt waist dresses and polo coats instead of fancy dress. His day clothes are clean cut and svelte and his evening wear is always glamorous and sexy. He took part in the Versailles show of five American designers in 1973.

HAMNETT, Katharine

Born Gravesend, England, 1948.
Born into a diplomatic family, her father being air attaché to various British embassies in Europe, Hamnett was educated at Cheltenham Ladies College. From there she moved to the St. Martin's School of Art in London to study fashion. Finding her course less than stimulating, she spent a great deal of time discussing textiles and art with Bernard Neville, the aesthete and textile designer. At this period her great love was the cinema. While at college she worked as a freelance designer and she continued to do so after she graduated in 1970, working in partnership with Anne Buck for Tuttabankem. When this firm closed she freelanced for French, Italian and Hong Kong firms.

In 1979 she founded Katharine Hamnett Ltd., and since then this firm has grown as a fashion influence, producing clothes that have made her the most copied of English designers, her influence being especially strong in Italy. She has shown in Paris and Milan. Her clothes are based on workwear and she designs in a similar spirit to KAMALI in New York. Hamnett is a feminist and a supporter of the peace movement. Her spring/summer 1984 line was inspired by the anti-nuclear women's protests at the Greenham Common airbase in England. In 1982 she introduced a successful men's range based on the same relaxed and undemanding approach.

HANAI, Yukiko
See JAPANESE DESIGN

HANDLEY-SEYMOUR, Mrs
This firm of ultra-conservative and ultra-exclusive gown and mantle makers was founded before World War I and was *the* dressmaker for London and county society during the 1920s and 1930s. The reason for its smartness was that Mrs. Handley-Seymour had received the royal warrant from Queen Mary and, as royal dressmaker, clothed that august figure almost exclusively. The most famous creation was the robe for Queen Elizabeth at the coronation of George VI in 1937. Other members of the royal family were dressed by Handley-Seymour too. Notably, she created the wedding dress and trousseau for the Duchess of York's wedding in 1923.

HARDWICK, Cathy
Born Seoul, Korea, 1933.
Hardwick's real name is Kasuk Surh. A direct descendant of Korea's last monarch, Queen Min, she went to America after studying music in Japan. At twenty-one she opened a boutique in San Francisco for which she designed most of the ranges, although she had no design training. Moving to New York in the late 1960s, she established Cathy Hardwick and Friends, there in 1972. The firm is now known solely as Cathy Hardwick.

HARP, Holly
Born Buffalo, New York, USA, 1939.
Born into a financially comfortable family, Harp 'dropped out' of education and went

to Acapulco. She began to design sandals and also her own clothes and decided that she would like to be a fashion designer. She studied art and costume design at North Texas State University, before opening a boutique in Los Angeles, with a $10,000 loan from her father, in 1968. She opened a boutique in Henri Bendel in 1972 and started her wholesale line in the following year. Her approach to design, which has attracted such rich free spirits as Ali MacGraw, Barbra Streisand, Liza Minnelli and Faye Dunaway, is best summed up in her own words. She has described her clothes as a release and an entertainment: 'I deal in nostalgia'. Her romantic and theatrical approach to design seems especially appropriate for her base, which is Hollywood. However, lest she be considered merely an impractical dreamer, it must be added that she has also designed on a practical level for Simplicity Patterns. Her clothes are always wearable, desirable and imaginative.

HARTNELL, Sir Norman
Born London, England, 1901.
Died Windsor, England, 1979.
Educated at Cambridge, where he became involved with the Footlights revues as a performer and costume designer, Hartnell was expected to become an architect, but instead became more and more interested in dress design. He began work with 'Madame Désiré', a court dressmaker, but was soon sacked. He showed his designs to LUCILE, who promptly published them under her own name; and his work was rejected by REVILLE; so finally, in desperation, he and his sister decided to open on their own. His father paid one year's rent

Above right: *Lady Smiley's presentation dress created by Hartnell in 1928. White silk tulle spangled with diamond-shaped sequins is arranged in pointed flounces with a long train at the back.*

Right: *Sir Norman Hartnell designed these peeresses' dresses for the coronation in 1953. They have his trademarks (glass bugle beads, crystals, paillettes and sequins) but not his customary full skirts as they were to be worn under ceremonial robes.*

on premises in Bruton Street in 1923. To begin with things were very difficult because Hartnell was not French and in those days being French or, at least, having a French name, was almost essential for success in fashion. To overcome this by achieving French acclaim, he took his collection to Paris in 1927. His show was an overwhelming success. In 1930 he again showed in Paris and received orders from many North American customers. He also worked in the theatre and designed costumes for many Cochrane revues.

Hartnell's long association with the British royal family began when he made three dresses for Queen Mary. This led to the commission to design the Duchess of Gloucester's wedding dress in 1935 and in 1938 he designed Queen Elizabeth's wardrobe for her visit to Paris. This had to be re-fabricated at the last moment, owing to the death of the Queen's mother. Though a period of mourning was decreed, Hartnell overcame the problem by creating an all-white wardrobe which caused a sensation in Paris. Also sensational and influential in Paris were the romantic, Winterhalter crinolines that he created for the Queen's evening look. From this point until his death, Hartnell was continually involved in dressing the royal family and his work included the wedding dress and coronation robe of Queen Elizabeth II, as well as wardrobes for most of her foreign tours.

In addition, Hartnell made elegant, well-tailored couture suits and coats and lavish evening gowns for his many private customers. In 1947 he received the Neiman-Marcus Award and in 1977 he was knighted. He wrote his autobiographical *Silver and Gold* in 1955 and *Royal Courts of Fashion* in 1971. He is best remembered for his sumptuous evening gowns, especially those for royal state occasions, which exemplified his admission that 'I am more than partial to the jolly glitter of sequins'.

HAWES, Elizabeth

Born New Jersey, USA, 1903.
Died USA, 1971.
Hawes is rather a maverick in the story of American fashion. She studied at Vassar, before following a design course at Par-

son's School of Design in New York. She moved to Paris in 1925 and worked as a 'pirate' sketcher, before being appointed Paris stylist for the American stores, Macy's and Lord and Taylor's. She also worked briefly for GROULT, before returning to America in 1928 to open her own establishment. Her clothes were in the CHANEL mould, soft, naturally proportioned and gentle, and were therefore in a sense out of their time, since SCHIAPARELLI's hard silhouettes and accented shoulders were the current vogue. In 1932 Hawes contracted to design several collections for various manufacturers. She retired in 1938, the year when her autobiography, *Fashion is Spinach*, was published.

HAYWARD

Hayward was a London couture house, active in the first decades of the 20th century and patronized by royalty. The firm created dresses for the trousseau of Princess Mary on her wedding to Viscount Lascelles in 1922, although the prize of the wedding dress went to REVILLE. The house was in no sense avant-garde. Its fame rested on the 'suitability' of its creations and the high level of its craftsmanship.

HEAD, Edith

Born California, USA, 1907.
Died Los Angeles, USA, 1981.
The doyenne of Hollywood designers, Edith Head had a career which spanned the fifty most exciting years of the cinema. After receiving her MA at Stanford, she taught languages and at the same time studied costume design at night school. She began at Paramount Studios in 1923 as a sketcher for GREER and, later, BANTON. She was made Studio Design head in 1938, when Banton retired. Through the thousands of costumes she designed for men and women in films her influence on the American fashion consciousness has been considerable. She won eight Oscars for work ranging from *The Heiress* in 1949 to *The Sting* in 1973. She designed for Vogue Patterns and Pan American Airlines. She believed that good clothes were not good luck but hard work, and saw their job as counter-balancing personality.

Barbara Stanwyck was dressed by Edith Head in 1941 for her part in The Lady Eve. *Second only to Adrian in influence, Edith Head designed film costumes which were first rate fashion in their own right.*

HECHTER, Daniel

Born Paris, France, 1938.
The ability to know what is right for the moment is the basis of success in the mass-market field. This ability is particularly important when catering for the volatile and unpredictable youth market. Daniel Hechter's empire has grown enormous and powerful because he has exactly this sense of what is wanted now. After various jobs, including cub reporter, salesman and storeman, he began working with Pierre d'Alby, from whom he learned a practical and pragmatic approach, not only to the design of clothes, but also to their promotion. With very little money, he and a friend, Armand Orustein, decided to set up alone and the Hechter group was founded in 1963 with the creation of his women's line. Fresh, young and iconoclastic, it set the tone for the Hechter house style. 1965 saw the introduction of his children's line, which owed its success to a colourful and witty use of materials and shapes unlike

Daniel Hechter's Winter 1983–84 collection included these large square-cut skirts with hand holds for the wearer to control their movement.

any previously seen in children's wear. In 1968 his menswear followed. So, in five years, Hechter had covered his particular market: the young, often married with children, who had style and dash but not a great deal of cash. Hechter is to clothes what Terence Conran and Habitat are to interiors for the young and upwardly mobile. Since the early 1970s he has colonized virtually all areas of fashion design, producing ranges of tennis and ski clothing, sunglasses, shoes, training wear and household linen. In 1982 he even entered the field of school supplies.

1983 saw the Hechter signature on a range of furniture. His market is worldwide. He exports to forty-seven countries and his line is licensed in Europe, Australia and North and South America. He also has a chain of Hechter boutiques throughout France, Europe and North America. He says 'I go for the free and easy', designing for the woman with 'nerve' who knows what she likes and how to wear it.

HEIM, Jacques
Born Paris, France, 1899.
Died Paris, France, 1967.
The year before Heim's birth, his parents founded a high-fashion furriers and it is

Above: This Jacques Heim dress from 1935 has an interesting cross-over top in velvet which fastens to a skirt in a strongly patterned print.

Below: Using a silk, wool and Bri-nylon gauze fabric Heim created a black draped tunic dress cut in one for Summer 1960.

there that he began his career as a designer when he was twenty-six. In the 1930s he opened in the Avenue Matignon, with his wife as *directrice*. Although his is a name largely ignored today, he was an important and original designer in his time, with several 'firsts' to his credit. He introduced cotton as a haute-couture fabric for beachwear and pareos; his 1937 'Heim-Jeunes Filles' line was the first to be dedicated to the young; he helped popularize the bikini; and between 1946 and 1966 he opened his own chain of boutiques. From 1958 to 1962 he was President of the Chambre Syndicale de la Couture. His son, Philippe, took over direction of the firm on his death.

Major perfumes: J'Aime (1950); Shandoah (1966).

HELYETT
See ITALIAN READY-TO-WEAR

HERBERT, Victor
Born Leicester, England, 1944.
After studying at Loughborough College of Art from 1961 to 1965, Victor Herbert

Victor Herbert created a jogging suit in purple and turquoise lurex material for informal evenings, 1979.

spent two years at the Royal College, where he specialized in fashion. He left in 1968 with first-class honours. He worked as a freelance designer for firms such as Littlewoods, British Home Stores, Stirling Cooper and Bruce OLDFIELD. He also became well-known as a fashion illustrator. In 1977 he started his own company in partnership with Christine Ruffhead, specializing in sportswear and knitwear. Herbert has also introduced a very successful men's range. He sees himself as working for the individual: 'I aim to make clothes that people can really wear'. His influence on high-street fashion through his freelance work for other fashion houses is quite considerable, and he works as a colour consultant and fashion forecaster for several firms, including an Italian knitwear company. In 1980 his influence on high-street fashion was acknowledged by the award of 'British Designer of the Year' presented by *Woman* magazine. He also plays an active part in design education.

HERMAN, Stan
Born New York City, USA, 1932.
After studying at the University of Cincinnati, Herman worked in the New York rag trade while attending the Traphagen Fashion School. After a stint as a nightclub entertainer, he returned to fashion in 1959 as designer at Mr. Mort. In 1978 he started his own dress house, Stan Herman. In 1965 he won the Coty award for 'Young Contemporaries' design; in 1969 he received a 'Winnie'; and in 1974 he was awarded a Special Award for lingerie.

HERMÈS, Thierry
The original Hermès was a saddler who set up business in Paris in 1837. Over the years the business expanded to take in boots, jewellery, toilet articles and accessories, all with the 'horsey' theme best seen in that famous silk scarf which is still in production today. In 1920 the founder's grandson, Emile Hermès, instituted a modern design policy which resulted in the development of well-designed luggage and couture clothes. In the early 1930s Hermès sport was introduced in its own store in Paris. Today the empire stretches to most major cities of the world.

HOLAH, David
See BODY MAP

HORN, Carol
Born New York, USA, 1936.
Educated at Boston and Columbia Universities in fine arts, Horn began as a retail stylist, then designed sportswear for Bryant 9. In 1966 she joined Benson & Partners. After four years she moved to Malcolm Starr International before founding Carol Horn Habitat. Her design philosophy is based on the contemporary feel for relaxed and natural shapes. In 1975 she received the Coty American Fashion Critics' Award.

HOWELL, Margaret
Born Tadworth, Surrey, England, 1946.
Howell followed the four-year course in fine arts at Goldsmith's College in London from 1966 to 1970. From there, with no specialist training in fashion and no preliminary experience with other designers, she launched into fashion in 1971 with a range of accessories under her own label. In 1972 she added clothes. In 1974 she began to work in conjunction with Joseph. In the 1970s she and her sister also had their own shop in Chelsea. Her business was subsequently run with her husband, an industrial designer. Her clothes were very English and included a range for men as well as women: wool, tweed, Melton cloth, brogues and gym slips were all used as inspiration for her traditional approach to dressing, which proved sufficiently successful to support her own-name shops in London and on Madison Avenue, New York. At the end of 1986 the firm of Margaret Howell went into liquidation.

HULANICKI, Barbara
Born Poland, 1938.
Along with her husband, Stephen Fitz-Simon, Barbara Hulanicki created a shop, a look and an attitude towards style which made her name famous in the 1960s. The daughter of a Polish diplomat, she moved to England with her family on the outbreak of World War II. She studied fashion illustration at Brighton School of Art and began her career as a fashion artist. Her beginning as a dress designer was in cheap mail-order: cheerful, easy clothes which were featured in magazines appealing especially to young readers. The success of her mail-order designs encouraged her to open a boutique, called Biba, in 1963, in Abingdon Road, London. From the beginning it sold not just clothes, but an approach to style. Its success was so considerable that in 1969, after several moves, the Biba organization took over the Art Deco building that had formerly been Derry & Toms department store in Kensington High Street. Here was sold a lifestyle and an attitude which were very individualistic and very much a reflection of Barbara Hulanicki's personal tastes.

The store had an all-black interior and walking through it was rather like being on an ocean liner of the 1930s or on the set of an early Noel Coward play. Hulanicki's love of Art Nouveau, Art Deco, dark colours (such as plum, prune and black) and slinky materials (such as crêpe and shiny satin) was apparent everywhere. The furnishings, furniture, menswear, make-up and women's clothes sold at Biba had the same feel as a 1930s Dietrich film: decadent, camp and unreal. The success of the store was instant. Tourists came especially to see it but, alas, too few of her stolid adopted countrymen could happily live in such an exotic way. Sales could not cover costs. In 1975 the store closed and the business ceased trading.

Barbara Hulanicki and her family moved to Sao Paolo in Brazil in 1976 to start all over again. In 1977 she signed an agreement with CACHAREL to have her clothes, made in Brazil, marketed under his name. An attempt to re-open in London in 1978 was not a success, but in 1981 she began to produce a 'Minirock' range for children. Its very name tells the story: Barbara Hulanicki had been too much a person of her time to move on. Her elegant, super-sophisticated, dressing-up clothes seemed irrelevant to the realistic late 1970s and early 1980s, just as their slinky, skinny appeal was lost on Punk-dominated London. Her autobiography *From A to Biba* was published in 1983. In the same year a Hulanicki range was re-launched: where there is life there is hope.

I·J

INABA (*See* JAPANESE DESIGN) · IRENE · IRIE · ITALIAN READY-TO-WEAR · JACKSON · JAECKEL · JAEGER · JAMES
JAPANESE DESIGN · JEAN LOUS (*See* LOUIS) · JENNY (*See* PARIS COUTURE) · MR. JOHN · JOHNSON · JONES · JOURDAN · JULIO

Jones

James

INABA, Yoshie
See JAPANESE DESIGN

Incorporated Society of London Fashion Designers
See FASHION ORGANIZATIONS, p. 297

IRENE
Born Montana, USA, 1907.
Died Los Angeles, USA, 1962.
Irene Lentz Gibbons studied the piano at the University of Southern California, but it did not sufficiently interest her, and so she followed a design course at the Wolfe School of Design. She opened her own shop on the campus of U.S.C., where the film star, Dolores del Rio, became a client. More introductions to the stars led to her opening a shop in Hollywood and a couture salon in the Bullocks Wilshire store. Her clientele were all stars and as she became increasingly involved with their personal wardrobes, so she came to be consulted about their screen wardrobes. She designed costumes for films at most of the major Hollywood studios, including R.K.O., Columbia and United Artists, before succeeding ADRIAN as chief designer at M.G.M. in 1942. She was also head and chief designer of Irene Inc., her highly successful dressmaking firm which produced two ready-to-wear lines a year and was supported by 25 US department stores.

IRIE, Sueo
Born Osaka, Japan, 1946.
Irie graduated from Osaka Sogo Fukoso Gakium in 1970. Very shortly afterwards he moved to Paris where he became part of the Jungle Jap boutique of KENZO Takada to whom he was design assistant. He was given the job of designer for Studio V in 1980 and he presented his first collection in May of that year.
See also JAPANESE DESIGN.

ITALIAN READY-TO-WEAR
Italy has over 100,000 registered dressmaking establishments which range from the grandest *alta moda* houses to the little seamstress around the corner. In the middle is a band of highly prestigious fashion wholesalers whose products have become world famous under their own or invented names. They rarely acknowledge the name of a designer but, in fact, this is where their strength originates. They are above the ordinary 'rag trade' level because they employ top designers to create their ranges for them. These ranges are original and have a strong design signature. This is not surprising when one considers the calibre of designer employed. By no means are all Italian: French and English designers play an important part at this level in the Italian fashion field. MONTANA designs for Complice and Cadette, VARTY creates the Byblos range. Also exceptional is the use made of Italian talent. Several famous designers are prepared to produce ranges in addition to the one using their own name. Their names are often kept secret (though the secret is sometimes an open one) and are acknowledged on the label only rarely. It is a form of 'moonlighting' which has proved highly lucrative for the designers and the manufacturers. It maintains a design standard and ensures a creative input which has helped make Italian casual clothes some of the best in the world. Of the internationally known firms, in addition to those already mentioned, Callaghan and Jenny are designed by VERSACE and Erreuno by ARMANI. Thus the two top Italian ready-to-wear designers are involved in this very Italian approach to design.

Basile
One of the better known firms, Basile was founded in Milan in 1969. Aldo Ferrante, was a businessman and an ex-salesman. He was employed by KRIZIA and MISSONI as sales agent and distributor, until in 1967 when, with his partners Tositti and Gigi Monti, he founded F.T.M. (an amalgam of their initials). In 1969 F.T.M. (sometimes written Effetieme) took over the firm of Gianfranco Basile which was a small menswear manufacturer making clothes anonymously for other companies. They quickly transformed it. With ALBINI as designer, Basile came to prominence in the seventies, and continued as an important wholesaler under the design guidance of Muriel Grateau. Basile has employed a variety of designers including TARLAZZI and VERSACE. Ferrante moved on to form a

A big, relaxed scale characterizes this throw-away look from Basile's Summer 1984 collection. It has classic proportions which can be worn by anyone.

second company, Ferrante Collections, a co-operative venture, where he continues the Basile luxury sportswear and evening pieces look. Basile came under the direction of Gigi Monti in 1979 who hired SOPRANI as designer and Nando Miglio as show producer.

Cadette
Cadette was founded in Milan in 1966 by Enzo Clocchiatti and Christine Tidmarsh. He was a graduate in economics who had worked in Vienna, Milan and Rome; she was an ex-model for Yves SAINT LAURENT. They employed ALBINI as their designer, and their success was immediate. In 1969 they stopped showing in Florence and opened a boutique and showroom in Milan. By 1974 a Cadette boutique had opened in Paris. The line is currently designed by MONTANA.

Genny

Arnaldo Girombelli began his fashion empire in Ancona in 1961 with a small workshop, named after his first child, to produce skirts and blouses. A decade of steady success was followed by a period of expansion. A meeting with VERSACE in Florence in 1974 led to his employment as the designer of the Complice line. His first collection in 1975 set the tone – it was original and imaginative and complemented the classic 'Genny' look. He also became involved with the 'Byblos' line which had been introduced in 1973. It was a young range, as its name (taken from a St Tropez hotel) suggested. Versace designed the Byblos line from 1975 to 1977 when Guy Paulin took over. Since 1981 VARTY has designed Byblos, which is now an independent company directed by Sergio Girombelli. MONTANA has designed Complice since 1980.

Since Arnaldo Girombelli's death in 1979 his wife Donatella has controlled the firm. Her policy follows that of her husband: she employs the best designers and is not afraid to let the fact be known. Her attitudes had their reward in 1984 when she was honoured by the White House, for whom she produced a 'Princess Grace of Monaco Foundation' fashion show. Other Genny ranges include Montana Donna, Montana Uomo, and Malisy – a young, avant-garde label. Genny produced 800,000 garments in 1983 and increased sales by 25 per cent – proof of the firm's stature in Italy and worldwide.

Ghirardi

Giovanni Ghirardi's high-fashion specialist leather firm was founded by his grandfather, Alfredo Melloni, as purveyor of leather goods and harnesses to the upper classes. During the Italian Monarchy the house of Melloni was the exclusive supplier to the royal House of Savoy. Ghirardi, born in 1937 in Milan, took over the management of the business from his father and began to update it, while maintaining quality levels. Its name is now synonymous with a high-quality range of fashion accessories.

Helyett

Since its foundation in Milan in 1972, Helyett has made a name for itself by employing designers of a very high calibre and using the latest mass-production techniques and high-quality fabrics to produce an up-to-the-minute, fashionable look of quality. It has been particularly noted for its high standards, especially in its silk blouses. Both Walter ALBINI and Luciano SOPRANI have been designers for Helyett and their tradition is carried on by Franco Moschino.

Maxmara

Now a flourishing and considerable manufacturing firm, Maxmara was founded in 1951 by Doctor Achille Maramotti. His first collection consisted of two outfits: a suit and an overcoat. Although trained as a lawyer, Dr Maramotti had a dressmaking background. His mother had founded a tailoring school in 1923. Since its foundation the firm of Maxmara has become known for its classic but highly imaginative styles designed by Anne-Marie BERETTA. The firm now has many branches: Sportsmax, begun in 1969, is the sports range and is designed by Guy Paulin; Marella is created by Laura Lusuardi and, in addition, I Blues and Penny Black are lively young co-ordinated ranges which have considerable influence in Italy.

Pims

One of the longer lasting Italian ready-to-wear firms, founded in Rome in 1968, Pims has succeeded by consistently producing fashionable clothes which in design, colour and price appeal to the young woman looking for good quality prêt-à-porter. Luciano SOPRANI, when working freelance, designed Pims. The line is currently created by an English design team and the clothes continue to sell well in boutiques in Italy and abroad.

San Lorenzo

The firm was founded by Paula San Lorenzo's mother in Turin in 1945, as a high fashion atelier. In 1968 the firm showed a high fashion collection in Rome with considerable success but a knitwear collection shown at the Pitti Palace, Florence, in 1973 pointed the way to the firm's future in ready-to-wear. From sweaters San Lorenzo expanded to include a complete range. Enrica Massei had been designing all the San Lorenzo collections for her sister Paula San Lorenzo but in 1977 she set up on her own and Paula and her mother continued San Lorenzo with a variety of designers. They are business women and they have had considerable success in producing middle-of-the-road clothes which sell well in Europe, America and Japan.

Timmi

Founded in Milan in 1978, Timmi is a design organization which, as part of the Soxs Italia firm of Milan, does several collections. The Timmi range is geared to separates and it has been designed by people of the calibre of BERETTA in the past. The present designer is Sonia Gattei.

Touche

Touche is a family business, founded by the Salmeri family in Milan in 1974. It has always specialized in lively, up-to-the-minute casual looks which have, since its inception, been designed by COVERI.

Varied stripes circled by an outsize belt are topped with a white collar and tie in this Summer look for 1984 by Touche.

JACKSON, Betty

Born Bacup, England, 1940.

Betty Jackson followed a three-year course in fashion at Birmingham College of Art from 1968 to 1971 and then worked as a freelance illustrator in London. In 1973 she joined Wendy DAGWORTHY as an assistant designer and remained with her until 1975. She then moved to Quorum and worked there as a designer from 1975 to 1979. For the next two years she designed for Coopers. She started to work under her own name in 1981. Her clothes, which are young and are based on classic themes developed and re-scaled, sell very well in America and Europe (especially Italy). They represent an essentially English, albeit updated and heightened approach to dressing.

For Summer 1983 Betty Jackson created a large scale elongated T-shirt pulled in at the waist.

JAECKEL

Jaeckel was a company established in New York in 1863 to provide elegant and expensive furs for New York society. Jaeckel also provided a selection of models chosen in Paris. The company had the exclusive American rights to them and often presented them with trimmings of its own furs.

JAEGER

The respected and well-established firm of Jaeger was founded in 1884 by Lewis Tomalin, who had translated and published the German Dr. Gustave Jaeger's book on health culture. The main argument of Dr. Jaeger's book was that natural animal hair, i.e. wool, was healthy, whereas cotton and linen were not. Tomalin accepted this view and his first shop was founded to spread 'Dr. Jaeger's Sanitary Woollen System'. The shop was solely a purveyor of health clothes up until the 1920s, when fashion began to enter. There is now a world network of Jaeger shops which showcase a very English look, using tweeds and colours which are traditional but *chic*.

JAMES, Charles ☐

Born Sandhurst, England, 1906.
Died New York, USA, 1978.

With a British army officer for a father and an American for a mother, it is perhaps not surprising that James lived a peripatetic life, criss-crossing the Atlantic, never having a real home and spending most of his years living in hotels. After Harrow, from which he was expelled for the usual reason at the age of eighteen, he spent a brief period at the University of Bordeaux. He then moved to his mother's home town, Chicago. At the age of nineteen he set up there as a milliner, calling himself Boucheron. Despite an unnerving habit of fashioning his hats on the heads of his customers, he was quite successful and was able to move to New York in 1928, where he made hats and a few dresses for private customers.

By the end of 1929 James was in London and in the next ten years he ranged between Europe and America: 1933 saw him back in the States; in 1934 he estab-

lished a salon in Paris; in 1937 he was living in London at the Dorchester and in the same year he showed for the first time in Paris. POIRET is reputed to have said to him, 'I pass you my crown. Wear it well.' Although he had been deposed many years before, Poiret recognized James' quality. So did BALENCIAGA, who called him 'the world's best and only dressmaker', and DIOR, who claimed that James had inspired his 'New Look'. By 1940 James had returned to New York and set up as Charles James Inc. He began a very fruitful, though not always smooth, association with Elizabeth Arden. He designed clothes for her exclusively until 1945, when they dissolved their partnership.

In 1947 James was back in Europe, showing in Hardy AMIES' salon in London and also in Paris. But for the next ten years he worked largely in New York. In 1958 he retired from couture and he spent the 1960s lecturing and conducting seminars at the Rhode Island School of Design and the Pratt Institute. He was also famous for his informal, all-night sessions at his studio or hotel. He was always obsessive about documenting his work and over a ten-year period the fashion illustrator, ANTONIO*, made drawings of all his masterpieces to be kept as a permanent record. In this way James spent the last few years of his life, living in the seedy Chelsea hotel, drug-addicted and suffering from diabetes and kidney disease, and finally dying there of pneumonia.

Charles James was fashion's Michelangelo. His clothes were sculptural. He was also its Leonardo, for his mind worked like an artist's and an engineer's. His work was in the classic couture tradition and yet his approach was thoroughly radical. He designed unique creations for individual customers and yet used the same design over and over again. He saw himself as a couturier and yet, as early as 1949, tried to set up machinery for the widespread merchandizing of his designs. His 'Charles James Services', which unfortunately failed, was the forerunner of the present-day 'designer's label' industry. He was an innovative genius who did not believe in fashion seasons or looks. Whereas other couturiers changed their designs every six months and discarded the old in favour of the new, he worked on his designs for

Three characteristic American looks by Louis dell'Olio and Donna Karan for Anne Klein (far left), Calvin Klein (left) and Norma Kamali (above).

A sure hand with pattern and colour produces fun fashion for the young in Kenzo's 1982 collection.

Kenzo's calypso dresses for his
Summer 1984 collection show why he
has been a power in Paris since his
arrival in the seventies: they are
colourful, witty and wearable.

The Japanese colour sense and
approach to pattern are exemplified by
this dress from Kenzo's 1984
collection.

The relaxed look of American fashion is crystallized in these two outfits from Calvin Klein's collection for Summer 1984. A look for long-limbed, healthy girls, its simplicity is deceptive: understatement with this amount of style requires skill.

Mariucca Mandelli's fun knitwear featuring animals has been a welcome part of the Krizia collections over the past years. They are witty and strong and fully deserve their place as status knits as this example from 1982 shows.

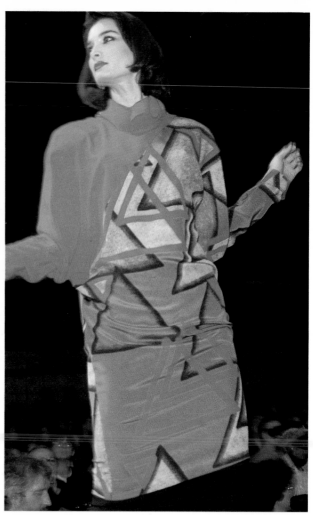

Above: *Geometrically patterned silk shows Lagerfeld's bold and unerring sense of scale in this dress from the Chloe Summer 1984 collection.*

Left: *Lagerfeld for Chloe, Winter 1983–84: how a genius can steer close to the edge of fancy dress and avoid the pit. The elements in this elegant outfit would bring disaster in any hands less skilled. As it is they are a triumph for Lagerfeld's verve and style.*

Above: *Lagerfeld's accessories have always been a strong part of the Chloe look but even without them his clothes have total authority and immense style.*

Right: *This perfectly restrained and understated pants suit from Lagerfeld's first collection under his own name (for Autumn 1984) shows that masterly cut is more important than fussy detail.*

A tropical print is used by Lancetti for this simple shift which makes its impact with its colour and scale.

Ralph Lauren uses bold Madras mixes for a tunic and skirt in his collection for Summer 1984. The look is completed by leather boots and large hats.

As colourists the Missoni's have been supreme since they began. Their look is unique and instantly recognizable: if men and women grew fur the sensible ones would want it to be like a Missoni jacket.

Pattern and texture given a masterly treatment by Miyake in 1983. The scale and colour of this outfit are totally convincing.

Not only the surest Japanese hand in Paris, Miyake is now one of the world's major designers. These uncompromising trousers from his 1982 collection show his strength.

Typical early eighties Japanese looks from Miyake's Spring 1984 collection: layers, colour and pattern are used with subtlety, assurance and strength.

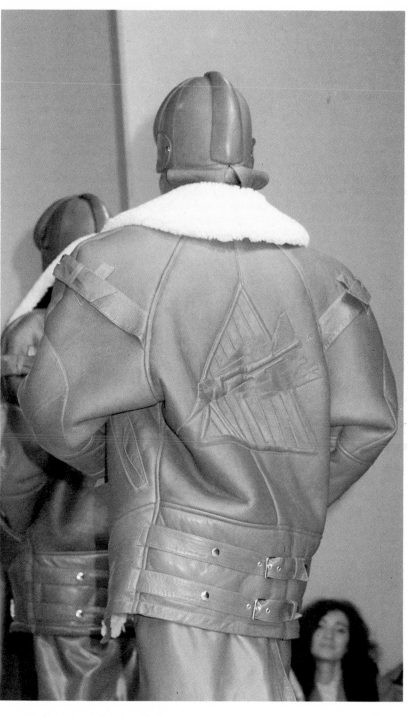

Montana's leather jacket from his 1983 collection shows his skill in using strong masculine lines and scale to produce a feminine look.

Left: *The matelot look from Montana, 1979.*

The two sides of Montana: good clean fun in his bright and wholesome striped outfits for day; Barbarella-fantasy women in hotly coloured dresses for sexy glamorous nights.

The Thierry Mugler Hollywood vamp evening look in which he satirizes fifties glamour through exaggeration is well seen in this shiny satin example from 1982.

Below: A courageous sense of scale and inspired placing of colour blocks produces an image of great strength in this seven-eighths coat from Mugler's 1982 collection.

Below left: An amazing fabric is used extravagantly by Mugler to produce a dress which seems determined to make a camp statement on taste and vulgarity.

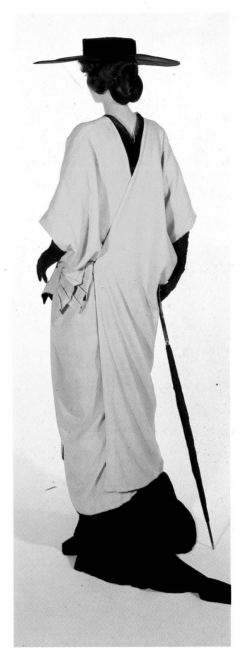

Above: *A wedding gown by Jean Patou drawn for the fashion periodical Art-Goût-Beauté in July 1923. The gown is of a simple, medieval appearance and the whole group has a pure 'sweetness and light' aura far removed from the flappers of the time.*

Right: *A beautifully simple fashion statement by Poiret. Cut, line and colour all show why he was considered one of this century's greatest couturiers.*

An unusual fabric treatment from Pucci in this restrained evening look shows the colour sense which made him famous.

Above: *Mrs Everitt D. Collins wearing a Charles James masterpiece at a charity ball. This ball gown of satin is stunning in concept and realization: there is nothing quite like the huge draped and bouffant flounce in any other designer's work.*

Right: *A suitably architectural setting for Charles James' monumental evening dresses which look so secure in their powerful stillness that, paradoxically, the architecture looks ephemeral and insubstantial by comparison.*

years. They remained on the market, not just for a season, but for decades. He developed about two hundred thesis designs with an intellectual, almost scientific, precision and logic and these were the basis of all his work. He created a master pattern, or 'sloper', which he viewed in the same way as one would 'the basic chassis in the automotive industry'. This was his design module, with interchangeable parts for every section of a garment (sleeves, bodice, armhole etc.) which could be combined to produce thousands of variations. He worked over his designs for many years, calling dresses back to be modified in the light of new discoveries and, in many cases, never finishing them.

In the 1920s and 1930s he developed spiral draping, a spiral zip on his famous 'Taxi' dress, a ribbon ball dress, a figure-eight skirt, and the directional white-satin, padded, quilted jacket which Dali called 'the first soft sculpture'. In the 1940s and 1950s his tailoring became severely mathematical in its precision and he perfected the grand ball dresses for which he is probably best remembered. They were very stiff and very sculptural, with superbly-built bodices and foliate forms for necklines. They came to their apogee in his clover-leaf ball gown of 1953, of which James said, 'I had intended it to be the last and final statement and it was composed of several parts previously developed as separate designs'.

This complex, contrary and eccentric man had no illusions about his worth. He knew he was the greatest couturier of the century. He saw his clothes as works of art whose rightful resting place was a museum. He saw himself as a fashion researcher and viewed everything he did with ruthless logic. 'All my seams have meaning' and 'cut in dressmaking is like grammar in language', two of his many comments, reveal his attitude to fashion. All that mattered to him was his work. He sacrificed everything to it. Quarrelsome, vituperative, self-destructive, his relationships with friends and colleagues were often disastrous. Forever in litigation, either suing or being sued for piracy, breach of contract or misuse of designs, he often made his customers wait for years for a dress to be delivered – and they had to pay him huge amounts of money. He was a tragic figure, but he was a truly great (possibly *the* great) designer. MAIN-BOCHER's view – 'If the right dresses are put next to one another they would be like a scale on the piano. Each grows into the other' – seems perfectly to fit the *oeuvre* of Charles James.

JAPANESE DESIGN

Perhaps the most interesting design development at the beginning of the eighties was the emergence of Japan as a major fashion influence on the West. Although KENZO, MORI and MIYAKE had been well-established in Paris since the early seventies it was not until 1982 that a concerted Japanese onslaught was launched. Whereas the earlier Japanese designers in Paris had, to a greater or lesser degree, worked within an occidental fashion matrix, the new designers produced clothes which were entirely oriental in spirit and inspiration. Their impact on the West was immediate: in its repercussions their first showing could be described as fashion's Pearl Harbour. Kansai YAMAMOTO, Yohji YAMAMOTO and Rei Kawakubo of COMME DES GARÇONS chose Paris as their launching pad because it was the traditional home of fashion and is still the major Western fashion centre. But the clothes they showed made few concessions to traditional Western ideas of dress, chic or beauty. They brought an alien way of looking at women, clothes and even life. These clothes were as much a statement of philosophy as they were of design.

The Japanese 'spearhead' designers have permanently altered fashion in the West. They have introduced a new dimension reflecting their cultural history and their attitude towards the nature of clothing the human body. Japanese history is, in cultural terms, spare, frugal and organic. It reflects the long period of isolation that Japan enjoyed for a portion of its history: the 300 years of the Edo period, during which the influences from outside the country were almost nil. Only the Portuguese, who landed in 1543, were allowed a foothold. The resulting period of unprecedented peace and isolation enabled the particular Japanese attitudes to art and design to develop.

Japanese design history hardly exists in Western terms. Whereas in the West, design and fashion tend to be a reaction to what has immediately gone before and are frequently seen as a contradiction of previous modes, Japanese design and fashion have concentrated on refining, not on changing, what existed already. Japanese designers have not and do not work on the same basis as Western designers: they do not have an endless appetite for change; and they do not look back to previous periods in search of inspiration, because there is no previous period in the Western sense. There is nothing on which to base a revival because the form of dress evolved by the Japanese was the result of a philosophical attitude not a search for novelty. It has not altered as a concept for hundreds of years.

While Western designers were creating Empire lines, crinolines and bustles the Japanese were developing and refining their timeless solution to dress: the kimono. Many-layered, elaborate and sensual, it is, in essence, unchanging. It is also the basis of all Japanese fashion thinking. It has evolved and is complete.

This is also true of the philosophical attitude of modern Japanese designers and their influence lies in this attitude. They are not 'creative', trend-setting and novelty-conscious as Western designers are. Their attitude to designing clothes is based on their evolutionary approach to design generally. Here lies their difference. Japanese design ideas have become a world force and will remain so because they have introduced a completely new attitude towards clothing the figure. In the West, clothes design has always been linear and vertical. Designers start (even in their roughest sketches) from the neckline and work to the hem. Front and back, left and right sides of a garment must balance and reflect each other. The Japanese, however, view the garment horizontally, asymmetrically, and in the round. Tops, bottoms or sides are hardly considered in Japanese clothes. They are peripheral to the design. This concept is the new dimension which has been introduced to the West: as it is slowly understood and assimilated by Western designers, it will prove to have a permanent effect on creative attitudes.

Japanese designers have given the rest of the world a new theme on which to play many variations. With this new theme, originality – in the sense of novelty and uniqueness – becomes irrelevant. Western designers have always been assessed on their individuality and, as a result, their idea of the shape of women is always changing. With the Japanese theme, which is (perhaps more logically) that

The layered look, Japanese style, by Junko Koshino for Winter 1983–84.

there is only one shape, this major guide to assessing a designer disappears and traditional Western methods of assessment become inappropriate. Designers working on the traditional Japanese basis do not produce designs that are individually and instantly recognizable as a particular person's handwriting, as in the West.

With the Japanese, fashion begins to move into the philosophical world of architecture or music. With shape gone, or at least taken for granted, what is left is scale, proportion, texture, and a stringently disciplined approach to colour. Japanese design has a control and order which have always been part of Japanese visual attitudes whether they be shown in their gardens or in their presentation of food. The Japanese creative rhythm is thorough, logical and inevitable. Also, because it is part of a continuing tradition it can be remarkably subtle by Western standards: Japanese architects actually

The Japanese look for 1984 is epitomized by this simple, ultra-casual dress by Koshino.

include light as an architectural element. Similarly Japanese fashion designers are elemental. Theirs is a new approach, and the Western involvement with changing skirt lengths and fashion details is of scant interest. Paradoxically, their designs are forward-looking because they are rooted in the past and share the timeless quality of the kimono.

The fashion energy which, some predict, could transform Tokyo into the fashion frontier of the nineteen-nineties, is generated from fabrics. Miyake has said 'The most important part in making clothing is to start to design the fabric'. Fabric design is seen as the most fundamental job of the dress designer: Kansai Yamamoto spends as much as 70 per cent of his time on textiles.

The force and vitality of Japanese design comes in large part from the Bunka College of Fashion in Tokyo and its professor, Chie Koike, who was trained at the Chambre Syndicale school in Paris. She has evolved an essentially practical education which has as its primary aim the production of technicians. The vast majority of her students follow the two- or three-year practical courses and only a few go on to the one-year design course. The college is overcrowded but teeming with enthusiasm: the visitor must step over students who are eagerly cutting out even on the corridor floors! Unlike their Western counterparts fashion students in Japan are not excited by individual acclaim. It is important to them that they live up to the Japanese ideal of the individual having credence only when part of a group, working for the common weal. Japanese fashion schools are reputed to produce about 10,000 graduates each year: their future influence on world design must be considerable.

Although it is obvious that the Japanese school of design has already had a real impact on international fashion it would be a mistake to see the handful of designers who show abroad as constituting the whole picture. Japan has its own vast, indigenous fashion identity which, in 1983, had a business turnover of $30 billion. Huge multi-faceted manufacturers specialize in vertical operations whereby the manufacturer not only makes the clothes but also retails them. The Jun group manufactures over 20 brands and has 600 stores in Japan. The Renown group, named after the uniform of the British sailors on H.M.S. *Renown*, has an annual sales turnover of $1 billion. It produces 40 brands of clothing but has diversified to include Renown homes and even a chain of Italian restaurants called Renown Milano. Of individual designers the story is the same: Kansai Yamamoto has a vertical operation whereby his firm is responsible for its own design, manufacture, wholesale and retail.

Of the many designers working and normally only showing in Japan who are achieving an international status through their sales abroad, **Kei Mori**, son of Hanae Mori, designs for Studio V; **Yoshie Inaba**, a Bunka graduate, works for Bigi; **Isao Kaneko** designs for Pink House and **Yukiko Hanai** creates the Madame Hanai range. In case it be thought that the East–West design traffic is all one way it must also be remembered that the German designer **Jürgen Lehl** has worked in Tokyo for the past fourteen years. He began in the Japanese way by designing fabrics for four years before launching his own ready-to-wear line in 1974.

The interplay of oriental-occidental influences will continue. At the moment each side is having an inordinate influence on the other. The young Japanese are as eager to assimilate Western, and especially American, culture as the rest of the world. The West has avidly taken up the outward form of Japanese dressing. The clothes which have so excited Western fashion circles are almost a P.R. exercise for the old Japan. Presented as avant-garde they are in many respects a clinging to the past. This is perhaps right in that Japan's long isolation for much of its history makes the Japanese susceptible to new influences (the impact of the West has become almost cataclysmic in the last decade) and yet has given them such a strong cultural identity that it must re-emerge as the country's dominant force. No amount of Western influence will alter Japan's deeply ritualistic and formal culture which its garments so clearly represent. Japanese clothes are not casual. Like many aspects of the country's culture they are to be viewed coolly, from a distance.

JEAN LOUIS
See LOUIS, Jean

JENNY
See PARIS COUTURE

MR. JOHN
Born Munich, Germany, 1906.
Mary Pickford, Sophie Tucker, the Duchess of Windsor — there is hardly a star, or fashionable international woman, who has not bought at Mr. John. His mother was a German, his father an Italian, and they emigrated to the United States after World War I. Mr. John studied medicine briefly at the University of Lucerne and then moved to Paris to study art at the Sorbonne. While there, he sold sketches to Parisian couturiers. He returned to New York in 1926 and in 1929 opened his own millinery business in association with

A zany melange of patterns for Summer 1984 from Betsey Johnson, America's doyenne of the unexpected.

Fred Fredericks. The firm was called John Fredericks. His success since then has been spectacular, not only in terms of originality, but also in terms of output. He has designed hats for over 1,000 films, including the bonnets worn by Vivien Leigh in *Gone With The Wind*; he has created every type of hat for private customers; he has designed original accessories and dresses, scarves and bags for women; and he has produced a scent called, appropriately enough, 'Chapeau' and a range of men's ties and shirts. In 1943 this industry was rewarded by a Coty award. In 1948 he dissolved his partnership with Fredericks and continued alone. In addition, he has amassed an historic collection of hats, ranging from ones worn by Lady Hamilton to those of Sarah Bernhardt. His customers loved him: one described him as 'such a doll' and pointed out that she always left his salon with more gifts than things for which she had paid.

JOHNSON, Betsey
Born Wethersfield, Connecticut, USA, 1942.
Quaint, unique, nonconformist, uninhibited: all of these words have been used to describe Betsey Johnson and they are all correct. She has been labelled 'anti-fashion' in her design approach, but in reality she is anti-Seventh Avenue. Having studied fine arts at Syracuse University, she was made guest editor on *Mademoiselle* magazine in 1964. At this time she was working on sweaters for friends, an activity which led to a contract designing for Paraphernalia in 1965. Her clothes were bought by assorted ex-First Ladies, film stars and models. She started her own boutique, 'Betsey, Bunky and Nini', in 1969, and in 1978 she founded Betsey Johnson to produce her own sportswear and dresses. In 1971 she received the Coty American Fashion Critics' award, 'Winnie'. She now operates from her own shop and has a thriving mail-order business.

JONES, Stephen
Born West Kirby, England, 1957.
Witty, outrageous, daring and directional are all words used to describe the millinery of Stephen Jones: all are apt. Fantasy and an enormously confident sense of style combine to create dazzlingly original hats which, according to their designer, 'make themselves'. After a foundation year at High Wycombe School of Art from 1975 to 1976, Jones studied at St. Martin's School of Art. He graduated in 1979 and began to make hats for his friends, who tended to be in the pop world and included Steve Strange, Boy George, Jeremiah of Haysi Fantazee, Spandau Ballet and Duran Duran. He opened his first shop in September, 1980, but moved to an atelier in Wardour Street in July, 1981. There he concentrated on a growing personal clientele which ranges from the Princess of Wales to Grace Jones. Stephen Jones also creates hats for several British and French designers, including Benny ONG, Zandra RHODES, Steven LINARD, Jean Paul GAULTIER and Thierry MUGLER.

JOURDAN, Charles
Founded France, 1920.
The eponymous founder of the firm, Charles Jourdan, began his business in the French footwear city of Romans in 1920 and by 1939 his factory was producing 400 pairs of shoes a day. After World War II he was joined by his three sons and together they turned the firm into a 'name' with a world-wide reputation. By 1963 they were producing 650,000 pairs of shoes a year, including a special range for DIOR, with whom a contract had been signed in 1959. In the early 1970s Charles Jourdan was bought by Genesco and it moved into the production of other accessories as well as shoes. In 1979 a ready-to-wear range with an emphasis on leather was produced. In 1980 a Swiss group took over the company, but retained the original name. Charles Jourdan shoes are sold all over the world, either in fashion stores or in Charles Jourdan shops, of which there are seventeen in the United States, nine in France and several in most of the major cities of Europe and South America.

JULIO
Born America, 1955.
Julio's father was an officer in the US army and the family moved around North and Central America during Julio's adolescence. Julio arrived in New York in 1974 to begin his own business. One of his first customers was Bendel's and he also catered very successfully for private customers. In 1976 his firm became the house of Julio, but after six successful years he was forced to close. In January, 1981, he began again with a new company called Julio Espada, which produced clothes with the Julio signature: simple, unornamented and conceived as individual pieces rather than as complete outfits. He went out of business after about a year, but is now back in again doing a small collection of unusual swimwear.

K

KAISERMAN · KAMALI · KANEKO (*See* JAPANESE DESIGN) · KARAN · KASPER · KAWAKUBO (*See* COMME DES GARÇONS) · KENZO
KHANH · KIAM · KIRKPATRICK · KLEIN, A. · KLEIN, C. · KLEIN, R. · KLINE · KLOSS · KOIKE (*See* JAPANESE DESIGN) · KOSHINO
KRIZIA · KUMAGAI

Klein, C.

Kenzo

Klein, R.

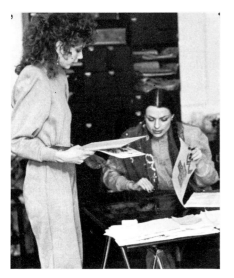

Kamali

Krizia

KAISERMAN, Bill

Born New York City, USA, 1942.
Although he studied drama and is without design training, Kaiserman has had lasting success in the fields of both menswear and women's wear. While working part-time as a clothes salesman in a man's shop, he began to design men's hats. These he introduced under the 'Rafael' label. From such a modest, slightly eccentric, beginning he moved on to leather and suede wear for men and then added shirts and cashmere. By the early 1970s his safari leisure suits had made him an important name in menswear. He then moved into the women's market, still using the 'Rafael' name, to produce a very individual line of casual sportswear and sophisticated day-clothes, made to exacting standards in Italy. They have the same restrained elegance as his menswear and are made in subtle and luxurious fabrics and colours. Kaiserman's clothes reflect the best face of American fashion: beautifully-cut garments which fit the middle-class American woman's lifestyle and work perfectly. His endeavours in the menswear field have been amply recognized. He received the Coty American Fashion Critics' award in 1974 and 1975 and the following year was elected to the Hall of Fame. In 1978 he received a Hall of Fame Citation for his continued contribution to American men's fashion.

KAMALI, Norma ☐

Born New York City, USA, 1945.
Norma Kamali's father owned an ice-cream parlour in Manhattan, where she was brought up. She trained as a fashion illustrator at the Fashion Institute of Technology, from which she graduated in 1964, but began her working life with an airline job which enabled her to spend many weekends in London. She was influenced by London designers like Ossie CLARK and Barbara HULANICKI. She married a Persian and she and her husband opened a shop in 1968 to sell imported English and French clothes in New York. Soon afterwards she began designing her own line, which, although she held no shows, quickly became known for its originality. Kamali Ltd. lasted for ten years. In 1978 she and her husband were

The beautifully simple cotton sweatshirt look which Norma Kamali has made her own. No-problem clothes to live in from her 1983 collection.

Norma Kamali's 1981 look included these vastly over-sized striped shirts worn with loafers and ankle socks for a schoolgirl image.

divorced and OMO Norma Kamali was established (OMO standing for 'On My Own').

Women's Wear Daily has called Kamali 'the arbiter of inventive clothes' and they are right. Her clothes are young, modern and very 'now' and, although she is an adventurous designer, she is never on the lunatic fringe. They are up-to-the-minute because, instead of simply doing two collections a year, she adds new things to her range almost weekly. She has introduced influential looks such as padded jumpsuits, duvet coats, lycra outfits and, probably the most copied, the Ra-Ra skirt. By using materials like parachute fabric and, especially, cotton sweatshirting, she has turned sportswear into streetwear and in the process she has been copied as much as COURRÈGES was in his time. Her empire is based on fleeced cotton and her huge and quilted sleeping bag coats.

In 1982 she introduced 'The Package', a range of all-white holiday clothes in a disposable fabric called Tyvec, which is like very soft nylon paper and can be machine-washed up to twelve times before being discarded. With such radical and original thinking, Norma Kamali seems set to continue as a catalyst and even an iconoclast in the American fashion scene. In 1983 the Council of Fashion Designers of America voted her the outstanding designer of the year. *Time* magazine summed her up as creating 'A combination of 1960s Carnaby Street funk and the locker room'.

KANEKO, Isao

See JAPANESE DESIGN

KARAN, Donna ☐

Born New York, USA, 1948.
Karan's real name is Donna Faske. Her mother was a model and her father a haberdasher. She was obsessed with fashion from a very early age. She attended Parson's School of Design, but did

not finish her course, since a summer job with Anne KLEIN led to a permanent post as designer there. She and Louis DELL'OLIO, who co-designed with her, won the Coty 'Winnie' in 1977 and the Hall of Fame Award in 1982. They jointly received a Coty award for Womenswear in 1984. In 1985 she left to produce her own name range. Her pared-down approach to capsule wardrobe dressing based on separate pieces has quickly put her at the forefront of American design.

KASPER, Herbert

Born New York City, USA. 1926.
Kasper was studying English at the University of New York when World War II interrupted his studies. Service in the army took him to Germany. When he was de-mobilized, he enrolled at Parson's School of Design. After leaving Parson's, he spent two years in Paris, where he worked for FATH and ROCHAS. When he returned to America he worked for several Seventh Avenue firms, designed hats and produced costumes for Broadway revues. In 1953 he joined Joan Leslie. He is now vice-president of the firm. He has received the following Coty American Fashion Critics' awards: 1955 'Winnie'; 1970 Return Award; 1976 Hall of Fame. His forte is high-fashion looks which reflect current trends, but are pared down to high-street levels of acceptability.

KAWAKUBO, Rei

See COMME DES GARÇONS

KENZO ☐

Born Kyoto, Japan, 1940.
Kenzo's name is Kenzo Takada. With MORI, he was in the vanguard of the Japanese move into Paris, and his influence and importance like those of his compatriot, MIYAKE, cannot be over-estimated. His enormous success has helped to encourage other Japanese designers, whether in Tokyo or Paris, who are also producing a very strong, national look which appears to be absolutely right for the times. His parents were hoteliers, but he studied art, not catering, and won top prizes at his art college. He began work

in Japan, but Paris was always his goal. When he was 'bought out' of his apartment by his landlord, he used the money to visit Paris in 1964. Beginning by selling designs to FERAUD and designing several freelance collections, in 1970 he opened his own shop, Jungle Jap, so called because it was entirely decorated with jungle patterns.

Although Kenzo is an admirer of CHANEL, VIONNET and BALENCIAGA (which designers are not?), his work has none of the classicism of the first two, nor the baroque splendour of the latter. However, it does have in common with them all the simplicity and purity of design which is the *sine qua non* of good design, whether couture or *prêt-à-porter*. His designs, largely

Left: For Spring 1982 Kenzo produced flounced and bowed 'little girl' dresses of great charm and wearability.

Below: For Winter 1983-84 Kenzo loosely layers and uses various small scale patterns for dress, vest and stockings.

based on traditional Japanese clothing, are always full of new ideas, always young and always very wearable. He became a 'name' almost immediately with his first collection. For financial reasons it was made in cotton, often quilted, and young fashion leaders took to the look instantly. His real impact was made with his revolutionary and totally contemporary knit-wear, which revitalized the knitwear industry. Kenzo is a trend-setter whose influence is felt in all areas of fashion. Smilingly, inscrutably silent, he is a pro-lific producer of ideas. He makes hundreds of sketches for each collection, three-quarters of which are never made. When not working, he is travelling or gambling — both of which pastimes are obsessive. This

Above: *Cashmere layering for uncomplicated and casual shapes by Kenzo.*

Right: *Kenzo at his most Japanese. Like his fellow countrymen in Paris, for Winter 1983–84 Kenzo produced a look which was decidedly ethnic, taking elements from several tribes.*

small, unassuming Japanese, whose empire now includes men's clothes, is always smiling and, indeed, he has every reason to be so.
See also JAPANESE DESIGN.

KHANH, Emmanuelle
Born Plain, France, 1937.
Emmanuelle Khanh is married to the Vietnamese furniture designer, Quasar Khanh. She was a model at BALENCIAGA and GIVENCHY before starting to design in 1959. Her first job was with CACHAREL, but by 1963 she was designing her own clothes and almost single-handedly bringing the youth fashion movement to Paris. She was a revolutionary force and her design philosophy is summed up in her

remark: 'This is the century of sex. I want to make the sexiest clothes'. Her rebellion against haute couture and her determination to make soft and gentle clothes had a considerable effect upon fashion in France and, indeed, the world. *Look* featured her on its cover and American stores began to buy in considerable amounts. Like those of Biba her clothes, when she was first making her impact in the late 1960s, had an exaggerated 1930s feeling: big collars, droopy reveres and long clinging jackets. The look was given its final touch of distinction by the largest possible pair of spectacles. A very individualistic designer, Khanh survived the 1960s and continued to produce feminine clothes which, because they are soft and relaxed, remain sexy and seductive.

KIAM, Omar
Born Monterey, Mexico, 1894.
Died New York City, USA, 1954.
Born Alexander Kiam and taking Omar from a nickname given to him by his classmates, this American ready-to-wear and film designer began his career as a stockboy in a millinery firm at the age of eighteen. Two years later he was promoted to the post of designer. In 1912 he arrived in New York, where he freelanced as a designer under his Omar Kiam name. He designed dramatic clothes and furs and it is not surprising that in 1935 he signed a contract with Samuel Goldwyn to design for such stars as Merle Oberon and Loretta Young, both on and off the screen. He worked in Hollywood for many years and the theatricality of his designs perfectly suited the mood of the place and the times. In 1941 he signed a contract to produce designs for a large ready-to-wear manufacturer in New York, in addition to his West Coast enterprises. He won a Coty American Fashion Critics' 'Winnie' in 1946.

KIRKPATRICK, Gayle
Born Mississippi, USA.
After studying art at Memphis, Tennessee, Kirkpatrick began to work in advertising and fashion-illustration. He moved to New York in 1957. After one year he was working as a sketcher on Seventh Avenue. He

then went on to design sporty, non-establishment clothes which brought him a Coty award in 1965. In some respects ahead of his time Kirkpatrick introduced the African look and the 1940s revival. He used nailheads on leather long before Punks and ALAÏA had been heard of. As a sportswear designer, his contribution to American looks has been an important one.

KLEIN, Anne ☐
Born New York City, USA, 1923.
Died New York City, USA, 1974.
Anne Klein's real name was Hannah Golofski. She began as a sketcher on Seventh Avenue, at the age of fifteen, in 1938. By 1948 she and her first husband,

Left: A silk and wool tweed blazer, a white silk blouse with detachable black collar and a black gabardine pencil skirt. Polished dressing by Donna Karan and Louis Dell'Olio for Anne Klein, Spring 1983.

Below: Louis Dell'Olio and Donna Karan create a distinctive look for Anne Klein, Summer 1984, with loose-necked shirts, big jackets and culottes in linen.

Ben Klein, were able to form their own company, Junior Sophisticates. In 1968 she and her second husband founded Anne Klein and Company and Anne Klein Studio, both of which became part of the Takihyo Company in 1973. After her death in 1974 the firm continued with Donna KARAN and Louis DELL'OLIO as designers. She was a respected member of the American fashion scene and her work and achievements received recognition in many awards: the Neiman-Marcus Award (1959 and 1969); the Coty American Fashion Critics' Award (1955); a 'Winnie' (1969); a Return Award; and election to the Hall of Fame (1971).

Anne Klein was a pioneer and an innovator who helped to change the concept of 'young dressing' by taking a fresh and individual look at what the young were like and how they lived their lives. She designed clothes to fit their life-style. She replaced cuteness with sophistication, while retaining freshness. Her clothes in the young, sporty field in the 1950s and 1960s were to what had gone before as *West Side Story* was to *Carousel*. She understood very early the American woman's need for a blazer, a good pair of trousers and some skirts, all competitively priced and well-designed. This understanding laid the basis for her great success. She was one of the designers invited to show at the Grand Divertissement at Versailles in 1973.

KLEIN, Calvin

Born New York City, USA, 1942.
Klein graduated from the Fashion Institute of Technology in 1962, worked for a time as a coat designer on Seventh Avenue, then started on his own when his friend, Barry Schwartz, the manager of a Harlem supermarket, lent him $2,000 in 1968. He began with three dresses and six coats, which Mildred Custin bought for Bonwit's. Klein delivered them to the store himself and they began to sell instantly. Since then the business set up by Klein and Schwartz has grown to such an extent that his name is now known all over the world.

His first coats were young classics, inspired by Yves SAINT LAURENT, but using American colours. Since then he has found his own distinctive style, which is more European than that of many of his New York colleagues. He eschews gimmicks and over-designed looks and designs simple, classic clothes in mohair, cashmere, wool and suede. His colour sense is subtle in an almost Italian way. Supple, elegant and understated, his clothes fulfil his comment: 'I like clothes that slide when the body moves'.

In addition to his ready-to-wear, furs, shoes, bags and bed-linen, menswear, make-up and, of course, scent bear the Klein label. Handsome, married and divorced, he has one child (who survived a kidnap attempt). Calvin Klein has, for many, the charisma of a superstar. His designer jeans have become an almost talismanic status symbol. The whole new

Checks and spots are teamed with solid colour in this Calvin Klein three piece outfit for Summer 1983.

approach to fashion based on jeans-inspired dressing may prove to be his most lasting memorial. Klein was the first designer to win the Coty American Fashion Critics' Award in three consecutive years. In 1973 he was awarded a 'Winnie', in 1974 a Return Award and in 1975 he was elected to the Hall of Fame. In the same year his fur designs won him a Coty Special Award. His fashion philosophy follows on from Claire McCARDELL's soft, supple and sexy sports clothes and, like her, he makes clothes which have a safely realistic wearability.

The low slung blouson and large pleated skirt are 'signature' looks from Roland Klein in Summer 1983.

KLEIN, Roland

Born Rouen, France, 1938.
After studying from 1955 to 1957 at L'École de la Chambre Syndicale, where his contemporaries were SCHERRER and GIUDICELLI, Klein went to work for that other son of Normandy, Christian DIOR. He was with him from 1960 to 1962 and there, in the tailoring room, he learned the basis of couture, which is cut. In 1962 he moved to PATOU where he was LAGERFELD's assistant. This was a highly educative experience for Klein, who considers Lagerfeld to have been the greatest influence on

An elegantly understated evening look from Roland Klein's 1974 collection.

his work. He left Patou in 1965 and moved to London to learn English. He joined the firm of Marcel Fenez and became managing director in 1973 with his own label. He opened his own shop in 1979. His background and training in the traditions of French couture are evident in his clothes, which are elegant, unfussy, well-cut and correctly made.

KLINE, Don

Born Near Pittsburgh, Pennsylvania, USA.

A slight rarity in America, in that he is a highly successful milliner in an age when hats are not considered an important part of a woman's appearance, Kline graduated from the Fashion Institute of Technology in 1969 and began work for the hatter, Emme. After a brief flirtation with sportswear he returned to millinery, selling his hats to Bendel's and Bergdorf's. In 1976 he began doing ready-to-wear and in 1978 he added furs. His retail boutique was opened in 1977. In 1973 he received the Coty Special Award for hats. His hats are popular with some of America's best-known designers, who use them to complete their look.

KLOSS, John

Born Detroit, Michigan, USA, 1937.

Kloss' real name is John Klosowski. After studying architecture in Detroit and finance in New York, he enrolled at the Traphagen School to study fashion. His student work was so impressive that he was offered a job in Paris by the American couturier, Bugnand. He worked for him briefly. While he was in Paris Nina RICCI offered him a job, but he preferred to return to New York. By the age of twenty-one he had set up on his own. Bendel's studio, part of the Henri Bendel store, manufactured and distributed his designs: his was the first 'single-designer' boutique the store set up. Kloss became known for his designs for Cira, the sleep and loungewear manufacturers, and he won the Coty Special Award in 1971 and 1974 for lingerie. In 1973 he became one of the Kreisler group. He now designs dresses, lingerie, tennis clothes and home-sewing patterns.

187

KOIKE, Chie
See JAPANESE DESIGN

KOSHINO, Hiroko
Born Tokyo, Japan, 1938.
Well known in Tokyo, where she has been an established designer for several years, Koshino first showed in Paris, as part of the increasing Japanese presence in that city, in 1983. Her designs are based on the traditional Japanese kimono, but they are voluminous in scale and layered. The ethnic feel is continued with obi sashes and bamboo and bird prints. Silk, cotton and linen, used for overlarge tops, dresses and trousers, are the essence of her look.
See also JAPANESE DESIGN.

KRIZIA
Founded Milan, Italy, 1954.
The firm of Krizia, with Mariucca Mandelli as its head of design and her husband, Aldo Pinto, as business manager, is one of the longest-established fashion houses in Milan. Mandelli was originally a primary school teacher, but she had always been interested in dressmaking and in the early 1950s she became increasingly frustrated with the clothes that she saw in the shops in Milan. This resulted in her making up her own designs with a friend, Flora Dolci. They began with skirts, which Mandelli personally took around Italy to sell directly to the shops. She thus obtained a valuable feed-back from street level, experience on which she was able to capitalize. By 1954 her venture had grown to include a *première* and six workers. Krizia, a name taken from Plato's dialogue on women's vanity, had its first exhibition in 1957. It immediately attracted the interest of press

Left: *For Spring 1982 Mariucca Mandelli for Krizia took college blazer stripes for a simple side buttoned dress and added an amusing neckline treatment.*

Below: *Krizia wit and flair are seen at their best in this accordion-pleated evening look.*

and buyers. Even at this early stage the originality and wit of Mandelli's designs was apparent. Dresses made of photo-printed cloth, with a fruit motive, showed that youthful fantasy of approach which is still apparent in her work today. In this early period, Walter ALBINI worked for Krizia and was the chief design collaborator for three years. More recently LAGERFELD has worked as design consultant to the firm, which now produces 10 collections a year and has 17 boutiques and 21 licensees.

Kriziamaglia has been very influential in the field of knitwear, especially in its use of unusual yarns, arresting colour combinations and new techniques: the animal sweaters of 1980 had an enormous influence and the idea was copied world-wide. Mariucca Mandelli has proved to be a lasting and formidable talent, producing young, humorous and carefree clothes which have been an inspiration to many designers. The Krizia themes are always witty and the clothes have *panache*. Their humour frequently makes one smile with pleasure, a rare and welcome thing in fashion. Mandelli has a Milan apartment, a Lake Como home and a place in Sardinia. She has been known to call herself a socialist.

KUMAGAI, Tokio
Born Sendai, Japan, 1948.
Tokio Kumagai, the Japanese shoe designer, graduated from the Bunka college of design in 1970. His designs won him a prize which included a trip to France, and he arrived in Paris in the same year. Almost immediately he found work. He designed ranges for CASTELBAJAC, Pierre D'Alby and Rodier, before moving to Italy to work with CERRUTI. He returned to Paris, where he opened his first boutique in 1980 in the Place des Victoires. This was followed by a second boutique in the rue du Faubourg Saint-Honoré. His fame as a shoe designer rests on designs based on the work of artists such as Dali, Kandinsky, Pollock, Mondrian and MAN RAY*. He reproduces their art in hand-painted versions on his shoes, using a wide range of materials. These abstract and surreal designs have become collector's items.
See also JAPANESE DESIGN.

L

LACHASSE · LAFAURIE (*See* PARIS COUTURE) · LAGERFELD · LANCETTI · LANE · LANVIN · LAPIDUS · LAROCHE · LATIMER · LAUG
LAUREN · LA VIOLA · LECOMTE (*See* PARIS COUTURE) · LEHL (*See* JAPANESE DESIGN) · LELONG · LENA (*See* EDINA AND LENA)
LEONARDI (*See* BIKI) · LESER · LEVINE · LEVI STRAUSS · LINARD · LONDON DESIGNER COLLECTIONS · LOUIS · LOUISEBOULANGER
(*See* PARIS COUTURE) · LUCAS · LUCILE

Lagerfeld

Lancetti

Lanvin

Left: *Lauren*

189

LACHASSE

Founded London, England, 1928.

The couture firm of Gray, Paulette and Shingleton set up Lachasse as a boutique-style offshoot for sports and country wear. The firm's first designer was Digby MORTON and the new establishment was an immediate success. Morton produced classic English tweeds, cut in a softer more sophisticated way than previously and able to

A modified 'New Look' suit from Lachasse. The precision of cut in the jacket is a hallmark of this firm which, although it has had several different designers, has always been known for impeccable tailoring.

'be worn with confidence at the Ritz'. His success encouraged him to start his own business in 1933. Hardy AMIES succeeded him at Lachasse – he wrote a description of a dress which so impressed Mrs. Shingleton that he obtained the job. He remained until 1939. After World War II a milliner, MICHAEL, was appointed and became the only designer to have his name on the label: 'Michael at Lachasse'. On Michael's departure, Mr. Owen became the designer, a post which he held until 1974. During his time CLIVE was employed to design blouses and Peter Crown, the present designer, became increasingly involved in design. Crown took over from Owen in 1974 and is now chairman, managing director and chief designer. In the 1960s and 1970s Lachasse was exclusively haute couture, but in 1981 a mini-boutique was opened. Peter Crown compares Lachasse to an elegant octopus. It has taken in many businesses, especially milliners, which have brought in skilled workroom technicians and customers. In addition to dressing Princess Marina and Lady Edwina Mountbatten, Lachasse has dressed films, television shows and the theatre. Once, no less than three productions on the London stage at the same time had Lachasse costumes. Lachasse is one of the longest-surviving fashion houses in the world and continues to serve an international, aristocratic clientele. The firm was a member of the Incorporated Society of London Fashion Designers.

LAFAURIE, Jeanne

See PARIS COUTURE

LAGERFELD, Karl ☐

Born Hamburg, Germany, 1939.

Lagerfeld's mother was German, but his father was Swedish. His background was wealthy, his family having made a milk fortune. He arrived in Paris at the age of fourteen and by the time of his sixteenth birthday, having won, along with Yves SAINT LAURENT, an International Wool Secretariat competition in 1954, he was working for BALMAIN. Not happy with the atmosphere at Balmain, he left within three years to become a freelance designer for various firms, including KRIZIA. An ex-

High style in this Chloë outfit for Winter 1979 by Lagerfeld. The perfect scale of the hat and accessories enhances the purity of the coat's cut.

perienced, highly professional designer, he joined Chloe in the early 1960s and was given an almost total *carte blanche*. In 1965 he began designing furs for the FENDI sisters. His freelance activities have also included knits for Ballantyne, clothes for Alma, shoes for Mario VALENTINO, men's clothes for Club Roman Fashion and, most recently, CHANEL couture – a job he was offered, but which he rejected, in 1973.

Lagerfeld is one of fashion's polymaths. His expensive, exquisite clothes for Chloe were almost couture standard. Ultra shapely, they were noted for hand-work and extravagant beading and were at the top of the de-luxe ready-to-wear market. Ever since his 1972 Deco collection, which brought world-wide acclaim for his black-

Above: *Winter 1983–84 saw Lagerfeld using soft checked wool for draped and caped suits which were elegant and flattering. This gently tied jacket is a good example of the perfection which this look can achieve in the hands of a master.*

Right: *Lagerfeld cuts and trims his 1984 Chloë collection in an extravagant and witty trompe l'oeil 'dressmaker' collection. The hair completes the fantasy.*

Scissors-belts and bobbin-bracelets enliven Lagerfeld's final collection for Chloë for summer 1984. Scottie-dog printed silk skirt, two-tone jacket and halter neckline add up to an irreverent but amusing look.

and-white prints and brilliant bias cutting, his collections have been more and more influential. His furs for Fendi are equally successful and important. Exotic, inventive, they have a baroque magnificence. Talking of fashion, Lagerfeld has referred to 'intellectual sexiness', which perfectly describes the clothes he designs. His influence is considerable because he is not afraid to make a real fashion statement: he is uniquely confident, takes new directions courageously and never looks back. His collections show a total concept and, when he takes a new point of view or introduces a changed silhouette, he does so boldly and with complete conviction. In the autumn of 1983 he produced his last collection for Chloe (now designed by

Guy Paulin) and took over complete responsibility for Chanel ready-to-wear, working with the stylist Gilles du Four, in addition to the couture, which he had designed for two seasons. In March 1984 he presented his first collection under his own name.

Lagerfeld's shows are incredible: hair, make-up and accessories all make a strong statement and mean something in putting over his new message. With his love of the 18th century, his fans and his pigtail, Lagerfeld is a stylish figure. But, above all, he is a design genius whose clothes startle, but never shock. His skill and taste are revealed by the cheap vulgarity of those who try to copy his clothes without possessing his disciplined flamboyance.

LANCETTI, Pino

Born Perugia, Italy, 1932.

Lancetti moved to Rome after studying fine art at the Art Institute of Perugia. In 1950 he began selling sketches to designers such as SIMONETTA, SCHUBERTH and FONTANA. He worked in ceramics before joining Princess Giovannelli as a designer in her high-fashion house. He then worked for CAROSA before opening his own house in 1961. In 1963 he created his 'Military Line', which made his name as one of the major Rome-based Italian designers. Highly respected in his own country, but not well known outside it, Lancetti is a craftsman and perfectionist. As a colourist he is exceptional and his print designs, which he evolves in a remarkably creative partnership with Etro, the famous Como silk manufacturers, influence designers not only in Italy, but also in London, Paris and New York. They prompted *Women's Wear Daily* to refer to his creations as clothes for a 'gypsy wonder woman'.

Lancetti's clothes are strong and colourful, as one might expect from a trained painter, and his evening looks, based on subtly coloured silk chiffon prints, are extraordinarily beautiful. Although he is really in the couture tradition, he produces a line of ready-to-wear called 'Lei'. Shy and retiring, but with considerable artistic integrity, Lancetti is an underrated creative force in Italian fashion.

LANE, Kenneth Jay

Born Detroit, Michigan, USA, 1932.

After studying at the University of Michigan and the Rhode Island School of Design, Lane began work in the art department of *Vogue* magazine. A meeting with Roger VIVIER led to a job as his assistant with Delmar shoes. Lane also worked as Vivier's assistant in Paris, working on shoes for Christian DIOR. In 1963 he began to experiment with jewellery in his spare time. Photographic coverage in the magazines meant that only a year later he was concentrating on jewellery design, for which in 1966 he won a Coty Special Award. It was followed by a Neiman-Marcus Award in 1968. Since 1972 his company has been privately owned. It is known for the daring and original mixture of precious gems and plastic, which Lane considers to be *the* modern medium for jewellery design.

LANVIN, Jeanne

Born Brittany, France, 1867.
Died Paris, France, 1946.

Jeanne Lanvin's world-renowned house was based modestly enough on clothes designed for her daughter and the daughters of friends. From such beginnings she became a name which, through her famous perfumes such as 'Arpège' and 'My Sin', is still widely known today. Efficient and imaginative, she was apprenticed to a dressmaker when only thirteen and became a milliner with Talbot's at the

Left: *Klimt-inspired embroidery was used to stunning effect in this afternoon coat designed by Lanvin in 1919.*

Below: *The Lanvin evening look for 1951: figure-hugging, embroidered and be-jewelled. This is an evening dress for romantic poses more than ballroom activity.*

Left: *Castillo uses pure silk to create a dramatically elegant Spanish look for Lanvin. Purity of line and controlled proportions ensure that an entrance in this theatrical ensemble would silence all cocktail chat.*

age of twenty-three. She developed her children's clothes into a commercial proposition and, just before World War I, began to introduce adult clothing, often based on a mother-and-daughter theme. By the end of the war, at the age of fifty-one, Jeanne Lanvin was the head of a prosperous couture establishment. Although she cannot be claimed as a major design talent or, indeed, a consistent design originator, she answered a need felt in many quarters. Her romantic picture dresses were in some respects above and beyond the vagaries of current fashion changes. Her fame as a designer was consolidated by her introduction of the chemise in the early war years: it was a pointer to the future, not least in the reception it got from the young, who were soon to edge into the

Three young and not-too-serious ways with knickerbockers from Lanvin. The right-hand coat is exceptionally interesting and well cut.

to Paris in his early twenties and opened his own small house to produce clothes for individual customers. He also designed for mass-production manufacturers, and early on produced a safari jacket which sold in its millions. Lapidus was much involved in the menswear revolution of the early 1960s and was in at the beginning of the unisex movement. He is essentially a practical designer who feels that creativity without technology is meaningless in modern terms. He understands that the designer is only as good as his manufacturing, distributing and retailing areas. This attitude has ensured that his designs are distributed world-wide, either in his own boutiques or in selected outlets.

LAROCHE, Guy

Born La Rochelle, France, 1923.
Laroche's family was in the cattle farming business and he entered fashion with no

An example of late fifties fashion from Guy Laroche. A simple top spreads into a bouffant skirt with baroque twists and swags reminiscent of eighteenth century curtain treatments.

position of fashion leaders, ousting their plump mothers. Lanvin is generally claimed as the first designer to open a boutique for men (in 1926).

Lanvin's administrative ability was recognized in 1937, when at the age of seventy she was appointed president of the Haute Couture committee of the Paris Exhibition. Two years later she was elected the Paris representative at the New York World's Fair. It was fitting that on her death the firm was taken over by her daughter, Princesse de Polignac – the very daughter whose dresses had, years previously, been the catalyst for the career of Lanvin, the dress designer. As designer she employed CASTILLO who, in 1963, handed over to CRAHAY. Crahay is now design director and creates the haute

couture lines. Maryll Lanvin, wife of Bernard Lanvin, the company president, designs the ready-to-wear collections. The Lanvin menswear range is designed by Patrick Lavoix.

Major perfumes: My Sin (1925); Arpège (1927); Scandal (1931).

LAPIDUS, Ted

Born Paris, France, 1929.
Lapidus is the son of Russian emigrés. His father was a tailor. Lapidus spent time in Japan studying technology at a Tokyo technical school, concluding this in 1949. He believed that the advanced technology which had put Japan in the forefront of radio and camera production should be brought to bear on fashion. He returned

Guy Laroche sprints into the future with a selection of looks from his 1957 collection. All five outfits are characteristic of the late fifties, with lines which were acceptable everywhere.

formal design training, although he had gained some experience as a milliner. He worked in America on Seventh Avenue for three years and then returned to Paris. After working for DESSÈS for eight years, he started on his own in 1957 with a small collection which he showed in his apartment. By 1961 he had his own couture house and boutique; menswear followed in 1966; one year later he introduced a scent. Laroche's name is licensed to a wide range of products for men and women and

Guy Laroche used black wool and silk for this high-waisted cocktail dress in his Autumn 1958 collection. The sophisticated elegance of the pared-down dress is enhanced by a provocative hat and formal suede gloves.

Skilful cutting makes this Prince of Wales check dress and jacket by Guy Laroche in 1958 a good example of the art of Paris in the late fifties. The trompe l'oeil *effect of the jacket, although appearing contrived to our eyes, shows great mastery.*

Delicate gathering creates a scallop effect on this high-waisted dress by Guy Laroche, which is feminine and flattering. It is from his 1963 collection. The false eye lashes and exaggerated hair style characterized the period.

For Spring 1963 Guy Laroche used black silk chiffon to create a short evening dress with a cape bordered in satin ribbon. The look is relaxed but elegant.

he has a network of international boutiques. In the late 1960s he sold a large interest in his business, first to Bernard Cornfeld, and later to L'Oréal, the hair product manufacturers. Laroche designs young clothes in the spirit of the moment.

Major perfume: Fidji (1966).

LATIMER, Hubert

Born Atlanta, Georgia, USA, 1927.
After studying design in Los Angeles and spending a period with the American ready-to-wear firm of DIOR (Christian Dior New York), Latimer joined Mollie PARNIS in 1973. He was her assistant designer until 1977, when he established his own firm. He returned to Parnis in 1979. His clothes are worldly and ageless – not for him the endless search for novelty.

LAUG, André

Born Alsace, France, 1932.
Died Rome, Italy, 1984
After a brief period in Paris working with RICCI and COURRÈGES, Laug moved to Italy, where he became ANTONELLI's designer. He opened his own house in Rome in 1968. He presents his high-fashion range there and his ready-to-wear line in Milan. Like many Rome-based designers, he designs for a very specific market. His clientele are wealthy. They require the look of the moment in a wearable form and this is Laug's forte. He presents beautifully cut, intelligently fabricated clothes, using the best materials and the most subtle colours. His look is *chic*, his silhouette is classic, and his making-up is of a very high order. He is one of that band of worthy clothes-makers who create garments to be worn with confidence and charm and who, although they and their clothes are often over-shadowed by louder fashion voices, continue the traditions of dressmaking by producing perfectly beautiful, well-bred clothes. When Mrs. CHASE* said of PIGUET and MOLYNEUX that they made 'clothes designed to be worn by ladies, not to take your breath away', she could have been talking about Laug and the others in that band of internationally admired craftsmen who are frequently underestimated by a sensation-hungry press.

LAUREN, Ralph ☐

Born New York City, USA, 1939.
Lauren's real name is Lipschitz. He is currently one of the very big names on the American fashion scene. His background is not unlike that of Italy's colossus, ARMANI. He had no design training, but after studying business methods at night school while selling ties at Brooke Brothers, he became assistant buyer at Allied Stores. Again, like Armani, he designed men's clothes before he began a women's wear range. In 1968 'Polo by Ralph Lauren' was created to produce very understated men's clothes combining English taste with American dash. Three years later his women's range was born: as a result of the success of his men's range, Bloomingdales asked him to design a few pieces for women, keeping the same relaxed feeling. Since then he has not looked back – scents, luggage, boyswear, his cheaper men's range, 'Chaps', and, perhaps the most audacious coup of all, 'Polo Western Wear' in 1979. Although there was very little design in this range it was hugely successful. Its 'Wild West' feel answered some deep nostalgia, latent not only in American men and women, but in many other parts of the world.

Lauren has developed his work by digging deeper into the prairie, homesteader tradition. He has produced quilted patchwork skirts, jumpers based on early samplers, and denim: the whole American frontier scene in fact. Whether or not this is fashion design is debatable, but its popularity is beyond question. All of these looks have sold to a phenomenal extent despite their very high prices. Ralph Lauren has the ability to create a look which has world-wide appeal. In 1973 his men's clothes for *The Great Gatsby* were very influential and his *Annie Hall* costumes in 1978 created a way of dressing which is still a potent influence today.

In 1973 Lauren received the Neiman-Marcus Award and the Coty American Fashion Critics' Award has come to him no less than six times: the 1970 Men's Award, the 1973 Return Men's Award, a 1974 'Winnie', the 1976 Hall of Fame Men's Wear, 1976 Women's Wear Return Award, and the 1977 Hall of Fame

Ralph Lauren's quintessentially American look: Madras plaid shirt and stone washed denim jacket are combined to create a relaxed, no fuss style. Note the jacket fastenings which are reminiscent of Bonnie Cashin's of twenty years earlier.

For 1984 Ralph Lauren uses linen to create a pre World War I look which is nostalgic and retrospective. These are clothes for playing a role: romantic, soft and feminine.

Women's Wear. His love of tweed and natural materials, his treatment of them in a sophisticated way, and the sheer wearability of his clothes suggest that for a very long time Ralph Lauren will continue to make a very special, very American contribution to fashion. His inspirations are all American and he seems to be his own catalyst. His style has been copied everywhere.

In 1986 he took over the Rhinelander building in New York to sell his uniquely popular look. He also opened a shop in Paris, in addition to his London shop.

LA VIOLA, Claudio
Born Milan, Italy, 1948.
La Viola's father was a lawyer, but Claudio rebelled against the legal profession and at the age of sixteen began designing his

own shirts and jackets and having them made up. In 1966, when he was only eighteen, he rented a store in Milan which he called Barba's. In 1976, having worked as a design consultant to various firms, he joined forces with Pierluigi Rovescalli and Tiziano Gusti to create 'La Viola'. His adventurous, fresh approach to men's and women's sportswear proved a considerable success and he now designs several collections in addition to his own. These include knitwear, leatherwear for men and women and, perhaps best known, 'Incontro by Viola', which is a high-class women's wear line. In addition, he has various franchises, for accessories that include ties, scarves and jewellery.

LECOMTE, Germaine
See PARIS COUTURE

Left: The American folk heroine, homespun and wholesome, as seen by Ralph Lauren in his 1982 collection.

LEHL, Jürgen
See JAPANESE DESIGN

LELONG, Lucien
Born Paris, France, 1889.
Died Biarritz, France, 1958.
Like PIGUET, Lelong was less a designer than a co-ordinator, responsible for encouraging and employing such luminaries as DIOR, BALMAIN and GIVENCHY. In fact, he wished Dior to take over from him as head of the firm, but he did not get on with Balmain, who called him 'a dealer in dresses', not a designer.

Lelong came from a fashion background, his father being a successful dressmaker. It was for him that Lelong produced his first collection, when he was only fourteen years old.

After being invalided out of the army in World War I, he opened his own establishment with 12 sewers, a fitter and a vendeuse. By 1926 he was employing 1,200. During the 1920s and 1930s he became famous as a designer and as a member of sophisticated Parisian society. He was early on the scene with perfume and established Parfums Lelong in 1926. By 1934 he had created a ready-to-wear line separate from his couture: one of the earliest designers to do so. As his fame grew, so did his house style. The woman who dressed at Lelong could be sure of the highest quality of workmanship allied to a distinguished line of elegantly acceptable day dresses and understated evening wear. His look was ladylike.

During World War II, Lelong's courage and determination came to the fore. Having been made the President of the Chambre Syndicale de la Couture in 1937, he had the responsibility of dealing with the Germans, as the spokesman of French couture, when they overran his country. In 1940 the German authorities wanted all French couture to be moved to Berlin and re-created as a German industry. Lelong went to Berlin and finally persuaded the Germans that it was an impossible dream: Paris fashion must remain

Miss Europe of 1930 looking serious in a Lelong dress and coat of silk, the dress having a demure pleated lace collar to enhance the lady-like look.

A masterly way of tailoring striped wool in this suit from the house of Lelong in 1941. The jacket length, the large pockets and the totally unrelated hat are all typical of the fashion of the time.

French. Having succeeded, he re-opened in 1941 with Dior and Balmain as designers. By doing so he helped keep the flame of fashion flickering in its rightful home. After the Liberation, he went to America to persuade buyers to return. At first he was only partly successful, and their return over the following two years was gradual. Only when his protégé, Dior, introduced the 'New Look' in 1947 did they come flooding back. Ironically, that was the year of Lelong's retirement.

Major perfumes: The house of Lelong produced no less than 27 fragrances, seven in 1939 alone. The best known survivors are Indiscret (1936) and Sirocco (1947).

LENA
See EDINA AND LENA

LEONARDI, Elvira
See BIKI

LESER, Tina
Born Philadelphia, USA, 1911.
A sadly underpraised innovator on the American fashion scene, Tina Leser began her career in 1935, when she opened a store in Honolulu to sell her own designs to friends and tourists. Her hallmarks were the use of beautiful and often unconventional fabrics and her emphasis on play clothes. After the Japanese attack on Pearl Harbor, she returned to New York in 1942. In 1943 she began to concentrate on glamorous sportswear. She specialized in hand-painted prints long before PUCCI, developed harem pyjamas long before GALITZINE, and produced toreador pants long before SAINT LAURENT. From 1943 to 1953 she worked with a business associate. Then, in 1953, she started her own business. Her eclectic approach to the ethnic looks of the world, her use of Chinese brocades, Japanese kimono silks, Indian sari cloths, Hawaiian hand-painted prints and Mexican satins were often pioneering. She is also credited with designing the first cashmere dress. Her honours range from a Coty Fashion Critics' Award and a Neiman-Marcus Award in 1945 to a US Department of Commerce Citation in 1957.

LEVINE (Herbert and Beth)
Founded USA, 1949.
The Levines played an important part in the American shoe business from 1949 to their semi-retirement in 1975. Their contribution to shoe design is especially strong in the field of boots: they created the stretch boot, thereby lightening the traditionally heavy article. At the other end of the scale, they were responsible for many variations on the lightweight sandal, including one made of vinyl. A Neiman-Marcus Award in 1954 was followed by the Coty American Fashion Critics' Award in 1967 and 1973.

LEVI STRAUSS
Levis are not only a word in a dictionary. They were the precursors of a uniform which transcends class, nationality and age. The original Levi Strauss arrived in San Francisco during the Gold Rush of the 1850s to sell tents to the prospectors, but since trousers were needed more desperately than tents, the enterprising entrepreneur cut up his tents and had the material made up into simple, functional and hard-wearing trousers for prospectors. The demand was enormous and his fortune was made. The trousers were to fulfil the need for hard, tough workwear and, to prevent tearing at the stress points, Levi-Strauss introduced rivets in 1873. They became a trademark. He would be amazed to learn that, since the 1960s, his humble workwear has become so sexy and glamorous that it actually won a Coty Special Award in 1971. Levi Strauss remains a family firm.

LINARD, Stephen
Born London, England, 1959.
Linard studied fashion at the Southend College of Technology from 1975 to 1978 and graduated with a diploma in fashion design. From 1978 to 1981 he followed a fashion course at the St. Martin's School of Art, from which he graduated with first-class honours. He immediately joined Notre Dame X and designed for them for two seasons before deciding to work alone. His first collection under his own name was shown in Paris as well as London in the spring of 1982. He introduced his

menswear in Paris in the spring of 1983. The rapid rate of success of Stephen Linard reflects his originality: he is in that special British mould of eccentricity and inventiveness which includes Antony PRICE, Vivienne WESTWOOD and Zandra RHODES. Although all very different in their approach to design, they have in common a creativity which springs from their own fantasies. Linard designs a total look with an overall image (including hair and make-up) exactly as on the drawing board. His 'Gangster' and 'Immigrant' collections showed how attuned he is to the attitudes and fashion demands of the urban young in Great Britain at the beginning of the 1980s. In 1983 the Japanese firm, Jun, decided to back Linard and provided him with a design studio in London and a show outlet in Tokyo.

LONDON DESIGNER COLLECTIONS
Founded 1975.
This co-operative of London designers, which has included some of the more interesting young British fashion designers to emerge in the years since its foundation, is organized and run by Annette Worsley Taylor. Members are elected and work at the top end of ready-to-wear. In addition to their individual fashion shows, they show their collections at an exhibition twice a year. By banding together, costs are reduced and efficiency and impact increased. Current members and associates include BELLVILLE SASSOON, Benny ONG, Bruce OLDFIELD, Christopher TRILL, EDINA AND LENA, Gina FRATINI, Hardy AMIES, Thea PORTER, Wendy DAGWORTHY, Zandra RHODES, Jean MUIR, MAXFIELD PARRISH, Roland KLEIN and Jacques AZAGURY.

LOUIS, Jean
Born Paris, France, 1907.
Louis Berthault, which is Jean Louis' real name, began work in Paris with DRÉCOLL after studying at an art school. With the compensation he received from a taxi accident, he crossed the Atlantic and arrived in New York in 1935, unable to speak any English. He was hired by Hattie CARNEGIE and one of his first designs was bought by the film star, Irene Dunne. After this promising start he remained with Carnegie for seven years and during that time he designed for the Duchess of Windsor and Gertrude Lawrence. Hired by Columbia Pictures in 1943 as their head designer, he was responsible for creating some of the most glamorous, high-fashion film costumes of the 1940s. Perhaps the most famous were for the Rita Hayworth movie, *Gilda*. He was nominated twenty-two times for Oscars for his work in films. He left Columbia in 1958 to open his couture salon in Los Angeles to provide clothes for the stars' private lives and he made them as glamorous and costly as those they wore in their films. His venture thrived and he was able to establish a wholesale dress business also.

LOUISEBOULANGER
See PARIS COUTURE

LUCAS, Otto
Born Germany, 1903.
Died Belgium, 1971.
After a period spent in Paris and Berlin to learn the milliner's trade, Lucas moved to London, where he opened his Mayfair salon in 1932. From that time until his sudden death in an aeroplane crash his business grew ever more successful and his hats were bought by major shops on both sides of the Atlantic. They were also bought by private customers such as the Duchess of Windsor and they were frequently seen in films of the 1940s and 1950s. Lucas' creative ability was matched by his business prowess: in the year before his death (at a time when hat-buying was almost extinct) his turnover was more than 55,000 hats.

LUCILE
Born London, England, 1862.
Died London, England, 1935.
Lucile's real name was Lucy Kennedy. The House of Lucile was the most successful London-based couture establishment of the century. In its heyday it had thriving and influential branches in New York, Chicago and Paris. Its founder, a sister of the popular novelist, Elinor Glyn, was married at eighteen, but soon divorced. She was a tough and visionary business woman. In the 1890s she and her mother set up as dressmakers, working from their home in Davies Street, London. Slowly her name was spread by word of mouth and she began to employ girls to help her. Soon she became sufficiently well-known to start trading under the rather exotic name of Lucile. After the turn of the century she married Sir Cosmo Duff Gordon and, as Lady Duff Gordon, her prestige increased sufficiently for her to be dressing London's very grand ladies who were entranced by her romantic, floating chiffons topped with large hats. She also designed costumes for the theatre, most notably for Lily Elsie in *The Merry Widow* in 1907. She rapidly became an international name. By 1909 she was reputed to be earning £40,000 a year – an enormous amount for the time. In that year she opened her New York branch and in 1911 she followed the bold lead of WORTH and REDFERN by opening a salon in Paris. She ensured attention in that chauvinistic city by her choice of mannequins, who were always tall, elegant and severe. Dolores and Hebe, the two most famous, were six feet tall.

Socially her life had its difficulties. She and her husband were passengers on the fatal *Titanic* maiden voyage and, although they survived, gossip implied that they had used their wealth and social position to secure places in the lifeboats. Although the rumour was totally unfounded, it had its effect on her business which, after World War I, began to wane. Her clothes were too exotic for the new times and her house slowly faded from the scene.

Lucile's achievements were considerable and she deserves to be remembered, not only for her romantic and theatrical creations, but also for her vision in seeing the opportunity to expand to North America (one of the first European couturiers to do so) and her success in tapping the burgeoning market there. She has been compared to POIRET and certainly she was fond of exotica like turbans and tassels, but her soft and gentle colour schemes were much more feminine than his. They shared the same fate, dying almost unnoticed by the world of fashion in which they had once played such an important part. Lady Duff Gordon's autobiography, *Discretions and Indiscretions* was published in 1932.

M

McCARDELL · McFADDEN · MACKIE · MAD CARPENTIER (*See* PARIS COUTURE) · MAINBOCHER · MANDELLI (*See* KRIZIA)
MANGONE · MANGUIN · MANNING · MARCOVICZ (*See* ZWEI) · MARTIAL ET ARMAND (*See* PARIS COUTURE) · MATSUDA · MATTLI
MAXFIELD PARRISH · MAXMARA (*See* ITALIAN READY-TO-WEAR) · MAXWELL · MICHAEL · MICHIKO · MILLINERS (French)
MIRMAN · MISSONI · MIYAKE · MOLYNEUX · MONTANA · MORENI · MORI, H. · MORI, K. (*See* JAPANESE DESIGN) · MORTON
MUGLER · MUIR

McFadden

Mainbocher

Maxfield Parrish/Nigel Preston

Missoni

Miyake

Molyneux

Mugler

Muir

199

McCARDELL, Claire

Born Maryland, USA, 1905.
Died New York, USA, 1958.

Claire McCardell is a justly honoured name in American fashion, considered by many as *the* American ready-to-wear designer of the century. She was from a comfortable background, her father being a banker and state senator. After studying illustration at Parson's, she spent a year in Paris. In 1929 she became a model and assistant designer for Robert Turk Inc. She moved with Turk to Townley Frocks in 1931. After his death she took over the job of designer and in 1938 she produced her first classic of simplicity: the waistless, dartless, bias-cut tent dress christened 'The Monastic'. Its large popularity and its easy copy-ability bankrupted Townley Frocks, but it ensured a job with Hattie CARNEGIE for McCardell. She worked with Carnegie from 1938 to 1940 and was given carte blanche to create a line called 'Workshop Originals'. In 1940 she returned to Townley Frocks to design under her own name. Then began her most productive period, the years in which she virtually founded the *American* look in clothes: sporty, relaxed, casual and comfortable. Clean, functional design, fitness of purpose and respect for material were the philosophical tenets of the McCardell look and they were used to create clothes based on an understanding of the attitudes and way of life of the American woman.

McCardell produced instant classics, right for their time and yet still perfectly fashionable today. Working with denim, jersey, ticking and cotton calico, she adapted workmen's and children's clothing and re-created high-waisted 'Empire' dresses in an utterly modern and relaxed way. Her trademarks were functional metal fastenings like rivets, gilt hooks and eyes, seams with top stitching and the shoestring ties which criss-crossed the bodice of her 'Empire' line dresses. She had many 'firsts' to her name. In 1942 she invented the diaper bathing costume; in 1944, to circumvent wartime restrictions, she created the flat ballet pump which has remained permanently on the fashion scene; in 1943 she took dancer's leotards and created the forerunner of today's ubiquitous body stocking and tights; and, in 1942 she created perhaps

The look which made Claire McCardell a leader in American fashion: these dateless dresses were designed in the fifties but still look right today and can be worn by anyone regardless of age.

A characteristically beautiful hand-printed chiffon over-tunic is given a pleated yoke by Mary McFadden. It is combined with ankle-length pleated pants, wrapped at the waist with gold lurex cords.

the most enduring of all her 'looks', 'the popover', a wrap-around dress, unstructured and unwaisted, that was a fashion favourite for the next twenty years.

In 1944 McCardell received the Coty American Fashion Critics' 'Winnie' and she was posthumously elected to the Hall of Fame in 1958. In 1948 she obtained the Neiman-Marcus Award and in 1956 the Parson's Medal for Distinguished Achievement. In 1955 *Time* magazine featured her on its cover in recognition of her 'artist's sense of colour and sculptor's feeling for form'. A year later she published *What Shall I Wear?*. Her achievement, which has been such a lasting inspiration in American design circles, was to take simple and relaxed materials and shapes and, avoiding all hint of the homespun or

crude, elevate them to a level of glamour and sophistication while retaining their integrity and fitness. Like CASHIN, she created totally unpompous clothes for women who were liberated but not lax.

McFADDEN, Mary

Born New York, USA, 1936.

Mary McFadden was brought up in Memphis, where her father was a cotton broker. He died when she was ten and she and her mother moved back to Long Island. Her education included a year at the Sorbonne and a year at the Traphagen School of Design in New York. She also took a degree in sociology at Columbia University in 1962. In the same year she became public relations director for Christian DIOR New

York. She married a DeBeers executive and moved to South Africa, where she became an editor of South African *Vogue*. In 1968 she re-married and moved to Rhodesia, where she founded a workshop for African sculptors and artists. She returned to New York in 1970 to work as a special projects editor for *Vogue*. Her entry into designing was almost by chance. To use rare African and Chinese silks she designed three tunics which were subsequently featured in *Vogue*. Bendels bought them and she was in business. That was in 1973. By 1976 Mary McFadden Inc., her own company, was established.

McFadden's clothes are designed for the individualistic, very rich woman who likes wearing luxurious, beautifully printed and coloured silk tunics. Her cut is austerely classic and her clothes have a very well-bred, understated style. They are a true reflection of their creator, whose approach to fashion is analytic, intellectual and precise. Her systematic and disciplined attitude to fashion has been called 'chillingly meticulous' by *Women's Wear Daily*. The trademarks of the McFadden look are slim tunics and dresses with knife pleats, silk pyjamas and much quilting. They exemplify the thinking behind her remark, 'I want my women to float'. Her jewellery is large and barbaric and uses combinations of brass, gold, precious stones and ceramics. She holds a Coty American Fashion Critics' 'Winnie' (1976) and a Return Award (1978), in addition to the Neiman-Marcus Award which she received in 1979, the year of her election to the Coty 'Hall of Fame'.

MACKIE, Bob

Born Los Angeles, USA, 1940.

After studying art and theatre design, Mackie obtained work as design assistant to Jean LOUIS and, later, Edith HEAD. His name is best known in conjunction with his design partner, Ray AGHAYAN, and the television stars, Cher and Carol Burnett, for whose shows he and Aghayan have designed many memorable costumes. Like Head, BANTON and Jean Louis, Mackie and Aghayan understand the medium of film and its particular demands on the designer. The fashion sense of the clothes for the screen must be enlarged without being

distorted, and a good design must combine a contemporary and timeless quality. Together they have won an Emmy Award four times for their costumes for TV shows and have had three Academy Award nominations. As well as designing swimwear for Cole of California, Mackie produces a high-gloss, glamour line of ready-to-wear clothes.

MAD CARPENTIER

See PARIS COUTURE

MAINBOCHER

Born Chicago, USA, 1890.
Died Munich, Germany, 1976.

Mainbocher's name should be better known outside the fashion historian's

field than it is. He was the first American designer in Paris and, before that, an influential fashion journalist. He designed the Duchess of Windsor's wedding dress and created clothes which typified all that was best in American design. His real name was Main Rousseau Bocher. He studied art in New York, Paris and Munich, but really wished to be a singer. To keep himself while studying singing he did fashion sketches, first for *Harper's Bazaar* in Paris and then for *Vogue*. By 1922 he had abandoned the idea of singing. He left his post as Paris fashion editor at *Vogue* to become editor of the French *Vogue*. His career as a journalist was distinguished: he invented the 'Vogue's Eye View' column and discovered the artist, ERIC*, and the photographer, HOYNINGEN-HUENE*. He abandoned this lucrative and

The Duchess of Windsor, photographed in 1937 wearing a supremely elegant Mainbocher dress which relies for its impact on the simplicity of perfect cut, in the grand couture manner.

Below: A 1971 Beaton photograph of a Mainbocher evening dress from 1936. The demurely embroidered flowers give a jewelled richness to an otherwise severely simple creation.

influential career in 1929, when, quite suddenly, he decided to open his own couture house. His contacts gained him almost instant recognition. His clothes had the same classic elegance of those of MOLYNEUX, but his real mentors were LOUISEBOULANGER, AUGUSTABERNARD and VIONNET. The latter's bias-cut formed the basis of many of Mainbocher's lines. He closed his successful Paris house at the outbreak of World War II and moved to New York, where he re-opened his doors in 1940. From then until his retirement thirty years later, he produced elegant and very costly clothes to enhance the backs of elegant and very costly women who, if not always ladies, certainly appeared to be so in Mainbocher's exclusive creations. At the other end of the scale were his simple and effective uniform designs for such strangers to high fashion as the WAVES and the American Red Cross.

As a designer Mainbocher must be taken seriously in a European context. His elegantly simple dresses relied on a luxurious use of fabric and a crispness of cut essentially in the great tradition of French haute couture. Although his American opening was largely financed by the Warner Corset Company, all other commercial offers were modestly rejected by Mainbocher, who refused to sell his name to wholesalers or his toiles to down-market copyists. There was more than a touch of pride in the maestro's stringent vetting of customers and press and his tyrannical insistence that magazines must always be laid out with two Mainbocher outfits on facing pages. Promiscuous mixing with the work of other designers, even the greatest, was not allowed. Clearly, Mainbocher was a sophisticated and worldly designer and businessman. No simple Chicago lad, he!

MANDELLI, Mariucca
See KRIZIA

MANGONE, Philip
Born Southern Italy, 1890s.
Mangone learned how to cut and sew from his father, who emigrated from Europe and opened a workroom in New York. He was appointed designer to a wholesale company when he was only nineteen and sent to Paris. By the age of twenty-seven he had his own business. It was popular for its beautifully cut coats and suits. He was especially successful in the 1940s, when America was cut off from French designers. Although not an originator, he has been credited with introducing the swagger coat.

MANGUIN, Lucille
See PARIS COUTURE

MANNING, Eldridge
Manning was a New York designer who worked during the 1920s. He designed fantasy evening dresses which were nostalgic and romantic with their beaded bodices and sweeping silk skirts.

MARCOVICZ, Gioia Meller
See ZWEI

MARTIAL ET ARMAND
See PARIS COUTURE

MATSUDA, Mitsuhiro
Born Tokyo, Japan, 1934.
Matsuda's father worked in the Japanese kimono industry and he had a considerable influence on his son, who became interested in the idea of creating Western-style clothes designed on traditional Japanese principles. Having graduated from Waseda University, Matsuda attended the famous Bunka Fukuso Gakuin, where he studied fashion alongside KENZO Takada. After graduating in 1962, they both worked as designers for the Sanai company, then went to Paris in 1965. Matsuda stayed in Paris for six months and then returned to Tokyo via the United States. In 1967 he founded his own company, Nicole, named after a model in *Elle* magazine whose image Matsuda had adored when a teenager. In 1968 the first Nicole boutique was opened in Aoyama. 'Monsieur Nicole', Matsuda's men's line, followed in 1974. Two years later he launched 'Madame Nicole', a more sophisticated women's line. Matsuda has always

Matsuda updates the granny look with his cobweb-fine knits and layered skirts to produce an endearingly youthful appearance enhanced by schoolboy shoes.

considered New York more important than Paris and it was there that he opened his first American boutique in 1982. In the same year he established a Matsuda boutique in Hong Kong. He now has five companies, thirty boutiques and more than fifty franchises. He publishes his own newspaper, *The Nicole Times*, which presents his looks and approach to fashion in a way easily assimilated by his clients. His clothes are well tailored, often humorous and tread a careful path between oriental and occidental matrixes.
See also JAPANESE DESIGN.

MATTLI, Guiseppe Gustavo
Born Locarno, Switzerland, 1907.
Died London, England, 1982.
One of fourteen children, with twelve sisters, Mattli was apprenticed to an oil

A typical Matsuda outfit shows a masterly control of layers, levels and scale, all of which are used to westernize a Japanese approach to design.

Matsuda makes an interesting statement about layering, texture and scale in this easy-to-wear outfit from his 1983 collection.

company in Geneva in 1925, but he moved to London the next year to learn English. From there he went to Paris and worked for PREMET. He opened his own business in London in 1934. By 1938 he was taking his collections to Paris. He became a member of the Incorporated Society of London Fashion Designers in the 1940s. After the war he continued to make couture clothes until 1955, when his company went into liquidation. His ready-to-wear lines continued into the 1970s. He was a regular fashion contributor to *Reynolds News* in the 1950s.

MAXFIELD PARRISH
Founded London, England, 1972.
The house of Maxfield Parrish was founded by designer Nigel Preston, who was born in Reading, Berkshire, in 1946. He at-

tended Dartington Hall, where he studied painting and graphic art. From here he moved into the field of interior design. Toying with music and making his own clothes led, in the classic way, to his making clothes for musician friends. By the end of the 1960s he was designing clothes for pop singers such as Suzy Quattro and Emerson, Lake & Palmer. From this basis Maxfield Parrish was created. It soon became synonymous in London with suede and leather clothing. The success of the firm is based on Preston's subtle colour-sense and his ability to create classic, relaxed designs with exceedingly soft skins cut like cloth. A Maxfield Parrish cloth collection was instituted in the spring of 1983. The clothes are carried by the better-class American and European stores as well as by top London stores.

MAXMARA
See ITALIAN READY-TO-WEAR

MAXWELL, Vera
Born New York City, USA, 1904.
Of Viennese parentage, Maxwell studied ballet and became a model in a fashion house. Her interest in fashion was kindled and she taught herself to draw, design and make clothes. She visited London where, under the influence of traditional men's clothing, she studied tailoring. She returned to New York and worked as a designer for sportswear and coat firms. Vera Maxwell Originals opened in 1946. Her firm was aptly named, since she is considered part of that small group of original American designers, which includes CASHIN and MCCARDELL, who were largely uninfluenced by Paris and produced simple, timeless, sporty clothes of essentially American inspiration. She is famous for her weekend wardrobe of 1935, her riding jacket suits and her no-zippers, no-buttons, no-hooks 'speed' dress of stretch nylon and polyester. In 1951 she won a Coty Special Award followed by a Neiman-Marcus Award in 1955. In 1970 she had a retrospective at the Smithsonian Institute, Washington, D.C. She is still running her own business.

MICHAEL of Carlos Place
Founded London, England, 1953.
Closed London, England, 1971.
Michael Donellan, having worked at the sportswear firm of LACHASSE, where he followed Digby MORTON and Hardy AMIES, founded his own couture firm in 1953, using his Christian name and address as the title of his house. He was a member of the Incorporated Society of London Fashion Designers and his tailored elegant looks were successful until the collapse of London as a couture centre after the 'swinging sixties'. Michael died in January 1985.

MICHIKO, Koshino
Born Osaka, Japan, 1950.
One of a triumvirate of designer sisters, Michiko studied fashion at the Bunka College of Fashion in Tokyo and graduated in 1974. By 1975 she was in London,

determined to begin a fashion career in the West. The following year she showed her first collection under her own name at the LONDON DESIGNER COLLECTIONS. Her show was successful and during the next two years she developed international outlets, including licences in Japan. By 1982 she had a knitwear, luggage, and denim line and a children's collection which was introduced in Japan. In the same year she opened a showroom in Milan.

See also JAPANESE DESIGN.

MILLINERS (French)

Barthet, Jean
Faubourg Saint-Honoré, Paris.
Barthet presented his first collection in 1949 and by 1965 he was generally considered the foremost milliner in the world. His exquisite and exclusive creations were the epitome of Gallic flair and were bought by elegant women from all over the globe. He created hats for many films, including *Les Demoiselles de Rochefort*. He revolutionized his designing in the 1980s with his work for UNGARO, MONTANA and MUGLER.

Paulette
Avenue Franklin Roosevelt, Paris.
Paulette opened her own milliner's establishment in 1939 and continued to work throughout World War II. She became famous in 1942, when she created wool jersey turbans for girls who were forced to cycle by wartime petrol restrictions. Her skill and practicality were shown by her elegant and *chic* solution to the problem. Scarves and draping were a frequent feature of her designs. She was still working for private clients and producing hats for the collections of the couturiers into the late 1970s.

Reboux, Caroline
Rue de la Paix, Paris.
Born in the 1830s, Reboux lived until 1927. Her father was a journalist and she was born and brought up in Paris. She had all the wit and panache of her city and introduced these qualities into her millinery.

Madame Reboux, like Charles Worth, was 'discovered' by Princess Metternich. She opened her 'smart establishment' at 23 rue de la Paix in 1870, and was one of the top milliners in Paris before World War I. She was still considered the best in the 1920s, when her cloche hats were in demand as the 'only' possible way to crown an elegant couture outfit. In the 1930s famous fashion beauties like the South American, Sra. Martinez de Hoz, were still favouring the romantic, broad-brimmed hats created by Reboux to complement elegantly draped dresses by VIONNET. Throughout the 1920s she was part of the Paris 'Holy Trinity': CHANEL for clothes, Antoine for coiffure, and Reboux for hats. She worked with everyone from WORTH to SCHIAPARELLI and her hats crowned every aristocratic head in Paris. The demi-monde, however, was firmly excluded from her shop. Her successor in the business was Lucienne Rebate.

Saint Cyr, Claude
Faubourg Saint-Honoré, Paris.
In 1937 Saint Cyr opened her first establishment in Paris, soon to be followed by one in London and one in Tokyo. Her designs were always supremely elegant, with the simplicity of a sure taste. In many respects she was the most famous milliner in Paris in the 1940s and 1950s.

Svend
Rue de Ponthieu, Paris.
After working with Jacques FATH from 1947 to 1951, Svend moved to Jacques HEIM and Pierre BALMAIN. A Dane, he was considered by many to be the most creative and imaginative milliner in Paris during the 1950s.

Valois, Rose
Rue Royale, Paris.
After working with Caroline Reboux, Valois opened on her own in 1927. On her retirement in 1970 her establishment closed.

MIRMAN, Simone ☐
Born Paris (after World War I).
Simone Mirman was the daughter of a dressmaker and she was apprenticed to a milliner at the age of fifteen. Her sister was apprenticed to a dressmaker, since their mother hoped that they would work together. This plan was wrecked by Simone's elopement to England, when not yet twenty, with Serge Mirman, who was later a director of DIOR and helped set up Dior-London. They arrived in London in 1937. Mirman had trained in Paris with

Three rings of white satin, topped with navy blue straw, make this Simone Mirman confection almost good enough to eat.

Rose VALOIS and in England she worked for SCHIAPARELLI's London branch, where she was in charge of the workroom. In 1939 Schiaparelli closed and after the war, in 1947, Simone Mirman opened her own establishment in Belgravia. Her long association with the British royal family began in 1952, when she was requested to prepare a selection of hats for Princess Margaret. In 1965 she began to make hats for the Queen and she has continued to do so. She has worked with the royal dressmaker HARTNELL, and also DIOR-London and Yves SAINT LAURENT-London. She was an Associate Member of the Incorporated Society of London Fashion Designers. She used to make about 125 hats a season, but she now makes about 150 models a year. She works with six girls and designs and trims all her hats herself. She never sketches, but works on the block directly. In 1982 Christies of London held a sale of her hats, which were eagerly bought by museums and private collectors.

MISSONI (Tai and Rosita) ☐
Founded Milan, Italy, 1953.
Tai (Ottavio) Missoni was born in Yugoslavia in 1921, the son of an Italian sea-captain and a Serbian countess. Rosita's family background was industrial: her father's firm made bedspreads. They met

in London, where she was studying English and he was competing as a member of the Italian team in the 1948 Olympics. He had a business producing track suits, which he had begun in 1946, shortly after his release from a prisoner-of-war camp. His track suits were the official Italian Olympic team's uniform and were worn all over Italy. He is credited with the invention of leg zips on track suits, although he had no design training. They were married in 1953. They decided to work together and, beginning with four knitting machines, produced anonymous knitwear to be sold under the names of other firms. They used various designers, including Emmanuelle KHANH, before Rosita decided to take over design responsibility. Tai Missoni is highly competitive, as befits a sportsman, and he and his wife have moved knitwear out of the unglamorous area of 'basic but boring' into the high glamour, startling and sophisticated central fashion stage. In this they were pioneers who altered, albeit slightly, the face of fashion. In doing so, they have created an international status symbol and become exceedingly wealthy. Throughout the fashion industry they are a much-loved couple and, together with their two sons and daughter, look likely to remain permanent, even traditional, fixtures on the international fashion scene.

The basis of the Missoni empire is the graph paper on which Tai works in watercolour to produce his inventive geometric patterns. His fresh, but subtle, colour sense is used to produce the stitches for Rosita to work on. She creates the shapes and the line — although she does not sketch. Working with assistants, she drapes the knitted lengths on the model. The line is always kept simple. The Missonis have produced many classics since their first 'put-together', produced in 1970, became their trademark. Production is limited and prices are very high, but this does not affect sales. As a result, the family is able to live in a relaxed, very affluent style in their villa in the hills of Lombardy. In 1973 the Missonis received the Neiman-Marcus Award and their 1978 Exhibition at the Whitney Museum in New York, where their designs were hung like works of art, showed how timeless and continuing their contribution to knitwear is.

MIYAKE, Issey ☐

Born Hiroshima, Japan, 1935.

One of the early Japanese exports to Europe, Miyake studied art at Tama University, from which he graduated in 1964. The following year he moved to Paris to study at the Chambre Syndicale de la Couture Parisienne. 1966 saw him commence a two-year period as assistant designer with Guy LAROCHE. In 1968 he moved, in the same capacity, to GIVENCHY. During 1969 and 1970 Miyake was in New York designing Geoffrey BEENE's ready-to-wear. In 1971 came his first individual collection, shown in Tokyo and New York. He presented his first collection

in Paris in 1973 and since that time all Miyake collections have been presented there. In 1976 he presented 'Issey Miyake and Twelve Black Girls' in Osaka for six days to a total audience of 15,000. The next year his 'Fly with Issey Miyake' show in Tokyo and Kyoto was seen by audiences totalling 22,000. Miyake claims that the Paris student revolution of May, 1968, had a radical and far-reaching effect on his design philosophy. He realized that traditional Parisian attitudes to fashion were inappropriate for the modern woman and he began to loosen up his designs. He moved into layering and wrapping and very successfully combined traditional

Autumn 1979: Miyake brings together eclectic elements to create a cross between Davy Crockett and a principal boy. Sleeves and trousers are shirred in a way that exploits the texture and pattern of the material.

Below: *The epitome of Japanese approaches to fashion: Miyake makes a statement about texture, pattern scale and form in this outfit from his March 1983 collection.*

A magnificently scaled and textured statement from Miyake, in March 1983. This uncompromisingly direct approach has put him in the forefront of Japanese designers showing in Paris.

Japanese design approaches with African-type fabrics to produce one of the first anti-fashion looks.

Miyake's development has been steady, his originality consistently independent of other designer's work and his influence on younger, anti-status clothes designers considerable. His claim is that he is 'taking the spirit behind the kimono' in all his work. He has cheaper ranges of clothes, more normal and wearable, which retail under the names of Issey Sport and Plantation. In 1978 he published *Issey Miyake East Meets West* and in the following year his achievements as a designer were acknowledged by an award from the Pratt Institute. He had already won the 1974 Japan Fashion Editors' Club award. In 1980 he moved into theatre design with his costumes for Maurice Béjarts' ballet *Casta Diva*. He is quite simply the best Japanese designer showing in Paris. His clothes are so good that even jaded fashion journalists covet them. Like LAGERFELD and SAINT LAURENT, Miyake is way ahead of the crowd.
See also JAPANESE DESIGN.

MOLYNEUX, Edward

Born London, England, 1894.
Died Monte Carlo, France, 1974.
Molyneux was a 'Jack-the-giant-killer' figure who, following the lead of WORTH, pitted British phlegm against French *je ne sais quoi*, and won. He began his life in fashion with LUCILE, for whom he worked as sketcher, travelling to her branches in New York, Chicago and Paris. He had a distinguished career in World War I as a captain in the British army. He lost one eye, sustained serious wounds three times, and was awarded the Military Cross twice.

In 1919 he opened his own house in Paris, thus initiating a design career which kept him a leading figure in Paris for more than twenty-five years. He was backed by Lord Northcliffe and patronized by the British Embassy. His style was almost a pastiche of English upper-class understatement and, especially during the 1930s, it was absolutely right for all those reacting against SCHIAPARELLI's robust and vulgar sense of fun. His clothes were discreet and lady-like and his simple classicism was based on a slow evolution of ideas which produced a consistently developed style. The ingredients were softly tailored suits, pleated skirts, printed silks, crisp white collars and a preponderance of grey, beige and navy. Impeccable standards were maintained by his exceptionally good fitters, many of whom moved to GRIFFE on Molyneux's retirement.

Molyneux's success is reflected in the fact that he had branches in London, Monte Carlo, Cannes and Biarritz, which were the places his sort of customers visited. Socially he was a flamboyant success: he opened two successful nightclubs with Elsa Maxwell, collected 18th-century and Impressionist paintings and was a personal friend of many of his distinguished clientele. His great *coup* was to make clothes for Princess Marina, including her wedding dress when she married the Duke of Kent. His clothes for Gertrude Lawrence in *Private Lives* made his name almost a household word, and it is often claimed that his costumes for the 1933 production of *The Barrets of Wimpole Street*, with their strong Winterhalter influence, were the forerunners of DIOR's 'New Look'.

Certainly Dior and BALMAIN (who

Captain Molyneux's skill is shown in this simple dress and cape of 1933. The impact is made by the cut and proportion which ensures a smart appearance even with a less than model girl figure.

worked for Molyneux) were influenced by his approach to fashion. With the outbreak of World War II Molyneux returned to London. He worked with the Department of Overseas Trade, for whom he mounted an exhibition of British fashion for South America and he joined the Incorporated Society of London Fashion Designers. After the war he returned to Paris, with GRIFFE as his assistant, but the increasing danger of blindness in his remaining eye persuaded him to retire and he closed his doors in 1950. His would have had an exemplary design life had he left it at that, but he was unwise enough to return in 1965. Comebacks are notoriously tricky to judge, as many a Hollywood star can sadly testify, and even with the help of John Tullis as his assistant, Molyneux could not re-establish his brand of elegant understatement. Unlike CHANEL, who managed to resyncromesh her fashion with the times, Molyneux was hopelessly at sea in a period when Paris was capitulating to the mini-skirt and his fellow countrymen were producing clothes of an unprecedented vulgarity to be snapped up by the eager and uneducated public who flocked to London to buy with uncritical adoration anything labelled 'young'.

Major perfumes: Numéro Cinq (1926); Vivre (1930); Rue Royale (1943).

MONTANA, Claude ☐

Born Paris, France, 1949.

Montana's mother was Spanish and his father was German. He began designing in London in 1971 when, having run short of money, he made jewellery using the unlikely combination of rhinestones and papier-mâché. Featured in the British *Vogue*, the jewellery was sufficiently successful to enable him to remain in London for a further year before returning to Paris. In Paris he began to work for a

Montana's way with leather in his 1979 collection: the girls stride out like medieval Japanese warriors. The image uses exaggerated shoulders, gauntlets and high heels to create a look which is disturbing as well as exciting.

Claude Montana's unerring sense of scale excites the photographers in his Spring 1983 show. The Montana trade marks are strong: bomber jacket, uniform hat, man's tie and propeller brooch create a powerful impact.

Cuddly fake fur softens the Montana impact although he uses his typical silhouette and proportions in his look for Autumn 1982.

French leather firm, MacDouglas. Montana's importance in the field of French ready-to-wear has increased throughout the 1970s and he is now a forceful influence. He produces a strongly individual, demanding silhouette by creating big, well-defined shapes. He is not afraid to produce things which appear ugly. His importance stems from his inspiration, which is male. He works most successfully with leather and, even when it is feminized, he treats it in a hard and masculine way, with massive details and strong colours (black, red, grey). Linked in spirit with uniforms and cowboy gear, his clothes are admired and coveted by the young *avant-garde*. His knitwear is rugged, heavy-gauged and strong. His men's range and the look he designs for the Italian firm, Complice, are also powerful and uncompromising. His boldly experimental approach was encouraged by an imaginative and creative partnership with the Spanish knitwear manufacturers, Ferrer y Sentis, with whom he signed a contract in 1975. With MUGLER and GAULTIER, he strides raunchily across the Paris fashion scene, and is one of that city's top designers, with a world-wide following.

MORENI, Popy
Born Turin, Italy, 1949.
After a period studying costume and design in Turin, Moreni moved to Paris when she was seventeen. She has remained there ever since. Her first job, from 1967 to 1972, was as designer for the Promostyl organization, but in 1972 she started up her own business, having previously designed the range for the Italian firm, Timmi. In 1976 she opened her own boutique. Her clothes are a very successful amalgam of Italian style and French practicality. They are young, not too serious and easily worn. She concentrates on sportswear, although she also has an evening line and does hat, shoe and jewellery ranges. Not surprisingly for an Italian, she is especially strong on colour.

MORI, Hanae
Born Tokyo, Japan, 1926.
A graduate in Japanese literature, married with two sons, Mori returned to college to learn the fundamentals of fashion design before opening a boutique in Tokyo. Her father, who was a doctor, had hoped that she would become a surgeon, but, helped by a husband who worked in textiles, she made the decision in favour of a fashion career. She had friends and contacts in Japanese film and theatre circles and began designing costumes for many productions. In 1955 she opened her first shop on the Ginza, Tokyo's high-class shopping street, selling her ready-to-wear line. With her husband's help she has become highly successful, especially in America, and she began showing her haute-couture collection in Paris in 1977.

Mori now has couture houses in Tokyo, New York (where she opened in 1973) and Paris and is a highly respected member of the international fashion scene. Her base is in Tokyo and she is very much a Japanese designer in her approach to shape and colour. Her evening wear, based on kimonos and made in soft silks printed with butterflies and flowers, is both sexy and refined, as only a Japanese woman could make it. Both her couture and ready-to-wear ranges are designed within the framework of Western styling, but they lean heavily on her Japanese cultural background. She uses her own specially woven materials, printed and dyed to her standard at Kyoto, the traditional home of dyed kimonos. In 1972 she designed ski wear for the Japanese Olympic team and in 1973 her international position was confirmed by the receipt of a Neiman-Marcus Award.
See also JAPANESE DESIGN.

MORI, Kei
See JAPANESE DESIGN

MORTON, Digby
Born Dublin, Ireland, 1906.
Died London, England, 1983.
Morton studied art and architecture in Dublin and London and in 1933 he joined the London-based sports firm, LACHASSE,

Sarah Churchill was photographed by Beaton in 1937 wearing a sleeveless evening gown of simple but skilled cut, by Digby Morton. Its elegance stems from its purity of line.

as designer. It was very successful throughout the 1930s and was especially noted for its tailored suits. In 1934 Morton opened his own couture house under his name. In 1939 he designed the uniform for the Women's Voluntary Service and he was a founder member of the Incorporated Society of London Fashion Designers set up in 1942 by the Ministry of Supply, for whom he worked to promote British fashion abroad. Other members included AMIES, STIEBEL, and MOLYNEUX. After the war Morton built up a world market, with particular success in America where he worked from 1953 to 1957. He designed the first 'Lady Hathaway' shirt for the American Hathaway Shirt Company and he designed and produced toiles for other US companies. In 1958, having closed his couture establishment, he became director of the London firm Reldon-Digby Morton. He retired in 1973.

MUGLER, Thierry ☐

Born Strasbourg, France, 1946.
The son of a doctor, Mugler began to take an interest in fashion in his teens, when he started to make his own clothes. He joined a ballet company in Strasbourg, but after a short while moved to Paris, where he obtained a job as a window-dresser for a Left Bank boutique. In 1968 he moved to London, where he remained for two years before returning to Paris via Amsterdam. He presented his first collection in 1971 under the name 'Café de Paris', and by 1973 he was designing under his own name. His approach to fashion in the last ten years has been unique, forward-looking and very strong. Although he likes to design 'clear of influence' and says that he respects only GRÈS from the past, his structured clothing seems to be in direct descent from the 1950s high-*chic* exemplified by the designs of FATH. He rarely sketches, since he prefers to construct clothes on live model

Traditional forties Hollywood elements are used in 1982 for Mugler's tongue-in-cheek comment on the trappings of glamour and their relation to taste.

Below: *Having fun in Mugler's up-dated forties look! Shoulder and hip emphasis exaggerates the femininity of the appearance to create amusingly sexy clothes for Autumn 1983.*

Digby Morton's luncheon dress in navy and white checked suiting has an intricately worked box-pleated skirt which forms a pocket on the hip. This look, from March 1947, was soon swept away by Dior's 'New Look'.

For Winter 1983–84 Mugler takes a long tunic and multi-belts it to wear over a long skirt. Hairstyle and accessories are used to complete a powerful and slightly disturbing projection of female power.

girls. His clothes are individual. They are aggressive and tough, while at the same time being vampy and tarty. The exaggerated line is even slightly sinister and menacing, but the look is always well-cut and designed. Many are frightened by Mugler's presentation, with its excessive and fantastic accessories, but underneath all of this are very well-constructed clothes. Mugler's 'Diffusion' is a much calmer version of his look and he also produces a range of men's clothes. He has a following among his fellow designers, including Azzedine ALAÏA and Jean Paul GAULTIER.

MUIR, Jean

Born London, England, 1933.

After a seemly education at a girls' school in Bedford, Jean Muir began her working life in a solicitor's office in London. From there she moved to Liberty to work in the stockroom. She then began selling lingerie, followed by sketching and selling in the made-to-measure department. This was her apprenticeship, a suitably practical one for a designer who is opposed to the notion of fashion as art and for whom making clothes is a trade with problems to be tackled in a workmanlike way. After a brief and unhappy period with Jacqmar, she was introduced by Aage THAARUP to the JAEGER organization, for whom she started to work in 1956.

Jean Muir designed for Jaeger for seven years. She began dressmaking under her own label, 'Jane & Jane', in 1962. 'Jane & Jane' became part of the Susan Small organization, and when it was bought by Courtaulds in 1966, Jean Muir decided to found her own company, with her ex-actor husband, Harry Leuckert, as co-director. Like Jane Austen and her little bit of ivory, Jean Muir limits her look to the materials and shapes that she knows. Not for her the big ball dress, the sweeping furs or the sexy swimwear. Instead, she uses the most liquid suede and the most clinging silk jersey to create beautifully simple shapes, flattering, elegant and refined. All have the Muir 'handwriting': her special way of cutting, stitching and seaming. She has described her work as having three sources: intuition, aesthetic appreciation and technical expertise and it is these which have made her one of the most respected designers working in Great Britain. Her hallmark is softness and she is superb at taking classic, tailored shapes and making them in soft fabrics. As she has said, 'I tailor matt jersey, I do not drape it'.

There are many who consider her the world's best dressmaker, unsurpassed for cut and detailing. Puritanical in her approach to fashion and obsessively professional, she believes in technical training as the only serious basis for a designer, training that should concentrate on 'more craft and less art'. She has received many awards, including the Ambassador Award for Achievement (1965); Harper's Bazaar

Trophy (1965); Maison Blanche Rex Awards (1967, 1968, 1974 and 1976); and the Neiman-Marcus Award (1973). In 1973 she was also elected a Fellow of the Royal Society of Arts, and in 1983 she was made a Commander of the British Empire (C.B.E.).

Jean Muir's way with jersey is justly famed. Here, from 1969, is an archetypal Muir with a skirt which hangs with the perfection of the folds in a Romanesque sculpture.

N·O·P

NARDUCCI · NICOLE (*See* MATSUDA) NORELL · OLDFIELD · OLIVE · OLIVER · OMAR KIAM (*See* KIAM) · ONG · OSTELL · PAQUIN
PARIS COUTURE · PARIS PRÊT-À-PORTER · PARNIS · PARTOS · PASQUALI · PATERSON · PATOU · PAULETTE (*See* MILLINERS)
PEDLAR · PERETTI · PER SPOOK · PERTEGAZ · PERUGIA · PIGUET · PFISTER · PIMS (*See* ITALIAN READY-TO-WEAR) · PINKY AND
DIANNE · PIPART · POIRET · PORTER · PREMET (*See* PARIS COUTURE) · PRESTON (*See* MAXFIELD PARRISH) · PRICE · PUCCI

Norell

Oldfield

Above: *Paquin*
Left: *Per Spook*

NARDUCCI, Leo

Born Massachusetts, USA.

Narducci's family was in the dressmaking business and, after spending two years studying business at Boston University and four serving in the Air Force, he enrolled at the Rhode Island School of Design, from which he graduated in 1960. After working as a sportswear designer and winning a Coty American Fashion Critics' Special Award for 'Young Contemporaries' design in 1965, he formed his own company in 1967. In 1971 it became Leo Narducci Ambiance. In addition to his moderately priced separates and at-home wear, Narducci does a range of accessories which includes jewellery, handbags and scarves. His licences include Vogue Patterns and a range of denim wear.

NICOLE

See MATSUDA

Neiman-Marcus Awards

See FASHION AWARDS, p. 302

NORELL

Born Noblesville, Indiana, USA, 1900.
Died New York, USA, 1972.

Norell's real name is Norman Levinson. When he was very young, his parents moved to Indianapolis, where his father established a haberdashery store. In 1919 he arrived in New York to study painting at Parson's; but he switched to costume design and graduated from the Pratt Institute in 1921. His working life began auspiciously enough with a commission to design costumes for Rudolph Valentino's film, *The Sainted Devil*, and this was followed by costumes for Gloria Swanson's film, *Zaza*, and a place on the staff of the Brooks Costume Company. In 1924 he made the move from costume to modern fashion design, when he accepted the post of designer for the dress manufacturer, Charles Armour. After four years experience at this level Norell was ready to move up-market. He joined the staff of Hattie CARNEGIE.

The experience Norell obtained with Carnegie was invaluable, not only because he learned so much from her taste, style

and fashion-sense, but also because he accompanied her on her trips to Paris. He was thus able to assimilate the European approaches to fashion, which were then far in advance of those in the United States. The Carnegie-Norell association continued in its productive way until 1941, when Norell joined the manufacturer, Anthony Traina, to form Traina-

Norell, a company with which he remained until 1960. The career shows the man: sixteen years with Carnegie and nineteen years with Traina suggest a high level of commitment, professionalism and loyalty. He gave himself time to develop and mature his creativity and, as early as 1943, his quality was recognized when he was given the Coty American Fashion

Opposite: *The American look in the hands of Norell is as pared down and sparse in its elegance as a greyhound.*

Below: *Norell's 1965 tweed suit is subtly scaled with its long jacket and low pockets topped off with a twenties-style cloche.*

with Charles JAMES, as *the* design talent in America. His reputation was equal to those of the top French designers. In fact, he expected the same treatment as the French. He showed before Paris and his clothes were featured in the magazines at exactly the same time as those of the French designers.

He was a trend-setter who originated many looks, including cloth coats lined with fur, long skirts with sweater tops for evening wear and, most far-reaching of all, his classically simple, sequined evening sheaths. His effect on general levels of taste in America was considerable and his influence on the American fashion industry was profound. In the film *Sweet Smell of Success* the waspish gossip columnist played by Burt Lancaster says of a woman in a club, 'The brains may be Jersey City, but the dress is Traina-Norell' — which made it clear that she had 'arrived'. The esteem in which his name was held in Europe gave the American industry a boost of confidence. It is no exaggeration to say that he and Hattie Carnegie were the father and mother of American high fashion. From their taste, talent and knowledge sprang modern creators like BLASS, HALSTON and GALANOS.

Norell once said that women could 'never be too simple during the day or too elaborate at night'. He thus encapsulated the New York approach to dressing which still pertains today. His sophisticated, relaxed clothes, made from glamorous and luxurious fabrics, were the equal of anything produced in Europe in his time, a fact acknowledged by the Metropolitan Museum of Art retrospective of his work in 1972. Norell suffered a stroke on the eve of the opening and died ten days later. This retrospective was the final honour in a long line of acknowledgements which he received during his career. Having been awarded the first 'Winnie' in 1943, he received the first Return Award in 1951, and in 1958 he was the first designer to be elected to the Hall of Fame. In addition to these recognitions from Coty, he received the Neiman-Marcus Award in 1942. In 1956 he was awarded the Parson's Medal for Distinguished Achievement; in 1962 he became the first designer to have conferred on him an Honorary Doctorate in Fine Arts by the Pratt Institute; and in

1972 he received the City of New York Bronze Medallion.

Norell was a man who had faith in American fashion: he was the founder and first president of the Council of Fashion Designers of America, established to promote design as an element of American art and culture and to develop a code of ethics within the industry. His influence was profound and lasting.

OLDFIELD, Bruce
Born London, England, 1950.
An orphan, Bruce Oldfield trained as a teacher and taught English and art before deciding to study fashion at the Ravensbourne College of Art. He spent the years from 1968 to 1971 there and then moved to the St. Martin's School of Art, where he

Silk crêpe and sequins are used by Bruce Oldfield for this evening dress from his collection for Spring/Summer 1984.

Critics' Award. He was the first designer to win the award. (He returned it in 1963 when GERNREICH received his.)

In 1960 Norell created his own firm, Norman Norell Ltd., and thus began his golden years. During his years with the Traina-Norell label his stature had grown, but it was the last twelve years of his designing life which established him, along

followed a one-year fashion course from 1972 to 1973. His working life began with freelance work in London. He also produced his own range for the American firm of Bendel's. In 1974 he sold sketches to Yves SAINT LAURENT and in the following year the first Bruce Oldfield collection was shown in London. By 1978 he had begun to build up his own private clientele as well as continuing his ready-to-wear collections. He is known for his made-to-measure evening wear, which he designs for the British princesses, the aristocracy and 'show-biz' stars.

OLIVE, Frank

Born Milwaukee, Wisconsin, USA, 1929.
Olive is a member of that dying breed: the milliners. Born on a farm, he studied fashion in Milwaukee and art in Chicago, then moved to California in the hope of becoming a costume designer. After working for a San Francisco dance company, he moved to New York in the early 1950s to become a stage designer. However, he did not begin to design costumes, because, having met NORELL, a fellow Mid-westerner, he took his advice and decided to make hats. He opened La Boutique in Greenwich Village, where he sold hats, scarves and blouses. From this grew his wholesale business with three lines: 'Olive Bar', 'Frank's Girl' and 'Frank Olive', his designer label. He managed to survive the hatless 1960s and he continues to manufacture his range of hats, along with beachwear, bags and blouses.

OLIVER, André

Born Toulouse, France, 1932.
After graduating from L'École des Beaux Arts in Paris, Oliver joined Pierre CARDIN in 1955 as his menswear designer. He has remained with Cardin ever since and now has his individual status as a designer within the organization. He has been responsible for both men's and women's ready-to-wear lines at Cardin and his evening dresses have always been especially strong. The partnership is unusual in that, far from working anonymously (as would be the case in other firms where the original designer is still alive and working), Oliver is given full credit by

Cardin and the two men acknowledge the applause together at the end of a show. In 1977 Oliver founded André Oliver Inc. New York, a prestigious men's shop.

OMAR KIAM
See KIAM, Omar

ONG, Benny

Born Singapore, 1949.
Of Chinese descent, Ong was brought up and educated in Singapore, where he took his A-level examinations. He then moved to London and in 1968 began a four-year course of fashion design at the St. Martin's School of Art. After graduation he did various freelance designing jobs in London before starting his own company, with outside backing, in 1974. His success is based on the fact that his clothes are modest, pure and pretty. They are seemly and conventional, well-made and young. In addition to his designer label he produces the 'International' collection and a cheaper line called 'Sunday'.

OSTELL, Richard

Born Barrow in Furness, England, 1959.
Richard Ostell is one of the group of young London designers who, having studied at St. Martin's School of Art (or Middlesex Polytechnic) set up almost immediately under their own label, Notre Dame X. They straddle the area between street fashion and the 'designer label' and create looks and an approach to fashion that are young, instant and uniquely English. Ostell studied fashion at St. Martin's School of Art from 1978 to 1981 and then began designing commercially. His success springs from the fact that his clothes are designed for a lifestyle and are, as he sees it, work clothes in the truest sense. Fabrics are essentially practical and are chosen to improve with wear. His shapes are big and easy.

PAQUIN

Founded Paris, France, 1891.
Closed 1956.
Madame Paquin, as she was invariably known, was married to a very successful

The strangely named 'Pouf-pouf' evening dress created by Paquin in 1922 is a perfect example of the look of the period.

businessman whose money provided the initial backing for her firm. Her training had been at Maison Rouff and from there she brought to her own firm an insistence on the highest levels of taste and refinement. Her romantic and glamorous clothes never slipped into vulgarity. Like LANVIN and VIONNET, her approach to design was practical and pragmatic; her shrewd common sense kept her in touch with what women wanted to wear and she realized that all change must be a gradual progression. She stands fair to be considered the first major female couturier, excluding the claim of Marie Antoinette's dressmaker, Rose Bertin. She was cer-

The Begum Agha Khan chose this Paquin outfit with integral cape shoulder and cross-over belt from the 1933 collection.

tainly the first woman dress designer to be awarded the *Légion d'Honneur*, which she received in 1913.

Mme Paquin's personal elegance exemplified her design approach and, together with her exceptional skill as a colourist, ensured considerable business success. She opened in London in 1912 and she also maintained branches in Madrid and Buenos Aires. Like POIRET and PATOU she was an excellent publicist and she often took her mannequins to the races and the opera, frequently dressing them all alike. A very public person, she and her husband were socially acceptable and were known for their lavish life style. However, pleasure never interfered with her work.

She was chairman of the 1900 Paris Exposition and from then until her retirement in 1920 she was a leader of Paris fashion – frequently hailed as its Queen, in fact. She was President of the Chambre Syndicale from 1917 to 1919. She employed over a thousand people and made a great deal of money by dressing society

ladies, courtesans and actresses. It was the house of Paquin which made up theatre costumes designed by BAKST and IRIBE*. Like Poiret, she sent her clothes on tour in America and her shows there were open to all who could afford a ticket. She died in 1936, but her house continued for another twenty years.

PARIS COUTURE

The strong traditions of Paris couture have stretched from before the beginning of the century up to the 1970s. Today the couture is confined to only a few grand houses and, even in the past, it was dominated by a handful of 'great' names. Nevertheless, there was, for the first sixty years of this century, a considerable number of smaller houses working to the highest standards and answering a real need for the many women who could not patronize the giants.

Augustabernard

Born Provence, France.

Augusta Bernard elided her name on opening her fashion house in 1919. Well-

The house of Paquin produced this complex draped evening dress in white silk jersey in 1954. The cape is of the same material, lined with cherry red taffeta.

A waisted tweed suit from the house of Paquin for Winter 1954–55. The gentle shoulders and interesting peplum detail make a silhouette typical of its time.

This elegant dress could almost be from a current Sonia Rykiel collection but is, in fact, from Augustabernard and was photographed at the races in 1929.

known and successful in the period between the two World Wars, she was an important member of the Paris fashion world when it was dominated by female designers. Her cut was impeccable and her hallmark was her deceptively simple, dateless clothes, all of which had a strong personality. She was a favourite of MAIN-BOCHER when he was fashion editor of French *Vogue*, and the memory of her clothes undoubtedly influenced him when he began to design. Slowly overwhelmed by financial problems, she retired in 1934.

Beer
Little is known of this almost-forgotten couturier except that he was the first designer to open a house on Place Vendôme, which he did in 1905. He was a dressmaker 'for ladies' and 'It's by Beer' meant a great deal in fashionable circles before World War I. The house was also noted for its discreet lingerie. The Beer fashion philosophy was 'conservative elegance for conservative patrons'. Much of the popularity of the firm was based on the aggressive sales techniques of Beer's chief *vendeuse*, who visited all the grand hotels of Paris to urge foreign tourists to come to the salon.

De Rauch, Madeleine
Madeleine de Rauch began designing sports clothes for herself in the 1920s. Friends asked her to make clothes for them and soon her unfortunately named 'House of Friendship' was opened in 1928. This developed in the 1930s into the House of de Rauch, which she founded in 1932 with her two sisters. It closed in 1973, but during its time it was noted for beautifully feminine, fluid clothes and its sporty day looks.

Groult, Nicole
Mme Groult, who was born in Paris in the 1880s, was the sister of the most famous couturier of her time, Paul POIRET, and his success, while overshadowing hers, at the same time helped her to develop and exploit her somewhat limited talent. She was very successful in the twenties and could claim a smart clientele of fashionable Parisiennes. Although she had only a fraction of her brother's talent, she prospered from the moment she opened in 1912 until she closed in the early 1930s. Also, although she made only a small amount compared to her brother's money,

Madame Groult (Poiret's sister) is seen here (centre) enjoying Biarritz sunshine in one of her own outfits from her 1925 collection.

she was infinitely wiser with it and was able to help support him in his penurious old age. She employed Elizabeth HAWES as a designer in the 1920s. Nicole Groult died in Paris in 1940.

Hallée, Jeanne
Although many dresses by the house of Jeanne Hallée have been saved, documentary evidence is sparse. One of Paris' prestigious houses from the turn of the century to World War I, it produced dresses which were clearly inspired by Watteau and 18th-century France, although after 1909, when the Ballets Russes appeared in Paris, Hallée changed to 'oriental' colours and textures and used looser shapes.

Jenny
Jenny opened in Paris in 1911, and the house was considered sufficiently important to take part in the Paris couture show at the San Francisco Exhibition of 1915, although now its name is hardly remembered. Jenny closed in 1938.

Lafaurie, Jeanne
The house of Lafaurie opened in 1925 and closed in 1958. Lafaurie was a couturier who enjoyed a long, if unspectacular, career as a designer of fashionable clothes in the mode of the moment. Her house was small and she catered only for private customers. Since she launched no perfume

or ready-to-wear lines, she is now almost totally forgotten. She should, however, be remembered (if for no other reason) as an employer of COURRÈGES and GOMA, both of whom she encouraged when they decided to form their own companies.

Lecomte, Germaine
Germaine Lecomte was born in Tourraine in the 1890s. She opened a 'medium' house in the rue Royale in 1920 and continued to produce couture clothes throughout the 1920s and 1930s.

Louiseboulanger
Apprenticed in 1913 at the age of thirteen, Louise Boulanger had an essentially practical training and experience. In her late teens she joined CHERUIT as an assistant designer and worked very closely with Mme Cheruit. When the house closed in 1922, she elided her first and last name and opened her own establishment in 1923. She remained a successful couturier until the outbreak of World War II. Her clothes were *chic*, her silhouette usually quite full, and her use of colour strong but subtle. She favoured 'heavy' fabrics such as moire and taffeta and, like VIONNET, used bias cutting a great deal.

Mad Carpentier
Named after its founders, Mad Maltezos and Susie Carpentier, this fashion house was opened in 1939. Maltezos and Carpentier had worked together at VIONNET and they continued their partnership throughout the war, despite all problems. Maltezos was the designer and Carpentier was the businesswoman. Although it produced little that was original, the house had high standards and the clothes found a ready market in post-war Paris. The house closed in 1957.

Manguin, Lucille
Manguin was the daughter of an Impressionist painter. She began by dressing dolls and selling them. She then founded her own dressmaking business, in 1928. She rigorously followed the couture tradition and was renowned for her perfection of detail. She is reputed to be the first designer to show her collections at night by candlelight. On her retirement in 1960 she opened an art gallery.

Martial et Armand
Although never more than a minor part of the Parisian couture scene, this house, like those of WORTH, LANVIN and PAQUIN,

was of sufficiently long standing to be represented in the Paris Couture section of the 1915 San Francisco Exhibition and the 1945 Théâtre de la Mode travelling exhibition. During the years in which the firm traded it was known more for its reliability and workmanship than for the originality of its creations.

Premet

This minor French couture house opened in 1911, and continued into the twenties. It was one of the exhibitors in the San Francisco Exhibition of 1915. Perhaps its greatest claim to fame lies in the fact that Premet trained Alix, known later in her career as Madame GRÈS.

PARIS PRÊT-À-PORTER

Ready-to-wear clothes in Paris were originally produced by haute-couture designers and were very much watered-down versions of their high-fashion lines. In 1960 eleven couturiers formed a group and began to show their *prêt-à-porter* collections two weeks before their couture collections. The original eleven were CARVEN, Claude Rivière, GRÈS-Special, Guy LAROCHE, Jacques GRIFFE-Evolution, Jacques HEIM-Vedette, Jean DESSÈS-Diffusion, LANVIN-CASTILLO, Madeleine de RAUCHE, Maggy ROUFF-Extension and Nina RICCI. From this group came the Association des Maisons Françaises de Couture-en-Gros which, by 1962, had twenty-nine wholesale house members. The shop, Maria Martine, owned by two Peruvians, Marcel and Federico Salem, was an important influence on the development of *prêt-à-porter* in that its customers included women who also bought from the grand couturiers. By 1963 the stylists, who designed only ready-to-wear ranges, had arrived and buyers and press slowly began to concentrate on their shows as being more important than those of the grand couturiers. Early stars included Emmanuelle KHANH and Karl LAGERFELD who, in the early 1970s, was reputedly working for twenty-five companies.

PARNIS, Mollie

Born New York City, USA, 1905.
While studying law at Hunter College in New York City, Parnis took a summer job with a blouse manufacturer. Intrigued by the fashion industry, she abandoned her studies and set out to be a designer. In 1933 she and her husband founded their own business, a ready-to-wear firm called Parnis-Livingston. He was a textile designer. She was head of the firm and her abilities as a businesswoman soon became apparent.

Mollie Parnis Couture is flattering and conservative and appeals to the well-off woman who is over thirty. She has dressed many of America's society women, including Mrs. Eisenhower, Mrs. Johnson, Mrs. Nixon and Mrs. Ford. Her Mollie Parnis Boutique Collection is a cheaper line which was designed by Morty Sussman until his death in 1979. There was also another cheaper line called 'Mollie Robert', begun in 1979 and aimed at the working woman.

Currently her 'couture' line is called, simply, 'Mollie Parnis', and is designed by George Samen. Her inexpensive line, 'Mollie Parnis Studio' is designed by Kenneth Pool. Mollie Parnis doesn't design directly any more but she oversees everything and is still very active in the business.

PARTOS, Emeric

Born Budapest, Hungary, 1905.
Died New York, USA, 1975.
After studying art in Budapest and Paris, Partos learned jewellery design in Switzerland. During World War II he served in the French army and the underground movement along with couturier, Alex Maguy, with whom he worked as designer after the war.

Emeric Partos moved to DIOR, an old friend, in 1947 and worked with him for three years creating suits and coats. In 1950 he joined Maximilian Furs as design consultant. He moved to his final job, fur designer at Bergdorf Goodman, in 1955. He will always be remembered for his original and daring treatment of luxury furs: mink dyed in stripes, removable sections of fur to change the length of a coat, intarsia fur flower on a fur coat. Emeric Partos received the Coty American Fashion Critics' Special Award for furs in 1957 — a suitable accolade for an outstanding tailor and craftsman.

PASQUALI, Guido

Born Verona, Italy, 1946.
The firm of Pasquali of Parabagio was founded in 1918 by Guido Pasquali's grandfather and Guido was involved in the factory early in his life, before studying mechanics and engineering at Bocconi University in Milan. He interrupted his studies when his father's ill-health made it necessary for him, at the age of twenty-one, to take over as head of the firm. His earlier experience helped him to reorganize and modernize everything, and his first job was to provide shoes for some of Italy's top designers — ALBINI, MISSONI and ARMANI. He has shops in Milan, Rome, Paris and Singapore and his range is bought by most of the prestigious stores of the world.

PATERSON, Ronald

Born Lanark, Scotland, 1917.
After an education in Scotland, Paterson moved to London in 1936 where he attended the Piccadilly Institute of Design. In 1938 he was 'discovered' by Elsa SCHIAPARELLI who gave him 1st and 2nd prizes in a national newspaper competition she was judging. Paterson recalls her: 'a terrifying woman, is all I can say'. However, with this start he obtained a job in a couture house. He remained here until World War II. After the war, in 1947, Paterson opened his own couture business starting with only twelve workers. He prospered and, by 1951, was employing a staff of 164. The house moved in 1966, because the building in which it was situated was subsiding. The new premises were too small to accommodate sufficient workers to cover the heavy overheads and the firm closed its doors in 1968. Paterson then worked on films, including two James Bond movies, before retiring to France. Here he worked on the decor and refurbishing of a chain of hotels for five years until his wife's illness decided him to return to England.

Although Paterson's couture house had a brief life it was a very successful one. Clients included royalty and the international jet set. In 1964 he won *The Sunday Times* Award and he was for some years Vice-Chairman of the Incorporated Society of London Fashion Designers.

PATOU, Jean ☐

Born France, 1887.
Died Paris, France, 1936.

'You're the Tops, you're a dress by Patou' wrote Cole Porter, confident that everyone would know who Patou was. In the late 1920s Patou was a world-famous name. After an awkward start – he was working on his first collection for his newly-opened shop called 'Parry' in 1914 when the war began – he opened after the war to instant acclaim. One of the 'new men', he turned his back on Edwardian fussiness and created clothes for active women, women such as the actress, Mary Pickford, and the tennis star, Suzanne Lenglen, who were achievers in highly competitive fields. Whatever he did was news and he produced such large collections that they were shown in two parts. Like CHANEL, he realized that the sporty, emancipated woman was the important customer of

the future and he devoted the morning of his shows to sportswear, active and spectator wear, plus beach and casual looks. His afternoon shows were for formal day wear and evening clothes.

Patou's clothes for sporting personalities had a permanent influence on fashion. To suggest that Chanel was the sole standard-bearer of the new simplicity is unfair to Patou, who should share a part of the honour. The reason why he has not been given such a 'good press' by fashion writers is almost certainly the mutual vendetta which raged between him and Chanel. Patou hated Chanel with an intensity equal to even that dedicated disliker's hatred of him. Patou and Chanel were jealous of each other's ability and each saw the other as an implacable adversary, even though their fashion philosophy was remarkably close. Chanel, however, had the ear of the press and the

De Meyer concentrates all interest on the back treatment for this photograph of a Patou evening dress which he took for Harper's Bazaar.

A day at the races in 1929, wearing Patou's crisply pleated skirt and soft jacket with extravagant fur trim.

Right: *The fifties conception of elegance is seen in this Patou dress for 1958. Spotted shantung, black velvet belt and back fastening make a sophisticated look which is given the final touch of chic by the simple hat.*

Pure silk shantung in honey blond is Patou's choice for an afternoon dress with raised waistline and a flared peplum for Summer 1960.

beau monde to a much greater degree than Patou, who even quarrelled with the American *Vogue* over the relative coverage of his and his rival's creations.

Patou was a showman and very pro-American. He admired American business methods and introduced them into his firm. He employed a large workforce and centralized production in his own establishment where he had workrooms for dyeing, weaving and embroidery. In 1925 he galvanized the fashion press by introducing six American models to show his clothes in a modern, sporty way. He is credited with being the first designer to lengthen skirts and re-place the waist in its natural position. This he did in 1929, and it had a profound effect on world fashion. His perfume, 'Joy', introduced in 1924, has been a best-seller ever since. At the time of his death in 1936 his house was one of the most famous and successful in Paris. It was continued under the direction of his brother-in-law, Raymond Barkas, and a series of designers including BOHAN (1954–1956), LAGERFELD (1960–1963), GOMA (1963–1973), TARLAZZI (1973–1976), Gonzalez (appointed 1977 to 1981) and Christian Lacroix, who was appointed in 1981.

Major perfumes: Amour Amour (1928); Moment Suprême (1933); Joy (1935); Caline (1946).

PAULETTE

See MILLINERS (French)

PEDLAR, Sylvia

Born New York City, USA, 1901.
Died New York City, USA, 1972.
Sylvia Pedlar's real name was Sylvia Schlang. She studied in New York with the intention of becoming a fashion illustrator but, taking a job to design a line, she discovered her true direction and founded her own firm, Iris Lingerie, in 1929. Sylvia Pedlar had perfect taste. In a field where vulgarity is often just an inch away, she was world-famous for her exquisite and elegantly sophisticated lingerie. She was an experimental and original designer who produced such decorative variations on the *peignoir* and the nightgown that even DIOR and GIVENCHY bought her creations — for what purposes is not revealed. She won the Coty Award in 1951 and 1964 and a Neiman-Marcus Award in 1960.

PERETTI, Elsa

Born Florence, Italy, 1940.
Peretti studied interior design in Rome and worked for an architect in Milan before moving to London, where she modelled clothes (in Milan she had been considered too tall to be a model). Arriving in New York, she became a top model, working with HALSTON and also SANT' ANGELO. He gave her design assignments and she began to design silver accessories and jewellery such as heart-shaped belt buckles and pendants of gemstone into which a fresh flower could be put. She also designed for Halston and was inspired by his simple, fundamental, perfectly-proportioned forms to produce complementary jewellery in simple organic shapes. In 1974 she began designing silver jewellery for Tiffany, who had not used that material for twenty-five years. She spends much of her year in Spain, where she has a studio and workrooms. In 1971 she received the Coty American Fashion Critics' Special Award for jewellery.

PER SPOOK

Born Oslo, Norway, 1939.
Per Spook arrived in Paris in 1957, aged eighteen, to study art. He studied at the École des Beaux Arts, then moved to L'École de la Chambre Syndicale to learn the practice and theory of fashion design. On completing his course he joined the house of DIOR. He worked on a freelance basis with Yves SAINT LAURENT and FERAUD, then opened his own house in 1977. His first collections caused a sensation. He was rapturously acclaimed for his fresh, lively approach to shape and, especially, colour. In 1978 he won the Golden Needle Award of the Chambre Syndicale; in the following year he won the Golden Thimble. In 1978 his entire collection was stolen from two vans parked outside his house — a disaster which he managed to survive. His interests include painting and sculpture and he produces haute-couture and ready-to-wear collections.

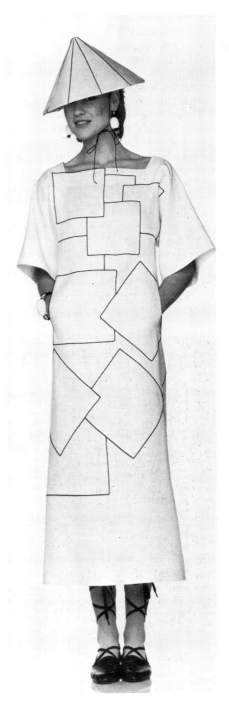

White linen was used by Per Spook for this dress with embroidered black squares in his collection for summer 1982. The dress is appropriately called 'Île de Wight'. The lampshade hat and wrapped legs cause mild concern.

PERTEGAZ, Manuel

Born Aragon, Spain, 1918.

Pertegaz is the other major Spanish designer. BALENCIAGA totally overshadowed his fellow countryman, who did not go to Paris but has worked all his life in Barcelona and Madrid, but Pertegaz showed the same classic and elegant approach to high fashion as the master did. Certainly he is Spain's greatest couturier after Balenciaga. He became a tailor's apprentice when he was only twelve and worked on men's clothes. This training gave him his lasting affection for tailored and structured looks. His real strength lay in haute couture and his clothes, like those of Balenciaga, reflect the drama and theatricality of Spain, while remaining austere and pure in line. His salon in Barcelona developed from the large apartment into which he moved in the early 1940s. His house in Madrid opened in 1968.

PERUGIA, André

Born Nice, France.

Perugia was one of the leading names in the minute band of world-class shoemakers. A craftsman, he learned the skills of his trade in his father's workshop in Nice, where he began working at the age of ten. Here all shoes were made by hand and Perugia thoroughly mastered the techniques required to make a delicate, but serviceable, shoe. However, the craftsman was an artist too and, at the age of eighteen, Perugia opened his own tiny shop in Paris. His intention was to create shoes which could be recognized as minor works of art in the way that all other aspects of Parisian haute couture were. Every shoe that came from his workroom was an individual, hand-made confection, perfectly balanced and shaped, often embroidered and sometimes jewel-encrusted. Such luxury naturally cost the customer a great deal of money. From the 1920s onwards Perugia provided shoes for the POIRET collections and thereafter he continued his association with the couturiers by making shoes for FATH and GIVENCHY. He retired in 1970 and went to live in Cannes, but his name is still wistfully recalled by those who remember the days when supreme craftsmanship was considered worth paying for.

PFISTER, Andrea

Born Pesaro, Italy, 1942.

Born of Swiss stock, Pfister moved with his family to Switzerland in 1945. He was educated there before attending the University of Florence to study art and languages. In 1961 he attended a shoe designer's course in Milan. Two years later he moved to Paris and began to style shoes for LANVIN and PATOU. In 1965 he presented his first collection under his name and in 1967 he opened his first shop in Paris. By 1974 he had his own shoe factory in Italy and he was also designing a range of bags, belts, scarves and jewellery. In the same year he opened his second shop in Paris. In 1976 he began to produce a ready-to-wear line of clothes. It is, nevertheless, as a shoemaker that he is best known. His shoes are colourful, inventive and young. They are sold worldwide in major stores and they have attracted many international private customers.

PIGUET, Robert

Born Yverdon, Switzerland, 1901.
Died Lausanne, Switzerland, 1953.

The son of a Swiss banker, in whose footsteps he was trained to follow, Piguet moved to Paris in 1918 with the intention of becoming a dress designer. In fact, he designed remarkably little. Although he was trained by REDFERN and POIRET, his house (founded in 1933) existed largely on designs provided by freelance designers. Of this group the most famous was undoubtedly DIOR who, along with BALMAIN, was selling designs to Piguet in the 1930s. In 1938 Dior was appointed as Piguet's regular designer. Other talents who were employed include BOHAN, GIVENCHY and GALANOS. The strain of producing collections was so great that after each show Piguet found it necessary to take a long recuperative holiday. He retired two years before his death. Piguet was a man respected for his refinement and reserve – the other side of the coin to his assurance and high elegance. His visual memory was prodigious and was used to full extent in his theatre designs. He dressed many productions by Guitry and Barrault, productions which starred actresses of the calibre of Edwige Feuillière. During World War II he defied the German government,

who wished Paris haute couture to be transferred to Berlin, by refusing to work outside Paris.

Major perfume: Bandit (1944).

PIMS

See ITALIAN READY-TO-WEAR

PINKY AND DIANNE

Pinky Wolman   *Born* Indianapolis, USA, 1946.

Dianne Beaudry   *Born* Indianapolis, USA, 1946.

Pinky, the extrovert, met Dianne, the studious, when they were both studying fine arts and fashion at Washington University in St. Louis. Dianne knew quite certainly that she wished to be a designer, but Pinky was more interested in illustrating. As there was no fashion illustration department, she studied in the design department. They graduated in 1967. Having decided to work together, they took Anne KLEIN's advice not to work as assistants but to 'go out and do it'. They did so and by 1970 they were sufficiently successful to be named Women of the Year by *Women's Wear Daily*. Working for Flo Toronto, a boutique which projected a unisex look, they brought the Europe of London and Paris to New York. Their clothes were much more European than American in feeling. In 1974 they moved to Milan and lived there for one year, doing freelance design work for such firms as FIORUCCI. They also worked in Hong Kong. In late 1975 they returned to New York and established Pinky and Dianne Private Label. Under this label they produced clothing that was less 'crazy' than their previous looks: 'Milan had refined us'. The clothes were made in Hong Kong. They appealed, then as now, to a wide range of young people, including entertainers like The Pointer Sisters and Elton John.

Since 1975 Pinky and Dianne have shown their collection in Milan and New York. They sell world-wide and their own boutique opened in Japan in 1984. Their men's and women's wear has been joined by 'P & D Sport', produced in Japan, and 'A.M.–P.M.', a range of intimate apparel. Their career has shown a strong sense of timing. They were part of the youth

Piguet's romantic, off-the-shoulder evening gown of satin is from his 1937 collection.

Right: *Yellow satin embroidered with paillettes is used in Autumn 1948 for an evening dress and stole by Piguet who tops it off with a feathered evening hat.*

A Poiret evening coat from 1920 sketched by Dufy who created many fabric designs for the couturier.

generation and when they began there were no rules. 'We were addressing our own peers' as Pinky put it. The essence of their designs has remained constant: fine silks and linens, signature prints, a masculine/feminine feel and a whimsical humour. They won a Coty American Fashion Critics' Award for Menswear in 1972.

PIPART, Gérard
Born Paris, France, 1933.
At the age of sixteen Pipart worked briefly for BALMAIN, having sold him some sketches, and then spent six months with FATH. He also worked for PATOU and BOHAN, before fulfilling his military service commitments. On returning to civilian life he continued to work as a freelance

designer for various firms, including Chloe. When Robert RICCI and CRAHAY separated in 1963, Pipart was appointed chief designer at Nina Ricci. He has remained there ever since, producing couture and ready-to-wear lines with great success. He draws on his vast experience as a freelance designer to create elegant, sophisticated and very Parisian clothes.

POIRET, Paul ☐
Born Paris, France, 1879.
Died Paris, France, 1944.
Every man's idea of the grand couturier, extravagant, arrogant and larger-than-life, Paul Poiret lived an extraordinary life. He began humbly, became rich, famous and autocratic, and yet died a pauper in a charity hospital. His father was a small-

time cloth merchant and, when he was still in his teens, Poiret was apprenticed to an umbrella maker from whom he used to steal off-cuts of silk to make oriental dresses for dolls. He taught himself to sketch and managed to sell some designs to Mme. CHERUIT at the Maison Raudnitz Soeurs. In 1896, having been consistently selling designs on a freelance basis to most of the top houses in Paris, Poiret agreed to work exclusively for DOUCET. This elegant, charming and refined man had a great effect on Poiret, who set out to emulate him. Doucet was, in fact, instrumental in helping Poiret to gain success when, after an unhappy period (1900–1904) with WORTH, he wished to work for himself. Doucet recommended the famous actress and fashion leader, Rejane (one of his own customers), to patronize his ex-designer.

Left: *The ultimate femme fatale in an outfit by Poiret in 1919. An extravagantly layered skirt (hair, fur or feathers?) makes her look as if she is wearing the scalps of her victims.*

Below: *Flower-embroidery, picture hat and chiffon sleeves are the unlikely ingredients for this frock designed by Poiret in 1920.*

She did and Poiret's name was made. That was in 1904 and during the next ten years Poiret's power as a fashion arbiter grew beyond even his ambitions and hopes.

Even at Worth Poiret had shown signs of the new spirit of fashion, which had displeased M. Jean, but interested his more forward-looking brother, M. Gaston Worth. Once on his own, Poiret's development was swift and determined. By 1906 he had loosened the shape of clothes and was producing soft, amorphous shapes. In 1909 the Ballets Russes arrived in Paris and Poiret's love of the exotic was stimulated. He began to produce his oriental line, using turbans, aigrettes and harem pants. He always refused to admit the influence of the Ballets Russes and BAKST on his designing at this time, but as BEATON* has said, this is 'reminiscent of the Cubists' denial that they had ever seen African art'.

Poiret's 'hobble skirts', brought out two years later, made him notorious. Although as a fashion they were only briefly successful, the public outcry they caused, with a condemnation from the Pope and hundreds of cartoons, brought Poiret world renown. Everyone wanted his clothes. In 1908 he had published an exclusive and beautiful book, with ten full-page coloured

A Poiret evening dress from 1933 in satin has velvet ribbons rippling down the back. Bias-cut and understated, this shows Poiret at his best.

illustrations by IRIBE*, called *Les Robes de Paul Poiret*; in 1911 he published a second book, *Les Choses de Poiret*, with illustrations by LEPAPE*. Not only was he now the most successful couturier in Paris, he was a huge social success. His garden club, L'Oasis, became the venue for lavish and exotic fancy-dress soirées and ever more extravagant entertainments.

Poiret toured Germany and Austria and returned to Paris excited by the new approach to design and craftsmanship which he had found there. Determined to put his own less rigid and less pedantic ideas into practice, he founded the Atelier Martine in 1911. Named after a daughter, this studio took untrained girls and allowed them to express their individuality in designs for textiles, wallpaper and furniture. The designs were then realized by skilled craftsmen. Atelier Martine had a real influence on design at the time, as did Poiret's encouragement of Dufy to embark on textile design. In 1912 he took his wife, his clothes and his model girls on a promotion tour of Berlin, Vienna, Brussels, Moscow and St. Petersburg. This was followed in 1913 by a tour of America.

Poiret disliked the United States: it lacked culture and sophistication and its designers blatantly plagiarized his designs.

On his return to Paris in 1914 he persuaded the other couturiers to join Le Syndicat de Défense de la Grande Couture Française to protect the copyright of their models. He was its first president. World War I forced him to close his doors and, after the war, he found that enthusiasm had waned for his lampshade tunics with wired hems, his ospreys, and the heavy tasselled capes and slave-market jewels which had become his hallmark. By 1924 his day was done. The post-war woman wanted CHANEL, of whom Poiret said, 'what has she invented? Poverty de luxe'. In emulation of Doucet, Poiret had built up a superb art collection. In 1925 he was forced to sell it. By 1929 he was bankrupt and penniless. His wife divorced him in the same year. The chain store, Printemps, offered him a job in 1933 to design ready-to-wear clothes, but the venture failed, due to his completely irresponsible attitude to money. Jacques Worth squashed a motion that the Chambre Syndicale

should give him a pension. He made a living taking small parts in films, wrote his autobiography, *My First Fifty Years*, in 1930 and moved to the South of France. During World War II he became so poor that he was forced to make himself a suit out of a beach *peignoir*. He died of Parkinson's disease.

What were the achievements of the man whom Cocteau described as 'like some huge sort of chestnut'? He claimed for himself that he had freed the bust, but shackled the legs and certainly he led the way in a general relaxation of shape, a loosening of the corsets and a reduction in the number of underclothes a woman had to wear. If he was not an outstanding innovator in terms of the cut and construction of a garment, he was the first couturier to make lecture tours and the first to launch a scent. He was a brilliant self-publicist, in the words of Ernestine Carter, 'adventurous, often ridiculous and outrageous, always courageous'. He dominated fashion and fashionable thinking for almost two decades. In many respects there is justification for seeing him as the great catalyst of 20th-century fashion. He changed the shape of the clothed female body, he banished the tightly corseted curves of the previous generation and he created the slender modern woman. Without this man, both 'shrewd and fatuous' as Mrs. CHASE* remarked, could there have been a Chanel?

Major perfume: Rosine (1911).

PORTER, Thea

Born Damascus, Syria, 1927.
Thea Porter was brought up in Damascus, where her father was a missionary and orientalist. Her work has always reflected this background. Just as Bill GIBB created a fantasy medievalism in his evening wear, so Thea Porter's look is fantasy orientalism. She had no design training and, in fact, read French at London University from 1949 to 1950. She returned to the Middle East in 1953 as the wife of an attaché at the British Embassy in Beirut. There she learned to paint. In 1964 she returned to London and opened a shop to sell Arabian and Turkish artefacts. It was a great success and from it developed the clothes designed by Thea Porter in antique silks and

fabrics. Since 1967 she has concentrated on clothes, especially evening looks, selling a top-quality ready-to-wear line and creating individual designs for private customers as different as Princess Margaret and Elizabeth Taylor. Chiffon, silk and velvet – trimmed, embroidered and beaded – are the signature of this dressmaker.

PREMET
See PARIS COUTURE

PRESTON, Nigel
See MAXFIELD PARRISH

PRICE, Antony
Born Bradford, England, 1945.
After a period following a general art course at Bradford School of Art, Price won a scholarship to the Royal College of Art, where he studied fashion from 1965 to 1968. Although he specialized in women's wear during his course, he decided to produce menswear for his final degree show. His designs won him a trip to New York. On his return he joined Stirling Cooper and worked as a designer with this firm from 1968 to 1974, when he moved to Plaza. Five years later he took over the shop and formed his own company, designing under the Antony Price label for the first time. He is much more than a designer of clothes: he is an imagemaker. The Stirling Cooper and Plaza shops were designed by him and the latter was unique in 1974, being based, as it was, on a display concept. There were no racks of clothes, just one garment (beautifully displayed on boards) which could be made to measure in the customer's colour choice. In this, Price predated ARMANI, who has since shown his clothes to the press and buyers in a similar way, by almost ten years. Price's over-all design skill is also seen in his 'packaging' of the singer, Bryan Ferry, and Roxy Music, for whom he designs record covers, stage sets and stage clothes. His influence on the rock music front is considerable, not only through his Roxy Music connection, but also through the clothes which he designs for other musicians.

Anthony Price's sexy 'services' look shows the excitement of uniforms as a form of provocative dress. The scale of the cap and the luxuriant hair ensure that the appearance is one of extreme femininity but not passivity.

In 1983 Price's 'Fashion Extravaganza' at the Camden Palace fulfilled a long-felt ambition: to show his clothes to the public, not just to the press and buyers. It was a great success, as Bill GIBB's similar exercise had been when it filled London's Albert Hall in 1977. Antony Price's clothes reflect his technical abilities and his interest in construction. They are body-conscious and highly structured and their roots are in Hollywood. They are blatantly sexual, whether for men or women, and they have glamour and theatricality. He is a unique talent in London and shows many of the design qualities of a modern Charles JAMES.

PUCCI, Emilio
Born Naples, Italy, 1914.
Marchese Emilio Pucci di Barsento is descended from the Russian and Italian aristocracy. He studied in Milan, then attended the University of Atlanta, Georgia, and Reed College, Portland, Oregon, where he received a master's degree in the social sciences in 1937. He also holds a doctorate in political science from the University of Florence, which was awarded in 1941. As if this were not strange enough for a designer, he was also a member of Italy's Olympic ski team in 1934 and an officer in the Italian air force during World War II. In 1965 he became a member of the Italian parliament. He slid into the fashion field almost by accident, as a result of being photographed in 1947, wearing ski clothes of his own design, by Toni FRISSELL*. This led to his designing women's ski wear for Lord and Taylor in the following year. He opened a shop on Capri in 1949 and in 1950 he founded Emilio, his couture house. That year he also opened boutiques in Rome, Elba and Montecatini.

Suddenly it was essential for the *chic* woman to own something by Pucci. His forte was simple silk jersey chemises and very strong prints using bold colour in abstract patterns. A Pucci print was immediately recognizable and, although often based on medieval heraldic banners of the sort waved at the Siena Palio, so utterly of the moment that it could be taken as a classic symbol of the late 1950s and early 1960s. His clothes during the 1960s were signed like works of art and his shifts are now collector's items. He was a brilliant colourist and his colours became *the* colours of the decade (hot pink, lime, blue, purple). Pucci's impact on the beaches and in the boutiques is well known, but it should be remembered that his protean talents have spread into many different areas of design, including pottery, motor cars and linens. He seemed able to capture the sun and fun of Italy in his prints and, along with GALITZINE, he can take the credit for creating the concept of relaxed, informal elegance in Italian fashion. He was presented with the Neiman-Marcus Award in 1954, a suitable recognition of the fact that, apart from SCHIAPARELLI in Paris, he was the first Italian to achieve international status.

Q·R

QUANT · RABANNE · RAHVIS · RAYNE · REBOUX (*See* MILLINERS) · REDFERN · REVILLE AND ROSSITER · RHODES · RICCI · RIVA
ROBERTS · ROCHAS · ROSE · ROSSI · ROUFF · RYKIEL

Rhodes

Above: *Ricci*
Left: *Rykiel*

QUANT, Mary

Born London, England, 1934.

A legendary name which personifies the youth revolution of the 1950s and 1960s, Mary Quant is now, sadly, secondary to the main fashion stream which she once led and her creativity seems to take second place to her commercial abilities. However, in the 1960s, Mary Quant's awareness and shrewd understanding of social changes made hers the most famous name in fashion ever to have come out of London.

She studied at Goldsmith's College of Art in London. There she met Alexander Plunket Greene. They were married in 1957, two years after opening the first Bazaar shop in the King's Road, London, in partnership with Archie McNair. This talented trio set a new standard in merchandising clothes for the young and made the King's Road a world-famous tourist attraction, which it remains today. Initially, Bazaar sold clothes designed by others but, frustrated by the manufacturers' lack of awareness of what the young customer required, Mary Quant began designing her own stock. She was so in tune with the mood of the moment that her clothes sold instantly. Whether she originated the mini-skirt is now an academic and unimportant question. She is certainly the designer who popularized it in Great Britain and, to a degree, in the United States. She was also one of the first designers to realize that the young no longer wished to dress like their mothers. She produced for them clothes that their mothers could not wear without looking disastrous. With her began the lucrative trade of designing specifically and exclusively for the teenage and early twenties market, one which, even today, is still a hugely growing industry. Her business began on a tiny scale, as she ran up her designs in her bed-sitter. The clothes she made were classless and iconoclastic. She was not afraid to violate previously-held canons of good taste. Her clothes were eagerly bought by a generation with considerable spending power for whom clothes were at the centre of existence. She herself said: 'by luck . . . by chance . . . perhaps even by mistake . . . we were on to a huge thing . . . a tremendous renaissance in fashion'.

In 1961 she opened her second Bazaar, in Knightsbridge, and by 1963 she was exporting to the United States. In that year she moved into mass production with her 'Ginger Group' line and she received a fashion award from *The Sunday Times*. In 1966, the year that she was honoured with the O.B.E. (Order of the British Empire), she founded her cosmetics empire, now a world-wide money-spinner. Throughout the 1970s her licences grew to include bed-linen, jewellery, carpets, men's ties and sunglasses. In 1973 the Museum of London gave her a retrospective exhibition, which seemed to imply that her days as a creative leader were drawing to a close. Whether one finds her contribution to fashion lasting or worthwhile is not important: no one can deny her claim to a central place in the cultural revolution which is still continuing today. Perhaps her sociological significance will, in the end, outweigh her reputation as a designer. Her autobiography, *Quant by Quant*, was published in London in 1966.

RABANNE, Paco □

Born San Sebastian, Spain, 1934.

Rabanne's mother was BALENCIAGA's chief seamstress and in 1939 his family moved from Spain, as did the maestro, to escape the Spanish Civil War. In Paris Rabanne studied architecture at the École Supérieure des Beaux Arts. He began in fashion as a freelance designer of handbags, shoes and embroideries. His interest in 'pop' art led him to create soft sculptures of plastic and feathers. His knowledge of architecture and his interest in sculpture are evident in his approach to fashion, an approach which was revolutionary in the 1960s and even now is ahead of the thinking of most designers. It is arguable that he has moved into a self-indulgent 'dead end', since much of the excitement of his clothes cannot be capitalized on in practical terms. Nevertheless, his influence has been seminal: VERSACE's experiments with chainmail are in direct line with what Rabanne was doing in the 1960s.

Rabanne's great interest lay in exploiting the potential of modern materials not previously considered possible for clothing. He worked primarily with plastic, making dresses of plastic discs linked by

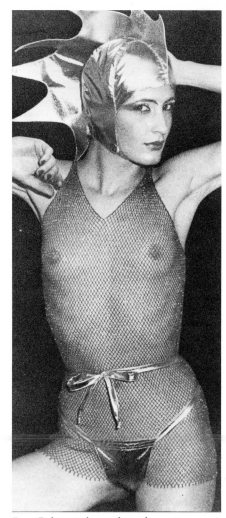

Paco Rabanne shows that when a designer's perfumes are hugely successful he can afford to take an unconventional approach to clothes! This outfit was launched on an unprepared public in 1981.

metal chains. He liked the incongruity of disparate materials and was one of the first to combine knits and fur. Welded or moulded garments were his forte. Paco Rabanne's work is in many museums, but whether it should be shown under 'sculpture', 'industrial design' or 'fashion' is arguable. What is beyond argument is the enormous success of his two perfumes, 'Paco' and 'Calandre', which help considerably towards funding his experiments.

Major perfumes: Calandre (1966); Paco (1973); Metal (1979).

RAHVIS, Raemonde

Born Cape Town, South Africa, 1918.
After a South African childhood and a period at a Swiss finishing school, Rae-monde Rahvis worked briefly as a model. Between 1935 and 1941, the date of the founding of the house of Rahvis with her sister Dorothy, she shared design prem-ises with others before moving into the elegance of a Mayfair salon. Her fashion house in Grosvenor Square was renowned for its magnificent marble staircase. She was a member of the Incorporated Society of London Fashion Designers. The Rahvis trademark was quality. Modern design, beautiful fabrics and haute-couture cutting produced luxurious evening looks and impeccably tailored day clothes. With this dedication to perfection, it is not sur-prising that icily elegant models like Barbara Goalen and Fiona Campbell-Walker were at one time Rahvis models. In addition to her haute couture, Rahvis designed for the theatre and the British film industry: she designed the clothes for *Room At the Top* and many other films. The house continues and, like LACHASSE and AMIES, it perpetuates the standards of the now almost totally defunct London high-fashion scene.

RAYNE, Edward

Born London, England, 1922.
The family shoe firm of H. & M. Rayne was founded in London in 1889 and provided shoes for a largely theatrical clientele. The scope was broadened by the opening of a shop in Bond Street in 1920. There are now three Rayne shops in London, 'shops within shops' and world-wide export agreements. Edward Rayne joined the firm in 1940, when he was eighteen, and he learned the trade by undergoing a full apprenticeship. He took over as managing director at the age of twenty-nine, when his father died. In 1961 he purchased a half share in Delman, the American shoe firm, and formed Rayne-Delman Shoes Inc. In 1973 Rayne was acquired by Debenhams, the British department-store chain which, three years later, bought out I. Miller, the American shoe company. Rayne shoes are elegant, sophisticated and well-crafted and they have always set a high standard for mass-produced footwear.

Twin dressing in 1930 in identical outfits from the house of Redfern. The whole look is delightfully soft and feminine but is not exactly a reflection of the times!

REBOUX, Caroline

See MILLINERS (French)

REDFERN

Founded London, England, 1841.
Closed late 1920s.
The house of Redfern, founded by John Redfern, is remembered chiefly as court dressmaker to Queen Victoria and Queen Alexandra. It was, in fact, a very large concern, and in its heyday it had branches in New York, Chicago, London and Paris.

Its beginnings were modest enough. Redfern first opened as a draper in Cowes, on the Isle of Wight. The girls who worked in his salon were exceptionally *chic* and always wore fresh orchid buttonholes. They were known throughout the town as 'Redfern's bunnies'. As Cowes grew in fashionability as a yachting centre, so Redfern expanded to include a ladies' tailoring department to attract the rich and fashionable who descended for Cowes Race Week. This venture prospered and with his sons Redfern opened a branch in London. In 1879 his efforts were crowned by the publicity he obtained for a jersey suit he made for the 'Jersey Lily', Lillie Langtry. From then on his business flourished and he dressed ladies from the grandest circles. By 1888 he was 'By Royal Appointment to Her Majesty the Queen and H.R.H. The Princess of Wales'. No higher success was possible in London and his couture house was added to his highly successful tailoring one. American branches soon followed and in 1881 he opened a salon in Paris, with John Poynter as its head. The Paris house continued to flourish after Redfern's death and it became a member of the Chambre Syndicale de la Haute Couture. Poynter remained as designer. Redfern was famed for its tailoring 'à l'Anglaise'. In 1916 the firm was responsible for the design of the first women's uniform for the International Red Cross.

REVILLE AND ROSSITER

Founded London, England, 1906.
Closed mid-1930s.
This couture house was founded by two buyers from Jay's, the now defunct London department store. Miss Rossiter was in charge of administration and Mr. William Reville was the designer. In 1910, four years after the firm began, it was appointed court dressmaker to Queen Mary. In those days the royal family was considered the arbiter of taste, if not exactly the leader of fashion. So, with a royal warrant, Reville and Rossiter automatically designed for the majority of London's society hostesses. In 1911 they designed the Queen's coronation robe and became a household name – admittedly in rather grand households!

Court dressmakers had to conform to certain rules: magnificence had to be tempered by seemliness and scandalously original creations were frowned upon. In a word, they had to be staid. That was the price exacted for the huge publicity which association with the palace automatically ensured, and although Reville and Rossiter continued as court dressmakers after World War I and were responsible for dressing a large proportion of society for 'the season', their days were numbered. Their sedately elaborate creations and

the sumptuous beading and embroidery they employed had an old-fashioned Edwardian feel that was out of tune with the times. They did not understand the new approaches upon which CHANEL and MOLYNEUX were soon to capitalize. Simplicity, wearability and ease were what women wanted after the war. They were no longer interested in stiff formality. As a result, by the end of the 1920s the firm

of Reville and Rossiter was in decline. In the late 1930s it merged with BUSVINE. Reville died in poverty, totally forgotten.

RHODES, Zandra ☐

Born Chatham, England, 1942.
Zandra Rhodes designs romantic and fantastic clothes which cannot be mistaken for the work of any other designer.

Pearl-sewn hems and furry trim add to the exotic pattern and complex layering of this dress by Zandra Rhodes from her March 1983 collection.

She is an excellent example of the importance of truth to purpose and courage. She is like her work: totally original and eccentric. Her mother had been chief fitter at WORTH in Paris and a lecturer in fashion at Medway College of Art. Zandra studied textile design and lithography at Medway and completed her education at the Royal College of Art, from which she graduated in 1966. She originally intended to be a textile designer and she set up her own print works to produce fabrics for British designers. She opened the Fulham Road Clothes Shop in order to sell dresses made of her own prints and in 1968, by which time she was convinced that she was the best person to interpret her fabric designs, she established her own dress firm. She was right. Her look has grown stronger over the years and it is now beautifully romantic, but with bite: 'outrageous' is a word frequently used to describe both clothes and designer.

Zandra Rhodes has reached her peak and found her level. One does not expect the shock of the new. What one expects, and gets, is a strongly personal, perfectly

worked-out approach to clothes. The approach must be applauded for its strength, even if it seems irrelevant to present-day needs. Her fabrics – chiffons, silks, tulles – are hand-printed with squiggles, zig zags and stars and float like butterfly wings. She has given us ruffled tulle crinolines, glamorized punk, uneven hems, bubble dresses – all with the strong Rhodes signature. She was named Designer of the Year by the British Clothing Institute in 1972. Her fabrics for furnishings are sold under the CVP label in London. Zandra Rhodes sees herself as an artist and markets a 'Works of Art Collection' in which each garment carries the message, 'This is one of my special dresses; I think of it as an art work that you will treasure for ever'.

RICCI, Nina

Born Turin, Italy, 1883.
Died Paris, France, 1970.
One of Paris' longest-running houses was opened in 1932 by Nina Ricci. It is headed today by her son, Robert, who works with

A very sophisticated fur and wool top coat by Nina Ricci in 1959 is given the added touch of a head-hugging cloche and long, supple leather gloves to complete the picture.

Gérard PIPART as his design chief. Madame Ricci (born Maria Nielli) was brought up in Turin, but moved to France with her family at the age of twelve. As a child she made hats and clothes for her dolls and when she was thirteen she began an apprenticeship with a couturier. Her talents were given practical development and her abilities showed themselves. At eighteen she was head of an atelier and by twenty-one she was a premier stylist. With this invaluable experience behind her, she opened her own house in 1932, encouraged and supported by her husband Louis, a jeweller. Her style was distinctive and quite different from those of other female designers such as CHANEL or SCHIAPARELLI. She understood the science of cutting and normally worked directly with the bolts of cloth draped on a model. But she was in no sense an originator of fashion ideas like her peers. Her house

Extraordinary hats by Stephen Jones add a touch of fantasy to these Zandra Rhodes silk dresses for Spring/Summer 1984.

'Triomphe de la vente', a cocktail dress from Nina Ricci's 1947 collection, complete with feathered hat, jewellery and long lace gloves.

A Nina Ricci two piece, from the 1963 collection, in light grey shantung with a hat of fine black straw.

Right: *An extremely elegant Nina Ricci outfit from 1962: heavy black silk crêpe is used for the dress and overskirt; the neckline and large hat are in sable.*

flourished because it provided *chic* clothes for elegant and wealthy women who had no special desire to be in the vanguard of fashion.

In 1945 Mme Ricci's son took over the management of the house and successfully extended its activities on an international scale. In 1951 Mme Ricci chose Jean-François CRAHAY to collaborate with her in designing the collections and from 1959 to 1963 he was entirely responsible for design. In 1963 he left the firm and Pipart became the designer. The name and the fortune of the house of Ricci have, to a considerable degree, been based on perfume: 'L'Air du Temps', in its Lalique *flaçon* with a frosted-glass bird as the stopper, is notable in a tradition which continued in 1980 with the introduction of 'Eau de Fleurs'.

Major perfumes: L'Air du Temps (1948); Farouche (1973).

RIVA, Heinz

Born Zürich, Switzerland, 1938.
Riva's mother ran a Swiss fashion house and encouraged his interest in design. After studying in Zürich, he went to Paris to study at L'École de la Chambre Syndicale. This was followed by a brief period of work in Paris and London, and in 1963 he joined GALITZINE in Rome as a design assistant. He opened his own house in Rome in 1966.

ROBERTS, Patricia

Born Barnard Castle, England, 1945.
In Great Britain Patricia Roberts' name is synonymous with all aspects of knitting, not only because of her knitwear collection, but also because of her stylishly produced pattern books which have done much to abolish the old-fashioned and dowdy image of home-knitting. She studied fashion on a four-year Diploma Course at Leicester College of Art from 1963 to 1967, then worked in the knitwear department of IPC Magazines. By 1972 she was a free-lance pattern designer and through *Vogue* magazine she was asked to supply knitwear for certain London shops. The demand quickly developed and she was soon producing a Patricia Roberts Knitwear collection to sell in better-quality stores throughout the world. Her first knitting shop under her own name was opened in 1976, followed by a second in 1979 and a third in 1982. All are in London and all carry her 'Woollybear' yarns as well as knitted garments. She shows twice a year at the London Designer Collections. All her garments are knitted by hand.

ROCHAS, Marcel

Born Paris, France, 1902.
Died Paris, France, 1955.
The house of Rochas was opened in 1924 in Faubourg Saint-Honoré and moved to avenue Matignon in 1931. Rochas was a lively contributor to couture, full of fantastic ideas and great enthusiasms. His enthusiasms, indeed, outran his judgement on occasions, the most infamous being in 1931, when eight women appeared at a party in the identical black satin Rochas dress, each of them having bought on the assumption that it was a 'one-off'. The tantrums and ensuing publicity made his name. Rochas' ideas were important and original. Many claim that he invented the

The Rochas' way with the 'New Look':
spotted silk and white lace creates a demure
dress with tiered skirt and three-quarter
sleeves which is very much in the spirit of
the late forties.

Left: *From 1925 to 1950. On the right*
Madame Rochas wears a suit from her
husband's 1950 collection while the
outfit on the left is from a Rochas
collection of 1925. The sleeve treatment
was a precursor of Schiaparelli's military
line, the collar is white lamb.

broad-shouldered military look before SCHIAPARELLI, although she is always credited with it. He could be said to have presaged the 'New Look' with his long skirts in 1941, his *bustier* of 1943 and his 'guipure' corset in 1946. He was the first couturier to put pockets in skirts and created two-thirds length coats. His perfume, 'Femme', in its black-lace packaging, is a classic. In 1951 he published *Twenty-five Years of Parisian Elegance, 1925–50.*

Major perfumes: Femme (1945); Madame Rochas (1960); Mystère (1978).

ROSE, Helen

Born Chicago, USA, 1918.

Helen Rose began work at the age of sixteen with 20th Century Fox. She then became designer for the San Francisco Ice Follies and remained with them for fourteen years. In the 1940s she returned to film work, first with Fox in 1943 and then, from 1944, with M.G.M. She became famous for her wedding gowns for stars such as Elizabeth Taylor, Grace Kelly and Debbie Reynolds. As a result of her costumes for *Cat on a Hot Tin Roof*, she set up her own manufacturing company.

ROSSI, Tita

Born Rome, Italy, 1922.

Tita Rossi's parents ran a fashion school and she followed the traditional family involvement in the world of fashion by opening her own high-fashion house in Rome in 1960. Although her name is not widely known outside Italy, she has for the past twenty years produced clothes of a very high standard of workmanship. They strongly reflect Italian tastes in exclusive clothes and she has maintained a high proportion of her countrywomen as customers. She has received many fashion

Maggie Rouff (on left) enjoying a night out with Les Girls!

Below: *A Maggie Rouff cocktail dress in pure silk shantung. It is called 'Mah Jong' and was shown in Spring 1960.*

awards, including the Gran Gala della Moda Italiana (1963) and the Premio Schubert (1978).

ROUFF, Maggie

Born Paris, France, 1896.
Died Paris, France, 1971.
Chevalier de la Légion d'Honneur and Conseilleuse du Commerce Extérieur, Maggie Rouff was an unspectacular, but convincing, success às a Parisian couturier. Her mother was Belgian and worked as DRÉCOLL's head designer. She began by designing sports clothes for Drécoll, then opened her own house in the former Drécoll premises in 1929 and was soon successful. After a tour of America she published *L'Amérique vue au Microscope*. She was also the author of the best-selling *The Philosophy of Elegance*. Her clothes were feminine, relaxed and wearable.

RYKIEL, Sonia   ☐

Born Paris, France, 1930.
Sonia Rykiel is the cool, sophisticated lady of Paris fashion. Untrained, she began her career in 1962, when she was pregnant. Frustrated by the maternity clothes she found in shops, she started to design her own. Her husband owned shops called 'Laura' and she continued designing in a small way for these outlets. By 1968 she had her own boutique in the Paris department store, Galeries Lafayette, then opened her own shop on the Left Bank. She has developed a very strong personal look, practical but sensual. Her softly fluid, coolly elegant designs have sometimes been absolutely right for the moment and sometimes not. But she has never changed her stance. Hers is a very strong, personal statement that has developed logically and consistently. It is based on soft jersey, crêpe and city knits and has now become classic. Her colours are beige, grey and black and her line is glamorously sophisticated. In 1979 she published *And I Would Like Her Naked*. Sonia Rykiel is Vice-President of the Chambre Syndicale du Prêt-à-Porter des Couturiers et des Créateurs de Mode. She is now one of the very best designers working in Paris and her feminine, wearable clothes are a world-wide success.

Sonia Rykiel's lady-like way with wool jersey is exemplified by this sophisticated but relaxed look from her October 1981 collection.

S

SAINT CYR (*See* MILLINERS) · SAINT LAURENT · SANCHEZ · SAN LORENZO (*See* ITALIAN READY-TO-WEAR) · SANT' ANGELO · SARLI
SCAASI · SCHARAFF · SCHERRER · SCHIAPARELLI · SCHLUMBERGER · SCHÖN · SCHUBERTH · SCOTT · SHAMASK · SHERARD
SHILLING · SIMONETTA · SIMPSON · SMITH, G. · SMITH, W. · SOPRANI · STEWART (*See* BODY MAP) · STIEBEL · SUPPON
SVEND (*See* MILLINERS)

Schiaparelli

Soprani

SAINT CYR, Claude
See MILLINERS (French)

SAINT LAURENT, Yves □
Born Oran, Algeria, 1936.
Yves Saint Laurent is *the* fashion genius of
the second half of the 20th century. A
master of colour, he has an unequalled
sense of form and is probably the most
reliable fashion barometer in Paris. In
his designs the very best of CHANEL and
BALENCIAGA melt together into a modern
form. He is the heir to their passionate
concern for cut, the basis of all haute
couture. John FAIRCHILD* called him 'the
complete innovator' and he was right.
Although Saint Laurent has been influenced by Chanel, Balenciaga and DIOR,
the real influence on his attitudes as an
artist are Proust, the Ballets Russes,
Picasso and Chinese painting. He takes
them all and produces, year by year,
perfectly beautiful clothes which can be
worn by *anyone*.

Saint Laurent's background was middle-
class. His first interest was theatre and
costume design. He came to Paris at the
age of sixteen and, after returning to
Algeria, he entered the International Wool
Secretariat design contest. In 1953 he won
third place, but in 1954 he was the first-
prize winner with a design for a cocktail
dress (made up by GIVENCHY); LAGERFELD
took second prize with a design for a coat.
Saint Laurent met Michel de Brunhoff,
director of French *Vogue*, before returning
to Oran. After graduating in modern
languages, Saint Laurent returned to Paris
and enrolled at the Chambre Syndicale
school in the autumn of 1954. In 1955
Brunhoff arranged a meeting with Dior.
After a fifteen-minute interview, Dior
offered Saint Laurent a job in what was,
at that time, the most prestigious fashion
house in the world. Saint Laurent set to
work to learn his craft at the side of the
maestro and, on Dior's death in 1957, he
took over the house, at the age of twenty-
one.

His first collection was a great success.
Subsequent collections proved less popular
and his Left Bank collection in 1960
was almost a disaster. Taking advantage
of his call-up for the Algerian war, the
house of Dior replaced him with Marc

Right: *An elegant draped tunic by Yves
Saint Laurent for Christian Dior-New York
in a wool and silk mixture is gathered into
a slim skirt. The outfit is all line — no
unnecessary detail takes away from the
purity of the style.*

Below: *An Yves Saint Laurent wool
cocktail suit for Christian Dior in 1960.
The skirt is tulip-shaped and the hip-length
jacket is decorated with bows to give an
overall effect of great refinement and
sophistication.*

BOHAN. After two-and-a-half months, Saint
Laurent was invalided out of the army. He
sued Dior for $40,000 and together with
his partner, business adviser and friend,
Pierre Bergé, opened his own house in
1962. From the beginning he was beloved
of the press, from *Women's Wear Daily*
downwards, although he has had many
disagreements with them. He banned
them from his 1965 shows because they
had been so unkind to his 1964 collection;
and after his 'Forties' collection in 1971
was labelled 'hideous' and 'a tour de force
of bad taste', he announced that August
1971 would be his last collection of
couture: 'haute couture cannot be mod-
ernized'. However, he continued to show
haute couture in 1972, although he
allowed only *Paris Match* to see his show.

There is no doubt that the way women
dress in the 1980s springs from the experiments which Yves Saint Laurent made
when he was searching for a style in the
1960s. By the early 1970s he had not only
found his style, he had changed the
appearance of women: he popularized a
day wardrobe which, relying as it did on
blazers, trousers and shirts, was basically
masculine. His evening wear, in contrast,

Left: *Glamour dressing by Yves Saint Laurent with a long-jacketed tweed suit, large gauntlets and lots of patterned fur. The silhouette tapers from broad shoulders and lapels to a straight skirt.*

Right: *A perfectly proportioned two-colour tunic by Yves Saint Laurent in an outfit of the greatest sublety shows why he is still the leader after over twenty years.*

was romantically feminine. He invented his own classics and they re-appear, subtly modified, but always absolutely right for the moment, season after season. Having taken over many of Balenciaga's workers, Saint Laurent has a uniquely supportive staff who can realize any idea that comes into his head. With them and the special genius of Bergé behind him, Saint Laurent has refined his approach to design. His clothes, in later years, have shown a marked and consistent style unique to himself, uninfluenced by any of his contemporaries. He now employs more than ten thousand people world-wide. His highly successful 'Rive Gauche' boutiques for his ready-to-wear were established in 1966; his menswear division, which is hugely popular, was begun in 1974; and a children's line made in the United States was introduced in 1978. His initials are now on just about everything to do with fashion: swimwear, sunglasses, scarves and bed linen are perhaps the most prominent. His perfume and cosmetic empires are huge, although eighty per cent of them is owned by Charles of the Ritz. 'Opium' and 'Y' (his first perfume, launched in 1964) are best-sellers for women, and for

men he has launched 'Pour Homme' and 'Kouros'.

Saint Laurent is, of all the French designers, uniquely sensitive to events around him and has been so since the 1960s, when he was heavily influenced by student political unrest and Left-Bank attitudes. He does, however, pay heavily for his sensitivity: Pierre Bergé is reputed to have said that 'Yves was born with a nervous breakdown'. Apart from his feminized male looks, seen most successfully in his ultra-*chic* smoking and tuxedo looks, his most noteworthy collections were probably his much-pirated 'Mondrian' look of 1965, his 'Rich Fantasy Peasant' line of 1976 and his 'Homage to Picasso' collection of 1979. Less successful were his see-through blouses of 1966 and his 'Longuettes' of 1970. However, his superb ability to mix the classic and the fantastic, for which *Time* magazine called him 'The Sun King of Fashion', is unequalled. So is his understanding of prints: he works with Abraham, the famous silk printers, to produce superb designs. In addition to his four large collections of about two hundred outfits a year, he has designed for the ballet and theatre – most notably, *Cyrano de Bergerac*, *The Marriage of Figaro* and, with ERTÉ, *Der Rosenkavalier*.

He received a Neiman-Marcus Award in 1958. In 1983 Diana VREELAND* organized a retrospective of his work at the Costume Institute of the Metropolitan Museum of Art. Only Balenciaga had been so honoured and Yves Saint Laurent is the first living designer to be featured.

Yves Saint Laurent, intense, highly-strung and emotional, is, without doubt, the greatest designer of his time. It must also be noted that he was the couturier who, in a sense, helped to weaken the position held by haute couture. As early as

1966 he realized, with his uncanny instinct for being in tune with his time, that a revolution was happening in the fashion world. His Pop Art couture collection of that year made an enormous impact because it worked against everything couture had stood for. Thereafter, understatement, elegance and taste could no longer be relied upon. The basis of future fashion was casualness and Saint Laurent was the first couturier to realize this. Nevertheless, it is his couture collections – the climax of his genius and the perfection of his style – which make him the greatest designer since Balenciaga.

Major perfumes: Y (1964); Rive Gauche (1970); Opium (1977); Paris (1983).

SANCHEZ, Fernando

Born Spain, 1930s.

Sanchez's father was Spanish and his mother Flemish, but his design education was French. He studied at the École Chambre Syndicale de la Couture in Paris and won a prize in the same International Wool Secretariat competition in which SAINT LAURENT and LAGERFELD won awards. This was followed by a job at DIOR designing lingerie, sweaters and accessories for the Dior boutiques. This job took him to New York to work with the Warner Company. He spent several years working between New York and Paris. He also began to make a name for himself with his adventurous fur designs for Revillon. He founded his own company in 1974 to produce lingerie and loungewear. For his work in the fields of lingerie and fur he won the Coty American Fashion Critics' Award. He has twice received a Special Award for his lingerie (1974 and 1977) and once a Special Award for fur design (1975). Sanchez launched a ready-to-wear line in the early 1980s, which has been shown in tandem with his loungewear and lingerie. All are in the same mood – sexy, dramatic and often vibrantly coloured.

SAN LORENZO, Paula
See ITALIAN READY-TO-WEAR

SANT' ANGELO, Giorgio
Born Florence, Italy, 1936.
A multi-faceted designer, one of America's avant garde, Sant' Angelo was brought up in Argentina and educated in Italy, where he studied law, industrial design and architecture. He studied with Picasso in the South of France and in 1962 moved to Hollywood to work for Disney. He began to work as a freelance textile designer for Cohn-Hall Marx and Marcus Brothers, two of America's leading fabric houses, and as a design consultant. His experimental work for Dupont led him to design fashion accessories made with Lucite. They were an immediate and widespread sensation. In 1966 he founded Sant' Angelo ready-to-wear and in 1968, the year of his first Coty award, he created di Sant' Angelo Inc. After his success with accessories, his next memorable fashion statements were his gypsy and patchwork looks. His influence on American fashion is considerable and consistent; he is involved in all aspects of design, including designing the film *Cleopatra Jones*. His couture clothes for the well-heeled are excellent examples of the relaxed fluidity characteristic of the best American designers. His second Coty award, a 'Winnie', came in 1970.

SARLI, Fausto
Born Naples, Italy, 1927.
Sarli's family lost all its wealth in World War II and to recoup the losses Sarli studied fashion in Rome. He won a design competition and in 1974 showed his first collection in Florence. He is based in Rome, but his clothes are made in Naples, under the control of his two elder sons. After fourteen years of success in designing women's clothes, he branched out with equal success as a designer for men.

SCAASI, Arnold
Born Montreal, Canada, 1931.
Scaasi's father was a furrier. His real name is Isaacs, but, considering the name to be too prosaic, he reversed it to make the title by which he has been known throughout his design career. He went to live in Australia when he was a teenager and he studied art there. He continued his studies when he returned to Montreal (specializing in design) and completed them in Paris at the Chambre Syndicale. He worked briefly at PAQUIN, then moved to New York in the early 1950s to work as a sketcher for Charles JAMES. After this sound apprenticeship, Scaasi opened his own wholesale business in New York in 1957. His success was almost immediate: he won a Coty 'Winnie' in 1958 and a Neiman-Marcus Award the following year. In 1963 he stopped making ready-to-wear and concentrated on haute couture, producing custom-made clothes for the rich and glamorous end of the market. He is especially admired for his grand evening dresses in luxurious fabrics, intricately cut and trimmed with fur and feathers.

SCHARAFF, Irene
Born Boston, USA.
Scharaff was basically a theatre designer who moved over to Hollywood. Her greatest successes were with M.G.M., for whom she designed costumes for several spectacular musicals. Through the medium of film she had a considerable influence, not only on millions of women world-wide, but also on American designers. She created costumes for many films, of which the most influential were probably *The King and I*, *Hello Dolly* and *Funny Girl*.

SCHERRER, Jean Louis ☐
Born Paris, France, 1936.
It is surprising that a couture house should be born in the 1970s, a period when everyone was convinced of couture's imminent death. Yet this is when the house of Scherrer was founded. It was able to establish itself because it was strongly backed by industrial supporters and it succeeded because the wives of prominent politicians, including Mme. Giscard d'Estaing, were customers. Scherrer was destined to be a dancer and trained in ballet at the Paris Conservatory. At the age of twenty he had an accident which damaged his back and made dancing as a career impossible. While recuperating, he began to experiment with fashion sketches. These were shown to DIOR, with the result that Scherrer joined Yves SAINT LAURENT as assistant to the maestro. He learned the intricacies of cutting and draping which are the bases of couture. When Dior died and Saint Laurent was chosen as his successor, Scherrer left. He found a real-estate millionaire to back him and set up opposite the house of Dior. He has had a considerable degree of success with his elegant and rather elaborate clothes at both ready-to-wear and couture level, and he sells very well.
Major perfume: Jean Louis Scherrer (1980).

SCHIAPARELLI, Elsa
Born Rome, Italy, 1890.
Died Paris, France, 1973.
'That Italian artist who makes dresses' was how CHANEL sneeringly described Schiaparelli and it is, in fact, a good description of this original and rather startling star of 1930s fashion. Her viewpoint was much more in line with the Surrealist artists' thinking than with traditional couture approaches. She was a sensational designer, not a sophisticated one. In place of a continuous development based on a design philosophy, she had a brilliant knack of producing the witty shape or the clever accessory which was perfectly in tune with the moment. Her very entry into couture was accidental.

The daughter of a Roman professor of oriental languages, she studied philosophy, married and moved to New York.

The Duchess of Windsor, photographed in 1937 by Cecil Beaton, wears a full-length dinner dress by Schiaparelli with extravagantly curled trimming from neck to hip line.

A pale blue outfit by Schiaparelli in 1938 shows the strong influence of Dali's surrealist fantasies and also foreshadows the torn, cut and shirred Japanese effects of the early eighties.

This Schiaparelli coat is posed by Beaton like an Egyptian hieroglyph to bring out the angularity of the design.

In 1920 her husband left her and she went to Paris with her daughter, but no money. She designed herself a black sweater with a *trompe l'oeil* white collar and bow which was knitted for her by an Armenian peasant. A buyer saw it, gave her an order, and she was in the fashion business practically overnight. She had found her métier. As a brilliant self-publicist and exploiter of novelty, for whom to be 'amusing' was more important than to be tasteful, she was given huge press coverage. By 1930 the little band of Armenian knitters with whom she had started had swollen to more than 2,000 employees working in twenty-six work-rooms.

In 1935 Schiaparelli moved to the Place Vendôme, where she opened one of the first couture boutiques. She sold sweaters, blouses, scarves and jewellery. The boutique's decoration included 'Pascal', a life-size wooden artist's figure, and a stuffed bear (which Dali had dyed shocking pink) with drawers in its stomach. Schiaparelli's originality had a permanent effect on fashion, and not everything she designed had merely the shock of surprise to recommend it. In 1933 she created the 'pagoda' sleeve which, in its new large dimension, became the pattern for several years. Wide padded shoulders, reminiscent of those on a guardsman's greatcoat, were thus invented and they remained the major fashion shape until DIOR's 'New Look'. Apart from this, Schiaparelli's genius lay in her ability to take something ordinary and transform it, with witty detail, into something amusing and new. She used tweed for evening; coloured plastic zips as decorative features on dresses; padlock fastenings on suits; and huge ceramic buttons in the shape of hands, butterflies or whatever else took her fancy. Her hats were notorious. She made them in the shape of a shoe, a lamb cutlet – whatever amused her. She is best remembered for the very strong pink which she introduced. She called it 'shocking pink' and indeed it was. Such a strong and violent shade had never been

A light-hearted look from the house of Schiaparelli in the mid-fifties updates the Italian Commedia dell'Arte costumes of the seventeenth century for a glazed cotton harlequin top.

Below: *This silk brocade evening jacket by Schiaparelli is patterned with her famous horses which were a feature of her circus collection.*

seen in couture before. Her perfume, 'Shocking', in a bottle shaped like a tailor's dummy, became world-famous.

Like Chanel, Schiaparelli was more than just a dressmaker. She mixed with intellectuals and artists and perhaps her most lasting contribution to couture was to involve artists in fashion. Cocteau and BÉRARD* both provided her with ideas for embroidery and hats, but it was with Dali that she developed the most productive partnership. They were an ingenious pair. They devised a skirt printed with a lobster, materials patterned with her press clippings, and even a coat based on Dali's *City of Drawers*, with pockets like drawers. She was the first to show collections with themes such as the zodiac or the circus.

All this *chic* outrage died with the fall of France in 1940. Schiaparelli left for the United States and remained there for the duration of the war. She re-opened in Paris in 1945, but although she continued until 1954, her day was over: fashion had moved forward. She closed her doors to spend her retirement in Tunisia and Paris. Her approach to fashion was slick, sophisticated and instinctive: her sense of humour was in strong contrast to the serious self-infatuation of Chanel and she had the courage to be outrageous. If POIRET was the fashion leader in the teens of the century, and Chanel dominated the 1920s, then Schiaparelli's vitality epitomized the 1930s. In 1940 she received the Neiman-Marcus Award and in 1954 she published her autobiography, *Shocking Life*. She was sufficiently well-known in intellectual circles for her name to appear in Louis MacNeice's poem, 'Bagpipe Music', where he writes of the Muse:

'With false eyelashes and fingernails of carmine
And dressed by Schiaparelli, with a pill-box hat.'

Major perfumes: Shocking (1937); Zût (1948); Succès Fou (1953).

SCHLUMBERGER, Jean

Born France, 1907.

One of a handful of world-class jewellery designers, Schlumberger began his working life as a member of the textile trade, after an education in Switzerland. In the late 1930s he made a living by mounting Dresden china flowers, found in the Paris flea market, to make clips and brooches. His originality and wit appealed to the iconoclastic SCHIAPARELLI, who employed him on a freelance basis to make outrageous costume jewellery for her. He began by using gold and precious stones and his jewellery was soon selling to such trend-setters as the Duchess of Windsor, Daisy Fellowes and Millicent Rogers. He joined the army in World War II, was evacuated at Dunkirk, and eventually reached America. He rejoined the theatre of war with the Free French, but, with the cessation of hostilities, returned to New York to work as a jeweller. In 1956 he joined Tiffany and Co. His work has a delicacy and strength which put him in the same class as the Renaissance jewellers of Italy. He has frequently been referred to as a latter-day Cellini or Fabergé. These claims may seem exaggerated, but what is beyond controversy is his virtuosity with gold, diamonds and emeralds and his revival of various almost-lost techniques. His work has fantasy without vulgarity and is refined without being vapid.

SCHÖN, Mila ☐

House founded Milan, Italy, 1958.

Mila Schön's parents were Yugoslav aristocrats who fled the Communists and went to Italy to live in Trieste. She moved to Milan and lived the life of a wealthy Italian: the nearest she got to fashion was as a client of BALENCIAGA. However, forced by financial circumstances to earn a

living, she opened a small atelier in Milan to copy Paris models. In 1965 she showed in Florence with considerable success. Since then she has become known as a designer who demands perfection. Originally her look was quite 'mannish', like that of SCHIAPARELLI, but it has since softened without losing any of the perfect cut which has always been the hallmark of her suits and coats. She works at the custom-made and top ready-to-wear levels. Schön uses double-faced wools and beaded evening looks to very sophisticated effect and has a second line, 'Mila Schön Due' and a man's range, 'Mila Schön Uomo'. In 1984 a swimwear range, 'Aqua Schön', and a sunglass range, 'Schön Ottica', were introduced. Hers is a respected name in Italian fashion because she upholds the highest level of design and execution within a classic design structure.

SCHUBERTH, Emilio Federico

Born Germany, 1904.
Died Rome, Italy, 1972.

Schuberth's working life began in Rome in 1939, when he opened a small hat shop. In 1940 he opened his dressmaking establishment and moved straight into the high-fashion world with his creation of the wedding dress and trousseau for the Princess of Savoy. A considerable showman, and a designer of high style, his private customers included all the Italian aristocracy and foreign clients as diverse as the Duchess of Windsor and Rita Hayworth.

SCOTT, Ken

Born Fort Wayne, Indiana, USA, 1918.

Scott studied at the Parson's School of Design in New York and then set off for Guatemala to paint and collect orchids. He moved to Europe in the late 1940s and, after some time in Paris, arrived in Italy. He opened in Milan and has remained there ever since. He is known for his colourful floral prints, which he designs himself. In the 1950s his scarves patterned with huge flowers were a status symbol. His ready-to-wear line, launched in 1964, is sold throughout the world. His line is loose, using tunics and kaftans, and his looks are typified by all-over flower prints.

SHAMASK, Ronaldus

Born Holland, 1946.

Shamask's boyhood, during the 1950s, was spent in the Australian outback and his first job was as a display designer in Melbourne. He moved to England, where he obtained work as an illustrator. From there he went to America, where he worked as a theatre designer, painter and interior decorator, while building up a private clientele for his clothes. Inspired by an exhibition of Charles JAMES' clothes, he became a disciple of the 'clothes as an art form' school of thought and, with his partner, Murray Moss, he concentrated on producing couture-level clothes. He began to sell them to prestigious stores in 1980, and since then he has become known for his intricate cut and for his pure, architectural shapes. The *New York Times* has compared him with Italy's master of structural clothes, Gianfranco FERRÉ.

SHERARD, Michael

Founded London, England, 1946.
Closed London, England, 1964.

The house of Sherard was a well-respected and well-patronized haute-couture establishment in London which specialized in the two fashion areas for which England is famous: well-tailored tweeds and romantic evening dresses. With the rise of ready-to-wear it became harder for couture to survive. The cost of handwork constantly increased and Sherard, like so many others in London, ceased to trade.

SHILLING, David

Born London, England, 1953.

One of London's most innovative milliners, David Shilling started designing Ascot hats for his mother when he was only twelve. Educated at St. Paul's, he had no formal fashion training and his first job was as an underwriter at Lloyds, where he worked from 1973 to 1975. In 1975 he opened his own shop in Marylebone High Street, where he originally sold not only hats, but also accessories (such as scarves and belts), blouses and wedding dresses. After his first season he decided to concentrate on hats. Known to the public for the extravagant and amusing

239

hats worn by his mother at Ascot, he is a much more serious and important designer than would first appear. The originality and wit of his designs are appreciated by other milliners who find his ideas inspirational. In 1983 he became the first milliner to have an exhibition of his hats tour provincial British museums. His work is in the permanent fashion collections at the Victoria and Albert Museum in London and Metropolitan Museum in New York. In addition to designing for private customers he creates hats and costumes for the theatre and cinema, and in 1984 re-introduced a line of clothes to his range.

SIMONETTA
(Duchess Simonetta di Cesaro)
Born Italy, 1922.
Of Italo-Russian parentage, Simonetta began designing clothes in the 1930s and became one of Rome's leading dressmakers. She married Alberto FABIANI in 1952. He was also a designer and they maintained separate, rival establishments in Rome for some years, before moving to Paris in 1962 and opening a joint establishment called Simonetta et Fabiani. In 1956 Fabiani returned to Rome, but Simonetta remained in Paris and set up her own boutique. After their divorce, she sold up in Paris and went on a religious pilgrimage to India, where she set up a leper colony before returning eventually to Rome.

SIMPSON, Adele
Born New York City, USA, 1903.
Adele Simpson represents the best aspect of Seventh Avenue. Her clothes are designed to delight, not dazzle, her middle-America customer, who wants an outfit of, but not before, its time. Her clothes are conservative without being old-fashioned. She studied dressmaking at the Pratt Institute and began her working career in 1925 designing coats and suits. At the age of twenty-one she was reputedly one of the highest-paid designers in the world. After various design jobs in the 1930s, she founded her own-name company in 1944 by buying out Mary Lee Inc., the firm for whom she had been chief designer.

Adele Simpson was one of the founders of the Fashion Group of America. Her collection of ethnic costumes and her fashion and costume library, containing more than 1,500 volumes, have been presented to the Fashion Institute of Technology. In 1946 she was presented with a Neiman-Marcus Award and in 1947 she received the Coty American Fashion Critics' 'Winnie'.

Simonetta creates an apron effect in crisp sheer black silk for her late fifties cocktail dress, the scale of which is given emphasis by the tulle-swathed flower pot hat.

For Autumn 1958 Simonetta created a short evening dress of airy wool and silk chiffon with front panels which sweep round to form an integral cape.

A very elegant wool and silk tunic line dress in black created by Simonetta for Autumn 1959. The seven-eighths tunic has a high belt and buttons down the side.

Zandra Rhodes is at her most extravagant with this gold evening dress. The operatic splendour of its shape and detailing is heightened by the magnificence of the material. It is from her 1981 'Elizabethan' collection.

The archetypal Rykiel look: feminine and subtly proportioned, its elements are cashmere and jersey and the 1982 example (left) is every bit as up-to-the-minute as the 1984 outfits (above).

Above: *Jean-Louis Scherrer created a sumptuously embroidered coat in sable beige cashmere, bordered with mink and hooded, to create an exotically pampered appearance for Winter 1980.*

Left: *An unexpectedly delicate dress from Paco Rabanne (1979). Fluid silk, hand painted by Eliakim Shpigel, falls from a deeply cut neckline edged with pearls.*

The drama of limited colour and strictness of line is exemplified in this strong statement by Mila Schön. Scale and proportions are enhanced by the richness of the orange and the snap of black at top and bottom.

Soprani's powerful leather statement uses masculine proportions but the over-all effect is strongly feminine. However, girls who dress like this know where they're going and it is certainly not back home for a night of knitting in front of the TV.

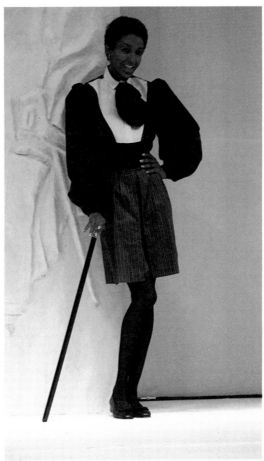

Negative-positive, masculine-feminine in a crisp outfit from Soprani for his Autumn-Winter 1982–83 collection.

Yves Saint Laurent has fun with colour and pattern in this semi-casual outfit from his Autumn 1978 collection. His pants are the most perfectly cut to be found in Paris.

Yves Saint Laurent's sensuous use of materials and colour give this boldly proportioned evening dress immediate and direct impact.

A classic Yves Saint Laurent look for the most sophisticated city streets. Strong colour and simple but perfectly balanced shapes are what help this sort of dressing continue year after year as the epitome of chic.

Ultimate glamour from the maestro of evening sophistication. Yves Saint Laurent's fitted and flared short dress is accessoried to emphasize what it is: the status dressing of the super rich.

Ungaro's mastery of colour and texture is shown in this svelte evening ensemble from his 1983 collection which has links with a traditional Khmer pattern.

Valentino is renowned for his sleekly sophisticated clothes aimed at the very elegant and well-groomed. This is an excellent example of the design skills which have given him world status.

Versace's amazingly fluid dress of steel glitters and glides with the body's movements. His development of this material was a major technological breakthrough in fashion.

Colour, proportion and materials add up to a strong fashion statement by Versace – but wouldn't these vaguely gaucho outfits frighten the horses?

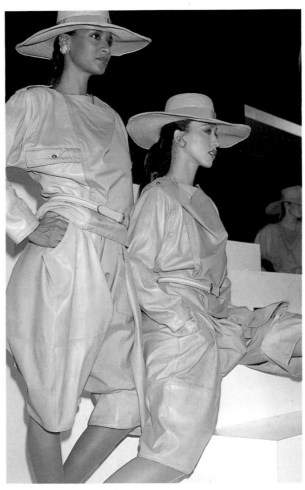

This pink satin shoe by Roger Vivier is as light and delicate as the butterflies surrounding it. Its subtle and uncluttered balance shows Vivier at the height of his power.

Left: *The perfectly tailored suit from Valentino's Autumn 1979 collection.*

Vivienne Westwood and Malcolm McClaren were in the vanguard of new dressing: their cheery iconoclasm is shown to perfection in this youthfully exuberant variation on the suit theme.

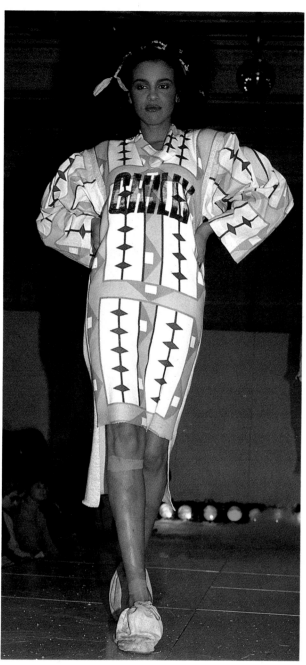

For their 'Savage' collection, Vivienne Westwood and Malcolm McClaren use sweat-shirting reversed so that the fluffy side is outside. The dresses are printed with slogans: 'Chilly' is New York slang; other words used were dressrock, gable and breaker. Great fun, young and anti-status fashion, these looks have considerable influence throughout the fashion world.

Right: *Kansai Yamamoto's colourful prints are wrapped and layered round the body. Strong pattern and colour blocks are enhanced by bold accessories.*

Classic Japanese elements are used by Kansai Yamamoto to create powerful statements which dazzled and excited western eyes when they appeared in Paris.

A shimmer of net flounces hazes this evening dress of red and pink in velvet and silk, which was created by Worth for the 1910–11 collection.

The standard Japanese shape, scale and form are seen here in an outsize look by Yohji Yamamoto, based on the classic kimono.

Yohji Yamamoto shows that Japanese clothes need not be frightening or difficult to wear. This outfit could be worn by any Sloane Ranger or preppy without causing too many raised eyebrows in shires or Hamptons.

Perfectly draped jersey by Yuki. This is a still, calm use of material to create a timeless, dateless and ageless look, reminiscent of Madame Grès' magnificent Grecian evening dresses of the thirties.

SMITH, Graham

Born London, England, 1938.

Having studied at the Bromley College of Art from 1956 to 1957, Smith moved to the Royal College of Art to follow a one-year course in 1958. On the completion of his education he spent the year 1959 in Paris, where he created hats for LANVIN. He returned to London in 1960 and became milliner to MICHAEL of Carlos Place. There he remained for seven years, designing elegantly formal hats as a seemly and sophisticated addition to the couture creations of Michael. In 1967 he set up his own business and he worked independently for the next fourteen years until he joined the Kangol organization as design director in 1981. He is one of London's most respected milliners and his designs are apt, whether produced for designers like Jean MUIR or for mass production by Kangol.

SMITH, Willi

Born Philadelphia, USA, 1948.
Died New York, USA, 1987.

After studying fashion illustration at the Philadelphia Museum College of Art in 1964, Smith won a scholarship to Parson's School of Design, where he studied from 1965 to 1968. His first jobs were as a freelance knitwear designer. In 1969 he became designer for a sportswear firm called Digits, where he remained until Willi Wear Ltd., his own company, was established in 1976. Willi Wear Men followed in 1978. He was one of several black designers to have come from Philadelphia. His clothes are stylish, sexy and fun.

SOPRANI, Luciano ☐

Born Reggiolo, Italy, 1946.

Born of farming stock and destined for the land, Soprani studied agriculture and farmed for a year-and-a-half before he contacted the Italian ready-to-wear firm of Max Mara in 1967 with the idea of becoming a dress designer. He was given a job and stayed there for eight years, becoming responsible for all the collections except Sportmax after only three years. In 1975 he stopped working full-time for Max Mara, although he remained a consultant to the firm for two more years. After a period as a freelance, he began to design for Pims and Helyett. By 1978 he had added 'Cori' to his range and 'Solo Donna' for G.F.T. In 1981 he signed his first contract for BASILE, to design a women's range. A year later he added Basile's menswear. The first collection signed Luciano Soprani was shown in the

A dramatic line-up from Soprani's 1982 collection shows variations on a fanned and harlequin theme for evening.

Left: The masculine look made desirably feminine by Soprani: a large-collared woollen overcoat goes over a man's jacket and pants for Winter 1983–84.

Below: The sort of work which has made Italy synonymous with the highest quality leather wear, this Soprani jacket is on a large scale and has enormous power.

autumn of 1981. He still continues to design for Basile but also has his own name men's and women's collections.

Soprani appears set fair as one of the coming supermen of Italian fashion. A steady development can be expected. His work is an amalgam of the approaches of FERRÉ, ARMANI and VERSACE – in other words, all that is best in Italian ready-to-wear fashion at the moment. He is a very Italian designer, who begins with good basic shapes, then adds intelligent details to produce a lively and original look which appeals greatly to sophisticates all over the world.

STEWART, Stevie
See BODY MAP

STIEBEL, Victor
Born Durban, South Africa, 1907.
Died London, England, 1976.
The son of a South African wool broker, Victor Stiebel was brought up in Natal. He arrived in England in 1924 to read architecture at Cambridge. While there he designed decor and costumes for the 'Footlights' revue. On leaving Cambridge he decided, on the advice of HARTNELL, to become a dress designer. From 1929 to

1932 he trained at the House of REVILLE. His own business was opened in London in 1932 at premises in Bruton Street. On the outbreak of war he enlisted in the army and eventually reached the rank of Lieutenant-Colonel in the Camouflage Corps.

In 1946 he re-established himself as a dress designer at Jacqmar in Grosvenor Street. A founder member of the Incorporated Society of London Fashion Designers, he served as Vice-Chairman and Chairman of the society. He re-opened his own house in 1958 in Cavendish Square, where he flourished until 1963, when, on the advice of his doctors, he closed his doors. He had for many years suffered from spinal trouble. *South African Childhood*, his autobiography, was published in 1968; he was working on a second volume when he died.

Stiebel's position in the London fashion scene of his time is reflected by the fact that he was chosen to design Princess Margaret's going-away outfit for her wedding to Lord SNOWDON* and, in addition, he dressed many other members of the royal family. In 1951 he designed a new uniform for the 'WRENS' and three years later did the same for the WRAF. A courageous man who battled for many years with ill-health, Stiebel was a colourist who produced romantic, understated, but assured clothes. He was especially known for his evening looks and his brilliant use of jersey and striped fabrics.

SUPPON, Charles
Born Collinsville, Illinois, USA, 1949.
A member of America's *jeunesse dorée* of the 1970s, Suppon was nominated for a Coty Award in his first year in business on his own! Having attended the University of Chicago, from which he graduated in 1971, he became assistant to Calvin KLEIN in the same year. After six years he began his own company, Inter Sport, to produce casual and sportswear lines for men and women. In 1978 he received the Coty American Fashion Critics' Award, 'Winnie'.

SVEND
See MILLINERS (French)

T·U

TARLAZZI · TASSELL · TAYLOR (*See* LONDON DESIGNER COLLECTIONS) · THAARUP · THOMASS · TIFFEAU · TIKTINER · TIMMI (*See* ITALIAN READY-TO-WEAR) · TINLING · TOUCHE (*See* ITALIAN READY-TO-WEAR) · TRIGÈRE · TRILL · TRUSSARDI · TUFFIN (*See* FOALE AND TUFFIN) · UNDERWOOD · UNGARO

Thomass

Trigère

TARLAZZI, Angelo

Born Ascoli Piceno, Italy, 1942.
Tarlazzi has always said that he feels more French than Italian, but admits that, despite working in Paris for so many years, his style was formed in Italy. At the age of nineteen he entered the firm of Princess Caracciolo in Rome, the important and influential high-fashion house called CAROSA. He stayed there for five years and eventually became chief designer. In 1966 he arrived in Paris and joined PATOU, where he worked with the firm's artistic director, Michel GOMA. After three years he travelled to New York, but could find no work. He returned to Europe to work freelance with Carosa before being called back to Patou in 1972. There he stayed until 1977, when he set up on his own to present his ready-to-wear line. His freelance work has also included collections for BIAGIOTTI and BASILE. He now has his knitwear made in Italy, but everything else is French. His clothes are a neat blend of Italian fantasy and French *chic*. They are amusing and display his sound sense of volume. He is always excellent when working with large, full shapes.

TASSELL, Gustave

Born Philadelphia, USA, 1926.
One of the classic purveyors of perfectionist clothing for ladies of refined manners and habits, Tassell studied painting at the Pennsylvania Academy of Fine Arts before doing his army training. After demobilization, he worked in New York for Hattie CARNEGIE, where he began as a window-display artist and ended up working as a designer. Miss Carnegie carried custom-made lines, and one of them was by NORELL, who had received his early training with her. These clothes, Tassell claims, inspired him to be a dress designer. In 1952, at the age of twenty-five, he left for Paris, where he kept himself alive by selling sketches to visiting Americans – including GALANOS, who was later to help Tassell set up his own business. In 1956 he set up in business in California to produce near-couture clothes of sophisticated simplicity and perfect finish. In his first collection he showed fewer than twenty models, but their pared-down lines were sensational, causing comment by what they left out at a time when most designers' clothes were elaborate and complicated. For sixteen years Tassell's high-fashion clothes were part of the California fashion scene, but in 1972 he closed down and moved to New York to take over Norell's house. For the next four years the label read 'Norman Norell by Tassell'. With the closure of the house he returned to designing under his own name. In 1961 he was the recipient of the Coty American Fashion Critics' Award.

TAYLOR, Annette Worsley

See LONDON DESIGNER COLLECTIONS

THAARUP, Aage

Born Copenhagen, Denmark, 1908.
Although now remembered largely as *the* royal milliner of London, Thaarup was more than that. He was an original, witty and daring designer of hats with a strongly Surrealist feel to them. He could be considered the SCHIAPARELLI of millinery. Like her, he designed with an irreverent, schoolboy *joie de vivre* and created amusing and surprising effects. His view was that anything was possible in making an elegant hat and he proved it by using plastic vegetables to trim a hat made for the Duchess of York.

Thaarup had hoped to be a teacher or priest, but his parents could not afford to support him during a long period of study. Instead, therefore, he studied commerce and became a millinery buyer for a Copenhagen store. In 1926 he moved to Berlin, where he worked in a store, before continuing to Paris. His chance came with a trip to India, where he set up shop and began to design hats for the rich English living in Bombay, Calcutta and Delhi. By 1932 he was in London, making hats for STIEBEL, having them photographed by BEATON and capitalizing on his creative and commercial abilities. He was soon making hats for everyone from the Queen down. He worked for the Board of Trade during World War II. After the war he was made chairman of The Associated Millinery Designers of London; he continued his royal associations and he also went into wholesale business with his 'Teen and Twenty' range for Marshall & Snelgrove.

By the late 1950s, however, no-one wanted hats any more. In 1958 he published his autobiography, *Heads & Tales*.

THOMASS, Chantal

Born Paris, France, 1947.
Although she had no formal training, Chantal Thomass was always interested enough in clothes to design her own to be made up by her mother. Her fashion career began in 1967, when she sold some dresses made from hand-painted scarves to Dorothée BIS. In the same year she married her husband, Bruce, who had been a student at the École des Beaux Arts and together they set up their own small firm, called Ter and Bantine. They designed inexpensive clothes for a very young, slightly wild market and were sufficiently successful to found Chantal Thomass in 1976, with Chantal as the creator and her husband as the administrator. The price of the clothes rose, but she kept her young, very pretty and feminine style. She reflects changes of mood with remarkable speed and her clothes always fit the mood of the moment: hence her success with the young.

TIFFEAU, Jacques

Born Chenevelles, France, 1927.
Tiffeau's early training in a Paris couture house was interrupted by the outbreak of World War II. After wartime military service he returned to Paris and worked with DIOR, who was a friend. In 1952 he arrived in New York, where he soon obtained work as a pattern cutter with the firm, Monte-Sano. In 1958 he joined with the daughter of the owner of Monte-Sano to create his own firm, Tiffeau-Busch. It produced young, sporty clothes. The firm closed in 1971 and Tiffeau returned to Paris to work with SAINT LAURENT. In 1976 he signed a contract to produce designs for Originala of New York and he has worked with BLASS on his 'Blassport' range. His abilities as a designer have gained him several awards: the Coty American Fashion Critics' Award in 1960 (a 'Winnie') and 1964 (a Return Award); the Neiman-Marcus Award in 1966; and the *Sunday Times* award in the same year.

TIKTINER

Born Nice, France, between the wars.
Tiktiner's real name is Dina Tiktiner
Viterbo. In the 1950s beach and play
wear by Tiktiner were a 'must' for the
côte d'azur set and even today the name
stands for sportswear which is modish and
smart.

Dina Viterbo began her family business
in Nice in 1949 and her success enabled
her to expand into general sportswear,
with factories in the South of France and
sales outlets throughout Europe and North
America.

TIMMI

See ITALIAN READY-TO-WEAR

TINLING, Teddy

Born London, England, 1910.
Tinling's life and design career have been
involved with lawn tennis since 1927,
when he began to work for the Lawn
Tennis Association at Wimbledon. He
opened his Mayfair fashion house in 1931
and his name was quickly made by his
designs for Suzanne Lenglen's appearances on the centre court of Wimbledon
in the early 1930s. He became world-
famous in 1949 with the lace-edged
panties he designed for 'Gorgeous Gussie'
Moran's appearance on the centre court.
They caused a *frisson* which it is hard to
comprehend these days, but the fuss and
photographs in the newspapers of the
world meant that Tinling had, from that
moment, an almost permanent career
designing dresses for centre-court stars.
His story appears in his autobiographical
White Ladies, published in 1963, and is
elaborated on in the second volume, *Sixty
Years in Tennis*, published in 1983. He was
chosen as Designer of the Year in 1971 by
the British Clothing Institute. In 1975 he
sold up and moved his business to
Philadelphia.

As a designer Teddy Tinling's fame rests
on his tennis outfits, although wedding
dresses for tennis stars have also been
part of his success. By specializing in an
area where his experience and knowledge
were unrivalled, he became the undisputed
expert in clothes for tennis and other activity sports.

*A classic high fashion look from Trigère's 1969 collection. Dramatically fitted and collared,
this wool coat is given extra dash by a glamorous fur hat.*

TOUCHE

See ITALIAN READY-TO-WEAR

TRIGÈRE, Pauline

Born Paris, France, 1912.
Trigère's parents arrived in Paris in 1905
in flight from the Sino-Russian war. Her
father was a tailor and her mother a
dressmaker. At the age of fifteen she was
apprenticed to MARTIAL ET ARMAND, but
she remained with them only briefly, since
she was so advanced that there was nothing they could teach her. She then worked
with her father until his death in 1932. In
1937, to flee war and persecution a second

Black and white impact in silk for Pauline Trigère's Spring 1983 dinner dresses.

time, the family moved to America. Trigère found work as Travis BANTON's assistant at Hattie CARNEGIE, then in 1942 began on her own. Her intellectual, self-disciplined approach to making clothes, together with her exceptional practical knowledge ensured that very soon she was producing highly individual clothes in the manner of the Paris designers. She works directly on the model, cutting and draping directly from the bolt, and the simplicity of her clothes is based on an intricate cut of which she is complete mistress. Her clothes are sophisticated and luxurious, nearer to couture than ready-to-wear in their design and fabrication. Trigère received a Neiman-Marcus Award in 1950, the Coty American Fashion Critics' 'Winnie' in 1949, and the Return Award in 1951. She was elected to the Hall of Fame in 1959. In addition, the city of

Paris honoured her in 1972 with its silver medal. Active and outspoken on behalf of American fashion, Pauline Trigère takes as her chosen talisman the turtle, which is a Chinese symbol for luck and longevity.

TRILL, Christopher

Born Lincoln, England, 1951.
Arriving in London in the late 1960s with the intention of studying for entry into Oxford, Trill decided instead to be a photographer. 'Brief but disastrous' is how he describes the attempt. He started making handbags to sell in the Portobello Road. His bags and belts were featured in *Vogue* and, after 1973, his market expanded rapidly to include top London and American stores. He also sells in Japan.

TRUSSARDI, Nicola

Born Bergamo, Italy, 1942.
The firm of Trussardi was founded in 1910. It was, as it remained until 1970, a manufacturer of high-quality leather gloves. Nicola Trussardi studied business and economics at the University of Milan and graduated in 1968. It was in 1970 that he began his career in the business and set about broadening its scope and developing its production. The name Trussardi is now associated with a wide range of luxury goods, all beautifully made to a high level of taste and costing a great deal of money. Not surprisingly, considering its background, the business is best known for its top-quality leather goods, especially bags, luggage and belts, but there are also Trussardi ranges of men's and women's ready-to-wear. These are traditional and very classic when compared with other Italian lines. In addition to the Trussardi boutiques in Milan, Rome, Florence, Paris, Geneva and London, the line is found in many luxury stores throughout the world.

TUFFIN

See FOALE AND TUFFIN

UNDERWOOD, Patricia

Born Maidenhead, England, 1948.
After a convent education, Patricia Under-

wood worked as an *au pair* in Paris and a secretary at Buckingham Palace. In 1968 she went to New York, where she studied at the Fashion Institute of Technology and then, with a friend, began to make hats. Featured in *Vogue* and bought by Bloomingdales and Bendels, her collections soon became well-known. In addition to her own range, she designs hats for Calvin KLEIN, Perry ELLIS and Mary MCFADDEN. Her skill lies in the way she takes classic simple shapes from the past — such as eighteenth-century milkmaids' hats, boaters, and nuns' coifs — and updates them.

UNGARO, Emmanuel ☐

Born Aix-en-Provence, France, 1933.
Ungaro's parents were Italian and his father, who was a tailor, taught him to cut and sew men's clothes. At the age of twenty-two he went to Paris to work for a small tailoring firm. This background in tailoring was the basis of everything that this *avant-garde* designer did years later when he had his own label. Equally important were the six years he spent working with BALENCIAGA, to whom he had been introduced in 1958 by COURRÈGES. When Courrèges left the maestro two years later, Ungaro took his place as chief designer. From Balenciaga he learned the dictum that 'we are artisans, not philosophers', which summed up Ungaro's already practical approach to clothes-making. In 1964 he went to work with on his own. His look was crisply modern porarily closed his doors and Ungaro, beginning with only six workers, opened Courrèges, but in 1965 Courrèges tem- and 'space-age', with an emphasis on tailored suits and coats. It appealed primarily to the young. From the beginning Ungaro had a close and productive partnership with Sonia Knapp, who designed his fabrics for him. Possibly as a result of her influence, his clothes softened and became much more fluid and flowing. His strength as a colourist has grown and his mixing of prints and layers has an 'Arabian Nights' glamour, a quality which his dresses share with those of the designer, LANCETTI. 'Ungaro Parallele', his *prêt-à-porter* line, was created in 1968.

V·W

VALENTINA · VALENTINO · VALENTINO, M. · VALOIS (*See* MILLINERS) · VARTY · VENET · VENTURI · VERSACE · VIONNET · VIVIER
VOLLBRACHT · VON FÜRSTENBERG · WAINWRIGHT · WEDGE · WEITZ · WESTWOOD · WOLMAN (*See* PINKY AND DIANNE) · WORTH

Valentino

Versace

Above: *Wainwright*

Left: *Vionnet*   Right: *Westwood*

263

VALENTINA
(Nicholaevna Sanina Schlee)
Born Kiev, Russia, 1904.

The Russian Revolution interrupted Valentina's training as an actress and changed her life. She and her family fled to France, and from there she went with her husband to America in 1923 as a member of the Russian Chauve Souris Theatre. Her particularly original approach to dressing, based on the dress of Russian country folk, gained notice from being so contrary to current fashion and by 1928 she was running her own dressmaking establishment. She created costumes for many stage productions and they were especially successful: Brooks Atkinson said in a review that 'Valentina has designed clothes that act before a line is spoken'. Valentina's customers, who included society women and stage and screen personalities, were attracted to her sense of the drama of simplicity, seen at its most telling in her all-black evening looks. She is often quoted as having said, 'Mink is for football, ermine is for bathrobes' — exactly why is not known! She retired in 1957.

VALENTINO
Born Voghera, Italy, 1932.

Valentino's full name is Valentino Garavani. He is the golden boy of Italian haute couture, and his name is as well-known as that of Agnelli. After an undistinguished school career, he studied fashion and French in Milan, before moving to Paris at the age of seventeen to follow a course at the Chambre Syndicale de la Couture. At the age of nineteen, in 1950, he was given a job by Jean DESSÈS. He remained there for five years, before moving to Guy LAROCHE as a general design assistant. He returned to Rome in 1959 and opened his own business in the prestigious Via Condotti. He had achieved a modicum of success and had moved to his present headquarters in Via Gregoriana when he decided to show in Florence in 1962. His show was seen by I. Magnin buyers, who liked it, bought heavily and made his name.

Since then Valentino has dressed most of the rich and famous women in the world and has maintained a loyal following for his glamorous and elegant clothes. He designed Jacqueline Kennedy's dress for her wedding to Aristotle Onassis and thirty-eight other clients ordered the same dress — an unprecedented thing at haute-couture level. In 1969 he opened his first ready-to-wear boutique in Rome. Now he has more than a hundred throughout the world. His menswear range began in 1972, his decoration and household fabrics outlet, Valentino Più, followed in 1973 and he began to show his ready-to-wear line in Paris in 1975. This he still does, while his *alta moda* showings take place in Rome. He has worldwide franchises covering sunglasses, leather goods, tiles, jewellery and much else. An Alfa Romeo car has

The epitome of glamour dressing from Valentino's Winter 1983–84 collection in this fine wool suit with full skirt, fur-trimmed jacket and chic hat.

Valentino's city coat for Spring 1984 is gently gathered at the yoke and tops a strongly blocked outfit of checks and solid colour.

For Summer 1984 Valentino gives a gently shirred soft suit a crisp hat and sharply cuffed gloves to create a city look of great sophistication.

been styled by Valentino and his perfume, launched in 1978, sells throughout the world. His clothes are refined and lady-like, with beautifully fabricated and tailored day looks and 'big-evening' ball dresses. He can take much of the credit for the revival of the romantic and glamorous evening looks of the late 1970s and early 1980s.

Valentino's ideas of *chic* and glamour are taken from the 1950s Hollywood look. Urbane and elegant, his clothes match his life-style. In the 1980s it can be said that his time has come. His approach to high-quality, high-fashion dressing is exactly in accord with the feelings of his rich clients and he and his partner, Giancarlo Giammetti, are lionized all over the world. Valentino the man and the designer personifies the sophistication of the old-style couturier. He lives in baroque style in a villa outside Rome and is regularly found at the watering holes of the super-rich.

VALENTINO, Mario

Born Naples, Italy, 1927.

Valentino's father, Vincenzo, was a well-known Neapolitan shoemaker and Mario followed in his footsteps after studying politics and economics. His first work was for I. Miller, the American shoemaker, but he left New York for Rome and set up as a high-class shoemaker, making shoes by hand for such famous customers as Sophia Loren and Ava Gardner. In 1965 he returned to Naples and proceeded to broaden his production and markets. He eventually had Mario Valentino shoe shops in six countries as well as Italy. Since 1973 the business has expanded to include high-class leatherwear, handbags and belts, and a women's range at one time designed by ARMANI but now done by VERSACE. His is a respected and trusted name in Italian fashion circles.

VALOIS, Rose

See MILLINERS (French)

VARTY, Keith

Born Darlington, England, 1952.

Many English-trained young designers make a living by working on the Continent,

but few actually manage to make a name for themselves. Keith Varty has succeeded on both counts. He trained at the St. Martin's School of Art and then took a postgraduate course at the Royal College in London. From there he went as a designer to the French firm of Dorothée BIS. He spent four-and-a-half years with Bis before moving to Italy. In Milan he worked for two seasons with COMPLICE, then moved to their 'Byblos' label. His success in the highly competitive Italian fashion field is due in no small measure to his ability to 'pick up' the mood of the moment and exploit current design thinking in an imaginative, amusing blend of Anglo-Italian fantasy.

VENET, Philippe

Born Lyon, France, 1929.

At the age of fourteen Venet was apprenticed to Pierre Court, who dressed the best backs in Lyon. He remained there for six years and then moved to Paris in 1951. He worked for SCHIAPARELLI, along with GIVENCHY, who employed him in 1953 at his own newly-founded house as his master tailor. After nine years with Givenchy, Venet opened his own house in 1962. The basis of his collections is always his beautifully tailored coats. He has a ready-to-wear line, boutique and menswear range. His clothes are elegant, easy-to-wear and sophisticated, although no longer in fashion's vanguard.

VENTURI, Gian-Marco

Born Florence, Italy, 1950s.

Having studied at the Istituto Tessile in Prato and gained a degree in economics and commerce from Florence University, Venturi spent some time in travelling the world before taking his first job with the Italian textile firm of Lebole. His designing career began with Erreuno. His own label soon followed and he is now responsible for several collections in addition to the one bearing his name.

VERSACE, Gianni ☐

Born Calabria, Italy, 1946.

Versace's mother was a dressmaker and his early training, while working with her,

can be seen throughout his development as a designer: his clothes are dressmaker clothes. He is one of Italy's best designers and the one most respected by his countrymen. With his clean design approach he must be considered one of the most modern designers working today. His simple shapes, his sophisticated wrapping, his unerring sense of proportion and fit, together with his inspirational sense of colour, create an overall head-to-toe look which is influential all over the world. Versace designed the GENNY and COMPLICE labels for the Girombellis (who also make the Versace label for him) and the 'Callaghan' label for Signora Greppi. Broadly speaking, 'Genny' was leather and suede, 'Complice', evening and day clothes and 'Callaghan', knitwear, often with a leather trim. Having developed the different aspects of his talent with these three firms he combined them all, as it were, to produce his own Versace collection.

Versace is an originator, notably in the

Leather has always played an important part in Versace's collections. These suits from 1979 are a very relaxed and accommodating way to dress. The hats (in hand) are modelled on sportsmen's protective headshields.

Left: *Masculine elements are used by Versace in October 1982 to make a gentle and softly feminine way of dressing.*

Right: *Versace's Spring/Summer 1984 look has the spirit of India and the sexiness of Italy in this linen dress, resembling a sari.*

Left: *Versace's miraculously fluid and sensual way with his metal fabric shows that it has the soft pliability of silk jersey and makes up into body-hugging dresses of the greatest seductiveness.*

development of new fabrics – for example, his softly sensuous metal dresses which can be sewed by machine. His leatherwear for men and women has been enormously important and popular for many seasons. He considers DIOR and CHANEL to have been uncreative, but admires POIRET and VIONNET. Like Vionnet, he cuts on the bias most of the time and drapes the material directly on to the model without sketches or designs. For 'recreation' he designs costumes for the La Scala and Béjart ballets. Many people consider him the only truly creative designer in Milan and his clothes are sufficiently in demand to enable him to live in some grandeur in a villa overlooking Lake Como.

VIONNET, Madeleine

Born Aubervilliers, France, 1876.
Died Paris, France, 1975.
The name of Vionnet, though it is barely known outside, is legendary within fashion

circles. Even today, designers who understand what dressmaking is really about see her in an undimmed light as one of fashion's true immortals. Although she lived to be almost one hundred years old, she practised under her own name for less than twenty years. It was, however, during those years, in 1926, that she evolved a totally new way of manipulating fabric with her introduction of the bias cut. It is for this that she will always be remembered. Her unrivalled technical knowledge which enabled her to use cloth in such an original and strong way was based on a long and thorough training as a seamstress before she opened her own house.

How different matters are today, when, after a couple of terms at an art college or some undemanding work, many young people consider themselves to be fully-fledged designers. Madame Vionnet would have found the notion absurd. Her apprenticeship began when she was twelve.

By the time she was sixteen she was working in the rue de la Paix with a well-known dressmaker called Vincent. There she stayed until she was twenty. She married a Russian refugee called Nechvolodoff at eighteen, had a child who died, and was divorced when she was nineteen. The following year found her in London working in a tailor's workroom in charge of twelve men. She remained in London for five years and, at the age of twenty-five, returned to Paris to take up a post with CALLOT SOEURS. She worked very closely with one of the sisters, Madame Gerber, for whom she made toiles. This woman profoundly influenced Vionnet, who considered her to be a great artist, greater even than POIRET. In 1907 Vionnet left Madame Gerber to join DOUCET. Here, she always claimed, she abolished corsets before Poiret. She presented clothes with mannequins who were barefooted or sandalled. In 1912 she opened her own house, but just as her success was grow-

A severely sophisticated dress and cape in grey jersey, created by Vionnet in about 1933. The whole outfit is cut on the bias, by the woman who invented this technique.

Lilac lawn is used by Vionnet for this delicately petalled dress of 1932 to create a lady-like afternoon outfit.

ing, World War I forced her to close. It was not until 1922 that she re-opened, in large premises on the avenue Montaigne. She remained here until 1940 when the lease ran out. She quarrelled with her backer and decided to retire.

Vionnet's approach to clothes was basically that of a classicist. As with GRÈS, draping was the foundation of her skill. She did not sketch. She worked directly with the material on a lay figure. Her skills with toiles, which she learned with Madame Gerber, enabled her to drape and cut with a unique flair and skill. She knew precisely what she could and could not achieve with fabric and scissors. Technically, she was probably without equal until the advent of BALENCIAGA.

Vionnet was happiest creating individual dresses for private customers, among them Mme. Citroën and the Rothschilds, but she also had to sell toiles to be copied in America and Europe. Although she is remembered for her bias-

Vionnet concentrates on back interest in this evening dress where the material is gathered over the hips and falls in a panel.

cut, draped and handkerchief-pointed dresses, she never allowed her fashion intelligence to ossify. In 1934, sensing that she was out of step with the new romanticism resulting from MOLYNEUX's costumes for *The Barretts of Wimpole Street*, she had the courage, determination and business sense to throw away her almost-completed collection, two weeks before her opening. She remade the entire collection and managed to show on time. She was the complete professional. Her understanding of fabric and the subtlety of her construction put her in the vanguard of dressmakers. Her 'looks' were clinging skirts, bare backs, fluttering *crêpe de chine*, satin evening dresses and superbly draped Grecian folds.

The influence of Vionnet on dressmaking techniques was unparalleled, and sprang from her philosophy that 'you must dress a body in a fabric, not construct a dress', a remark which could have come from any of the current Japanese designers whose approach to clothes is considered so new and revolutionary.

VIVIER, Roger ☐

Born Paris, France, 1913.

Vivier is the Fragonard of the shoe world, whose light-hearted and rococo creations lift the spirits. He studied drawing and sculpture at L'École des Beaux Arts before working for a shoemaker. His early education was important, as his shoes, under their decorative details, have the taut, controlled harmony of sculpture. It is almost as if the basic shoe is an armature on which Vivier builds his fantasies. His exceptional style and ability were soon recognized. He established his own firm in 1932 and was soon making shoes for discerning women throughout the world. Delman invited him to New York to produce an up-market range for them. In 1953 he became shoemaker to Christian DIOR, for whom he created two collections a year. His work with Dior was truly inspired and his evening shoes of this period were exquisite: jewelled and embroidered on satins and cut velvets, always in the most refined and streamlined shapes. In 1963 he again formed his own company and in 1974 he moved to the prestigious rue Royale, from which base

These extravagantly bejewelled and embroidered evening shoes were created by Roger Vivier for Christian Dior in 1961. They have the splendour of Louis XIV's Versailles and are masterpieces of the shoemaker's art.

he created shoe collections for many of the top haute-couture houses in Paris. He won a Neiman-Marcus Award, the Daniel & Fischer Award, and the Italian Riberio d'Ora Award, richly deserved by the creator of this century's most beautiful shoes.

VOLLBRACHT, Michaele

Born Kansas City, USA, 1949.
Vollbracht came from an army background and he spent his youth moving all over the United States. He moved to New York at the age of seventeen and enrolled at the Parson's School of Design. From there he went to Geoffrey BEENE to work on Lynda Byrd Johnson's wedding designs. He then went to work as a designer on 'Beene Bazaar', but eventually left. Then there began a see-saw period: he moved to work with Donald BROOKS, then back to Beene, and returned to Brooks before joining Norman NORELL, with whom he worked until the designer's death in 1972. The next two years were spent illustrating for the New York department store, Bloomingdales, before starting on his own with a fashion benefit show featuring silks printed in Italy to his own designs by Bellotti. He had met

Bellotti through MIYAKE. Vollbracht's impact was considerable, but his activities were stopped by a split with his business backers. In 1981 he set up a new company. His look is still based on hand-painted designs, which he has printed on silk by Bellotti. They are mostly figurative, although he also creates abstract and random prints. They are not for the shy.

VON FÜRSTENBERG, Diane

Born Brussels, Belgium, 1946.
Von Fürstenberg's parents were divorced when she was thirteen and she was sent to boarding school. She studied in England, Spain and Switzerland, where she read economics at the University of Geneva, and became fluent in five languages. She married Prince Egon von Fürstenberg in 1968 and moved to the United States in 1969. She began her business with a small range of jersey dresses which had been made for her in Italy. She sold them to stores directly herself. They were an immediate success and she became a known designer almost overnight. Sexy, *chic* and easy to wear, these dresses were absolutely right for their time and they had the added appeal, especially potent to Americans, that they were designed by a princess! Von Fürstenberg's empire expanded and, in addition to her range of women's clothes, she developed a highly successful line of cosmetics, including scent, jewellery, handbags, furs, shoes, wallpaper, stationery, table-linen and designs for Vogue Patterns. She is divorced from Prince von Fürstenberg. She no longer designs under her own name but still has clothing licensees and a cosmetics line. She is also currently doing a line of furniture for Sears.

WAINWRIGHT, Janice

Born Chesterfield, England, 1940.
Having studied fashion at the Kingston School of Art, from which she graduated in 1962, Wainwright followed a postgraduate course at the Royal College of Art until 1964. Her first job was with the Simon Massey company, for whom she designed under her own label. Her own company was formed in London in 1974. Throughout her career she has laid great

Janice Wainwright's pagoda dress in crêpe, from her Winter 1975-76 collection, spirals around the body from a decorative yoke.

emphasis on materials and she is actively involved in the design and colouring of the fabrics she uses. She has frequently used embroidery on silks, wools and jersey and the softness of these fabrics gives her clothes the fluidity of line and softness of silhouette which are her hallmarks. Her sales are world-wide and she produces two collections a year of day and evening wear.

WEDGE, James

Born London, England, 1937.
After two years service in the British navy, Wedge studied art and fashion at the South Wessex College of Art. He then went to the Royal College of Art to specialize in millinery. In the mid-1950s he became milliner for the couture house of Ronald PATERSON, before setting up on his own. In addition to providing hats for male and female private customers, he designed them for films such as *Blow Up*.

He expanded by opening two boutiques in London's King's Road, 'Top Gear' and 'Countdown'. As the market for hats dwindled, he became interested in photography and it is as a fashion photographer that he now earns his living.

WEITZ, John

Born Berlin, Germany, 1923.

Although educated in England, Weitz has spent his adult life in America. He is the antithesis of the narrow specialist. His interests include motor racing (he was a driver in the 1950s), sailing and writing. He has written a novel based on the fashion world, *The Value of Nothing* (1970), and an executive dress and behaviour guide called *Man in Charge* (1974). His approach to design reflects his sporting interests. His early apprenticeship was in Paris with MOLYNEUX. He arrived in America in 1940. After army service he worked as a designer for several firms. In 1954 he began designing his own collections and produced practical, young and sporty clothes for men. He used his criteria for menswear for his women's lines, which he started soon afterwards, and created casual easy-to-wear, sporty clothes with a masculine flavour. In the 1960s he pioneered a ready-to-wear couture scheme whereby individual dresses were made for a client who chose the style and material from a range of swatches and sketches: the old dressmaker concept, in fact. Since 1970 he has concentrated his efforts on menswear and his middle-class clothes for the middle classes have been successful all over the world. He is reputed to have said that he concentrated on menswear because it was impossible to become famous as a women's designer unless one were French or Italian! He received a Coty American Fashion Critics' Award in 1974.

WESTWOOD, Vivienne ☐

Born Tintwhistle, England, 1941.

Decadent, degenerate and irrelevant are all words that have been used in the attempt to describe Vivienne Westwood and her peculiarly original contribution to clothes. They are all meaningless. No matter how one reacts to her clothes or attempts to describe them, she is, without

dispute, one of the most influential designers currently working in London. Her international significance is as great as QUANT's was in her day. Whether what she does with clothes is to be considered fashion is not the question. Her influence has been considerable, not only at street-level, but also on other designers.

After only one term at Harrow Art School Westwood left and trained to become a teacher, which is how she earned her living before meeting Malcolm McLaren. It was through her association with McLaren that she gradually slid into the world of fashion. Together their approach is largely anarchic, inspired by rebellious urban youth: Teddy Boys, Rockers and Punks. Their shop in the King's Road, London, has had several names, each of which reflected the cultural influence of the moment: 1971, Let it Rock; 1972, Too Fast to Live, Too Young to Die; 1974, Sex; 1977, Seditionaries; 1980, World's End. In 1982 it was joined by a second shop, called Nostalgia of Mud, which, slightly inappropriately, was sited in the refined and mildly unreal St. Christopher's Place in London's West End. Until the end of the 1970s Westwood's clothes were largely based on leather and rubber fetishism, Punk Rock, bondage and S & M. They reflect the values exemplified by Malcolm McLaren's pop group, *The Sex Pistols*. At the beginning of the 1980s 'New Romanticism' and 'Pirate' looks were introduced and immediately had an impact on world fashion.

The latest Westwood looks have included torn, misaligned garments, perverse 'little girl' looks, and even crinolines. They make their wearers look like victims of some terrible holocaust, but, surprisingly, happy and contented victims. Vivienne Westwood is London's most creatively courageous designer although she cocks a snook at London as a fashion centre by showing in Paris. Her first show there in the spring of 1983 was her 'Witches' collection. She is, creatively, part of that increasingly-exposed underbelly of modern dressing which includes COMME DES GARÇONS and several other major Japanese forces. They could equally easily represent the real future of dressing or merely prove to be an interesting cul-de-sac.

Vivienne Westwood and Malcolm McClaren produced their 'Pirate' collection for Winter 1981–82 with a bold use of patterns and layers to create a totally swashbuckling, buccaneer appearance.

Vivienne Westwood and Malcolm McClaren top off their pirate look with an uncompromising theatrical hat and hair treatment.

WOLMAN, Pinky
See PINKY AND DIANNE

Woman Designer Awards
See FASHION AWARDS, p. 305

WORTH ☐

Founded Paris, France, 1858.
Closed 1954.
For almost a century the house of Worth, founded by the Englishman, Charles Frederick Worth, thrived in Paris. It was at the height of its power, under the leadership of the founder and his sons, Jean Philippe and Gaston, before this century began and it continued as a strong force for the next thirty years. Jean Philippe (1853–1924) and Gaston (1856–1926) took over the firm on the death of their father in 1895. They had both worked with him for many years, Jean Philippe as a designer and Gaston as an administrator.

Jean Philippe was not overshadowed by his father. He was a very good designer in his own right and designed for the Spanish, Italian, Dutch and Russian royal families before World War I, as well as for just about every woman of note in *la belle époque*. His attitude to his customers was very like that of his father. He was the creator and they were to be guided by his choice of what was suitable for them. Gaston was much more practical and saw that, with wars and revolutions, the traditional Worth customer was disappearing. Simple, less opulent clothes to attract a broader, less rarefied, clientele were essential if the firm was to survive. To achieve this end he engaged POIRET, who was perhaps an odd choice as a designer of simple lines. Jean Philippe disliked Poiret's design approach and eventually had him sacked. He himself retired in 1910 and Gaston's son, Jean Charles, became the house designer.

Like his uncle, Jean Charles was a good designer and he kept the name of Worth in the vanguard of fashion throughout the 1920s. The sophisticated, relaxed elegance of his clothes appealed to members of American and European high society, actresses and the mistresses of millionaires. He retired in 1935, though he did not die until 1962, at the age of eighty-

Miss Barbara Grey photographed on the set of Call Me George *at the Garrick Theatre wearing a dress by Worth 'brought over from Paris by aeroplane this morning'.*

A woollen suit by Worth with a great deal of Persian lamb trimming on the jacket collar, hem and up the sleeve, photographed at the races in 1930.

This Worth outfit from his 1928 collection is in green and red with gold thread and green and red beads for all-over decoration.

one. Roger Worth, the son of Jacques, became designer at the age of twenty-seven and, when his father died in 1941, head of the firm. The fourth generation continued the dynasty. Maurice was in charge of administration and Roger was head of design. On Roger's retirement in 1952, Maurice took control of everything and in 1954 he accepted a take-over bid from PAQUIN. So ended the longest-running house in the history of haute couture.

Through four generations the high standards set by Charles Frederick, the father of fashion, had been maintained by his descendants. The London branch of Worth, opened in Queen Victoria's time, continued under non-family management until the early 1970s. The Worths played an important role in the organization of Paris haute couture: Gaston was the first president of the Chambre Syndicale de la Haute Couture Française and Jacques held the same post twice, from 1927 to 1930 and from 1933 to 1935. He also founded L'École Supérieure de la Couture in 1930 as an establishment to train apprentices and thus maintain the high standards of couture workmanship.

Major perfumes: Dans La Nuit (1924); Je Reviens (1932).

Y·Z

YAMAMOTO, K. · YAMAMOTO, Y. · YUKI · ZORAN · ZWEI

Yamamoto, K.

Yamamoto, Y.

Zoran

YAMAMOTO, Kansai □

Born Yokohama, Japan, 1944.

Kansai Yamamoto's early training was in civil engineering, which he concentrated on at high school. He left school in 1962 to study English at Nippon University. He worked as a designer for Hisashi Hosono Studio before establishing his own firm in a small way in 1971. In the spring of that year he presented his clothes in London at a spectacular show which he orchestrated on stage like a conductor with musicians. In 1972 his show in Tokyo had an audience of 5,000 people. His Paris debut took place in 1975. Since then he has continued to show in Paris. His clothes

Total originality characterizes this Kansai Yamamoto outfit seen in Paris in 1978. It exemplifies the schism between old and new approaches to clothes: a few years previously it would have been totally inconceivable that something like this would appear on the runways in the French capital, the traditional home of high fashion.

For Spring 1983 Yohji Yamamoto enlarges his proportions to a Brobdingnagian extent to make the wearer look like a little girl wearing daddy's clothes.

For Spring/Summer 1984 Kansai Yamamoto takes a traditionally inspired wave print for his skirt and teams it with an asymmetric sailor top and ankle socks to create a young fashion look.

are licensed in Europe and the United States. In 1979 he staged a huge disco-fashion show in New York and he has signed agreements to produce menswear, bags, household linens and stationery. His work is an exciting mixture of ancient oriental and modern occidental influences and always shows a strong colour flair and sense of form, using boldly-patterned, abstract shapes and powerful colour combinations.

See also JAPANESE DESIGN.

YAMAMOTO, Yohji □

Born Japan, 1943.

After graduating from Keio University in 1966, Yamamoto went on to study fashion at Japan's prestigious Bunka College of Fashion in Tokyo under Chie

Koike, who had studied at the Chambre Syndicale School in Paris with Yves SAINT LAURENT. Yamamoto followed the general two-year course from 1966 to 1968, studying all aspects of the clothing industry. By 1972 he had his own company and in 1976 his first collection was shown in Tokyo. In 1981 he established his company in France and opened a boutique in Les Halles in Paris. Since that year he has shown his collection as part of the Paris fashion week. Like Kawakubo of COMME DES GARÇONS he is in the forefront of that 'new' dressing which holds in contempt the traditional 20th-century view of female clothing as a means of emphasizing the figure in order to titillate. Yamamoto's woman is draped and wrapped to disguise her body. She concedes little to accepted ideas of sexuality. Her clothes are func-

tional and ruthlessly unglamorous. Like most of his compatriot designers Yamamoto largely eschews evening clothes; his looks are business-like and down-to-earth, whilst making a strong statement about colour and pattern. His inexpensive range of clothing, aimed at the young and care-free, carries a label in English which says that 'There is nothing so boring as a neat and tidy look'. Whether this is to be viewed as a philosophical statement or an apologia depends upon one's ability to leap the culture barrier between East and West. These are clothes for pragmatists, as are all those designed by members of the Japanese school of fashion.
See also JAPANESE DESIGN.

YUKI

Born Miyazaki-ken, Japan, 1940.
Originally trained as a textile engineer, Yuki worked in animation in Tokyo before arriving in London. From there he went to the Art Institute of Chicago, where he studied architecture and interior design from 1962 to 1964. Returning to England, he studied fashion at the London College of Fashion from 1964 to 1966. In 1966 he became design assistant to MICHAEL of Carlos Place and two years later he joined HARTNELL. In 1969 he moved to Paris to work with CARDIN. Freelance work in Europe and America was followed by the launching of his own collection in 1972. In 1976 he won the Yardley Designer of the Year Award. A retrospective of his work was held at the Victoria and Albert Museum in 1978 – the first designer to whom this has happened. As well as having licences for jewellery, ties and leather goods, he has also been involved

Above: *Yohji Yamamoto's archetypal Japanese look from his Winter 1983–84 collection. Layers, flaps and pockets in anti-logical arrangements suggest that the wearer is a survivor of some hideous disaster who has snatched up any items of clothing available in the confusion.*

Right: *Yohji Yamamoto uses heavily textured knitted surfaces and asymmetric collars and hems to create his Winter 1983–84 look.*

Yohji Yamamoto's very young way with casual dressing: an asymmetric torn and shirred top is lightly harnessed by a cross-over belt. The pants have a half skirt. The effect is of a gentle karate outfit.

Yuki's Japanese inspiration was seen in his first couture collection Autumn 1972. The wearer is cosseted as if in a luxurious sleeping bag.

in theatre and television design. His couture and ready-to-wear lines are fluidly sculptural in the GRES mood.

ZORAN

Born Belgrade, Yugoslavia, 1947.
Having obtained his degree in architecture from the University of Belgrade, Zoran moved to New York in 1971. He became a name in fashion in 1977 when a friend saw his designs and introduced them to Bendels, the New York fashion store. They were written up in *Women's Wear Daily* and, from that moment, Zoran had arrived. His approach to design is minimalist, in the HALSTON mode but even more radical. His first collections were based on rectangles and squares in *crêpe de chine* and other luxury fabrics, and his designs have evolved from this into utterly simple shapes. They have a minimum of detail, but are created in the most luxurious and sensuous materials. 'I start from the body,' he has said. 'There's nothing requiring fitting. Either it's your size or it's not.' The casual simplicity of his clothes might, at first glance, appear obvious, even boring, but it stems from a fine appreciation of proportion and a mathematical precision of design. Zoran's expensively relaxed look is achieved by an eye finely attuned to balance and scale. Such sophisticated simplicity is only for the very rich, who crowd into his Sullivan Street loft in New York City to rub shoulders with Ali Mac-Graw, Lauren Hutton and other stars. Zoran's showings are informal and so *chic* that even very grand press ladies feel honoured to sit on the floor and nibble cheese while the models slide among them.

Mindful of the sort of lives his customers live, Zoran has produced a jet-pack collection of ten pieces that pack into a small bag. Their owner can look casual and glamorous wherever her schedule takes her. As far as possible, Zoran avoids everything extraneous. He prefers not to use buttons and zippers. His colour range is severely limited and his basic colours are red, black, grey, white and ivory. His simple sweatshirts, T-shirts and jogging pants wrought in cashmere and sold for huge prices, can suggest either a perfect understanding of the way we live or the ultimate perversity. It largely depends upon one's bank balance.

With the growth of fame has come the realization of the importance of commerciality, and Zoran has begun to refabricate in cotton knit down to a price. Taking four tee-shirts, two skirt lengths, trousers, a cardigan and a hooded top he has created a complete wardrobe. If his day materials are frequently 'unglamorous' cotton jersey and flannel, his evenings are still ritzy, in satin, velvet and, inevitably, cashmere. Not surprisingly, his sensuous clothes are coveted on both sides of the Atlantic.

ZWEI

Fiona Dealey, *born* Hockley, Essex, England, 1959.
Gioia Meller Marcovicz, *born* Hanover, Germany, 1955.
Founded London, England, 1982.
Fiona Dealey originally began to study painting at Lancaster Polytechnic, but after six months she transferred to St. Martin's School of Art to read fashion. She graduated in 1981. Gioia Marcovicz began her training with an apprenticeship in an haute-couture house in Munich, but after three years she left to set up her own small business for private customers. She came to London in 1977 to learn commercial pattern-cutting in various fashion houses. The girls met in 1982 and, finding their approach to fashion to be the same, they decided to work together. They formed Zwei (German for two) in June, 1982, and showed their first collection in October of that year. Since then their clothes have sold in Germany, Switzerland and America as well as in England. They designed modern working clothes which were efficient and practical, although body conscious and sexy. Their collections always had a strong emphasis on knitwear and used plain fabrics with limited colours. They have now dissolved their partnership and the firm has ceased trading.

THE IMAGE MAKERS

AGHA · ANTONIO · AVEDON · BAILEY · BEATON · BENITO · BÉRARD · BLUMENFELD · BOUCHÉ · BOUËT-WILLIAUMEZ · BOURDIN
CHASE · CLARKE · DAHL-WOLFE · DE MEYER · DRIAN · ERIC · EULA · FAIRCHILD · FRISSELL · GRUAU · HORST · HOYNINGEN-
HUENE · IRIBE · KLEIN · LANDSCHOFF · LEPAPE · LIBERMAN · MAN RAY · MUNKASCI · NAST · NEWTON · PARKINSON · PENN
SEEBERGER · SNOW · SNOWDON · STEICHEN · TURBEVILLE · VERTÈS · VREELAND · WEBER

Chase

Fairchild

Snow

Vreeland

Liberman

AGHA, Mehemet Fehmy

Born Turkey, 1898.

Agha was working in Paris in the twenties for the Dorland Advertising Agency under Walter Maas. When Maas was asked to set up a German *Vogue* in 1928 he took Agha with him. His talents were so evident that, when the German magazine collapsed, the multi-lingual Agha was taken to New York to be Art Director of *Vogue, Vanity Fair* and *House and Garden.* He transformed them. He got rid of italic type, placed photographs asymmetrically and, above all, was not afraid to leave lots of white space on the page. Under his guidance Condé NAST* magazines became modern. He retired in 1943, having permanently left his mark on the company's publications. His successor was Alexander LIBERMAN* who, ironically, had been sacked by Agha at the very outset of his career.

Antonio

ANTONIO (Lopez) □

Born Puerto Rico, 1943.

When he was a child, Antonio's Spanish parents moved to New York. After studying at the High School of Industrial Art, Antonio attended the Fashion Institute of Technology from spring 1961 to autumn 1962. In 1964 he introduced himself to the couturier, Charles JAMES, in a New York restaurant. The result of this meeting was that James asked the young artist to make a drawn record of all his clothes. Often working late at night, Antonio, who had previously worked largely on Seventh Avenue at a very commercial level, was given a unique education. The great designer taught him to appreciate the sculptural quality of clothes and this had a lasting effect on the Spaniard's drawing. In the early seventies he moved to Paris where he became the central figure in a group of American ex-patriots there. Since the mid-seventies his fame has grown and his style, always eclectic and varied, has settled a little. An Antonio drawing can always be recognized by its firm graphic basis whether it be of the precision of his Bloomingdale's or La Forêt advertisements of the late seventies or of the freedom of his work for the Italian fashion magazine *Vanity.* It is the creative partnership he has with this magazine's editor Anna Piaggi

which has produced work of such quality that every issue is a collector's item.

Antonio can be considered the father of the rebirth of fashion illustration in the eighties: his influence on students and fellow fashion artists is enormous and it is a testimony to his considerable technical skill that so many attempt to copy his style and so few succeed. His work has flair, accuracy and realism. It comes as no surprise that he lists Boldini and Ingres as the artists who have influenced him.

AVEDON, Richard

Born New York, USA, 1923.

Avedon's parents owned a dress shop, so that he grew up surrounded by fashion. Having learned photography in the Marines, he became a student of Brodovitch, who was art director at *Harper's Bazaar.* He worked for *Harper's Bazaar* from 1945 to 1965, when he moved to *Vogue,* for whom he still works. The film, *Funny Face,* was based on his life and he acted as consultant and stills photographer for it. He is one of the handful of fashion photographers with an international reputation. His photographs have speed, wit and verve and his model girls look not only real, but

fun. He has always experimented with new techniques and he has worked with the world's top models, especially successfully with Suzy Parker in the 1950s and Lauren Hutton in the 1970s. His work is exuberant and versatile and second only to that of PENN* in its influence: his energetic and unpredictable images still have enormous impact even on those who know nothing about fashion.

BAILEY, David

Born London, England, 1938.

Bailey's contribution to fashion photography is largely to do with attitude. His women, like those of AVEDON*, have an immediacy and freshness, but, unlike the American photographer's work, Bailey's images have a strongly sexual feeling. His girls gaze at us provocatively. He has been involved in creative partnerships with Jean Shrimpton, who became *the* face of the early 1960s, Twiggy, who became even more famous, Penelope Tree and Marie Helvin. His first work was for the *Daily Express* and in 1959 he worked as an assistant to the fashion photographer, John French, before beginning on his own. He has worked regularly for British,

Bailey

Beaton

French, and Italian *Vogue* and he also directs television commercials. His *Goodbye, Baby and Amen*, published in 1969, summed up a whole era and his book, *N.1*, published in 1981, evokes the atmosphere of that part of London with memorable imagery. They are the most interesting of several publications bearing his name.

BEATON, Sir Cecil

Born London, England, 1904.
Died Wiltshire, England, 1980.

Sir Cecil Beaton was a man of many talents. He was educated at Harrow and Cambridge. He took his first job in 1928 as an illustrator for *Vogue*, and it was then that he began a long and productive col-

laboration with the Condé NAST* organization. Illustrator, photographer, costume and scenery designer, camp chronicler of the passing social scene and diarist, he brought elegance and creative flair to everything he did. As a photographer he recorded the royal family, worked for the Ministry of Information during World War II and, with his fondness for theatrical lighting and Surrealist and romantic backgrounds, created many memorable fashion photographs. His designs for ballet, opera, stage and films showed an ability to assimilate historic styles and his wide understanding of the history of taste and fashion.

Beaton achieved success in all his chosen fields, but his most important and lasting contribution to fashion could well

prove to be his fashion exhibition at the Victoria and Albert Museum in 1971. His publications include *The Book of Beauty* (1930), *Cecil Beaton's New York* (1938), *The Glass of Fashion* (1954) and his *Diaries* (published between 1961 and 1973). His film designs for *Gigi* (1958) and *My Fair Lady* (1964) won him Academy Awards. He designed sets and costumes for many theatrical productions, including *Lady Windermere's Fan*, *The School For Scandal*, *My Fair Lady* and *Coco*. In 1956 he received the Neiman-Marcus Award, in 1957 the C.B.E. and in 1960 the French Legion of Honour. His final honour was the knighthood bestowed on him in 1972. After a stroke in 1975, he lived in semi-retirement until his death.

Benito

BENITO, Eduardo Garcia

Through his covers for *Vogue*, Benito has given us the quintessential 1920s woman. With her small, neat head and long neck, her father was Brancusi and her mother, Modigliani. Her education, or that of her creator, was from LEPAPE*. Benito's *Vogue* covers, 'icons of their time', frequently consisted only of a head: shingled, bird-like, and frequently cloched, it was the archetypal image of the flapper. His technique was strong and simple, which gave his drawing a monumental purity even when, as frequently, he was being boldly experimental.

BÉRARD, Christian

Born Paris, France, 1902.
Died Paris, France, 1949.
Bérard is undoubtedly one of the most neglected geniuses of the century. As a painter, costume designer, interior decorator and fashion illustrator, he was im-

mensely influential in Paris during the 1930s and early 1940s. As an arbiter of taste and a judge of style, his advice and approval were courted by all. His influence in couture was considerable, especially on DIOR and SCHIAPARELLI, for whom he designed scarves and fabrics. His training was in architecture, but he was known in Paris as a painter. Gradually he spent less and less time on painting and more and more in the ephemeral worlds of illustration, fabric-designing and decor. His colour sense was uniquely fresh. He was able to combine the most unexpected and even vulgar shades to produce totally new and sophisticated schemes which are now considered standard combinations.

As a fashion illustrator Bérard worked both for *Vogue* and *Harper's Bazaar*. Whether working with watercolour or Japanese brush and Indian ink, his style was painterly and evocative: vulgar precision was not what he aimed for. The elegant understatement of his illustrations was too imprecise and subtle for many: hence Randolph Hearst's crass gibe of 'faceless Freddy', which referred to the fact that Bérard frequently considered it unnecessary to delineate facial features. As a painter he was associated with Neo-Romanticism and his attitudes are seen in

his most lasting memorial, his stage and film work. His designs for Cocteau's *La Machine Infernale* and *La Belle et la Bête* are still powerful and impressive, forty years later. By the cognoscenti he was adored. Though he was frequently dirty and addicted to opium and low life, he found society's doors always open to him. Artistic and fashionable life fed on the vitality and inventiveness of his inspiration in all areas of design.

BLUMENFELD, Erwin

Born Berlin, Germany, 1897.
Died Rome, Italy, 1969.
Before World War I Blumenfeld worked as a dress designer. Then, under the influence of the Dada movement, he began to write and paint. He moved to Holland in 1918 and ran a shop there until 1935, when his business became bankrupt. He moved to Paris to become a photographer. His work with French *Vogue* began in 1938, but in the next year he moved to *Harper's Bazaar*. He spent much of World War II in prison camps in France. After the war, he moved to America, became an American citizen and recommenced his career as a fashion photographer. His work was always strong and clear and he created some classic

Bérard

Blumenfeld

images. Although he produced excellent and inventive photographs, he apparently disliked the world of fashion and the work which he produced for it. His photographs will be remembered for their technical skill and their daring: he posed models on the Eiffel Tower, reversed images and printed negative and positive images together. His work was always arresting and challenging.

BOUCHÉ, René
Born France, 1906.
Died London, England, 1963.
A master of line who, with the utmost economy of gesture, created illustrations of total elegance and sophistication, Bouché was a subtle observer of the fashion scene and, at heart, a portrait painter. Every drawing was like a portrait of a particular dress. Bouché seemed to capture the personality of the dress, the designer and the wearer with his strong, pure lines. His line was economic and his eye looked at contours. He worked quickly, usually using pen-and-ink and wash, although some of his most successful work were the soft and unemphatic drawings done in charcoal, Conte crayon or pencil. He experimented with Japanese bamboo pens and Japanese

brushes to produce semi-abstract illustrations of power and elegance. Apart from his fashion work for *Vogue*, for whom he worked from 1941 onwards, he also was an extremely successful painter and portraitist.

BOUËT-WILLAUMEZ, Count René
Bouët-Willaumez' drawings, always signed R.B.W, were soft and liquid. Although his line was not of the same calibre as that of BOUCHÉ* and ERIC* (of whom he was intensely jealous), his technique had style and panache. His preferred media were pen-and-ink and wash and with them he achieved a marvellous feeling of speed and movement. A sense of arrested life created by a line totally in control was the hallmark of a R.B.W drawing. His work was featured in *Vogue* throughout the 1930s and 1940s and he also did a considerable amount of drawing for advertising. Like his contemporaries, he always worked with a live model.

BOURDIN, Guy
Born France, 1935.
Bourdin is the man who put sex and violence into fashion photography. His

images shock. He was extremely popular in the 1970s and his work seemed to epitomize the preoccupations of that decade. An impoverished artist, he discovered the work of the American photographer, Edward Weston, in the 1950s while he was on military service in Dakar. On demobilization, he tried to obtain a job as assistant to MAN RAY*. He did not succeed, but he was able to spend a lot of time with the photographer in his studio. Bourdin began to work for French *Vogue* in 1960. He now does editorial work almost exclusively for them and is allowed considerable freedom in his choice of clothes and models. He is also largely responsible for deciding how they are to be photographed. His advertising campaign for Charles JOURDAN shoes, which he began in 1966, is famous. So was his Bloomingdale's lingerie brochure. The image he projects in his photographs is obsessive and sexy, yet strangely cold and remote.

CHASE, Edna Woolman
Born New Jersey, USA, 1877.
Died New York, USA, 1957.
Edna Woolman Chase was brought up by Quaker grandparents and their ideals and standards remained with her all her life: she believed in hard work, professional honesty and self-awareness. The doyenne of fashion editors, she began at *Vogue* in 1895 at the age of eighteen and remained there for fifty-seven years. When she began working for it, *Vogue* was only two years old. Her job was in the subscription department. When she retired in 1952 she had held the post of editor-in-chief of American, British and French *Vogue* for thirty-seven years. Her influence on fashion and its special brand of journalism was immense. It is no exaggeration to say that modern fashion magazines look and sound as they do largely because of Mrs. Chase.

She trained artists, writers and photographers and was involved in appointing staff to all the *Vogue* magazines for many years. Her views were strong and carefully worded and they almost always prevailed. Her partnership with Condé NAST* was the most productive proprietor/editor relationship in fashion-magazine history and their influence far transcended the comparatively limited readership of the

Bouché

Bouët-Williaumez

279

magazine. Together they made *Vogue* the symbol of quality in fashion and fashion journalism. Mrs. Chase's sane, but witty, writing can be seen at its best in her autobiography, *Always in Vogue*, published in 1954. She received the French Légion d'Honneur in 1935 and a Neiman-Marcus Award in 1940.

CLARKE, Henry
Born California, USA.
Clarke began his career as a display manager for I. Magnin in Oakland. In 1948 he obtained work in *Vogue*'s New York studio, building sets. He followed Brodovitch's famous course at the New School for Social Research and then moved to Paris. His first jobs were as house photographer for DESSÈS and MOLYNEUX, but he later worked for *Femina* and British *Harper's*

Bazaar. He signed up with Condé NAST* in 1951 and has worked for French *Vogue* and lived in Paris ever since. Like those other Brodovitch protégés, AVEDON* and PENN*, Clarke produces elegant and sophisticated work which projects an image of feminine, glamorous women.

DAHL-WOLFE, Louise
Born San Francisco, USA, 1895.
Louise Dahl-Wolfe joined *Harper's Bazaar* in 1936 and remained with that publication for the rest of her working life. Having studied at the San Francisco Institute of Design, she worked in New York from 1921 to 1923 as an electric-sign designer and as a decorator's assistant. She became interested in photography and colour theory and, after spending time in Europe and Africa between 1927 and

1928, returned with her husband to California. Two years later she was photographing the Smoky Mountain people of Tennessee. These documentary photographs were published in *Vanity Fair* in 1933 and their impact was sensational. Three years later she became a fashion photographer. Her compositional skill and colour sense reflected her early training as a painter and, together with her sensitive eye, enabled her to produce fashion photographs of great subtlety and calm.

DE MEYER, Baron Adolphe
Born Paris, France, 1868.
Died Los Angeles, USA, 1949.
De Meyer studied painting in Paris before moving to London in 1895 and marrying Donna Caracciolo, reputedly Edward VII's illegitimate daughter. In 1901 he was

Clarke

Dahl-Wolfe

ennobled by the King of Saxony. He published a luxurious limited edition of photographs of the Ballets Russes in 1914, before fleeing to America on the outbreak of war. He began to work on *Vogue* for Condé NAST*, who was impressed by his European taste and connections. *Vogue* readers were informed of his grandeur and his cost and they were doubtless suitably awed. De Meyer must have cut an exotic figure in the New York of the time, with his courtly European manners and his hair dyed bright blue! He was the first *artistic* photographer and his photographs of New York society beauties wearing the latest fashions were feminine, romantic and idealized images of luxury. In 1918 De Meyer moved to *Harper's Bazaar* on a high salary and returned to Paris. His back-lit, luminous photographs, with their soft-focus technique, were flattering, ethereal

Drian

De Meyer

and romantic. They set an international standard to which all other photographers aspired. But during the 1920s De Meyer's fame waned. He was out of tune with the times and his work looked old-fashioned. Sacked in 1932 by *Harper's Bazaar*, he was unable to regain employment with *Vogue* and he died neglected and forgotten.

DRIAN, Étienne
Entirely self-taught, Drian was only fifteen when he first exhibited at the Salon de la Nationale. He worked briefly as a fashion designer before settling into his métier as a decorative artist. His work, always life-like and convincingly drawn, is in line with that of Boldini, Sargent and Toulouse-Lautrec. His elegant women enhanced the pages of most fashion journals during the 1920s. They were first seen in the prestigious and exclusive *Gazette du Bon Ton* between 1913 and 1915. His lightly sophisticated and intelligent graphic approach was seen in his etchings, poster designs, illustrations and decorative screens.

ERIC

Born Illinois, USA, 1891.
Died New York, USA, 1958.
Carl Erickson always signed his work 'Eric'. He was discovered by MAINBOCHER when he was editor of French *Vogue*. They worked closely together in the 1930s and, although Eric was of Swedish American stock, his drawings of the period perfectly reflected French elegance and style. His line epitomized the patrician way of life of the *haut monde* of Paris. In appearance he was the classic *boulevardier*, always wearing a bowler hat (even when drawing) and bow ties and was frequently accompanied by a large brown poodle. He always sketched from the model and his work for *Vogue* right up to the late 1950s puts him second only to BÉRARD* as a fashion illustrator.

Like Bérard, he was an artist first and a fashion illustrator second. He understood the feel of materials and knew how the clothed body moves; he was also a close observer of figures within a social context. His fashion illustrations invariably had the feeling of a moment observed. He used no sterile formula or stylized tricks. He looked at clothes, understood them and drew them as they were.

EULA, Joe

Having studied at the Art Student's League in New York, Eula decided to take a course in fashion. From there it was a short step to specialization in fashion illustration. His work has always been noteworthy for its economy of line, allied to a total conviction which enables him to express the substance of style in a very direct way. He usually works on a very small scale and, in the last few years, he has produced marvellously free, impressionistic watercolours, which have speed and panache and, eschewing complicated details, express the personality and feel of the clothes. His

Eric

Eula

multi-coloured, mixed-media portraits and fashion illustrations for Italian *Harper's Bazaar* are the work of an artist of considerable talent. He has matured into a uniquely gestural chronicler of the fashion scene.

FAIRCHILD, John

Born New York, USA, 1927.

After Princeton, John Fairchild joined the Fairchild organization, a trade-publication empire founded by his grandfather, as a retail news reporter for the New York City area. After this experience, he moved on to head the London bureau and then became head of the Paris bureau from 1955 to 1960. It was in Paris that his abilities really became evident. His approach to the sacred cow of Paris fashion appeared, in the hallowed halls of haute couture, to be brash, unsubtle and iconoclastic. His articles were often partisan, but they were always written in a lively informal way, gossipy and fresh. They soon became compulsive reading. He broke the rules whenever he wished to and did so with wit and panache. As a result *Women's Wear Daily* ceased to be viewed as yet another dull trade paper: its snappy approach under his leadership, as its publisher and editor-in-chief, made it compulsory reading for anyone involved in the garment industry. It is now considered the Bible and Fairchild, like Moses, brings 'the word'. He is a king-maker, he is still partisan and he still injects huge gulps of vitality into the fashion industry through his newspaper. *W.W.D.*, as Fairchild likes it to be called, is respected for its judgement, involvement and style. It uses the best fashion illustrators to pinpoint 'the look' and brilliantly sums up the mood of the fashion moment with its wittily coined expressions and phrases.

In 1970 a glossy, coloured, fortnightly newspaper called *W* was launched. It became an immediate success. Snobbishly glamorous and shamelessly extolling the advantages of wealth, it is read all over the world. A male equivalent, *M*, followed. The least glamorous publication, *Daily News Record*, the trade paper for menswear, is a respected and trusted mouthpiece. In 1975 Fairchild received the French Legion of Honour. He published

Frissell

Gruau

The Fashionable Savages in 1965. Although he has mellowed, his critical acumen has not been blunted: Fairchild's frown can make couturiers quake even yet.

FRISSELL, Toni

Born New York, USA, 1907.

Toni Frissell was one of the world's top fashion photographers. Her sporting interests affected the way she photographed clothes: she liked casual, outdoor shots of sporty girls at ease with their clothes and surroundings. She took MUNKASCI*'s spontaneity one stage further, to produce refreshingly casual and practical images which had the immediacy of a snapshot. She worked as a painter and trained as an actress before joining *Vogue* in the early 1930s as a caption writer. Her photographs for *Vogue* were always taken in the open air and she specialized in low-angle shots. She ceased working in fashion in 1946.

GRUAU, René

Born Rimini, Italy, 1908.

Gruau moved to Paris in the 1930s and soon became immersed in the fashion world. It was at this time that he began to develop his unique style. His drawing has simplicity and directness plus considerable panache, but, although highly stylized, it is always full of vitality. The figure is always silhouetted with a continuous black line, which gives the design considerable strength, and the rest of the drawing is delicate and free. Much of Gruau's best work has a considerable sense of movement and speed. He reached his apogee in the 1950s and his drawings of today (especially those for advertisements of DIOR's perfumes) retain a very 1950s elegance. Therein lies their charm. Gruau's presentation and lay-out have always been of a high level, with a boldness and directness which have enormous impact.

HORST, Horst P.

Born Germany, 1906.

After a broad education, Horst began working for an export firm in Hamburg in the early 1920s. He went on to study under

Walter Gropius and then joined Le Corbusier as a student in Paris. He met HOYNINGEN-HUENE* and became his intimate friend and model. He became a Condé NAST* staff photographer in 1932 and took over Hoyningen-Huene's job as *Vogue*'s Paris photographer in 1934, when his friend defected to *Harper's Bazaar*. From then until the outbreak of World War II Horst split his year between New York and Paris. After the war, he remained based in America. His photographs were always dramatically lit and exuberant: he loved *trompe l'oeil* effects and his pictures were often witty. He published his work and that of his mentor in *Photographs of a Decade* (1946) and his work was again seen in *Salute to the Thirties* (1974).

HOYNINGEN-HUENE, Baron George

Born St. Petersburg, Russia, 1900.
Died Los Angeles, USA, 1968.
Hoyningen-Huene arrived in Paris as a refugee from the Russian revolution, and worked as a film extra and a sketcher in his sister's dressmaking firm. From the first job he learned lighting and camera techniques, from the second how to look at clothes. In 1925 he began to work in *Vogue*'s Paris studio as a designer of studio sets for fashion photographs. He soon became French *Vogue*'s main photographer. His considerable importance and influence as a fashion photographer are based on his respect for the garments he photographed, his ability to create a unique sense of space and atmosphere within his picture frame and his dramatically Surrealist lighting. He placed his models in realistic situations, but he also often mixed dummy mannequins with live models. In 1934 he moved from *Vogue* to *Harper's Bazaar*, having apparently taken offence at the clause in his new contract which said he must 'desist from calling attention to himself'. The story goes that he upset a bowl of spaghetti over Dr. AGHA*, *Vogue*'s art director, and promptly telephoned Mrs. SNOW*. In 1946 he moved to Hollywood, where he worked as a colour consultant to the film industry. His work as a fashion photographer is characterized by an elegant perfectionism.

IRIBE

Born France, 1883.
Died Paris, France, 1935.
Iribe's real name was Paul Iribarnegaray. Illustrator, stylist, designer, *bon viveur* and womanizer, Iribe was an important figure in the artistic and fashionable circles of Paris even before World War I. In 1906, when he was only twenty-three, he established his own newspaper, *Le Témoin*, and in 1908 he illustrated *Les Robes de Paul Poiret*, a sumptuous limited edition of POIRET's oriental fashions. His illustrations for this book had a considerable influence on illustrators and art directors and set a pattern of drawing which remained constant for over ten years. Unfortunately, Iribe proved so difficult to work with, and so elusive, that Poiret could never see him direct. All business was transacted through a mysterious lady, and since Iribe's drawings were delivered very late, if at all, Poiret used LEPAPE* to illustrate his second volume in 1911. Nevertheless, Iribe's influence was enormous – the 'rose Iribe' was widely copied and became a key motif in Art Deco.

Hoyningen-Huene

In 1914 Iribe left Europe for America. By 1919 he was working in Hollywood with de Mille. He was a great stylist and his influence, like that of BÉRARD* some years later, was pervasive: he designed furniture for the home of DOUCET and pendants for Lalique. He was considered a great lover and had an affair with CHANEL, whose money was used to finance the reappearance of Le Témoin in 1930 (with Iribe as director and principal illustrator). His working life was a success story, from the beginning, when at the age of seven-

impact: it reflected his iconoclastic attitudes. As a young man he worked in Paris with Léger, executed abstract and kinetic works which were exhibited throughout Europe, and experimented with photographic techniques. He worked for Vogue from 1955 to 1956, producing dramatic results with innovations like wide-angle lenses and multiple flash. A sort of mischievous AVEDON* or PENN*, Klein photographed women who looked elegant without hauteur: sharp, ironic and street-wise, they presaged the model girls of the 1970s.

On leaving Vogue, Klein concentrated on film-making, producing documentaries and writing and directing films. He lives in Paris.

LANDSCHOFF, Herman
Born Munich, Germany, 1905.
Having studied design, Landschoff became interested in photography and opened a photographic laboratory in Paris in 1933. Up to the outbreak of World War II, he worked for French Vogue and Femina. He

Iribe

teen he drew for the famous newspaper, L'Assiette au Beurre, through his fabric designs for Bianchini-Ferrier, down to his costumes and sets for de Mille's Ten Commandments. His skill as a draughtsman, his taste and his knowledge placed him at the centre of all aspects of the decorative arts.

KLEIN, William
Born New York, USA, 1928.
Something of a maverick in the world of fashion, Klein was originally an artist and had little interest in the world of clothes and glossy magazines. For this very reason his fashion photography had considerable

Klein

Landschoff

moved to America in 1941 and began to work for *Harper's Bazaar*. His photographs are characterized by a light-hearted approach and an enormous feeling of movement. He was the first photographer to feature blurred backgrounds to give a sense of speed.

LEPAPE, Georges
Born 1887.
At the age of twenty-four, having studied at the École des Beaux Arts in the Atelier Corman, Lepape was chosen by POIRET to illustrate his second publication, *Les Choses de Paul Poiret*, published in 1911. Lepape's drawings of Poiret's creations for this spectacular, full-colour volume made his name. Following in the footsteps of IRIBE*, who had illustrated Poiret's first volume, Lepape found his drawings much sought-after by art editors. He was one of Lucien Vogel's team of illustrators on the luxuriously self-indulgent and original *Gazette du Bon Ton* and his work appeared regularly in magazines such as *Vanity Fair*, *Femina*, *Harper's Bazaar* and *Vogue*. His covers for

Man Ray

Vogue dominated newstands in the 1920s and early 1930s. In addition, he designed sets and costumes for plays and revues. Lepape was a bold colourist with a strong sense of design. The influences on his work were the Ballets Russes, Cubism, Modigliani and Brancusi. He popularized and made familiar many modern art innovations by adapting them to his work. His decline was brought about by the advent of the relaxed and natural drawings of ERIC* in the 1930s, which suddenly made Lepape's techniques look tired and old-fashioned.

LIBERMAN, Alexander

Born Kiev, Russia, 1912.

After a brief period (1921–1924) spent in London, Liberman studied architecture at L'École des Beaux Arts in Paris and graduated in 1930. He remained in Paris, working on the magazine *Vu* from 1931 to 1936, winning the Gold Medal for Design at the 1937 International Exhibition in Paris. In 1941 he arrived in America and obtained a job as Art Director of *Vogue*, despite an initial feeling that Dr. AGHA* had that he was not right for the magazine. In 1943 Liberman took over Agha's job of Art Director for all Condé NAST* publications. He became Editorial Director in 1962.

His influence on publishing, and especially fashion journalism, has been benign and widespread. Under his guidance American *Vogue* remains in the vanguard just as it was in the days of Condé Nast and Agha. In addition to his work in publishing, Alexander Liberman has a distinguished record as an artist and photographer. His paintings are in the Permanent Collection of the Museum of Modern Art in New York and that museum also exhibited his photographs in a one-man exhibition in 1959. He holds the French Légion d'Honneur. His book *The Artist in His Studio* was published in 1960 and a biography, *Alexander Liberman* by Barbara Rose, appeared in 1981.

MAN RAY

Born New York, USA, 1890.
Died Paris, France, 1977.

Man Ray moved to Paris in 1921, met POIRET, for whom he did fashion photographs, and was soon deeply involved with the Dada and Surrealist movements. Enigmatic and strange, he was one of the central figures of the art world of the 1920s and one of its most inventive photographers. His fashion work for *Harper's Bazaar* in the 1930s was exceptional and highly influential. It used the process of solarization to give a bizarre and dramatic light to his pictures. Man Ray did not take fashion photography particularly seriously. He used it as a means of support for his art and experimental photography. For this reason he broke many of the 'rules' and produced highly creative

images with a Surrealist influence. His 'rayographs' which reproduce the effect of a photograph being sent by radio waves, illustrate his dictum that 'inspiration, not information, is the force that binds all creative acts'.

MUNKASCI, Martin

Born Romania, 1896.
Died New York, USA, 1963.

When he was eighteen Munkasci joined a sports newspaper in Budapest and in 1923 became a news photographer. In a short time he was Hungary's most successful photo-journalist. In 1927 he began working for German newspapers and magazines. *Harper's Bazaar* lured him to America in 1934 and his work was soon a regular and lively part of that magazine. Munkasci was one of the most influential and original fashion photographers of the century. He brought the realism, movement and immediacy of sports photographs into fashion shots and he made history with his shots of girls running along the beach or actively participating in sports activities. No one had done this before and in many respects Munkasci must be considered the father of action fashion photography.

NAST, Condé

Born Montrose, Colorado, USA, 1873.
Died New York, USA, 1942.

Condé Nast's grandfather was a Lutheran clergyman who emigrated to New York, aged 21, and his father was in the diplomatic corps. He studied philosophy and maths at Georgetown university, obtaining his Master's degree in 1894. In 1900 he became advertising manager of *Collier's Weekly*, thus beginning his life-long association with magazines. He realized quickly that the keystones of a fashionable magazine were 'exclusivity, affordable luxury and the highest quality'. In 1909 he bought *Vogue* and set about putting into practise these precepts. His timing was perfect: American society was expanding; there were plenty of people not in Mrs. Astor's 'famous 400' who had money, pretensions and ambition; they needed a guide to dress and behaviour – and Condé Nast gave it to them in *Vogue*. His business acumen is seen in the fact that, although

Munkasci

his magazine was the epitome of snobbishness, he retained the Vogue Pattern Service. In this he understood the American dichotomy: the desire for thrift and practicality even in luxury. *Vanity Fair* was bought in 1913, *House and Garden* in 1915.

The success of *Vogue* is a reflection of the creative partnership between Condé Nast and Mrs. CHASE*. She became editor in 1914, and ruthlessly imposed her standards on staff and magazine, with the total approval of Nast. Together they planned and controlled British *Vogue* (founded 1916) and French *Vogue* (founded 1920). Nast was also co-publisher of the *Gazette du Bon Ton* from 1920 to 1925 and owner of *Jardin des Modes* (founded 1921). His failures were Spanish *Vogue*, which only lasted from 1918 to 1923, and German *Vogue*, founded in 1928 but abandoned after a few issues. Throughout his life,

Condé Nast insisted upon using the very best talents available and the list of *Vogue* and *Vanity Fair* contributors over the years constituted an artistic and intellectual *Almanach de Gotha* which far transcended the ranks of those involved purely in fashion. Before the Wall Street crash he gave magnificent parties which were like the pages of *Vogue* brought to life. After the slump he hit financial problems and with them came a character change. His last years were marred by his increasing irritation and refusal to listen to any views which did not coincide with his own. His final magazine venture was with *Glamour* which he began in 1939, three years before his death. It can be said that his far-sighted and imaginative approach to magazine publishing created modern fashion journalism. The broad guidelines which he and Mrs. Chase evolved are still observed by wise magazine publishers throughout the world.

NEWTON, Helmut

Born Berlin, Germany, 1920.

Newton began to take photographs when he was twelve years old. After a long apprenticeship in Berlin and wide experience with many magazines during the 1950s and 1960s, he finally developed his own very strong and arresting style, which is an amalgam of sex and aggression. Since the beginning of the 1970s, his work for French *Vogue* has presented a bold and personal statement which uncompromisingly reflects the feelings of the decade and makes him the most important photographer of his time. His models are hard, but elegant; they are sexually desirable, but belligerent; and although they are rich, they are often found in squalid surroundings. Newton shocks the viewer by producing images which come very close to pornography: violence and perversion are presented as almost normal, everyday aspects of life. Technically, his photographs are stunning.

Newton

Parkinson

PARKINSON, Norman

Born Roehampton, England, 1913.

Norman Parkinson is the much-loved and respected doyen of British fashion photographers. He was educated at Westminster School, where his great interest was art. On leaving school, he became apprenticed to the court photographers, Speaight. He set up on his own as a portrait photographer and from this base began to work for *Harper's Bazaar*. During the war he worked with the RAF on reconnaissance photography over France. He joined *Vogue* in 1948 and remained with the Condé NAST* organization until 1960, when he became an associate editor of *Queen*. Since 1964 he has worked as a freelance, mainly with *Vogue* and *Elle*. He lives in Tobago.

In the 1930s, Parkinson's work had the freshness of MUNKASCI*'s. Like Munkasci, he photographed models out-of-doors, walking, running and jumping in a natural way. The spontaneity and humour of these early photographs have remained the hallmark of his work throughout his career. His choice of model girls has always been one of his strengths as a photographer – they are up-to-the-minute, fresh and able to evoke the 'mood' of his pictures. An exhibition of his work was held at the National Portrait Gallery, London, in 1981.

PENN, Irving

Born New Jersey, USA, 1917.

Like AVEDON*, Penn was a student of Alexei Brodovitch, art director of *Harper's Bazaar*, who had a great influence on photography through his lectures at the New York School for Social Research. After working as a freelance artist for *Harper's Bazaar* from 1937 to 1939 and living as a painter in Mexico, Penn began, in his own words, 'a close and continuing collaboration' with *Vogue* in 1943, a collaboration which still continues. Penn's war service took him to India and Italy, two countries full of colour, cultural impact and light, which clearly had their effect on his photographer's eye. He returned to *Vogue* after the war and his work there was characterized by a painterly quality and a clarity and calm that made him the most influential and important fashion photographer of the

Penn

post-war period. His photographs capture the quality of the 1950s and 1960s as no other photographer's work does. *Inventive Paris Clothes*, his photographic essay based on Diana VREELAND's* exhibition, was published in 1977 and *Flowers* followed in 1979, but perhaps his most influential book was the earlier volume, *Worlds in a Small Room*. His work is simply beautiful.

SEEBERGER, Frères

The three Seeberger brothers, Jules (*born* 1872), Louis (*born* 1874) and Henri (*born* 1876), were originally trained as artists. Led by Jules, they moved over to photography in the early 1900s. In 1909 they began to do location fashion work by photographing the designs of the couturiers worn by society women at fashionable gatherings in Paris and spots such as Biarritz, Deauville and Le Touquet. Jules retired in 1928, but his brothers continued until 1939. Louis' sons took over the business after the war. The photographs of the Seeberger brothers provide a unique record of the elegant clothes created by Parisian couturiers for well-dressed society women

Seeberger

for over sixty years. In 1979 a selection of their work was made by Celestine Dars and published under the title, *A Fashion Parade*.

SNOW, Carmel White

Born Dublin, Ireland, 1887.
Died New York, USA, 1961.
Brought up in New York, Carmel Snow joined *Vogue* in 1921 as fashion editor and remained there until 1932, working with the editor Mrs. CHASE*. In 1932 William Randolph Hearst asked her to be fashion editor of his newly-acquired *Harper's Bazaar* and she remained there as editor-in-chief for the rest of her working life. Her brilliance as a fashion journalist rested to a certain degree on her ability to spot and encourage talent. Despite her flair and intuition, however, she made a dramatic mistake in firing ERTÉ, whose cover designs for *Harper's* had projected such a strong image. She understood the movements of fashion and was able to explain them lucidly to her readers. Hers was a didactic role and every month *Harper's* taught the women of America, in firm

*Man, I've flipped ! ***

*** Yes, it is *rather* exciting news**

Snowdon

tones, how to look at themselves, their clothes and their life-styles. Against all opposition she championed causes in which she believed, and she should always be remembered for her determined encouragement and promotion of BALENCIAGA at a time when other fashion journalists were unable to understand him.

Although she considered herself illiterate and uneducated, she had a professional intuition attuned to the most subtle nuances of fashion. The electric rivalry between her and Mrs. Chase spurred them both on to produce a level of fashion reporting and extravagant, but informed, presentation which has been only rarely surpassed. She retired in 1956, lived briefly in Ireland, and then returned to

New York, where she worked on her memoirs, *The World of Carmel Snow*, published in 1962. In 1941 she received the Neiman-Marcus Award, in 1949 the French Légion d'Honneur, and in 1954 the Italian Star of Solidarity. These last two awards were in recognition of her work as fashion and textile consultant to the two countries concerned.

SNOWDON, Earl of
(Anthony Armstrong-Jones)
Born London, England, 1930.
Educated at Eton, Snowdon went up to Cambridge to read natural sciences, but he loathed the course and almost immediately switched to architecture. He did not graduate, but came down and obtained work as an assistant to the ballet and society photographer, Baron. He worked for the *Daily Express* as photographer of theatrical events and slowly moved into fashion photography. In the 1950s he began to work for the English *Vogue* and he soon developed a style full of movement and arrested disaster: his model girls had fun knocking over bottles and finding themselves marooned in mid-stream. After his marriage to Princess Margaret, he moved away from fashion into documentary work for *The Sunday Times* and portraiture. He likes photographic anonymity and has said, 'I never want to put my stamp on anything'. He has produced books on London, Venice and, with *Private View*, the London art scene.

STEICHEN, Edward
Born Luxembourg, 1879.
Died New York, USA, 1973.
Steichen was the grand old man of fashion photography and far and away the most important fashion photographer of the century. His family moved from Europe to America in 1881 and he was brought up in Milwaukee. At the age of fifteen he was apprenticed to a lithograph company there and he began to paint and take photographs. He met Alfred Stieglitz in New York in 1900 and joined his Photo-Secession Movement when it was founded in 1902. In 1911 he did a series of fashion photographs for the French magazine, *Art et Décoration*, featuring POIRET's cre-

ations, and he became involved with modern art and the works of Picasso, Matisse and Rodin. He devoted much of his time to developing his painting until, in 1918, he destroyed all his work and turned his back on painting in order to concentrate on photography. He joined *Vogue* in 1923 and in the same year began to work for J. Walter Thompson. At *Vogue* he replaced Baron DE MEYER* and within a year had changed the look of fashion photography for ever. Gone were De Meyer's softly lit, romantically pictorial images; in their place Steichen created unromantic, unsentimental pictures which reflected the new Modernism. His independent, witty-looking girls were perfect reflections of the 1920s – none more so than Marion Moorehouse, with whom he had the first of those creative partnerships between photographer and model which have been a feature of the art over the years. He imposed his own style on all fashion photography and his persuasive influence was seen throughout the 1920s in every fashion magazine.

Steichen closed his New York studio in 1938. During World War II he was an official US government war photographer, becoming director of all naval combat photography in 1945. In 1947 he became director of the Department of Photography at the New York Museum of Modern Art,

a post he held until 1961. He was responsible for many important photographic exhibitions there, including the now legendary 'The Family of Man' show. He was awarded the Presidential Medal of Freedom.

TURBEVILLE, Deborah
Born Massachusetts, USA, 1938.
Deborah Turbeville arrived in New York in 1956 and worked for two years as a model and assistant designer for Claire MCCARDELL, before being appointed an assistant editor of *Ladies' Home Journal*. In 1963 she became a fashion editor at *Harper's Bazaar*. After attending a fashion photography seminar given by AVEDON* in 1966, she became fashion editor for *Mademoiselle*, though she continued to work as a freelance photographer for *Harper's Bazaar*. In 1972 she moved to Europe as a freelance and worked for *Nova* in London. Her work throughout the 1970s developed a strong personal style. She creates a mysterious and slightly menacing atmosphere with model girls who look strangely sad and vulnerable in their limp, enigmatic poses. There is an ambivalence in her work which is disturbing. Although different, it is every bit as haunting as that of NEWTON* and BOURDIN*.

Turbeville

VERTÈS, Marcel
Born 1895.
Died 1961.

Vertès' fashion illustrations represent a delightful, witty iconoclasm. His nervously darting, broken lines show the hand of an artist, not an illustrator – the quality of the line is always more important than the exact delineation of detail or conveyance of fashion information. When Vertès used colour he produced work of considerable subtlety and delicacy. His humour, which frequently inclined towards the whimsical, and occasionally the inoffensively suggestive, was seen in everything he produced, whether it was meant to be fantasy or straightforward fashion reporting. In fact, straightforward reporting did not interest Vertès. As a result, he has left us a clear artistic record of 1930s *chic* of the kind that Dali and SCHIAPARELLI were noted for. Born in Hungary, he worked for years in Paris before moving to America in 1940. His covers for the American *Harper's Bazaar* were outstanding and his work on the film, *Moulin Rouge*, the story of Toulouse-Lautrec, won him two Academy Awards.

VREELAND, Diana
Born Paris, France, 1906.

On the outbreak of World War I, Diana Vreeland moved with her parents to America. She married in 1924 and, except for nine years in London from 1928 until 1937, her married life was spent in New York. Her life in Paris as a child had been passed in the artistic and fashionable world. She was exposed to stars like Diaghilev and Nijinsky and the foundations for a life in fashion were laid very early. In 1937 Carmel SNOW asked her to join *Harper's Bazaar*. Within six months she was made fashion editor and with Mrs. Snow and the legendary art editor, Alexei Brodovitch, she set about making *Harper's Bazaar* a stylish and important magazine. She became famous for her 'why don't you . . .' column, in which she made amusingly outrageous suggestions to fire the

Vertès

imagination of her fashionable readers, expressing herself in radical and memorable terms.

Having worked for *Harper's Bazaar* for twenty-seven years, Vreeland left in April, 1962. In January, 1963, she became associate editor of *Vogue*. She was soon made editor-in-chief and remained with *Vogue* until 1971. Admired for her originality and her commitment to fashion, she used *Vogue* to educate the taste of her readers. She was able to inspire her colleagues and to communicate her flair and quality to them so that, during her editorship, the photography, lay-out and writing in *Vogue* reached a very high level. On leaving *Vogue* she became adviser to the Costume Institute of the Metropolitan Museum of Art. Here her influence continues through the regular and important exhibitions she mounts. Outstanding examples have been the Balenciaga Retrospective, the Glory of Russian Costume, and The Manchu Dragon exhibitions. The opening nights are the highlight of the season and the

very expensive tickets are eagerly sought after. Vreeland is now the undisputed Muse of Fashion, whose every pronouncement, like those of the Delphic Oracle, is eagerly chronicled. In 1970 she received the French Order of Merit and in 1976 the French Legion of Honour. In 1977 she published (with PENN*) *Inventive Paris Clothes* and in 1981 she published *Allure*.

WEBER, Bruce

Born and raised in a small American town, Bruce Weber's background was safely upper middle class. He went to a private school where, as he admits, he lived a closeted life. From childhood he remembers his grandmother taking marvellously intimate family pictures. Study at film school in New York, where he trained in film and acting, was followed by a stint as an actor – his hero was Clint Eastwood, which is why his dog is called Rowdy. To make money he did some modelling whilst waiting for the 'break'. His sister was PR for David Bowie and Weber accompanied them across America photographing backstage as the group performed in high schools and halls. He made his name as a photographer working for *Gentleman's Quarterly* – 'G.Q.' – during the seventies and then with British *Vogue*.

With these magazines he has done pioneering work. His model girls and boys look like real people photographed doing real things. So sure is his eye for colour and composition that a Weber shot is instantly recognizable. His photographs have not only changed fashion photography, they have also had an enormous influence on the style of the young: he can be considered the best and most original image creator since the fifties. Weber's 'snapshot' style (which can take weeks of planning and hours of shooting) in which his models so often seem like young puppies, active, alert or lolling exhausted, is a paradigm for his times. He has replaced glamour and glossy sexiness with realism and warmth.

FASHION UPDATE

In this new and revised edition of the *Directory*, I have taken the opportunity to update existing entries so that each one gives the reader the very latest information. Only in this way can the *Directory* continue to be what I originally intended it to be and what it has, to my great pleasure, become: a valuable reference for professional and general readers. The first edition of the *Directory* received a gratifying welcome from the fashion press and the industry and I have been pleased at how many people working in the profession have come to trust and rely on it. I have wished for some time that the *Directory* could be more available to young students of fashion and I am very pleased that this paperback edition now makes this possible at a price they can afford.

In addition to revising existing entries I have broadened the scope of the book by adding this supplement which includes all the latest designers in Britain, Europe and America, some of whom were still at college when the first edition appeared. As a result I can say with confidence that there is no more up-to-date reference book of fashion designers than *McDowell's Directory*. The supplement also makes the span of designers mentioned greater than that of any book currently available. *McDowell's Directory* contains details of the earliest designers, many of whom were in danger of slipping into oblivion, as well as the latest.

The response to my original entries on Italian and Japanese fashion which were in the nature of broad examinations rather than delineations of individuals, has been so favourable that I have included two more broad surveys on Viennese and Russian design – which I hope will be of value to readers.

AGNÈS B.

Born Paris, France, 1941.
Agnès B's father was a barrister in Versailles and she trained at the Ecole des Beaux-Arts to become a museum curator. Married at seventeen, she was divorced at twenty and, having two children to support, took a job on *Elle* magazine. Soon after she began as a freelance designer for Dorothée BIS and Pierre d'Alby before opening her first boutique in 1976, in a converted butcher's shop in the then unfashionable Les Halles district of Paris. The firm of Agnès B is a family one, involving her second husband and her children. There are now over twenty Agnès B boutiques across the world and in 1981 she received the Ordre National du Mérite for her services to the French foreign trade balance. Her range includes men's and children's wear as well as women's clothes. Of the latter she has said 'if it is too expensive, it doesn't exist.' Her relaxed and easy shapes bear out her comment that fashion bores her. She designs clothes to out-last the ephemeral mood of the moment and be wearable for many years – by women of all ages.

BARNES, Jhane

Founded New York, USA, late 1970s.
Jhane Barnes was born in Maryland. Clothes she made for school friends sufficiently impressed her high school principal that he commissioned her to design and make uniforms for the school band. After high school she studied fashion at the Fashion Institute of Technology in New York and, whilst still a student, received an order for 1,000 pairs of trousers after a retailing executive had noticed a model in a restaurant wearing a pair which Barnes had designed. She set up as a menswear designer and soon developed her own style as a minimalist. She has since begun to design womenswear on the same principles. Jhane Barnes was awarded a Coty Award for menswear in 1980. She was not only the youngest designer to be so honoured she was the first woman to receive a menswear award. In 1984 she received a Coty Return Menswear Award.

BARRY, Margaret

Born Ireland 1890s.
Died London, England, 1940s.
Margaret Barry began as a milliner in 1914 with a small shop in Dublin. This expanded into a dress shop and became very successful. In the early 'thirties she moved to London and opened an exclusive dressmaking establishment in Bond Street. It flourished until World War II and was patronised because of the Barry skill with beautiful and exclusive Irish tweeds which she made up into well-cut suits for town or country.

BENETTON, Luciano

Born Treviso, Italy, 1935.
The firm Benetton was founded in 1966 by Luciano Benetton and his sister Giuliana.

He was a shop assistant and she a garment factory worker. Their combined talents on both sides of the counter have made their firm, based in the village of Ponzano, near Venice, a world-wide success. Benetton is Italy's biggest single manufacturer of casual clothing. It has over 4,000 franchise shops in fifty-seven countries, produces over forty million garments per year and, in 1985, announced profits of forty-two million dollars. No wonder that the firm (still family controlled by Luciano, Giuliana and their brothers Carlo and Gilberto) has been affectionately dubbed 'the fast food chain of fashion'.

Benetton's stock-in-trade is basically sweaters and jeans. What makes it special is its own original concept for selling. Once revolutionary, it has now been adopted by most chains. The Benetton success is a packaging and retailing one. The formula is twofold: clothes using simple styles and strong colours, and shops which are distinctively designed and sell only Benetton products. Benetton was one of the first manufacturers to combine fashion and 'high-tech' industrial approaches, such as computer-designed patterns and colour ways for sweaters. All design and marketing are co-ordinated. Indeed, Benetton's whole approach to design is co-ordinated. The firm has been especially influential in the use of colour, creating many unusual combinations which have been plagiarised by the garment industry world-wide. Despite the wholesale copying of their approach to colour, design and co-ordinated retailing, Benetton are still first in the field.

BLAIR, Alistair

Born Freetown, West Africa, 1956.
Alistair Blair was educated in Scotland at Larchfield School, Helensborough. He arrived in London in 1974 to study fashion at St Martin's School of Art. Immediately after graduating he went to Paris as Marc BOHAN's assistant at DIOR. He worked with Bohan on the couture collection for one year and then moved to Hubert de GIVENCHY with whom he worked for two years. In 1980 he took up a post as designer at CHLOE and remained there for two years working with Karl LAGERFELD before moving on to work as assistant to Lagerfeld under the designer's own name. He then moved to New York to be in charge of Lagerfeld's

sportswear collection. In 1985 Blair left Lagerfeld and returned to London to design under his own name. His first collection, in Spring 1986, was very different from most of the design emanating from London at that time. Highly sophisticated and glossy, the Blair looks were more like those of Paris and Milan than London. They had a particular appeal for American buyers. Blair has expressed admiration for VALENTINO, especially his skill in producing 'lines from couture to sportswear in a very classy, very stylish way. In ten or fifteen years I would consider myself very lucky to have achieved that . . .'

BRUYERE, Marie Louise

Founded 1929.
Closed 1950s.
Bruyere opened in Paris in 1929 having worked for some years at LANVIN where she had learned her trade so well that her business flourished. She was able to move into new premises in 1937 to accommodate the growing number of clients for her heavily embroidered evening gowns. In the 'thirties her 'Zouave' trousers, topped with short embroidered jackets, were a trademark.

BYBLOS: *See* Varty.

CHLOE

Founded Paris, France, early 'sixties.
This high-class ready-to-wear firm has always had a policy of employing top designers to create its line. It began with Graziella Fontana, whose trademarks were feminity and softness allied to strong colour, but became a world-famous name in the era of Karl LAGERFELD who was design consultant from 1965 to 1983. In this period Chloe became synonymous with adventurous design produced to the highest levels of workmanship. The traditions established at this time were continued by Guy PAULIN. The present designer is Martine Sitbon.

COSTELLOE, Paul

Born Dublin, Ireland, 1945.
Whilst studying at the Chambre Syndicale school in Paris from 1967–8, Paul Costelloe began to design part-time for Jacques Esterel. When his course was completed, he worked full-time with Esterel for a year as

design assistant. He returned to London in 1969 and worked in the design department of Marks and Spencer for the next three years. During this time he was also involved in setting up design studios for the Italian chainstores La Rinascente and Upim. In 1972 Costelloe joined the New York firm of Anne FOGARTY as designer and remained there until 1975. He returned to Ireland in 1976, and set up his own design consultancy in Dublin the following year. His business was consolidated in 1979 when he went into partnership with Robert Eitel to develop the export market for the Paul Costelloe label. Since then the name of Costelloe has gained respect for clothes which are an amalgam of modern trends and traditional Irish materials. They have an appeal for women in many parts of the world, much as those of fellow Irish designer Sybil CONNOLLY have had.

ETTEDGUI, Joseph

Born Casablanca, Morocco, 1936.
Joseph, as he is always known, was educated at a French school and began his working life in 1959 as a hairdresser. He remained a hairdresser until he inaugurated his fashion enterprise, 'Joseph', in 1972. Since that date his story has been one of continuing success and he is recognised as a major force in London fashion. It is not easy to classify Joseph as, in addition to being a skilled retailer, he is also by way of being a designer. What *can* be said with confidence is that he has one of the keenest fashion intelligences in London. Added to his strong entrepreneurial abilities, this has been responsible for Joseph encouraging many young designers to create relaxed and accessible looks. The Joseph shops have helped many designers of the calibre of Katherine HAMNETT, whilst selling ranges designed for and masterminded by Joseph himself. His influence has been especially strong in knitwear. The Joseph empire now includes designer household goods and a restaurant – in both of which his special sense of style is benevolently apparent. Joseph has been a fashion luminary of 'eighties London as Mrs Berstein of Browns was in the 'seventies. His popularity rests on admiration of his skills, delight in his enthusiasm (which made him once confess that his greatest joy was to spend Sundays dressing the windows of his shops) and

appreciation of his sheer pleasure in show-casing beautifully designed clothes for young women living 'real' lives.

EXTER, Alexandra Alexandrovna:
See Soviet Design.

FRENCH, John
Born London, England, 1907.
Died Surrey, England, 1966.
Study at Hornsey School of Art was followed by work in a commercial art studio. In 1930 French moved to Positano to study painting. On his return to London in 1936 he began work in a photographic studio. During World War II French served in the Grenadier Guards. In 1950 he began to work as a fashion photographer for the *Daily Express*. Throughout the 'fifties his practice grew to include advertising photography and work with many top London fashion magazines, including *Harper's Bazaar* and *The Tatler*. His success was due in large part to his original 'bounced light' technique. This created a soft but perfectly clear print which reproduced extremely well on newsprint. He continued to refine his technique until his illness in late 1965. French's high professionalism and insistence on the minimum of 'tricks' when photographing fashion have not been without their influence on British fashion photographers. A retrospective of his work was held at the V & A in London during the winter of 1984 to mark his widow's gift to the museum of the French archive documenting a professional life of nearly 10,000 sittings.

GALLIANO, John
Born London, England, 1961.
Considered by many to be the first truly original designer to have appeared in London since the 'sixties, John Galliano's success began whilst he was still at college. He studied fashion at St Martin's School of Art and his degree show in 1984 not only obtained for him a first class honours degree, it also forcefully brought him to the attention of the fashion press. Most of them quickly recognised that he had something entirely new to offer fashion. Called 'Les Incroyables' his first collection was a re-working of clothing types and shapes common during the French Revolution and was the culmination of many months of research. Galliano used Revolutionary France as a peg on which to hang his own revolutionary clothes concepts which were no less than a redefinition of shape and function in fashion design. Multi-levelled and many-surfaced, these first clothes have been the template from which subsequent collections have grown. Galliano's work shows a remarkable consistency in its development and a rare maturity for a designer still well under thirty. Like those of Balenciaga, his clothes are not easy to understand or to wear. They are in their way every bit as severe and uncompromising as the Spanish designer's. Nevertheless, behind the courageously unconventional approach of Galliano lies a deeply-felt understanding of cloth and how it should be manipulated to work with the body without imposing itself *on* the body. This concept, shared with many young Japanese and London designers, is the leit-motif of Galliano's design.

GIGLI, Romeo
Born Faenza, Italy, 1949.
The influence of his father's antiquarian book business is freely acknowledged by Romeo Gigli. 'My ideas are all from pictures I have in my head from 15th and 16th century books,' he admits. Gigli did not go into the antiquarian book trade; instead he studied architecture for two years, and travelled regularly to Paris and London. In 1972 a Bologna store owner asked Gigli to design some clothes based on the 'way-out' fashions he had seen in those two capitals. In 1978 Gigli went to New York to design a men's range for Pietro Dimitri but he only stayed for one season: Dimitri wished him to sign an exclusive contract and Gigli decided against doing so. He returned to Italy and became a design consultant for several companies, including TIMMI. He started on his own in 1983 and his unstructured clothes with their emphasis on an elongated silhouette soon made him stand out from mainstream Italian fashion, although it must be remembered, they have a strong link with the design philosophy of Giorgio ARMANI. Gigli's shows have become cult affairs and his clothes are eagerly bought by wealthy young women world-wide. His designs are a synthesis of London post-punk street fashion and Japanese avant-garde style presented with Italian refinement and colour to produce clothes of extreme subtlety and elegance. His success has been phenomenal. Many fashion experts consider him the most important designer to have appeared in the 'eighties. His menswear is also increasingly influential.

JACOBS, Marc
Born New York City, USA, 1963.
Marc Jacobs followed his education at the New York High School of Art & Design, from which he graduated in 1981, with a course in fashion design at Parsons School of Design. During his time at college he worked as a salesman in the Charivari clothing store and, as part of a school project, designed sweaters which the store produced and sold. On leaving Parsons in 1984 he designed 'Sketchbook', a sportswear line, for Reuben Thomas and just one year later, set up his own label. He continues as head of his own firm under the aegis of the Japanese firm, Kahiyama.

LACROIX, Christian
Born France, 1951.
After a childhood spent in the South of France, in Provence and the Camargue, Lacroix read Classics and History of Art at Montpellier University. He moved to Paris to continue his studies at the Ecole du Louvre. Lacroix declares that his passion at that time was designing theatrical costumes. The drama of opera especially appealed to him. Instead of following the academic art historian's path and ending up as a museum curator, Lacroix chose fashion. He began his career as an assistant designer at HERMES and Guy PAULIN before a stint working in Tokyo. In 1981 Lacroix joined the house of PATOU. His couture collections for Patou have broken new ground in fantasy and theatricality and placed him at the forefront of modern couture. Lacroix's collections are deliberately anti-rational and, by taking 'fifties couture ideas and twisting them to his fantasy, he sets out to *épater le bourgeois*, whose fashion standards he deliberately satirises. The success of his stratagem has been considerable. By creating fantastically 'mad tea-party' shapes and scales, Lacroix ensures that his name is currently kept in the headlines. Whether it will remain so is yet to be seen but, apart from all the

braggadoccio, he has a highly original eye and a totally iconoclastic approach to fashion design. These have made him seem like a breath of fresh air in the stuffy and rather self-satisfied world of French haute couture. His clothes are witty and his shows are full of laughter. He opened his own-name fashion house in 1987.

LAMANOVA, Nadezhda Petrovna:
See Soviet Design.

McINTYRE, John
Born Liverpool, England, 1955.
Study at Birmingham Polytechnic was followed by a post-graduate year in the fashion department of the Royal College of Art, from which McIntyre graduated in 1979. This was followed by a period working as a designer in Italy for KRIZIA, COVERI and SOPRANI as well as doing freelance work for Swedish and Canadian firms. After this broad experience McIntyre returned to London and formed his own company to produce a womenswear range. This was later augmented by a menswear range. McIntyre has proved to be one of the more reliable British designers and he currently designs for Reldan in London and Albert Nippon in America.

MOSCHINO, Franco
Born Milan, Italy, 1950.
His father's industrial work did not interest Moschino and so at fifteen he joined the Accademia delle Belle Arti in Brera to study life drawing and ceramics. His first jobs were varied. He worked for publicity agents, was a computer programmer and dabbled in experimental theatre on an amateur level. In 1970 he began drawing for magazines and illustrating fashion collections. Through this work he met Gianni VERSACE for whom he illustrated many publicity campaigns. Moschino worked closely with Versace for two years and during that time he began to try his hand at designing. He gained invaluable design experience working for CADETTE, for whom he designed for eleven seasons, and MATTI, amongst other freelance design commitments. He showed his first own-name collection in 1983. It provoked immediate interest and, by the end of 1984, Moschino's name had assumed cult level. His complex and many-facetted approach

to fashion design is unique in Italy. In fact, his iconoclastic approach to breaking the rules of fashion puts him in the same league as LACROIX in Paris. Like him, Moschino believes in bringing out the humour in clothes, sending up the past and generally debunking the concept of glamour. Underneath all the humour of the shows, however, he creates clothes which are of the moment and it is upon that that his success is based.

OZBEK, Rifat
Born Istanbul, Turkey, 1954.
Rifat Ozbek spent three years at Liverpool University studying architecture but, having decided that designing clothes was more interesting, he enrolled at St Martin's School of Art to study fashion. He graduated in 1977 and took up his first job, with Walter ALBINI in Milan. He principally worked on the range which the Italian designer created for the upmarket Italian ready-to-wear firm of Trell. He returned to London in 1980 and began designing for the Monsoon Company, whose mass-market clothes were produced in India and Hong Kong. He remained with Monsoon for three years before deciding in 1983 to work on his own label. His success with Monsoon (during his time they had increased their retail outlets from six to fourteen) enabled him to get backing from a Geneva-based shipping company for his own firm. His first collection was greeted with enthusiasm. *Woman's Wear Daily* praised his clothes as 'slick, sophisticated and clean-cut, while still laced with a healthy dose of the unexpected.' Ozbek's future as a design presence seems assured although he may not necessarily remain in fashion. Whatever course he chooses his cultural range and intelligence should ensure that he remains in the vanguard of modish thinking.

PAULIN, Guy
Born Lorraine, France, 1945.
Paulin began his working life as a lift boy in the Parisian store, Printemps. He began to sell his sketches and worked briefly for Prisunic, another French department store chain, before beginning his freelance career. He worked as a design consultant for various manufacturers, including Dorothée BIS, in France. He also designed for American firms and, in Italy for BYBLOS

and MAXMARA. He designed under his own name in the late 'seventies before replacing LAGERFELD at CHLOE in 1984. He left Chloe in 1986.

POPOVA, Liubov Sergeyevna:
See Soviet Design.

PREMONVILLE, Myrene de
Born Pays Basque, France, 1949.
DEWAVIN, Gilles
Born Paris, France, 1957.
One of the few indigenous French design companies which specialise in young fashion and has made an impact outside its own country, Premonville and Dewavin has found itself a niche not unlike that found by RICHMOND/CORNEJO in London. Elegance of cut and clarity of line are lightened by fantasy touches which bring just the right degree of wit and style. Premonville and Dewavin clothes are extremely stylish without being stiff or pompous and they appeal to a young clientèle which wishes to be fashionable without dressing in expensive rags. Premonville, the designer, studied creative art in Paris before taking a job with Promostyl. A year spent in London working as a model and taking any fashion-related job available was followed on her return to Paris in 1975 by work as a freelance designer with FIORUCCI. She also continued to work with Promostyl and spent time as an assistant to Poppy MORENI before setting up with Dewavin in 1983.

RICHMOND-CORNEJO
CORNEJO, Maria
Born Santiago, Chile, 1962.
RICHMOND, John
Born Manchester, England, 1960.
Whilst studying fashion at Ravensbourne College of Art, from 1982–84, Maria Cornejo designed on a freelance basis for FIORUCCI who, after she graduated, offered her a full-time job in Italy. This offer was not taken up as she preferred to remain in London. John Richmond also produced commercial collections whilst he was a student. He studied fashion at Kingston Polytechnic from 1980–82 and, in his second year, created a capsule collection for Elle. In 1982 he designed two collections for Lana Lino before creating his own line, called '4 Sleeve', in 1983, as well as designing sections of the JOSEPH TRICOT

collections. Richmond/Cornejo began in 1984 to almost unanimous praise from press and trade. They now produce a knitwear collection for the Japanese manufacturer, Epoch 3, a menswear range and their own-name collection. Their early designs were perhaps over worked but their understanding of cut and their technical ability made their collections outstanding. Richmond/Cornejo clothes follow the course first trail-blazed by Vivienne WEST-WOOD and are based on an approach to fashion which is essentially British. In the designers' own words, they set out 'to crash through the gender barrier'.

RODCHENKO, Alexandr Mikhailovitch:

See Soviet Design.

ROEHM, Carolyne

Founded New York, USA, 1985.

Carolyne Roehm's clothes have found a place in the luxury market in America. They are glamorous and subtle and appeal to women similarly blessed. Roehm's childhood in Missouri was followed by a course of study at Washington University, St Louis. From there she moved to New York and began her fashion career designing for a firm which manufactured polyester dresses for Sears. In 1974 she went to work for Oscar DE LA RENTA. She worked with him for ten years, being involved in all areas but especially designing for his 'Miss O' and boutique collection. She opened her own business in 1985.

SOVIET DESIGN

After the October uprising the role of art in Russia was redefined: revolutionaries considered artists who fulfilled their traditional role in society to be little more than the effete kept boys of a corrupt and degraded society. The revolution swept them away along with their masters. In post-revolutionary Russia artists were to serve the people by improving the quality of everyday life. The Petrograd Futurist newspaper, *The Art of the Commune*, urged them to go into the factories to create objects which would have the only valid beauty: their functionalism. Textile and clothes design were to be part of this new approach and, almost uniquely to the Soviet Union, were considered worthy and legitimate areas of

concern for the artist. Almost all of the people producing textiles and clothes designs based on the artistic theories of Constructionism and Suprematism were painters. The only dress designer involved was Nadezhda LAMANOVA who had been a couturière in pre-revolutionary St Petersburg.

Revolutionary idealists and intellectuals, they approached dress design from the viewpoint of practicality. Only by functioning for the workers who wore them could their design be consistent with Marxism, the artists argued. As STEPANOVA suggested, post-revolutionary fashion was to do with the toil. The clothes designed by the artists could only be considered to have the status of an art form when worn 'during the process of work'. The artists wanted to find a new approach to dress which would be consistent with revolutionary ideals and free of historic attitudes. Status from clothes was inconsistent with this credo. All women were to be well dressed i.e. dressed in functional clothing designed with a rigorous logic and a severe control of 'artistic' impulses. Practicality was all-important but this did not mean sterility. On the contrary Soviet artists produced fabrics, textiles and clothes of considerable originality and vibrancy. Like modern Japanese designers the Russians began the process of re-thinking clothes design by creating new fabric patterns. Abstract patterns using industrial motifs were frequent. Tractors, factory chimneys, collective farms and totally linear abstraction were common. Constructionist clothes showed a marvellous control of patterns and shape. They were created for practical pursuits. At the core were working clothes and sportswear. Comfortable and relaxed, they required no special attitudes in the wearer. In 1919 Lamanova set up the Workshop of Contemporary Clothes Design which was one of the earliest training schools to teach design and practical skills for the garment industry. The Atelier of Fashion was set up in Moscow in 1923 and the House of Fashion design school followed later.

The Constructivist clothes created in Russia in the 'twenties showed a control of abstraction and shape far in advance of their time and more in line with recent fashion approaches in London and Japan. Soviet efforts were stunted by the poverty

which followed the Civil War and thus this completely fresh and idealistic approach to clothing the masses did not have the far-reaching effects it might have had. In some respects, the rest of the world has only just caught up.

Those involved in the experiments in dress represent a roll call of the very best creators working in Russia in the 'twenties and 'thirties.

Exter, Alexandra Alexandrovna

Born Kiev, USSR, 1882.
Died Paris, France, 1949.

Exter studied art in Kiev, graduating in 1906. She then took the first of many trips to Paris where she continued her studies and met and made friends with Apollinaire, Braque, Picasso and Marinetti. Her pre-revolutionary life included much travel: Kiev, Moscow, Paris and Rome. After the revolution her work became totally non-representational and she began to design costumes and scenery based on the spatial conceptions of Cubism. She also became interested in adapting Cubist theories to fashion, whether for mass production or individual items. She emigrated to France in 1924.

Lamanova, Nadezhda Petrovna

Born Shuzilovo, USSR, 1861.
Died Moscow, USSR, 1941.

Lamanova learnt the arts of couture at the Moscow School of Fashion and Clothes and by 1885 had opened her own atelier. Despite her previously held position in pre-revolutionary Moscow society she was accepted in post-revolutionary Russia and, in her turn, enthusiastically used her knowledge and skills to serve the new régime. She worked as an instructor at Narkompros and was head of the Contemporary Clothes Workshop set up in 1919 at her instigation. Her theoretical programme for Soviet fashion was published in 1921 and had far-reaching effects. Throughout her life she was involved in theatrical costume design and dressed many Soviet films, including *Alexander Nevsky* and *Ivan the Terrible*.

Popova, Liubov Sergeyevna

Born Moscow, USSR, 1889.
Died Moscow, USSR, 1924.

One of the undisputed artistic giants of the Soviet Union, Popova studied painting in

Russia and then travelled to Paris in 1912 where she worked with ex-patriot Russians for a year. Her obsession with Cubist theory and the dynamics of colour, form and movement led her endlessly to experiment. The resultant work, dynamic and powerful, included painting, collage, propaganda literature, textiles, theatre sets and costumes and fashion. In all fields her approach was revolutionary and her effect far-reaching. Her association with STEPANOVA at the First Textile Printing Factory produced textiles of originality and force. She designed clothes to accommodate abstractly patterned fabrics which she often used to highlight a dress made in a plain fabric.

Rodchenko, Alexandr Mikhailovich

Born St Petersburg, USSR, 1891.
Died Moscow, USSR, 1956.
From 1910–1914 Rodchenko studied at the Kazan Art School where he met his future wife, STEPANOVA. His involvement in all aspects of art and design made him a central figure in Moscow art circles. In fact, after the revolution he was the main organiser of artistic life in the city. He taught, chaired committees, joined theoretical groups and became totally dedicated to the concept of art as a driving force in the new Soviet society. In 1921 he gave up easel painting and concentrated on design: posters, books, textiles, photography, theatrical design and fashion were all included in his oeuvre. With TATLIN, POPOVA and STEPANOVA he formed the Productivist Group dedicated to the denial of pure art and the insistence on art as an essential aspect of everyday life. His clothes designs were essentially functional.

Stepanova, Varvara Fedorovna

Born Lithuania, USSR, 1894.
Died Moscow, USSR, 1958.
In 1911 whilst studying at the Kazan Art School, Stepanova met her future husband, RODCHENKO. She continued her studies in Moscow and from then on was involved with non-objective, Suprematist art as a painter and teacher. In 1920 she joined Inkhuk (the Institute of Artistic Culture). Her historic and important association with POPOVA began in 1921 at the First State Textile Print Factory in Moscow. Together they revolutionised the design of cotton

fabrics but this fruitful co-operation was cut short by Popova's death in 1924. Her strongly blocked abstract designs had a considerable influence on clothes design. Like her husband and TATLIN she believed that everything stemmed from the principles of Constructivism.

Tatlin, Vladimir Evgrafovitch

Born Moscow, USSR, 1885.
Died Moscow, USSR, 1953.
Tatlin's art training, frequently interrupted by stints in the Russian merchant navy, was cut short in 1909 when he was expelled from the Art Institute in Moscow. In 1913 he went to Berlin as a musician in a dance band and then on to Paris where he met, and was greatly influenced by, Picasso. On his return to Moscow in 1914 he became involved in the avant-garde art movement. He ran a design workshop from 1919–1921 with the precise title 'Studio for Volumes, Materials and Construction'. By the mid-'twenties he was deeply involved in design. He worked on the theory and practice of clothes and created the cut-out suit.

TATLIN, Vladimir Evgrafovitch:

See Soviet Design.

STEPANOVA, Varvara Fedorovna:

See Soviet Design.

VARTY, Keith

Born Darlington, England, 1952.

CLEAVER, Alan

Born Northampton, England, 1952.
Keith Varty studied fashion at St Martin's School of Art from 1969–71. He followed this with a post-graduate course at the Royal College of Art from 1971–73. Alan Cleaver followed a fashion course at Kingston Polytechnic from 1969–71 and spent two years at the Royal College of Art. He completed his post-graduate course there in 1974.

For the next six years Varty worked in Paris with Dorothée BIS whilst Cleaver worked as a freelance designer. In 1980 they joined forces in their own business based in Milan. From here they moved to the Ancona-based Italian ready-to-wear firm of Byblos, as joint designers. Their success in producing the firm's range of

menswear and womenswear has been considerable, both creatively and commercially, and they have made Byblos an internationally respected name. The skill of Varty and Cleaver lies in their ability to take the current young mood and develop it into an amalgam of the best of Italian and British design thinking. They create clothes which have an appeal for youthful sophisticates who want to be fashionable without being too avant-garde.

VASS, Joan

Born New York City, USA, 1925.
The success of Joan Vass is rather unexpected. She entered fashion late and yet has made a very strong impression on the American market. Her untypicality can be gauged by the fact that she not only holds a Coty prize, she has also been honoured by the Smithsonian Institution. Joan Vass is an academic. She studied at Vassar and at the University of Wisconsin, majoring in Art History and Philosophy. She did not begin designing until 1977. Before that time she was a curator at the Museum of Modern Art in New York, an editor for the art book publisher Harry Abrams and a regular contributor to *Art in America*. Her first designs, for unique sweaters, were on a cottage industry basis but now her name is synonymous with high-class, commercial knitwear. In addition to Joan Vass USA, her moderately priced range, there is also Joan Vass, New York, her couture range. The business is a family one and her stance is independent. An example of her attitudes is her comment, 'My clothes don't have a theme for the spring season. They're not a play or a book. They're clothes.' Vass won a Coty Award in 1979.

WIENER WERKSTÄTTE 1903–1932

The Vienna Workshop was founded in 1903 by the designers Kolo Moser and Josef Hoffmann with backing from Fritz Waerndorfer. It followed William Morris's Art Worker's Guild, founded in 1861, in placing emphasis on the marriage of artistic creativity and craftsmanship and deploring the lack of individuality in mass-produced industrial goods. In 1910 the Wiener Werkstätte opened a fashion department directed by Eduard Josef Wimmer-Wisgrill (born Vienna 1882, died Vienna 1961) who remained in charge until 1922; his successor was Max Snischek (born Dürnk-rut, lower Austria 1891, died Hinterbrühl, 1968) who directed the department until it closed.

The objective of the Wiener Werkstätte fashion department was to produce haute couture clothes in keeping with the Werkstätte belief that artists were the best designers. The designs were to have a Viennese, not Parisian, flavour. The first collection was shown in 1911 and most of the clothes were designed by Wimmer-Wisgrill, with additional items by Hoffmann. The Weiner Werkstätte pavilion at the 1911 Rome Exhibition attracted the attention of POIRET who visited Vienna and bought textiles designed by Hoffmann and Wimmer.

In 1913 the Wiener Werkstätte fashions toured Germany to great acclaim and journalists began to praise the Austrians for breaking the French fashion hegemony. National fashion was promoted by the Austrian Werkbund which produced *Mode Wien* in 1914. It was a gold-bound folder containing twelve folios of twelve hand-coloured fashion prints showing the national design style. Other Austrian societies of designers, artists and manufacturers sprang up to follow enthusiastically the lead of the Wiener Werkstätte in designing their own textiles and clothes without reference to Paris. More folders of designs were published. Wiener Werkstätte designs were now being shown regularly in Germany as well as in cities such as Stockholm and Zürich. The clothes which used Wiener Werkstätte fabrics were considered to have a quite separate design pedigree from those produced in Paris. They were described as having 'a quiet originality'. By far the majority were designed by Wimmer (who, on leaving the Werkstätte, taught for two years at the Chicago Art Institute) and Snischek themselves.

WOODWARD, Kirsten

Born London, England, 1959.

After spending five years in Vancouver, Kirsten Woodward attended a comprehensive school in Swansea before enrolling at the London College of Fashion in 1980. Having specialised in millinery she started to sell her hats at London's fashion 'supermarket', Hyper-Hyper, whilst she was still a student. In 1984 Karl LAGERFELD visited Hyper-Hyper, met her and asked her to design a collection to show with his clothes. She has continued to work with Lagerfeld, for his own and his CHANEL & FENDI collections, as well as various English designers, including BELVILLE SASSOON. Woodward also produces individually designed hats for private customers, including The Princess of Wales. Her specialities are extravagant creations with a strong surrealist feel. They are amusing without overshadowing the wearer or her clothes.

AUTOBIOGRAPHIES

Amies, Hardy *Just So Far*. Collins, London/New York 1954

Amies, Hardy *Still Here*. Weidenfeld and Nicholson, London 1984

Balmain, Pierre *My Years and Seasons*. Cassell, London 1964/Doubleday, New York 1965

Creed, Charles *Maid to Measure*. Jarrolds, London 1961

Daché, Lilly *Talking through my Hats*. Coward-McCann, New York 1946

Duff Gordon, Lady *Discretions and Indiscretions*. Jarrold's, London 1932

Dior, Christian *Talking about Fashion*. Putnams, New York 1954

Dior, Christian *Dior by Dior*. Weidenfeld and Nicholson, London 1957

Erté *Erté – Things I Remember*. Peter Owen, London 1975/Quadrangle, New York 1975

Ferragamo, Salvatore *Shoemaker of Dreams*. Harrap London 1957

Greer, Howard *Designing Male*. Hale, London 1952

Hartnell, Norman *Silver and Gold*. Evans, London 1955

Hawes, Elizabeth *Fashion is Spinach*. Random House, New York 1938

Hulanicki, Barbara *A to Biba*. Hutchinson, London 1983

McCardell, Claire *What Shall I Wear?* Simon and Schuster, New York 1956

Poiret, Paul *En Habillant l'Époque*. Grasset, Paris 1930

Poiret, Paul *King of Fashion: The Autobiography of Paul Poiret*. Lippincott, Philadelphia 1931

Poiret, Paul *Revenez-Y*. Gallimard, Paris 1932

Quant, Mary *Quant by Quant*. Cassell, London 1965

Schiaparelli, Elsa *Shocking Life*. Dutton, New York 1954

Thaarup, Aage *Heads and Tales*. Cassell, London 1956

Tinling, Teddy *White Ladies*. S. Paul, London 1963

Tinling, Teddy *Sixty Years in Tennis*. Sidgwick and Jackson, London 1983

Worth, Jean Philippe *A Century of Fashion*. Little Brown, Boston 1928

Dior 1955

FASHION ORGANIZATIONS

CHAMBRE SYNDICALE DE LA COUTURE PARISIENNE

This multi-faceted organization has, since its foundation in Paris in 1868, held a very influential place in the development of French fashion. It has been instrumental in setting standards and training attitudes in couture throughout the world for the last hundred years. Originally part of the French craftsmen's guilds organization, it began to assume its modern shape in the late 1880s, when Gaston WORTH organized the Parisian couturiers into the Chambre Syndicale de la Couture Française. In 1911 the Couture Parisienne established its Chambre Syndicale, to be headed by designers elected by their peers. The only female president ever to have been elected is Madame PAQUIN; Jacques WORTH held the role twice; and Lucien LELONG, who was president during World War II, played a crucial role in dissuading the Germans from moving the fashion centre to Berlin.

As early as 1915 French designers recognized the importance of a united front. The couturiers BEER, CALLOT SOEURS, CHERUIT, DOEUILLET, DOUCET, JENNY, MARTIAL ET ARMAND, PREMET, Raudnitz, PAQUIN and LANVIN exhibited jointly at the San Francisco Exhibition of that year. A similar joint effort took place in 1945, when the Chambre created the travelling exhibition, Théâtre de la Mode, to re-establish Paris as the world fashion centre after the war. The collection of dolls, dressed by fifty-three couturiers, travelled Europe and America with great success.

The Chambre's main job is to organize and oversee the twice-yearly collections. It arranges the calendar of showings, organizes press and buyer accreditation, issues entry cards and generally helps the couture houses to present an efficiently organized front in order to gain maximum sales and press coverage. Since 1920 couture designs registered with the Chambre have been accorded by French law the same protection from plagiarism as literary works, films and patent inventions. It has a school to train French and foreign students in the practical business of creating couture.

THE FASHION GROUP OF AMERICA

Founded in 1931 as a means of creating more opportunities in fashion for women, this organization had, as one of its founders, Claire MCCARDELL, the influential American designer of sportswear and casual evening wear, who at the time was working in the wholesale trade at Townley Frocks. Her participation is significant as she was not only one of the first major female designers in America, but was also one of the first designers anywhere to create clothes for normal women living everyday lives who wished to be smart but not *chic*. Her designs played a significant part in creating the climate which made the expansion of the Fashion Group possible. Over the years it has grown into an international organization spreading as far afield as Paris and Tokyo. The Group presents fashion shows abroad, with the backing of the government, arranges exhange programmes and career guidance, and gives professional and consumer advice.

FASHION HOUSE GROUP OF LONDON

In 1947 the Model House Group was formed by fourteen top London wholesalers to organize and regulate the dates and times of their showings. In the 1950s it was re-organized into an association of twenty-seven manufacturers and the name was changed to The Fashion House Group of London. These manufacturers, along with twenty-four Associate members representing accessory makers, put on collective dress shows. By 1960 their combined turnover was £14,000,000 a year, £2,000,000 of which was for export orders. Well-known manufacturers who were members of the Fashion House Group included Aquascutum, Brenner, Dereta, Frank Usher, Amies Ready-to-Wear, Linzi, Polly Peck, Rembrandt, Spectator Sports, Susan Small and Vernervogue.

INCORPORATED SOCIETY OF LONDON FASHION DESIGNERS

This organization was set up with the backing of the British government during World War II to promote British clothing exports. It grew from a co-operative venture in 1941, when British high-fashion designers who were working together anonymously created a joint collection to tour South America. The tour proved so successful that the Incorporated Society was founded in 1942. There were originally eight members: AMIES, HARTNELL, MOLYNEUX, MORTON, WORTH, STIEBEL, Bianca Mosca and Peter Russell. The chairman was Molyneux. Later members included CAVANAGH, CREED, MATTLI, MICHAEL, PATERSON, SHERARD, LACHASSE, Delange and Champcommunal. The original eight members co-operated with the government to promote the 'Utility' scheme of clothing, a product of the 1942 Board of Trade Civilian Clothing Order restricting the amount of material to be used in garments for the British market. After the war, in an effort to catch American buyers and boost sales, the London couture houses decided to show jointly in a London fashion-week immediately prior to the Paris showings. The government co-operated over cloth allocations, since the clothes were for export, and the venture was a success. London Fashion Week remained an important point on the buyers' calendar until the society ceased to function. Its demise came when its members were driven out of business by the advance of the ready-to-wear side of the business and the escalating costs of couture.

Only a handful of the society's members are remembered now. One of them is Victor Stiebel, who was born in South Africa in 1907 and died in London in 1975. Another is Michael, whose full name was Michael Donellan. He worked as Michael of Lachasse before opening his establishment in Carlos Place and becoming known as Michael of Carlos Place. He closed his doors in 1971. Peter Russell, whose Carlos Place premises were taken over by Michael, was active in the 1930s, but closed down in 1953. Michael Sherard opened in 1946 and closed in 1964. Elspeth Champcommunal designed for Worth's London branch and Bianca Mosca worked at Jacqmar. Hardy Amies and the house of Hartnell still function.

FASHION AWARDS

BATH MUSEUM OF COSTUME: 'DRESS OF THE YEAR'

In 1963 the Museum initiated a scheme whereby each year it would acquire a garment and accessories chosen from ready-to-wear collections by British fashion journalists. The choice of designer was to be left entirely to the journalist, the only restriction being that the designer had to agree to present the chosen outfit to the Museum. Since 1966 the choice has been made by a British journalist working for a newspaper or magazine published in the United Kingdom.

Year	Designer	Journalist
1963	Mary Quant	Fashion Writers Association
1964	Jean Muir for Jane & Jane	Fashion Writers Association
1965	John Bates for Jean Varon	Fashion Writers Association
1966	Michele Rosier for Young Jaeger	Ernestine Carter *The Sunday Times*
1967	David Bond for Slimma	Felicity Green *Daily Mirror*
1968	Jean Muir	Ailsa Garland *Fashion*
1969	Ossie Clark of Quorum	Prudence Glynn *The Times*
1970	Bill Gibb for Baccarat	Beatrix Miller *Vogue*
1971	Graziella Fontana for Judith Hornby	Serena Sinclair *Daily Telegraph*
1972	Biba	Moira Keenan *The Sunday Times*
1973	Jorn Langberg for Dior London	Alison Adburgham *The Guardian*
1974	Ottavio & Rosita Missoni	Jennifer Hocking *Harper's & Queen*
1975	Gina Fratini	Anna Harvey, *Brides*
1976	Kenzo Takada of Jap	Helena Matheopoulous *Daily Express*

Year	Designer	Journalist
1977	Kenzo Takada of Jap	Ann Boyd *The Observer*
1978	Gordon Luke Clarke; Nino Cerruti	Barbara Griggs *Daily Mail*
1979	Jean Muir	Geraldine Ransome *Sunday Telegraph*
1980	Calvin Klein	Michael Roberts *The Sunday Times*
1981	Karl Lagerfeld for Chloe	Vanessa de Lisle *Harper's & Queen*
1982	Nigel Preston at Maxfield Parrish; Margaret Howell	Grace Coddington *Vogue*
1983	Sheridan Barnett	Sally Brampton *The Observer*
1984	Betty Jackson; Body Map; Katherine Hamnett	Brenda Polan *The Guardian*
1985	Bruce Oldfield; Scott Crolla	Suzie Menkes *The Times*
1986	Giorgio Armani	Colin McDowell *Country Life*

The shoes of Manolo Blahnik were chosen in 1974, 1979, 1982 and 1983.

COTY AMERICAN FASHION CRITICS AWARD

Founded in 1942 by the cosmetics and perfume company, Coty, to encourage American fashion designers during the war, this award is now arguably the world's most prestigious. Awards for men's and women's wear are given annually on the recommendation of committees of journalists. The women's wear award is called a 'Winnie'; the menswear award (begun in 1968) is without name. Repeat awards are the Return Award and the Hall of Fame Award. In addition Special Awards are given to designers of furs, lingerie, jewellery, etc.

1943 **Winnie:** Norman Norell.
  Special awards – millinery: Lilly Daché; John Frederics.
1944 **Winnie:** Claire McCardell.
1945 **Winnies:** Gilbert Adrian and Tina **Special awards** – leather accessories: Phelps Associates; – millinery: Sally Victor. Leser (at-home clothes); Emily Wilkens (teenage clothes).
1946 **Winnies:** Omar Kiam; Vincent Monte-Sano; Clare Potter.

1947 **Winnies:** Jack Horwitz; Mark Mooring; Nettie Rosenstein; Adele Simpson.

1948 **Winnie:** Hattie Carnegie.
Special awards – furs: Joseph De Leo; Esther Dorothy; Maximilian.

1949 **Winnie:** Pauline Trigère.
Special awards – shoes: David Evins; – sportswear: Toni Owen.

1950 **Winnies:** Bonnie Cashin; Charles James.
Special awards – shoes: Mabel and Charles Julianelli: – lingerie: Nancy Melcher.

1951 **Winnie:** Jane Derby.
Return awards: Norman Norell; Pauline Trigère.
Special awards – prettiest dresses: Anne Fogarty; – sportswear: Vera Maxwell; – lingerie: Sylvia Pedlar.

1952 **Winnies:** Ben Sommers; Ben Zuckerman.
Special awards – concept of dressing: Karen Stark (of Harvey Berin); Sydney Wragge (of B. H. Wragge).

1953 **Winnie:** Thomas Brigance.
Special awards – children's designer: Helen Lee; – evening wear: John Moore (of Mattie Talmack).

1954 **Winnie:** James Galanos.
Special award – innovative cut: Charles James.

1955 **Winnies:** Jeanne Campbell; Herbert Kasper; Anne Klein.
Special award – millinery: Adolfo.

1956 **Winnies:** Luis Estevez; Sally Victor.
Return award: James Galanos.
Hall of Fame award: Norman Norell.
Special award – knitwear: Gertrude and Robert Goldworm.

1957 **Winnies:** Leslie Morris; Sydney Wragge.
Special award – furs: Emeric Partos.

1958 **Winnie:** Arnold Scaasi.
Return award: Ben Zuckerman.
Hall of Fame award: Claire McCardell (posthumous).
Special awards – influence on evening clothes: Donald Brooks; – jewellery: Jean Schlumberger.

1959 **Hall of Fame awards:** James Galanos; Pauline Trigère.

1960 **Winnies;** Ferdinando Sarmi; Jacques Tiffeau.
Special awards – innovative body clothes: Rudi Gernreich; – costume jewellery: Sol Klein (of Nettie Rosenstein); – beaded evening clothes: Roxane (of Samuel Winston).

1961 **Winnies:** Bill Blass; Gustave Tassell.
Hall of Fame award: Ben Zuckerman.
Special awards – deep-country clothes: Bonnie Cashin; – leadership in hair-styling: Kenneth.

1962 **Winnie:** Donald Brooks.
Special award – millinery: Halston.

1963 **Winnie:** Rudi Gernreich.
Return award: Bill Blass.
Special awards – leather design: Arthur and Theodora Edelman; – furs: Betty Yokova (of A. Neustadter).

1964 **Winnie:** Geoffrey Beene.
Return award: Jacques Tiffeau.
Special awards – lingerie (return special award): Sylvia Pedlar; – jewellery design: David Webb.

1965 **Special awards** – fabric design: Tzaims Luksus; – leadership in makeup: Pablo (of Elizabeth Arden); – furs: Anna Potok (of Maximilian); – foundation garments: Gertrude Seperack; – designers of young fashions (joint award): Sylvia De Gay; Edie Gladstone; Stan Herman; Victor Joris; Gayle Kirkpatrick; Deanna Littell; Leo Narducci; Don Simonelli; Bill Smith.

1966 **Winnie:** Dominic.
Return awards: Geoffrey Beene; Rudi Gernreich.
Special award – costume jewellery: Kenneth Jay Lane.

1967 **Winnie:** Oscar de la Renta.
Return award: Donald Brooks.
Hall of Fame award: Rudi Gernreich.
Special award – shoes: Beth and Herbert Levine.

1968 **Winnies:** George Halley: Luba (Marks).
Return awards: Bonnie Cashin; Oscar de la Renta.
Special award – fantasy accessories and ethnic fashions: Giorgio di Sant' Angelo.
Menswear award: Bill Blass.

1969 **Winnies:** Stan Herman; Victor Joris.
Return award: Anne Klein.
Special awards – millinery: Adolfo; Halston; – fabric design: Julian Tomchin.

1970 **Winnies:** Giorgio di Sant' Angelo; Chester Weinberg.
Return award: Herbert Kasper.
Hall of Fame award: Bill Blass.
Special awards – costume jewellery (joint award): Steven Brody (of Cadoro); Alexis Kirk; Cliff Nicholson; Marty Ruza; Bill Smith; Daniel Stoenescu; – tie-dyed fabrics: Will and Eileen Richardson.
Menswear award: Ralph Lauren.

1971 **Winnies:** Halston; Betsey Johnson (of Alley Cat).
Hall of Fame award: Anne Klein.
Hall of Fame citation: Bill Blass.
Special awards – lingerie: John Kloss (of Cira); – men's shoes: Nancy Knox; – world fashion influence: Levi Strauss; – jewellery: Elsa Peretti.
Menswear award: Larry Kane (of Raffles Wear).

1972 **Winnie:** John Anthony.
Return award: Halston.
Hall of Fame award: Bonnie Cashin.
Special awards – for excitement in menswear (special menswear awards): Robert Margolis (of A. Smile Inc.); Alan Rosanes (of Gordon Gregory Ltd); Alexander Shields; Pinky Wolman and Dianne Beaudry (of Flo Toronto); – patchwork and quality: Dorothy Weatherford (of Mountain Artisans).

1973 **Winnies:** Stephen Burrows; Calvin Klein.
Hall of Fame award: Oscar de la Renta.
Special awards – accessory design (joint award): Joe Famolare (shoes); Don Kline (hats); Judith Leiber (handbags); Herbert and Beth Levine (shoes); Michael Moraux (of Dubaux) (jewellery);

303

Celia Sebiri (jewellery); – original young fashion: Clovis Ruffin.
Menswear award: Piero Dimitri.
Menswear return award: Ralph Lauren.

1974 **Winnie:** Ralph Lauren.
Return award: Calvin Klein.
Hall of Fame awards: Geoffrey Beene; Halston.
Special awards – lingerie design: Stephen Burrows; Stan Herman; John Kloss; Fernando Sanchez; Bill Tice; – menswear: Sal Cesarani; John Weitz; – menswear award for jewellery: Aldo Cipullo.
Menswear award: Bill Kaiserman.
Menswear return award: Piero Dimitri.

1975 **Winnie:** Carol Horn.
Hall of Fame award: Calvin Klein.
Hall of Fame citation: Geoffrey Beene.
Hall of Fame award (for menswear): Piero Dimitri.
Special awards – fur design: Bill Blass (for Revillon America); Calvin Klein (for Alixandre); Fernando Sanchez (for Revillon America); Viola Sylbert (for Alixandre): – swimsuits: Monika Tilley (for Elon); – menswear award for leather design: Nancy Knox.
Menswear award: Chuck Howard and Peter Wrigley (of Anne Klein Studio).
Menswear return award: Bill Kaiserman.

1976 **Winnie:** Mary McFadden.
Return awards: John Anthony; Ralph Lauren.
Hall of Fame award: Herbert Kasper.
Hall of Fame award (for menswear): Bill Kaiserman.
Special awards – sportswear: American Sporting Gear; – menswear: Sal Cesarani; – menswear

award for neckwear: Vicky Davis; – women's wear: Barbara Dulien; – men's loungewear: Lowell Judson; Ronald Kolodzie; Robert Schafter.

1977 **Winnies:** Stephen Burrows; Louis Dell' Olio; Donna Karan.
Hall of Fame award: Ralph Lauren.
Special awards – contribution to American fashion: Geoffrey Beene; – jewellery: Ted Muehling; – lingerie: Fernando Sanchez.
Menswear award: Alexander Julian.

1978 **Return award:** Mary McFadden.
Special awards – outstanding contribution: AMF Head Sportswear Co.; – citation for continued contribution to American men's fashion: Bill Kaiserman; – exercise and sports clothing: Danskin Inc.; – shoes and boots: John Helpern.
Menswear award: Robert Stock.
Women's fashion awards: Bill Atkinson; Charles Suppon.

1979 **Winnie:** Perry Ellis.
Hall of Fame award: Mary McFadden.
Special awards – men's furs: Conrad Bell; – jewellery: Barry Kieselstein-Cord; – shoe design: Gill Truedsson; – crafted knit fashions: Joan Vass: – contribution to international status of American fashion: Geoffrey Beene; Halston; Calvin Klein; Ralph Lauren.
Menswear award: Lee Wright.
Menswear return award: Alexander Julian.

1980 **Winnie:** Michaele Vollbracht.
Menswear award: Jhane Barnes.

1981 Awards given to all nominees.
Women's apparel: Geoffrey Beene; Perry Ellis; Calvin Klein.
Accessories, lingerie and furs:

Barry Kieselstein-Cord; Alex Mate and Lee Brooks (of Alex and Lee); Fernando Sanchez.
Men's apparel: Jhane Barnes; Alexander Julian; Ralph Lauren.
Menswear special awards: Andrew Fezza; Nancy Knox; Robert Lighton.

1982 **Winnie:** Adri.
Return award: Norma Kamali.
Hall of Fame awards: Louis Dell' Olio, Donna Karan (of Anne Klein).
Special awards – Geoffrey Beene; Bill Blass.
Menswear award: Jeff Banks.
Menswear return award: Sal Cesarani.

1983 **Winnie:** Willi Smith.
Hall of Fame award: Norma Kamali.
Special awards – citations: Bill Blass; Alexander Julian; – citation for women's wear: Perry Ellis; – handbags: Carlos Falchi; men's scarves: Susan Hurton; – retail store: Selma, Jon and Barbara Weiser (of Charivari Workshop).
Menswear award: Alan Flussers.
Menswear return award: Perry Ellis.

1984 **Winnie:** Adrienne Vittadini.
Hall of Fame award: Perry Ellis.
Special awards: citations: Perry Ellis; Ralph Lauren; Donna Karan and Louis Dell'Olio for Anne Klein; Alexander Julian; – belts and jewellery: Barry Kieselstein-Cord; – jewellery: M & J Savitt; – belts: Robin Kahn; – retail: Milena Canonero (Standards of Norman Hilton & Company).
Menswear award: Andrew Fezza.
Menswear return award: Jhane Barnes.

1985 Award discontinued

NEIMAN-MARCUS AWARDS

Stanley Marcus, head of the famous department store, Neiman Marcus of Dallas, founded the Neiman-Marcus Awards in 1938. From the beginning, the criteria for the awards were broad, as exemplified in the citation. The awards are given to those who have rendered 'distinguished service in the field of fashion', so, unlike the recipients of the Coty Awards, those honoured by the Neiman-Marcus Awards could include personalities peripheral to the design world. The Coty Awards go solely to designers whereas the Neiman-Marcus Awards have been accepted by grand couturiers, fashionable figures and 'show-biz' personalities. Also, whereas Coty Awards are presented to designers working in America, Neiman-Marcus Awards are made regardless of nationality and cover the world. Judging is by a panel of executives, originally headed by Stanley Marcus, who work to a loose brief. The awards are regarded as a pretigious prize.

Year	Awardee	Year	Awardee	Year	Awardee
1938	Louise B. Gallagher		Mrs Faei Joyce		Sally Kirkland
	Mr John		Mr William Phelps		Vera Maxwell Incorporated
	Richard Koret		Adele Simpson	1956	Cecil Beaton
	Dorothy Liebes	1947	Christian Dior		Marie-Louise Bosquet
	George Miller		Salvatore Ferragamo		Guiliana Camerino (Roberta)
	Germaine Monteil		Irene Gibbons	1957	Mlle Gabrielle Chanel
	Dan Palter		Norman Hartnell	1958	Helen Lee
	Nettie Rosenstein	1948	Gen. Julius Ochs Adler		Jens Quistgaard
1939	Elizabeth Arden		Mme Henri Bonnet		Yves-Mathieu Saint Laurent
	Hattie Carnegie		Antonio Castillo	1959	Emme
	John Cavanagh		Claire McCardell		Piero Fornasetti
	Janet May	1949	Alice Cadolle		Anne Klein
	Clare Potter		David Evins		Rosalind Russell
1940	Edna Woolman Chase		Jacques Fath		Arnold Scaasi
	Lilly Daché		Mrs Robert Geissman (Merry	1960	Roger Jean-Pierre
	Elsa Schiaparelli		Hull)		Sylvia Pedlar
	Sylvan Stroock	1950	Bonnie Cashin		Dinah Shore
1941	Anthony Blotta		Fleur Meyer (Mrs Tom M. Meyer)		Edward Burke Smith
	Omar Kiam		Gloria Swanson		Claude Staron
	Eleanor LeMaire		Pauline Trigère	1961	Greer Garson (Mrs E.E.
	Max Meyer	1951	Mrs Ernestine Cannon		Fogelson)
	Carmel Snow		Jane Derby		Harry Rolnick
	Mme Tobe		Jacques Lesur		Count Fernando Sarmi
1942	Betsy Talbot Blackwell		Michelle Murphy		Roger Vivier
	Norman Norell		Ben Zuckerman		Sydney Wragge
	Voris	1952	Dolores Del Rio	1962	Sports Illustrated
1943	Adrian		Roger Fare		Jules François Crahay
1944	Brooke Cadwallader		Anne Fogarty		Estée Lauder
	Jo Copeland		Vincent Monte Sano		James Laver
	Ben King	1953	Charles James	1963	Georges Braque
	Countess Mara		Gilbert and Helen Orcel		Bud Kilpatrick
1945	Tina Leser		Ben Sommers		Margaret Clarke Miller
	Vera Marghab		Marchesa Olga di Gresy		Maurice Tumarkin
	Maurice Rentner	1954	James Galanos	1964–65	Geoffrey Beene
	Dr Francis Taylor		Herbert and Beth Levine		Mr and Mrs Arthur Edelman
	Mrs Thea Tewi		Emilio Pucci		Tzaims Luksus
	Louis A. Weinberg	1955	Pierre Balmain	1966	Mary Brosnan
	Emily Wilkens		Henry Dreyfuss		Mme Helen Lazareff
1946	John Gates		Mrs Florence Eiseman		Lucie Ann Onderwyzer
	Mrs Leland Hayward		Her Serene Highness Princess		Jacques Tiffeau
	Mr William H. Joyce		Grace of Monaco (Grace Kelly)	1967	Fiamma Ferragamo

Year	Awardee	Year	Awardee	Year	Awardee
	The Artisans of Florence		Bernard Kayman	1979	Giorgio Armani
	Valentini Garani		Anne Klein		Richard Avedon
	Giancarlo Venturini		Emanuel Ungaro		The Artisans of Baccarat
	Lydia de Roma		Gloria Vanderbilt		Perry Ellis
1968	Roland Jourdan	1973	Ralph Lauren		Mary McFadden
	Kenneth J. Lane		Mr and Mrs Ottavio Missoni	1980	Karl Lagerfeld
	Armi Ratia		Hanae Mori		Judith Leiber
	Oscar de la Renta		Jean Muir	1984	Jack Lenor Larsen
1969	Bill Blass Ltd		Levi Strauss and Company		Issey Miyake

THE SUNDAY TIMES INTERNATIONAL FASHION AWARDS

Sponsored by the London *Sunday Times* and organized by that newspaper's fashion editor, Ernestine Carter, the awards were for those designers of any country who, in the opinion of the international jury, had made the greatest contribution to fashion in that year. There were three jury panels: one for the USA, one for France and one for Great Britain. They met and cast their votes in Paris. The winners were flown to London with their collections for a gala presentation. The scheme ran for only three years. In 1966 it changed into the Under-23 Fashion Competition and in 1967 the category was broadened to include Europe with the first Euro Fashion Competition for Under-23-year-olds. Competitions and awards ceased after this date.

1963

US Jury: Eleanor Lambert (Chairman); Sally Kirkland (*Life Magazine*); Catherine di Montezemolo (*Ladies Home Journal*); Eugenia Sheppard (*Herald Tribune*); Diana Vreeland (*Vogue*); Nancy White (*Harper's Bazzar*).

French Jury: Marie-Louise Bousquet (*Harper's Bazaar*); Vicomtesse de Ribes Marie-France de la Villehuchet (*Jardin des Modes*); Helène Gordon-Lazareff (*Elle*).

British Jury: Ernestine Carter (Chairman); John French; Professor Janey Ironside; Martin Moss; Alison Settle.

WINNERS: **USA** – Norman Norell; **France** – Pierre Cardin; **Great Britain** – Mary Quant.

SPECIAL AWARD: Emilio Pucci, Italy; Alexandre (Hairdresser), France.

FASHION IMMORTAL: Gabrielle 'Coco' Chanel.

1964

US Jury: Eleanor Lambert (Chairman); Sally Kirkland; Eugenia Sheppard; Jane Stark (*Look Magazine*); Nancy White.

French Jury: Alice Chavane de Dalinassy (Chairman); Augustine d'Abadie (*Figaro*); Vicomtesse de Ribes Marie-France de la Villehuchet; Helène Gordon-Lazareff.

British Jury: Ernestine Carter (Chairman); Madge Garland; James Laver; Martin Moss; Alison Settle.

WINNERS: **USA** – Jacques Tiffeau; Bonnie Cashin; **France** – André Courrèges; **Great Britain** – Ronald Patterson.

SPECIAL AWARD: Princess Irene Galitzine.

1965

US Jury: Eleanor Lambert (Chairman); Sally Kirkland; Eugenia Sheppard; Virginia Steele (*McCall's*); Jo Ahearn Zill (*Look Magazine*).

French Jury: Alice Chavane de Dalinassy (Chairman); Augustine d'Abadie; Marie-France de la Villehuchet; Helène Gordon-Lazareff; Rebecca Hamilton (*Harper's Bazaar*).

British Jury: Ernestine Carter (Chairman); John French; Professor Janey Ironside; Alison Settle; Vernon Stratton.

WINNERS: **USA** – James Galanos; **France** – Antonio Canovas del Castillo; **Great Britain** – Michael.

SPECIAL AWARD: Hardy Amies, Great Britain (for menswear); Rudi Gernreich, USA.

'WOMAN' DESIGNER AWARD

An annual award founded in 1979 by the mass-circulation British magazine *Woman* to encourage national designers. Winners of the award are as follows:

1979	Jeff Banks	1983	Betty Jackson
1980	Victor Herbert	1984	Sheilagh Brown
1981	Terence Nolder	1985	Joseph
1982	Jeff Banks	1986	Rifat Osbek

GLOSSARY

This glossary contains brief definitions of the most frequently used fashion terms. It is by no means exhaustive, however, and those in need of further information or greater detail should consult more specialized sources.

aigrette   heron feathers worn on head in a tuft, often with diamond tiara.

alpaca   hair of the Peruvian alpaca which has given its name to a cotton/alpaca mixed fabric; also the name of a cotton/rayon mix fabric.

alta moda   Italian for high fashion.

angora   1. hair of angora goat, used in making mohair – used in a mixture with rayon or wool to create warm but light fabrics. 2. hair of angora rabbit used as a very soft knitting wool for sweaters.

aniline dye   strongly coloured organic dye, extracted from coal tar.

appliqué   French for applied or laid on; decoration laid on and applied to a base surface; in embroidery, a motif or design applied by means of stitches – a fabric applied to another fabric.

Argyle   plaid design of solid blocks or diamonds with a contrasting overplaid.

atelier   French for studio or workroom; a designer's workroom where designs are created and made up.

baguette   French for rod or small stick; a way of cutting diamonds in a rectangular shape with sloping sides.

bandanna   Hindu word for a dyeing process; large handkerchief (often with spots or figures) worn around neck or head.

bandeau   narrow band worn around the head.

barathea   smooth worsted or wool fabric originally used for overcoats and uniforms, now used as a suiting material.

basket weave   plain weave with two or more yarns used as one.

basque   French for short skirt; formerly this described a closely fitted bodice with seaming from shoulder to waist; now, a piece of material attached to the bodice at the waist (*cf.* peplum).

basting   large stitches used to hold fabrics temporarily in place.

bateau neck   boat shaped, horizontal collar.

batik   method of applying dyed designs to a fabric by coating parts of the design with wax so that only the uncovered parts take the dye.

batwing sleeve   long sleeve with a deeply cut armhole and a fitted wristband.

beau monde   French for the fashionable world.

Bedford cord   strong fabric in rib weave with raised lengthwise cords in wool, cotton, rayon or a mix.

bench-made   hand-made shoes created on shoe-maker's bench.

bertha   very deep collar falling over the shoulder from a bodice neckline, commonly falling to the waist.

bias   folding or cutting a material by taking a line diagonally across warp and woof thread running at a 45° angle to selvage.

bifurcated   forked, or divided, into two parts – applied to divided skirts.

binding   an enclosing edge or band to finish the edges of a garment for decoration, strengthening or protective purposes.

block   a mould used to make and shape a hat.

bloomer   pantaloons closed by elastic at knee level, named after the American cyclist and dress reformer, Mrs. Amelia Jenks Bloomer.

bolero   short jacket worn open in front and finishing above the waistline, with or without sleeves.

bouclé   French for buckled, or curled, used to describe woven or knitted surface which has a looped or knotted appearance.

box pleats   combination of two folds from opposite directions with turned-under edges which meet underneath.

braid   narrow strip of flat tape (silk, wool, linen, etc.) for trimming and binding.

Breton   hat with upward rolled brim originally worn by peasants of Brittany.

brocade   jacquard weave fabric with all-over woven design of raised figures such as flowers and foliage.

broderie anglaise   embroidery of small (usually floral) designs punched or cut, then oversewn.

buckram   stiff two-ply, coarsely-woven fabric filled with glue sizing, used for stiffening garments and lining waist bands.

buckskin   cream-coloured, close-weave woollen fabric, named after the suede-leather that was originally made from the skin of a deer.

cable knit   knit in raised, twisted lines.

cable stitch   embroidery stitch of connected loop strips using one thread.

cachet   style, individuality.

calico   plain woven cotton cloth named after Calicut, India, where it was originally produced.

cambric   fine glazed cotton used for linings and toiles; fine plain woven linen used for blouses, collars and cuffs; named after Cambrai in France where it was first made in the 14th century.

camisole   under-bodice usually with straight top and shoulder straps of the same material, ribbon or lace.

cape   sleeveless outer garment which hangs loosely from the shoulders to any length.

cap sleeve   a small sleeve which just covers the top of the arm.

cardigan stitch   a rib-stitch modified by tacking on one or both needles.

cashmere   luxury cloth made from the under-hair of Himalayan goats; cashmere shawls are made of fine wool and were originally made in Kashmir.

cavalry twill   strong double twill woven fabric of wool, cotton or rayon.

ceinture   French for sash or belt.

chain stitch   loop stitches with one thread which look like links in a chain.

chamois   soft, pliable leather from the skin of the chamois goat.

Chantilly lace bobbin lace with a fine background and designs outlined with silk threads.

charmeuse lustrous satin wave fabric.

chemise loose undergarment which hangs straight from the shoulder; now more commonly the name of a straight unbelted dress in any soft material.

chemisier French for shirt-maker; a ladies' shirtblouse.

chenille French for caterpillar; material of silk, cotton or wool with a tufted, velvety pile.

chi-chi over-feminine, fussy bad taste in clothes.

chiffon soft, diaphanous plain woven fabric of silk, rayon etc.

chinchilla soft fur from the chinchilla, a small South American rodent, originally a blue-grey colour.

chip straw inexpensive straw woven from strips of woody material, originally from Italy.

chiton ancient Greek tunic in two styles: 1. Doric – sleeveless tunic made from an oblong piece of cloth, folded double above the waist and pinned at the shoulders; 2. Ionic – loose gown with sleeves.

choker high collar necklace or neckline.

chrome leather leather treated with chromium salts in the tanning process.

ciré French for waxed; a treatment of fabrics with wax, heat and pressure to make them shiny.

classic clothing which is timeless and unchanging in essentials; which remains in style as a result of fundamental simplicity regardless of changes in fashion.

cloche French for bell; a close fitting hat which follows the shape of the head.

cloqué French for blistered; used of fabrics with raised and irregular surfaces.

coat dress tailored dress made on coat lines with front closing from neckline to hem.

cocktail dress short dress for wear in the early evening; normally made of wool or evening materials, plain or embroidered; originally designed for the cocktail hour.

coiffure French for hair arrangement.

collection all the garments shown by a designer in one season.

confection/confezioni French and Italian for ready made clothes.

coolie coat straight box-shaped coat reaching to mid-thigh with unshaped armholes.

coolie hat a one-piece hat sloping on a straight slant from a central point.

corsage French for bodice; a bouquet of real or artificial flowers worn at neck, shoulder or waist.

corset a figure-moulding, supportive undergarment of elastic; formerly stiffened with steel or whalebone.

costume jewellery jewellery using non-precious materials, usually in an exuberant way, to be sold comparatively cheaply.

cotton fabric made from yarn spun from the soft fibrous substance attached to cotton plant seeds, the best or most expensive kind being Egyptian or Sea Island; mercerized cotton is created by treating the fabric with a caustic substance – it is stronger, better able to take dye and much silkier than ordinary cotton.

couture French for sewing or needlework; now used to mean the top end of the fashion spectrum.

couturier French for dressmaker; now used of the top designers who present a collection each season primarily aimed at individual private customers.

covert cloth a hard-wearing wool-and-cotton-mix woven fabric, often waterproofed.

cowl neckline softly draped or folded material at the front of a neckline which falls across the bodice in a loose semi-circle.

crash coarsely woven fabric with rough texture due to knotted or uneven yarns.

cravat a scarf folded or tied in front with the ends normally tucked in.

crêpe originally a gauzy silk material; now can be of any fabric which has an uneven surface. The best-known are:
1. **crêpe de chine**, a very high quality silk material with a lustrous quality;
2. **crêpe georgette**, a sheer, fine-textured fabric of silk, silk and cotton or silk and rayon;
3. **marocain**, a ribbed fabric of silk or wool or a mixture;
4. **matelasse crêpe**, a fabric which looks quilted;
5. **Crêpe plissé**, which is permanently blistered or puckered in stripes, like seersucker.

crimp fine fluting or plaiting of fabric.

croquis French for a quick sketch; it is normally used in connection with a designer's working sketch or a fashion illustrator's drawing.

cross-stitch a decorative stitch which forms an X.

cross cut cutting across the warp of the material to make a cross-wise line.

crushed velvet velvet treated so that its surface is irregular and distressed.

Cuban heel a heel of medium height with a straight, uncurved fall.

culotte full-proportioned trousers which fall together to give the appearance of a skirt.

cut the way in which a garment is cut and made; how a garment hangs.

cutter the person who cuts the garment out of the material using a master pattern created by the pattern cutter for the designer.

dart a shaped tuck in the material of a garment to make it follow the line of the figure.

décolleté a very low-cut neckline exposing neck and shoulders as a bodice treatment for evening wear.

défilé French for a file or line; used in a fashion sense to describe a fashion show.

dégagé French for free, easy or relaxed dressing.

démodé French for unfashionable, outmoded; no longer stylish clothes and attitudes.

dentelle French for lace.

dernier cri French for the last word in chic, the most fashionable thing of the moment.

déshabillé French for undressed; used in the fashion sense for a négligée, house-coat or any informal, untidy intimate dressing.

diaphanous of fine, transparent material.

directoire in the style of the French Directoire (1795–1799) – low décolletage, high waist, tight sleeves and straight skirt.

dirndl a full skirt gathered on a waistband.

doeskin leather made from sheep skin (originally from a female deer).

dolman sleeve a sleeve with a very deep armhole which is gathered at the wrist; it is seamless, being cut in one piece with the bodice.

Donegal originally a handloomed homespun fabric using uneven yarns woven by Irish peasants; now a slubbed tweed.

double-breasted a form of front, usually for a jacket or coat, which overlaps sufficiently to allow two rows of buttons.

drape to hang fabric in loose folds; to create a dress on the body using this method.

drawstring   cord or ribbon inserted in the lining or hem of a garment to pull up fullness of material thereby fastening the garment.

dropped shoulder   extension of shoulder line so that it ends on the upper arm.

dummy   model or dress form used in draping or for displaying garments.

duster coat   a lightweight, unlined coat which wraps across the body and usually has no fastening.

écru   beige, the colour of unbleached linen.

embossed   raised design which stands up from the base fabric in relief, obtained by passing material through hot engraved rollers or, in the case of velvet by shearing it.

Empire line   named after the Empress Josephine, this is a high waisted line with a skirt which falls straight and loose from immediately below the bust.

ensemble   the French word meaning 'together'; used to refer to a complete outfit of dress.

epaulet/epaulette   originally a badge on the shoulders of uniforms consisting of a fringed pad; now an ornament or trimming on a dress or coat shoulder that gives a feeling of width.

espadrille   rope-soled shoe with canvas upper.

étoile   French for star; can refer to a star design or a type of satin.

Eton collar   a high, turned-over collar, stiffly starched.

Eton jacket   a short, open jacket with wide lapels which ends at the hip.

eyelet   small hole or perforation used as a decorative device or, with laces or twines, as a fastening.

fabric   any man-made or natural fibre material from which garments are made, having a front (or face) and back.

face   1. to finish off an edge with a piece or lining of the same or constrasting material; 2. the right or finished side of a fabric.

facing   1. fabric applied to the edge of a garment, frequently on the underside; 2. the lining for parts of a garment which are turned over such as collars or cuffs.

façonné   French for figured; used for fabrics with random woven motifs.

fagoting   a form of stitching or embroidering using thread, ribbon or braid in a straight or criss-cross formation to form an openwork trimming.

faille   a silk fabric with a slight sheen and a heavy crosswise grain which can be stiff or limp.

Fair Isle   a form of traditional multicoloured, smallscale patterned knitwear from the Scottish island of that name.

fancy work   embroidery or decorative needlework on a garment which is normally done by hand.

fedora   felt hat with a crease running from front to back of the crown and a soft brim.

fichu   a scarf or shawl draped loosely over the shoulders with the ends hanging down from a softly tied bow at breast level.

filament   thread or fibre which is the raw material for textiles.

filigree   very delicate open work of a lace-like quality.

finish   the surface of a fabric after treatments such as embossing, napping, steaming or glazing.

fitting   1. ensuring that a garment conforms to the figure; 2. the period spent with tailor or dressmaker to adjust a garment to ensure its correct fit, as in 'Madame has a fitting tomorrow morning to correct the sleeve length on her coat'.

flannel   soft fabric of wool with a slight nap.

flannelette   soft fabric of cotton with a slight nap.

fleece   the wool coat of sheep, cashmere goats, camels, vicuñas or llamas.

fleece lined   a garment lined with sheepskin, such as a coat, or shoes.

floating panel   a panel at the back or sides of a dress which falls free of the main garment.

flounce   a gathered strip sewn on to a garment and having its lower edge free; normally found in tiers on skirt or sleeves.

fly front   a piece of material attached to the garment by one edge which conceals the fastening.

forage cap   a small cap worn by soldiers when not in full dress uniform; any small cap resembling this.

foulard   a satiny-silk fabric, plain or printed (normally with small motifs); a handkerchief or scarf which is a square.

French chalk   soft chalk used to mark cloth, or which is rubbed on hands to prevent perspiration damaging delicate fabrics when handled.

frill   a narrow ruffle gathered and attached on one edge but left free on the other; normally found at neck or wrist of garment.

fringe   a border of threads, tassels or cords attached at one end and hanging loose.

frou-frou   French for a rustling sound hence used to describe a dress in a material (such as silk taffeta) or style (e.g. flounced and frilled) which will make such a sound when the wearer moves.

furbelow   a ruffle or flounce.

fustian   a napped fabric of linen and cotton or cotton and wool.

gabardine/gaberdine   a twilled, worsted fabric used for coats, uniforms or riding habits.

galoshes   protective overshoes of rubber.

galuchat   a type of sharkskin with a pebbly surface.

gamin(e)   French for tomboy or street urchin; used to describe women or dress of a boyish, mischievous type.

gather   to draw a material together to take in its fullness; if there are more than two rows of gathering the term shirring is used.

gaufré   French for fluted, crimped or embossed.

gauze   thin, diaphanous material in loosely woven cotton, silk or linen originally from Gaza in Palestine.

gigot   a leg-of-mutton sleeve.

gilet   French for vest; a decorative, sleeveless top like a waistcoat.

gingham   lightweight, washable fabric yarn dyed and woven in checks, stripes or solid colours; **champray** is a fine, linen-like gingham with coloured warp and white filling named after Cambrai, France.

glaze   to coat with a thin glossy overlay thus making the face of the material smooth, as in glazed cotton.

Glengarry   a woollen hat with the crown creased from front to back and bound with ribbon, the ends of which float loose behind.

godet   a piece of cloth narrow (pointed or rounded) at the top and wide at the bottom, set into skirts and sleeves to create fullness.

goffered   a fabric with a stamped or embossed pattern produced by application of heat.

gore   a shaped, set-in section, narrow at the top and wide at the bottom, which extends from waist line to hem of a skirt; a skirt can consist of anything up to 24 gores.

grain   the direction of warp and woof threads in a fabric which can be lengthwise, crosswise or diagonal (bias grain) across the warp and woof.

grosgrain   silk fabric corded from selvage to selvage, having heavy crosswise ribs.

guipure   heavy lace, large patterned with either no ground or a coarse net one.

gusset   triangular, tapered or specially shaped piece of material inserted into a garment for additional strength or to adjust the fit.

hang   the way a garment hangs on the figure.

hank   a coil of thread or yarn.

harem skirt   bifurcated full draped skirt.

Harris tweed   soft wool tweed named after the Hebridean island of Harris.

haute couture   French for high dressmaking, now used to mean high fashion.

herringbone   a weave in which the direction of the twill is alternated to give a zigzag effect resembling the backbone of a herring.

hobble skirt   a very narrow, long skirt which restricts walking.

hopsack   a rough-surfaced linen, cotton or rayon fabric.

hound's tooth check   a small design of broken checks.

interlining   an inner lining between the lining and the fabric of a garment placed there for warmth or shaping purposes and usually of cotton.

Inverness   a long cape fitted at the neck and hanging loosely from the shoulders.

inverted pleat   pleat like a box pleat in reverse.

jabot   a frilled or ruffled piece of material fastened at the neckline and worn down the front of the bodice, often of lace or lace-trimmed.

jacquard   a figure weave created with a jacquard loom, used for brocades and damasks.

jaspé   French for marbled; a fabric with streaked blended colours caused by weaving various twisted yarns of different shades.

jerkin   a short jacket with no sleeves and normally no lapels which finishes at waist level.

jodhpurs   full-cut breeches which narrow below the knee to become closely fitted to the leg, ending with a cuff at the ankle, sometimes having a strap to go under the foot; originally worn as riding breeches.

jute   the fibre from the jute plant which is mixed with silk, wool or rayon in fabrics.

kapok   silky fibre from the silk-cotton tree used as filling and padding in quilted garments.

knickerbockers   loose, full pants with fullness caught in a band just below the knee.

knife-pleats   narrow pleats sharply pressed.

lambsdown   heavy woollen knitted fabric with a thick nap on one side.

lambskin   leather from the skin of very young lambs.

lamé   fabric woven of gold or silver threads.

lapel   a front neckline treatment whereby the garment turns back or is folded over; if the turn back is very big the name rever is used.

last   the wooden form on which a shoe is shaped.

lawn   a soft sheer fabric (normally cotton) plainly woven, which is starched or sized.

leather   hide or skin of any animal which has been tanned and treated; the most frequently used are alligator, antelope, calf, chamois, cowhide, doeskin, goatskin, lambskin, lizard, pigskin, sharkskin, sheepskin, snakeskin and suede.

leatherette   trade name for imitation leather which is cloth or paper treated to simulate the grains and texture of the real thing.

leghorn   finely plaited straw which has given its name to a large brimmed hat – the straw was originally exported from Italy via the port of Livorno, which was called Leghorn by the English.

length   1. a vertical measurement from the top to the bottom of a garment or part of a garment; 2. the direction of the warp in a fabric.
The basic variations of garment measurements are: Coat lengths – **finger tip:** to ends of fingers when arms are hanging straight down; **hip length:** to hips at their widest point; **seven-eighths:** one eighth shorter than skirt underneath; **three-quarters:** one quarter shorter than skirt underneath.
Dress lengths – **ankle length:** falling to the ankle bone; **full length** or **floor length:** just skimming the floor when the wearer is standing straight.
Sleeve lengths – **elbow length:** just covering the elbow bone; **three-quarter length:** ending between the elbow joint and the wristbone.

line   1. the cut of a garment to create a particular outline or style (e.g. Dior's A-line): 2. a particular brand or class of goods supplied by a manufacturer; 3. to give a coat, dress or skirt a second, inner layer, known usually as the lining.

linen   strong fabric woven from flax and then bleached; normally of plain weave so it can be dyed or printed.

lisle   thread is made of fine twisted cotton and was used for stockings.

loafer   American name for a soft slip-on shoe with a flat heel, based on the moccasin worn by American Indians.

loden   an overcoat which falls loosely from a yoke; it is made of loden cloth which is coarse woven wool originally from the Austrian Tyrol and normally in dark green.

Lucite   trade name for a clear plastic material.

Lurex   trade name for a shiny yarn created by inserting aluminium foil between coloured plastic film.

lynx   the soft, long-haired fur of the European or North American lynx.

macramé   knotted bulky lace or woven cotton fabric.

madras   a firm, smooth cotton fabric usually in stripes or checks.

Magyar sleeve   a sleeve cut on the same lines as traditional Hungarian Magyar costumes; it is very full and is gathered tightly in at the wrist.

maillot   from the French word for tights; it describes a figure hugging, one-piece bathing costume.

maison   French for house, used to describe a business establishment – e.g. the house of Dior, Maison Dior.

maison de couture   a dressmaker's establishment.

mandarin coat   long embroidered silk coat which falls straight, after the style worn by Chinese mandarins.

mandarin collar   narrow collar which stands up from the tight-fitting neckline of a garment.

mandarin sleeve   a full, square cut sleeve like those on a kimono.

mannequin   1. display model of a human torso used to show or fit clothes on; 2. a girl employed by a fashion establishment to wear clothes for display to customers or press.

manteau   a cloak or cape.

mantilla   1. a traditional headcovering for Spanish women, consisting of a high comb in the hair which is draped with heavy lace; 2. a cloak.

mantle   a cloak or loose wrap normally without sleeves.

maquillage   French for make-up.

marabou   tail and wing feathers of the African marabou stork, used as trimming on hats, dresses or lingerie.

marmot   inexpensive fur often dyed to resemble mink.

marocain   ribbed crêpe, of silk, rayon or wool.

marten   soft fine fur of the stone marten.

martingale   a half belt placed at the back of a jacket.

matelassé   French for padded; it is a soft fabric with a raised or blistered surface, made of wool, silk, rayon or cotton.

matt   a dull, flat surface finish.

mélange   1. a fabric mixture consisting of a wool weft and a cotton warp; 2. a mixture of woven colours.

melon sleeve   a very full sleeve, normally short, which gathers into a band at the bottom.

melton   a thick, heavy material of wool, or wool and cotton, used for overcoats and jackets: the nap is raised and then shaved to create a smooth texture.

mercerize   a treatment for cotton which was evolved by John Mercer (1791–1866), an English calico printer – the cotton is treated with caustic soda or potash to make it take dye more easily and in the process it is given a surface sheen.

merino   the wool of the merino sheep; see **wool**.

midinette   French for shop girl; the name is reputed to derive from the fact that the shop girls of Paris all came onto the streets at midday (midi).

midriff   the diaphragm.

midseason   the show or sale time between the major spring and autumn shows.

milliner's fold   a method of stitching so that stitches do not show on the right side of the fabric – the edge of the fabric is folded four times and then caught with basting stitches.

millinery   hats and head-dresses made to be worn by women.

mink   a luxurious thick fur; most expensive is wild mink – the majority of mink is ranched.

mitre   a method of joining fabric or finishing a hem at a corner – a triangular piece is cut off the fabric, and the raw edges are turned in and sewn.

mitt   a fingerless glove.

moccasin   an American Indian's heel-less shoe made by gathering up a piece of soft leather in a U shape around the foot and attaching it to an upper piece.

mode   synonym for fashion.

model   1. a mannequin; 2. a girl who poses for photographers and artists or who shows clothes to customers and journalists; 3. a garment which serves as a pattern for making copies; 4. a garment made in limited numbers, using high-quality materials and carrying a designer's name label.

modelliste   a designer who works anonymously in a maison and whose clothes are shown under the name of the fashion house.

mohair   long, shiny, silky fur of the angora goat used to make very soft or light wool.

moiré   wavy, watery pattern effect on fabric, obtained by a process of crushing some parts of the material by passing it through special cylinders.

moleskin   a kind of fustian, with a thick, soft nap like the fur of a mole; a strong cotton fabric used for men's heavy-duty work clothes.

monkey jacket   a short, fitted jacket with lapels and ending at the waist.

monogram   a person's initials embroidered onto a garment, often used as a decorative device.

mousseline de laine   very lightweight wool muslin.

mousseline de soie   transparent gauzy silk fabric.

muff   a tubular device into which the hands are placed to keep them warm; it can be made of fabric, fur or skin and is often lined with wool, fur or feathers.

muffler   a heavy, thick woollen scarf.

muslin   fine cotton fabric, plainly woven, bleached or unbleached.

musquash   muskrat skins; the muskrat fur is long and glossy.

nacre velvet   velvet in two colours: the back one is colour and the pile another.

nap   the fibres found in certain fabrics which give a soft surface by lying smoothly, all in one direction.

neckband   a band fitting around the neck to which the collar is attached.

needlework   any sewing, embroidery or appliqué work.

negligée   any informal dress but normally refers to a soft, full-length garment worn indoors by women; it can be belted or loose.

net   open-work fabric of thread with mesh which can be in any size.

New Look, the   the silhouette launched in 1947 by Christian Dior – it had full skirts and tight bodices.

Norfolk jacket   a hip-length, fitted and belted jacket which is single-breasted, has patch pockets and is box-pleated at back and front.

notch   1. a triangular indentation on a pattern which must be matched to an opposite notch on the piece to be joined so that the fit is correct; 2. a triangular opening where a collar joins the lapel at the front of the bodice.

nub   texture caused by irregularities in thickness of yarns woven into fabric.

nylon   a strong synthetic compound made from coal. It is washable, quick-drying and elastic; it creases only slightly and takes all dyes.

obi   a broad Japanese sash worn as a belt; it is usually made of a heavy fabric like stiff silk or satin and is often embroidered or brocaded.

ocelot   a spotted fur from a large Central and South American wildcat: the markings are black on a tawny background.

off-the-shoulder   a neckline which leaves the neck, shoulders and upper arm bare.

oilskin   cotton, linen or synthetic cloth waterproofed by a process using oil.

ombré   colour which is graduated in tone.

openback shoe   a shoe with the back part of the upper cut away to reveal the wearer's heel.

opening   the part of a garment which opens to allow it to be put on – e.g. the placket of a skirt or the neck of a blouse.

open welt seam   like a tucked seam, this is used to panel a skirt or seam a jacket or coat; it is made by finishing with a tuck which is part of the seam.

open work   work with holes in the material such as punch work or lace.

opera cloak   a full length evening cloak.

opossum   long-haired fur of the American opossum, in shades of grey.

organdie/organdy   a very fine, stiffened muslin.

organza   sheer, fine fabric used in several layers for diaphanous evening gowns.

original a garment designed and made by a couture house and carrying the designer's name.

osprey the general name for feathers used in hat trimmings, originally from an osprey itself.

ottoman a strong, firm fabric with crosswise ribs.

outfit a complete ensemble normally for a specific occasion.

overblouse loose, full blouse which falls over the waist and is not tucked in.

overcheck a check pattern created by weaving one colour on top of another.

overskirt a top skirt worn over a dress skirt; shorter than the under skirt and frequently draped or open at the sides or front.

Oxford 1. a basket weave fine cotton; 2. a low-cut shoe with front lacing.

Oxford bags very wide-bottomed men's trousers especially popular in the 1920s.

padded shoulders a means of extending the shoulder line by padding which increases the appearance of height or width.

paille straw used for hats or handbags.

paillettes tiny, shiny discs sewn on a fabric backing to resemble fish scales; similar to spangles.

Paisley a swirling design of arabesques printed on fine wool or silk; shawls so printed, hailing from Paisley in Scotland.

pajamas/pyjamas a lounging-suit originally for sleep or beach wear, consisting of a loose, large-proportioned jacket and loose trousers.

panache originally a plume of upright feathers worn on a helmet; now used by the fashionable as a synonym for style.

Panama a man's hat of fine straw with a wide brim.

panel the front gore of a dress or skirt which can be a part of the dress (as in a princess line dress) or allowed to hang free of the garment.

panne satin satin, treated by pressure and heat to produce a high surface shine.

panne velvet velvet with pile flattened all one way to give a shiny surface.

pannier a bouffant, side drape, fullness-giving treatment for a skirt named after the baskets carried on each side of a mule or horse's saddle.

pantaloons trousers which are close-cut and terminate in a band at calf level.

pareo rectangular cloth, usually of cotton, worn as a skirt, loosely tied and falling open.

parti-coloured variegated in colour.

parure a set of jewels or decorative trimmings intended to be worn together.

passementerie trimmings of heavy embroidery using braids, beads or tinsels.

patch pocket a pocket sewn to the outside of a garment and being attached on all sides but the top.

patten a wooden sole fastened to a boot or shoe to protect it from mud.

pattern 1. a guide for cutting garments – it is measured and cut to shape from paper; 2. a block pattern is cut out of heavy paper or card and is used to fix the size of a shape before cutting and for grading sizes up or down; 3. a printed pattern is a commercially produced pattern – it is of tissue paper and contains instructions for lay-out and cutting; 4. a transfer pattern is an embroidery one in which the design is stamped on paper ready to be transferred on to the fabric by the application of heat, for instance by an iron.

pavé a setting for jewellery in which the stones are placed very close together.

pea jacket a loose, double-breasted jacket based on those worn by sailors and fishermen.

peau de soie dull, satiny finish silk used for trimmings on coats and dresses and facings on dress coats.

peccary fine grained pig skin.

pedal pushers straight trousers ending just below the knee.

peg-topped wide at the top and narrow at bottom; applied to trousers, skirts or pockets.

peignoir a dressing gown originally of terry towelling and for use at the beach; now used to describe an item of lingerie worn as a cover-up at home, in bedroom or bathroom.

pelisse a long straight cape.

pelt the hide or skin of any animal.

pencil skirt long, narrow, straight skirt.

pendant ornament or jewellery that hangs or is suspended, e.g. pendant earrings.

peplum a small ruffle or flounce extending from the waist to cover the hips.

pepper and salt tweed a mixture of twisted yarns, normally in black and white, woven together.

percale close, plain-woven cotton.

Persian lamb tightly curled fur of very young lambs.

petal collar a collar made of overlapping oval shapes arranged like petals.

Peter Pan collar a soft, rounded, turned down small collar.

petersham heavily napped woollen cloth, usually dark blue, used for heavy-duty coats.

petit point fine-needle small stitch.

petticoat woman's underskirt.

picture hat a wide-brimmed formal hat often trimmed with flowers or ribbons.

Pierrot collar a wide, softly ruffled collar reminiscent of that worn by the French pantomime character.

pigskin hard-wearing leather from the hide of a pig.

pile fabric surface of close threads that form an even surface.

pillbox a small round hat with straight sides and flat top.

pink to cut the edge of cloth in small, triangular notches; pinking shears are scissors which cut the fabric in a sawtooth design.

pin stripe a very fine stripe printed or woven.

pin tuck a pinch of fabric secured by stitching.

piping a narrow bias fold used as a finish on edges or a narrow piece of leather or suede sewn into a seam as a finish.

piqué a firm fabric, normally cotton, in a lengthwise cord effect.

placket an overlap of material covering the opening at waist or neck level which enables a garment to be put on.

plaid originally the national dress in Scotland, it is now used to describe any fabric in which the woven pattern is created by crossing bands of colour in various width to form variegated squares.

plait a braid in which strands are passed over each other in turn.

plissé French for gathered, pleated or folded.

plunging neckline a very deep V-cut dropping in some cases as low as the waist.

plus-fours loose, widely-cut knickerbockers reaching to mid-calf.

pochette French for small pocket; now used to describe a small handbag.

polka dots a regularly placed all-over pattern of uniform circular shapes of medium size.

polo shirt a short-sleeved sports shirt in cotton jersey having a knitted collar and buttoned placket.

poncho a square of material worn as a cape having an opening in the centre for the head.

poodle cloth a knotted or looped woven fabric similar to bouclé.

poplin a medium-weight, plain weave fabric made of cotton, silk or wool.

premier/première the head of workroom.

premier modelliste/première modelliste assistant to the head of an atelier.

prêt-à-porter French for ready-to-wear.

prick to trace a pattern or decorate a surface by means of tiny perforations.

princess line a dress or coat which is close-fitting and shaped without belt or other interruption, from the shoulder to the hem.

print fabric stamped with patterns using dyes and applied by means of screens, rollers or blocks.

proof to treat a fabric so that it is water resistant.

pucker a wrinkle or furrow in a fabric.

puff a method of gathering or shirring fabric to give it an enlarged appearance.

puff sleeve a full cut sleeve gathered at the bottom so that the material stands out.

punch work open-work embroidery.

purl/pearl a knitting stitch achieved by bringing the needle out across the thread or wool and holding it.

puttee a leg covering consisting of cotton ribbons wound round the leg from the ankle up.

quilt 1. to band together several thicknesses of fabric by sewing them along with the same number of layers of padding; 2. to outline a design on several thicknesses of fabric by running stiches.

raccoon a strong coarse fur from the animal of that name.

raffia straw made from the palm fibre used in making hats and bags.

raglan a loose covercoat with large, full sleeves, named after Lord Raglan (1788–1855) of Crimean fame.

raglan sleeve a full, wide sleeve with the armhole line extending from the neck.

raised a pattern or design which stands up in relief from the fabric surface.

ravel to pull out threads on the edge of the material to make a fringe.

raw silk fibre obtained from silkworm cocoons.

rayon a man-made textile using fibre made from regenerated cellulose.

redingote French word derived from English words riding coat; a tight-fitting, three-quarter or full length overcoat.

reefer jacket a boxy coat, normally double-breasted and finger-tip length.

rep/repp a strong plain weave fabric of cotton, wood or silk, its warp and waft threads being arranged alternatively coarse and fine.

resist a substance that repels dyes, used in resist printing by applying to cloth before dipping.

revers wider-than-normal lapels on coats or jackets.

rhinestone lustrous paste or glass imitation of real precious stones.

rib a raised ridge in fabric caused by alternating wales in two different directions.

rick-rack a flat woven trimming in a zig-zag form which can be of various materials and widths and is used as a decorative trimming.

robe de chambre loose dressing gown for men or women; that for women is usually long and of satin, silk or velvet.

robe de style a formal evening dress with tight bodice and very full skirt.

roll collar a high, turnover collar which stands away from the neck.

rolled hem a hem made by rolling the edge of the material and securing it with slip stitches.

rompers a one-piece garment consisting of bib top and short, bloused trousers.

rouleau a milliner's term for a roll of ribbon used as piping.

ruche a gathered or pleated strip of fabric used as a trimming.

ruff a pleated collar.

ruffle a gathered or pleated strip of fabric used as a trimming which is attached so that one or both edges are left free.

sable the fur of the sable, which is the most luxurious and valuable of all furs, the Russian variety being considered especially fine.

sac de voyage French for travelling bag.

sack a loose, unshaped dress hanging straight from shoulders to hem.

saddle stitch a decorative stitch frequently made using very narrow strips of leather.

salon a showroom.

sarsenet/sarsnet soft fabric of silk.

sari a wide scarf of silk or cotton, often decorated with gold, which is draped and wound around the body leaving one end free to place over the head; traditional Indian female dress.

sarong a wide piece of fabric, usually cotton and brightly printed, which is wrapped around the waist and tucked in on itself to make a skirt which normally falls to ankle length.

sartorial pertaining to men's clothes and accessories.

sateen a cotton fabric with a satin finish free from twill used largely for linings and underskirts.

satin a silk or rayon fabric with a smooth surface free from twill and normally with a high gloss face and matt back.

schappe silk originally yarn or fabric made from silk degummed by the schappe method of fermentation; now merely means spun silk.

scrim poor quality muslin-type cloth normally made of cotton.

sealskin the fur of a seal, normally dyed black or grey.

season 1. a period of several weeks in spring and autumn when new fashions are being promoted; 2. the period of high summer when English society follows traditional pursuits – e.g. Henley, Ascot – before moving north for grouse shooting.

seed pearl a tiny pearl used in embroidery and decoration.

seersucker a lightweight plain weave fabric having stripes or checks made by puckering parts of the surface.

self of the same material as the rest of the garment (e.g. self-belt, self-covered buttons).

selvage/selvedge the longitudinal edge of a woven fabric finished to prevent ravelling.

semi-fitted the bodice on a garment which is shaped loosely to the body but is not figure-hugging.

serge a piece-dyed simple twill woven fabric with a clear finish; originally made of wool but now using other fabrics.

shantung a plain weave silk which has surface irregularities or slubs.

sharkskin 1. leather from the skin of the shark; 2. a fabric with a firm surface.

shawl collar one where the collar and revers are in one uninterrupted piece without notches; normally falls quite low over the bodice.

shearling short-woolled sheep or lamb's skins which were sheared before slaughter, then tannned with the wool on.

sheath a straight and very tight-fitting dress which is often full length.

sheen the shine or lustre of a fabric.

sheer very lightweight fabric of degrees of transparency.

Shetland wool from the Shetland sheep; *see* **wool**.

shift a straight, narrow-cut chemise.

shirring three or more rows of gathering in a piece of material.

shirting fabrics such as cotton, linen, silk or flannel which have been traditionally used for making men's shirts.

shirtwaister a tailored dress like an elongated shirt, normally with a belt.

shot silk silk with different coloured warp and weft so that the surface colour changes with variations of light or movement.

showerproof a material or garment chemically treated to resist light rain.

shrinkage the amount a garment or fabric is reduced in size as a result of washing or dry cleaning.

shuttle the instrument used in weaving to pass the weft threads from side to side between warp threads.

silhouette the outline of a figure or garment.

silk a shiny yarn, produced by silkworms, which becomes white when degummed; the fibre is woven to produce a high quality, very light fabric.

silk gazar the trade name for a slightly stiff organza or gauze much favoured by Balenciaga for evening dresses.

single-breasted a means of closing coats and jackets down the centre front with one row of buttons.

single cuff a shirt cuff with no turnback.

size 1. the measure or dimensions of a garment expressed in inches, metres or symbols such as small, medium and large; 2. process for treating cloth.

skein a loosely tied coil of thread or yarn in a standard length.

sketcher a member of a design team who draws the designer's ideas before they are put into production or who records finished designs.

slacks trousers for women worn in casual or informal situations.

slash a cut in the material of a garment to reveal a contrasting material or the wearer's flesh underneath.

slip an undergarment worn with unlined dresses or skirts.

slipper satin a fine satin with a dull surface finish.

slip stitch used for hems, facings etc., when it is important that stitches are not seen on the right side of the fabric; the stitch is loose and concealed between two layers of fabric.

sloppy Joe a large, loose slip-on sweater.

slouch hat a hat with a soft crown and brim.

slubbed a fabric with thick lumps in places.

smock a loose full garment like a big shirt.

smocking a form of decorative stitching to hold the fullness of the fabric in a regular pattern.

smoking a man's jacket and trousers worn for evening; almost always black and with the revers of the jacket faced in a lustrous fabric; it is now often worn by women.

sneaker a casual sports shoe with rubber sole, canvas upper and central front lacing.

soie French for silk.

soignée well-groomed.

sombrero a large-scale, broad-brimmed hat.

sou'wester a broad-brimmed, high-crowned waterproof hat of rubber or specially treated material.

spangles small, shiny discs of metal used for decoration and embroidery.

spat an ankle-gaiter worn over the shoe – it passes underneath the sole and is buttoned up the side.

spencer a short often semi-fitted jacket which finishes at waist level.

stand-up collar a collar which stands up from the collar line and is unfolded.

stencil a piece of paper or thin metal on which designs are cut out; the design is applied to the fabric underneath by brushing, stippling or spraying due or ink through the spaces where the designs have been cut out.

stiffening a method of sizing fabric so that it is permanently crisp, using starch or glue.

stiletto a very narrow pointed heel resembling a stiletto dagger.

stock a band of cloth wound around the neck and tied; now usually ready-made, and fastened at the back.

stockinette an almost obsolete term for a plain knitted fabric.

stole a long scarf, often fringed ends, used as a shoulder wrap.

stone marten the fur of the European or Asian marten.

strand a single fibre, a filament of yarn.

stylist a person who organizes the look of a particular garment for show or photography by choosing and arranging accessories, backgrounds, lights or whatever.

suede a leather with a napped surface.

sunburst pleats close, all-round pleats on a circular full skirt.

surah a soft, lightweight silk fabric.

svelte/svelte lithe, slender and graceful.

swag a draped piece of material which falls in soft, full folds.

swagger coat a flared coat which hangs loosely from the shoulders.

swatch a small piece of cloth cut from the bolt to be used as a sample or *aide mémoire* concerning weight, texture and colour.

sweater a knitted top normally of wool or cashmere.

tack to baste or sew quickly with long stitches which are often temporary and should not show too prominently on the right side of the fabric.

taffeta a plain, closely woven smooth fabric which is slightly lustrous; the two most popular taffetas are probably faille and moiré.

tailleur a tailored suit or dress.

tailored a crisp look achieved by careful cutting and seaming using a firm fabric and keeping the design plain and close-fitting.

tailor's chalk soapstone used by tailors and dressmakers to mark cloth when garments are being made or altered.

tam-o'-shanter a Scottish hat with a full crown which overlaps a tight headband, named after the hero of a poem by Robert Burns.

tassel a covered, ornamental shape with threads hanging down; usually made in silk or wool.

Tattersall check a bold check named after the London horse market.

tatting knotted lace edging made by hand.

terry cloth a fabric with a raised loop forming uncut pile, made of cotton normally but can be made of other fabrics – e.g. wool or rayon.

tie-dye   a process whereby portions of fabric are so tightly tied before the dye is applied that it cannot penetrate: thus a pattern is created when the fabric is removed from the dye and untied.

tier   one of a series of flounces or ruffles on a garment.

tie silk   a fine, closely woven ribbed silk fabric used for neckties, blouses and dresses.

tissue paper   an almost transparent paper used for patterns and for wrapping: it can be white, black or coloured; black prevents metallic fabrics from tarnishing and blue prevents light fabrics from yellowing; the name derives from its original use to prevent tarnishing of layers of metal tissue fabrics.

toile   French for a fine linen fabric; now used to mean a garment made up in muslin to enable the designer to see how his design will look before cutting materials; or to mean a muslin copy of an existing garment which a manufacturer buys to copy from.

top coat   an overcoat.

top stitch   a visible stitch, functional and decorative, which is used as a stylistic device.

toque   a close-fitting brimless hat with a flat crown and straight edges.

tortoise-shell   the brown and yellow mottled, semi-transparent substance found on the shells of some turtles; used in making accessories and trims; now it is made of plastic treated and coloured to resemble the real thing.

towelling   a loose woven material, often of linen or cotton, having a high absorbency rate.

tracing wheel   a wheel with sharp points which is used to mark seams or construction lines prior to sewing.

train   an extended panel of a dress or skirt which trails behind; it may also be a length of material suspended from the back of the head, the shoulders or the waist.

transfer pattern   **1.** a carbon design transferred to cloth by heat application; **2.** perforated design transferred to cloth by rubbing colour through the perforations.

trapunto   a process whereby a design is stitched then given a raised effect by being stuffed with cotton.

trench coat   a loose-cut raincoat with many pockets and flaps, held at the waist with a self-belt.

trend   a movement in fashion thinking.

tricot   from the French word *tricoter*, to knit; it now is used for any knitwear or fabric woven to give the appearance of knitting.

trousseau   a bride's outfit including garments for her honeymoon.

tuck   a fold of fabric stitched into place on a garment.

tulle   a very fine silk, cotton or synthetic net.

tunic   an overblouse or coat reaching to hip length or below, normally cut slim or fitted.

turban   a close-fitting hat with softly draped sides and crown, based on the long strip of cloth wound round the head to create a traditional oriental head-dress.

turtle neck   a high, loose rolled neckline.

tussore   a soft, lightweight silk fabric.

tweed   originally a rough-surfaced, heavy fabric woven in Scotland; now used to describe any woollen weave effect using colours, checks or herringbone.

twinset   cardigan and jumper made to match or complement each other and to be worn together.

ulster   a large, loosely cut overcoat which is rain-repellent and can be belted (first made in Ulster, Ireland); it has a buttoned back flap in the skirt.

upper   the part of the shoe above the sole and heel.

vamp   the part of a shoe upper which covers the front (toes and instep) of the foot as opposed to the quarter which is the part of the upper covering the back of the shoe.

veil   piece of transparent fabric or lace worn over head or face and frequently suspended from a hat: often made of net or tulle.

velours   **1.** a heavy napped fabric resembling velvet; **2.** a velvety felt used for hats.

velvet   a cut warp-pile fabric with the cut ends forming the surface; originally of silk now also of rayon and cotton.

vendeuse   French for saleswoman.

vest   short, close-fitting sleeveless garment.

vicuña   very soft wool-type material made from the wool of the South American vicuxa.

voile   a lightweight, plain, semi-transparent fabric of cotton, silk, rayon or wool.

waistband   a band inside the top of a skirt.

waistcoat   a sleeveless, close-fitting garment, front-buttoned and extending to the waistline.

wale   the texture or weave of a fabric.

warp   the threads in a material which run lengthways and form the base through which the weft threads are woven.

wedge heel   a solid heel which is an uninterrupted continuation of the sole.

wellingtons   originally a type of riding boots which covered the knee in front but were cut away behind, named after the Duke of Wellington (1769–1852); now rubber boots loosely covering the calves.

weft   the threads in a material which run crossways and are woven through the lengthways warp threads.

welt   a strengthening strip stitched to an edge or border; in knitting, a secure edge made during or after the knitting process; in shoes, the strip of leather stitched to the shoe upper prior to attaching to the sole.

whipcord   normally a cotton or worsted fabric characterized by a bold, upright, diagonal twill weave.

wincey   a lightweight flannel material originally made with a cotton warp and a wool weft.

winceyette   a lightweight cotton material raised on one or both sides.

windbreaker/windcheater   a short, outdoor jacket with a fitted waistband made of heavy wool, gaberdine or waterproof material.

Winterhalter   a style of evening dress based on the paintings of Winterhalter (1806–1873), characterized by the off-the-shoulder necklines, narrow waists and very full, flounced skirts.

woof   the crossways yarn in a material, more commonly known as weft.

wool   the hair of the sheep or other animals, made into twine for knitting or weaving. The best known varieties are:
1. alpaca: a superior, fine quality wool from the South American animal of that name;
2. angora: the long, silky wool of the goat of that name, used to make mohair;
3. Botany: high quality wool originally from the Botany Bay area of Australia;
4. cashmere: the very soft underhair of Himalayan goats;
5. lambswool: the very fine, soft hair of young lambs;
6. merino: high-quality wool from the fleece of merino sheep, which were originally from Spain;

7. **Shetland:** the wool of sheep from the Shetland Islands, off the coast of Scotland – characteristically tough and hard-wearing.

worsted a yarn spun from combed wool.

wrap a loose, sleeveless outer garment without collar fastening.

wrap-around skirt a skirt with two unsewn edges which wrap or fold over each other.

yarn a product of considerable length and comparatively small cross-section, of fibres with or without twist; yarn is used in weaving or knitting.

yashmak the veil used by Moslem women to cover the lower portion of the face.

yoke a fitted portion of a garment, normally covering the shoulders, to which the rest of the garment is attached.

zig-zag a line, running in angular turns, alternating from side to side.

zouave a form of a very full skirt or trousers based on the quasi-Moorish trousers worn by the French infantry regiment of that name which originated in Algeria.

INDEX

New designers, included in the FASHION UPDATE section of this edition, do not feature in this index, but can be found easily in the supplement which is in strictly alphabetical order.

PICTURE CREDITS

We would like to thank all the designers who kindly contributed pictures of their work.

John Adrian   p. 147
Antonio   pp. 71, 276
Richard Avedon   p. 263
David Bailey   p. 277
BBC Hulton Picture Library   p. 211
Cecil Beaton/Courtesy of Sotheby's Belgravia   pp. 87, 90, 99, 111, 135, 145, 153, 177, 201, 208, 221, 233, 237, 263
Shirley Beljohn   p. 199
Bibliothèque Nationale   pp. 165, 192, 197, 206
Bridgeman Art Library   p. 67
British Museum   p. 26
Henry Clarke/© Harper's Bazaar U.K.   p. 280
Colorific   pp. 43, 53, 54, 57, 90, 148, 194, 195, 238
Courtauld Institute of Art   p. 26
Louise Dahl-Wolf/© Harper's Bazaar U.K.   p. 280
Design Council   pp. 65, 69
Christian Dior   pp. 87, 130
E.T. Archive   pp. 59, 122, 175, back cover
J. Eula/© Harper's Bazaar Italia   p. 282
Mary Evans Picture Library   pp. 32, 281
Fine Arts Society   p. 88
Fairchild Syndicate   p. 275
Sally and Richard Greenhill   p. 70
© Harper's Bazaar U.K.   pp. 80, 149, 176, 204, 218, 250, 275
Peter Hope-Lumley   pp. 63, 83, 84, 88, 91, 105, 112, 130, 138, 155, 190, 192, 194, 195, 199, 218, 230, 232, 234, 240
Illustrated London News   p. 222
William Klein   p. 285
Keystone Press   pp. 34, 35, 101, 272
Koball Collection   pp. 27, 32, 34, 81, 154
Landschott/© Harper's Bazaar U.K.   p. 286
Eleanor Lambert Division   pp. 111, 129, 185
Natalie Lamoral   pp. 56, 72, 73, 85, 108, 119, 135, 137, 141, 146, 169, 170, 172, 174, 182, 183, 184, 186, 188, 196, 205, 206, 207, 208, 209, 228, 232, 242, 251, 257, 266, 271, 272
Collection Dr Rupold Leopold, Vienna   p. 70
London Express News Service   p. 189
Man Ray/© Harper's Bazaar U.K.   p. 287
Mansell Collection   pp. 11, 60
Frank Martin/The Guardian   pp. 160, 186
De Meyer/Royal Photographic Society   p. 281

Simone Mirman   p. 67
Christopher Moore   pp. 63, 78, 79, 80, 82, 85, 96, 97, 98, 101, 116, 117, 118, 120, 121, 123, 124, 126, 136, 141, 152, 154, 158, 159, 162, 163, 164, 165, 166, 167, 168, 169, 171, 173, 174, 178, 179, 180, 184, 185, 190, 191, 196, 205, 207, 210, 224, 229, 242, 246, 247, 248, 249, 250, 252, 253, 255, 264, 265, 266, 273
Alec Murray   pp. 89, 150, 229
Muncaski/© Harper's Bazaar U.K.   p. 287
Musées Nationaux   p. 13
National Gallery of Scotland, Edinburgh/Bridgeman Art Library   p. 66
Helmut Newton/Condé Nast   p. 275
Nostalgia and Mud   p. 269
Norman Parkinson   p. 288
Irving Penn/© Condé Nast Publications Inc. c. 1950   p. 289
Pictorial Press   p. 99
Popperfoto   pp. 46, 142, 151, 153, 177, 209, 213, 221, 270
Rex Features   pp. 91, 139, 215, 226, 230
Sunday Times   pp. 93, 101, 103, 104, 146, 149, 210, 263, 268, 288
Seeberger Collection   pp. 133, 134, 215, 218, 220, 227, 231, 232, 270, 290
Snowdon/Condé Nast Publications Ltd.   p. 290
*Tate Gallery   p. 68
Tony Stone Worldwide   p. 65
John Topham   pp. 53, 64, 101, 106, 135, 139, 151, 231
Deborah Turbeville/© Harper's Bazaar Italia   p. 291
U.F.A.C./Jean-Loup Charmet   pp. 89, 102, 110, 111, 139, 149, 155, 189, 192, 194, 197, 218, 222, 229, 267
UPI   pp. 64, 93, 94
Vertès/© Harper's Bazaar U.K.   p. 292
Victoria and Albert Museum   pp. 32, 38, 69, 74, 125, 127, 143, 144, 155, 175, 214, 221, 223, 237, 238, 254, 267, 270, 285
Courtesy of Vogue © 1950, 1951, 1952, 1954; 1955, 1959, 1961, 1965 (renewed 1978, 1979, 1980, 1982) by Condé Nast Publications Inc.   pp. 89, 96, 146, 212, 275, 278, 279
Courtesy of Vogue © 1938 Bérard   p. 279, © 1938 Blumenfeld   p. 279, © 1938 Eric   p. 282, © 1933 Hoyningen-Huene   p. 284 by Condé Nast Publications Ltd.
Barbra Walz   pp. 63, 99, 145, 151, 157, 199
WWD   pp. 11, 84, 87, 135, 181, 182, 199, 200, 201

Publisher's note

The publishers would like to thank Arthur F. Abelman of Moses & Singer, Nancy Evans of *Glamour* magazine, Lorna Koski of *Woman's Wear Daily* magazine, Marjorie Miller of The Fashion Institute of Technology and Claire Streeter of Abbeville Press, Inc. for their assistance and advice in the preparation of this book.

* Composition in red, yellow and blue by Piet Mondrian / © DACS 1985.